IF YOU THINK YOU'VE HEARD IT ALL, YOU PROBABLY HAVEN'T HEARD THIS...

Essentially a nose with a dog attached, the bloodhound is the first animal whose evidence is legally admissible in court. A typical bloodhound's nose is lined with 230 million scent receptors—around 40 times more than the human nose—which are used in court to match scene-of-crime evidence to criminals.

Melvin Feizel Boothe of Pontiac, Michigan, hasn't cut his fingernails for 25 years. As a result, he now has a total nail length of 346 in. (931 cm.) for both hands—the longest nails of anyone on the planet.

Ashrita Furman—the man who holds the most Guinness World Records, with 54 as of March 2007—crawled a mile (1.6 km.) in 24 min. 44 sec. at Beardsley Park in Bridgeport, Connecticut, on October 18, 2006.

Accreditation

Guinness World Records Limited has a very thorough accreditation system for records verification. However, while every effort is made to ensure accuracy, Guinness World Records Limited cannot be held responsible for any errors contained in this work. Feedback from our readers on any point of accuracy is always welcomed.

Abbreviations & Measurements

Guinness World Records Limited uses both metric and imperial measurements (metric in parentheses). The sole exceptions are for some scientific data where metric measurements only are universally accepted, and for some sports data. Where a specific date is given, the exchange rate is calculated according to the currency values that were in operation at the time. Where only a year date is given, the exchange rate is calculated from December of that year. "One billion" is taken to mean one thousand million. "GDR" (the German Democratic Republic) refers to the East German state, which unified with West Germany in 1990. The abbreviation is used for sports records broken before 1990. The USSR (Union of Soviet Socialist Republics) split into a number of parts in 1991, the largest of these being Russia. The CIS (Commonwealth of Independent States) replaced it and the abbreviation is used mainly for sports records broken at the 1992 Olympic Games.

Guinness World Records Limited does not claim to own any right, title, or interest in the trademarks of others reproduced in this book.

General Warning

Attempting to break records or set new records can be dangerous. Appropriate advice should be taken first and all record attempts are undertaken entirely at the participant's risk. In no circumstances will Guinness World Records Limited have any liability for death or injury suffered in any record attempt. Guinness World Records Limited has complete discretion over whether or not to include any particular records in the book. Being a Guinness World Record holder does not guarantee you a place in the book.

GUINNESS WORLD RECORDS 2008

BANTAM BOOKS
NEW YORK • TORONTO • LONDON • SYDNEY • AUCKLAND

GUINNESS WORLD
RECORDS

EDITOR-IN-CHIEF
Craig Glenday

CONTENTS

★ BRAND-NEW RECORDS are indicated by a solid star, in both the text and record headings

☆ BROKEN OR UPDATED RECORDS are indicated by an open star, in both the text and record headings

Contents

INTRODUCTION

A Double Back-Spin on a Motorcycle ...
An Elephant with a Wooden Leg ... An Apple
the Size of Your Head ... It's Just Another
Year at Guinness World Records!

Perhaps the best thing about working on each new edition of the *Guinness World Records* book is the incredible variety we encounter on a daily basis. The world's **best-selling copyright book** wouldn't even exist if it weren't for the countless record breakers that are out there.

In the past 12 months in the U.S.A. alone, the Records Management Team—and particularly our Head of US Research, Stuart Claxton—have adjudicated records as diverse as the **largest game of bingo** (CA), the **most people reading simultaneously** (NY), the **largest gingerbread house** ever (MN), the **most custard pies thrown in one minute** (NY), and the **longest snowskate ollie** ever (CO)!

MEET THE RECORD HOLDERS Guinness World Records Day (see pp. 80–88) gave us a chance not only to celebrate record-breaking feats all over the globe but also to meet up with some record breakers as well. Cathie Jung (**smallest waist**, at 15 in.; 38.1 cm), Jackie Bibby (**most snakes held in the mouth**, 10) and Bryan Berg (**tallest house of cards**, over 25 ft.; 7.6 m) visited us in New York, where we toasted Guinness World Record holders everywhere!

POPCORN GIANTS Mickey Mouse and members of the Popcorn Giants team stand before the world's **largest popcorn sculpture** in the shape of the famous Disney character. Measuring 19 ft. 8.5 in. (6 m) and weighing 6,000 lb. (2,721 kg), the creation was part of *Food Network Challenge Guinness World Record Week,* which hit TV screens in October 2006. Find out more about this gastronomic extravaganza on page xiii.

Not only were we invited to take part in some fantastic events over the past year—such as the **X Games,** the **NBA All-Star Jam Session,** and the **Wild West Arts Convention**—but we were also asked to appear on countless TV shows such as *Live with Regis & Kelly, Food Network Challenge, Animal Planet's Guinness World Records: Amazing Animals, The Daily Show with Jon Stewart, The Late Show with David Letterman, The Ellen DeGeneres Show, Good Morning America, The Early Show, The Today Show,* and the *CW11 Morning News.* Many thanks to everyone who treated us so well on these occasions; we're certainly looking forward to returning to your screens again next year.

And let's not forget about **Guinness World Records Day!** This event has grown into a truly international phenomenon, and we played host to a multitude of weird-and-wonderful record challenges all over the world, from the northernmost wilds of Scotland to the southernmost beaches of Africa. From New York to California, and from Florida to Texas, the U.S.A. was most definitely a key part of this, the largest of international record-breaking celebrations!

Record-Breaking Year As soon as our famous book gets sent to the printers in May, the record keepers hit the road once more and continue the search for the world's most exciting content. The best part of this job is traveling around the country—and the world—meeting the record breakers face-to-face and judging their claims. It's an exciting process as, with over 50,000 letters received every year, we never know what we'll be witnessing

GWR SLOPESTYLE! The Guinness World Records Snowskate Park was one of the attractions at the X Fest this year, part of ESPN's Winter X Games held every year in Aspen, Colorado. Members of Premier Snowskates team and the public were invited to attempt to break several records, including the longest ollie and most consecutive kickflips! Pictured from left to right above are Jared Plays, Max Konopatzke, Justin Majeczky, Matt Plays, Justin Parsons, Phil Smage, Max Hilty, Rico Desjardin, Nick Ahrens, and Josh Seguin.

next! So, before you begin your journey through this year's edition, we thought we'd share with you a few of the highlights of our Guinness World Records year. Are you ready? Let's go!

Live with Regis & Kelly The most exciting time of the year for us is during the book launch, and for the last three years we've been thrilled to be a part of ABC's *Live with Regis & Kelly* for a special Guinness World Records week. Last year, it was Kelly throwing pies at Wilmer Valderrama—she broke the record for the **most pies thrown in one minute** (24). The year before that, it was Regis himself we recognized, for the **most hours spent on US television** with a staggering 15,188 hours! Who knows what will happen this year, but keep an eye out—we're sure it'll be spectacular!

Good Morning America! In the summer, Bill Weir, one of the hosts of ABC's *Good Morning America!*, surprised everyone (including himself!) by actually **flipping a pancake to the greatest height ever**—an outrageous 14 ft. (4.2 m)—outside their studios in Times Square.

Not only did Bill make history that morning, but he also added his name to the ever-growing ranks of US record breakers!

CUTTING EDGE Regis and Kelly once again played hosts to Guinness World Records week and it was one of the best years ever. Kenneth Lee (U.S.A., above) cut 23 apples in the air in one minute using a samurai sword; Don Claps (U.S.A.) completed the **most cartwheels in one hour** outside the studios, with 1,297; and Regis and Kelly participated in an attempt on the record for **most custard pies thrown in one minute** ... hurled at them by NASCAR drivers!

The Daily Show with Jon Stewart Guinness World Records' Editor-in-Chief Craig Glenday was a guest on the Comedy Central show back in August. In a hilarious exchange, Craig spoke about how the book is put together every year, and the many records he has personally witnessed, including measuring the world's **longest fingernails** (see p. 103) and the world's largest piece of peeled skin, which was sent in by a reader from China. Needless to say, this was *not* accepted as a Guinness World Record!

X Games Guinness World Records has been a part of ESPN's X Games for three years running and it's one of our favorite events in the record-breaking calendar. X Games 12 in Los Angeles was no exception—and what a thrill it was to witness firsthand Travis Pastrana's amazing double backflip on his motorcycle (**most backflips on a motorcycle**). We were more than happy to award him his certificate face-to-face!

SEE YOUR NAME HERE

Find out how to get your name in the next edition of *Guinness World Records* by turning to p. xvi. There, you'll find out what you need to do to get your record attempt registered. Good luck!

KING OF POP POPS IN One of the highlights of our year was undoubtedly a visit from the King of Pop, Michael Jackson. A long-term fan of the book, Michael popped into our London, UK, headquarters to pick up an array of certificates for his incredible musical achievements. He also insisted that he be awarded his record for **best-selling album** (*Thriller*) at the World Music Awards the following day, an honor we were more than happy to oblige!

We also flew to the Winter X Games in Aspen, Colorado, where the crew from Premier Snowskates got to attempt four Guinness World Records! Which ones were broken? Find out on p. 522.

Food Network October was definitely the most mouth-watering month of the year for us, as we made our debut on the *Food Network Challenge* series. Every night for the entire week, viewers of the series watched as over a dozen Guinness World Records were set or broken by individuals or teams of hopefuls vying for a spot in our famous book. Our US adjudicator Stuart Claxton traveled across the U.S.A.—literally—accompanied by the cast and crew of the show judging all manner of food records.

WHAT A CARVE UP! Guinness World Records judge Stuart Claxton was on hand for *Food Network Challenge Guinness World Records Week*, and traveled all around the U.S.A. to judge a dozen record attempts with the help of host Keegan Gerhard. From pizza juggling to creating massive sugar sculptures, from oyster shucking to pumpkin carving, it was all going down. Stephen Clark (U.S.A., above left far left) was one of the show's record breakers: he carved a pumpkin in just 24.03 seconds!

To launch the week, we joined Hyatt Regency Chicago pastry chef Alain Roby at FAO Schwartz, where he unveiled a most singular creation—the world's **largest chocolate sculpture**! The colossal chocolate confection—a replica of the Empire State Building, Rockefeller Center, and the Chrysler Building—measured a tooth-rotting 20 ft. 8 in. (6.29 m)!

You'll find a few fantastic food records—including some more set during the *Food Network Challenge* series—on pp. 190–197 of this year's Society chapter.

***National Geographic Kids* magazine** Providing kids with educational material that's also fun and inspiring is something that we support here at Guinness World Records, so we're more than happy to have an exclusive magazine partnership with *National Geographic Kids*. This awesome publication features an array of articles on the living world, and in every issue you'll find highlights from our very own GWR database.

Each year, the readers join forces to set or break a record, and last year, they successfully achieved the **largest gathering of plush toys.** Readers sent in a total of 2,304 toy animals, all of which were amassed in Washington, D.C., in December 2006!

Wild West Arts Convention Finally, just before the April deadline closed for applications for the 2008 edition, Craig Glenday, the *GWR* Editor-in-Chief, paid a visit to Claremore, Oklahoma, for the Wild West Arts Convention's annual Will Rogers International Expo 2007.

"What an amazing weekend!" reported Craig (pictured right with Western arts entertainer Mark Mulligan). "It was such a treat to spend time with talented, passionate supporters of these classic cowboy skills. I was honored to be able to award these achievements with official Guinness World Records certificates."

So, who's the fastest whip in the West? Who can perform the most Texas skips? Find out for yourself on pp. 514–518.

I hope this brief snapshot of our year has given you some idea of the lengths that we—and the record-breaking public—go to in order to create this exciting book each year. *Guinness World Records 2008* is itself a fascinating snapshot of the world we live in today, and we hope you enjoy reading about these inspiring, crazy, courageous, humbling, record-breaking people, pets, and places just as much as everyone here has enjoyed bringing it all together.

WAL-MART If Guinness World Records is known for recognizing superlatives in all shapes or forms, then there can be no bigger achiever in the U.S.A. than Wal-Mart, Inc. So we thought we'd honor this grandest of stores as the biggest seller of the *Guinness World Records* book! It's more than likely that the book you're now reading was bought in one of the 3,800 Wal-Mart stores, which not only make it the world's **largest corporation** but also the **largest private employer** in the world, with a staggering 1.8 million sales associates!

Over the years, it has become familiar to Guinness World Records for other, lesser known record-breaking feats as well. Did you know it displayed the world's **largest chalk pavement art** in 2002 in the Hanover store parking lot, measuring 33,391 ft.^{2} (3 102 m^2)? Or that the **largest inflatable structure** ever—a Power Rangers sculpture (pictured above right)—toured Wal-Mart stores in 1999? What about the **longest square-dance–calling marathon**? That took place at a Wal-Mart parking lot in Norfolk, Nebraska, in May 2000, when Dale F. Muehlmeier called for a throat-drying 28 hours! Finally, let's hear it for the **fastest check-out operator** in the world—Debbie O'Brien (above left), from a store in London, UK, scanned and bagged 50 items in a record time of 3 min. 31 sec.!

HOW TO BE A RECORD BREAKER

Guinness World Records Is the Global Authority on Record-Breaking Achievement. So If You Want to Get Your Record Approved by Our Adjudicators, Here's How...

Guinness World Records is a unique organization—no one else ratifies record-breaking achievement across such a wide range of subjects, and with the same degree of authority. That's why we get over 1,000 record claims sent to us every week!

We have over 50 years' experience of judging and collecting world record facts to help us produce this, the world's **biggest-selling copyright book.** A record is not a Guinness World Record until our team of experts has examined the claim and given the official stamp of approval.

If you want your record attempt verified immediately—or you want your official certificate presented the moment you successfully complete it—you can apply to have one of our trained adjudicators attend your attempt. On pages xviii–xix, Anthony and Kim reveal some of the equipment we might consider using at an attempt.

REGISTER ONLINE This year, we've completely redesigned our website, making it even easier to register your Guinness World Record claim.

You'll find us at www.guinnessworldrecords.com. Log on now to find out more—including how to monitor your claim as it progresses through our system.

TALKING YOUR LANGUAGE Guinness World Records has multilingual adjudicators who travel around the globe. Here, judge Sarah Wagner is inspecting the **longest line of pizzas** (611 ft. 2 in.; 186.3 m) in Treviso, Italy.

SIZE MATTERS No job is too large—or too small—for our adjudicators. If you think you've got the **largest glitter ball,** for example, and it beats Nigel Burrows's (UK) 16-ft.-wide (5 m) ball being measured here by GWR's Laura Hughes, let us know!

1. Go online If you want to break a record you've seen in the book or on television—or you want to set a new one—**the first thing you must do is contact us.** The easiest way is via our website (see opposite page).

2. Follow the rules Use the website to tell us as much as possible about your idea. If it's an existing record category, or a new idea that satisfies our basic record requirements, **we will send you the official Guinness World Records guidelines** that you must follow in order to achieve the record.

3. Gather the evidence You don't need a Guinness World Records official at your attempt, although you can apply for one using the website if you wish. Just be sure to **collate all the evidence we need.** If you've requested an adjudicator, he or she can approve your record immediately and will present you with your Guinness World Records certificate there and then, if you are successful. Otherwise, please note that it can take up to six weeks to have your evidence assessed professionally.

Finally, if you didn't request an adjudicator, you'll find out if you're a new Guinness World Record holder when your certificate is mailed to your home. Welcome to the gang!

ANY TIME, ANY PLACE, ANYWHERE . . . Guinness World Records travels the globe in our endless quest for exciting new records. Above, adjudicator Michael Whitty visits the Azteca Stadium in Mexico City, Mexico, to measure the **largest soccer shirt** (168 ft.; 51 m long).

A. LASER RANGE FINDER To measure distances, we might consider using laser technology: by timing the returning pulse of a laser beam, these handheld devices can provide exact distance measurements.

B. ENVIRONMENTAL GAUGE This device measures air temperature, humidity, altitude, and wind speed.

C. LASER THERMOMETER We use high-tech, noncontact, infrared temperature meters, which help us measure heat at a distance. They work by measuring an object's infrared energy radiation.

D. SOUND-LEVEL METER Got a loud snore or a deafening belch? To measure it accurately and objectively, we use a peak sound meter, which tells us in decibels the relative loudness of a sound.

E. VIDEO CAMERA We ask all claimants to videotape their attempts, just in case we need to go back and double-check any aspect of the claim.

F. DIGITAL CAMERA We expect you to take as many photos of your attempt as possible—indeed, the best option is to take a professional along to do the shooting. We use handy pocket digital cameras as well as larger, SLR-style digitals.

G. TWO-WAY RADIO RECEIVER We may use one of these at larger attempts to stay in touch with other adjudicators or the record organizers.

H. DIGITAL STOPWATCH The most basic piece of equipment for an adjudicator is a stopwatch accurate to 1/1,000 of a second.

I. BINOCULARS Binocular telescopes give three-dimensional (stereo) views of distant objects.

J. TRUNDLE WHEEL If we need to measure something that's too long for a tape measure—or something that doesn't follow very straight lines—then we use this simple device. It houses a clicker that counts every meter as the wheel turns.

K. TAPE MEASURE A tough, fabric, waterproof tape measure (metric and imperial).

MOST POPULAR RECORDS

☆ **Most people dribbling basketballs** This extremely popular record was broken twice in 2006. (Although the most times it has been broken in one year is five, back in 2003.) The first successful attempt of the year was on March 31, 2006, when a group of 910 people dribbled basketballs simultaneously at Meadowbank Sports Centre in Edinburgh, Scotland, UK. Just four and a half months later, 1,111 people beat the record at Flora Hill Secondary College in Bendigo, Victoria, Australia, on August 16.

☆ **Longest radio DJ marathon** On average, this record is beaten every four months! Current holder, Stefano Venneri (Italy), DJ'd for an incredible 125 hours on Radio BBSI in Alessandria, Italy, from April 26 to May 1, 2006.

☆ **Longest keyboard marathon** Charles Brunner (Trinidad and Tobago) played piano for 64 hours at the Hilton Hotel in Port of Spain, Trinidad and Tobago, from December 7 to 9, 2006.

☆ **Longest lesson** From October 20 to 23, 2005, Sanjay Kumar Sinha (India) taught a 73-hr. 37-min. lesson on English grammar to 59 pupils at the Bay City Club in Bandra, India. Two other people briefly held the title in 2005: David Specchio (China) for a 72-hour lesson, also on English, and Tomasz Marczak (Poland) for his 69-hour effort on language.

Largest pillow fight A total of 3,648 participants gathered at the University at Albany, Albany, New York, U.S.A., on April 17, 2005, to battle it out with feather pillows.

☆ **Longest hotdog** South Africans, Icelanders, and now Japanese have laid claim to this not-quite-all-American record! The All-Japan Bread Association made a 197-ft. 1-in.-long (60.3 m) frankfurter in Toyama-Ken, Japan, on August 4, 2006.

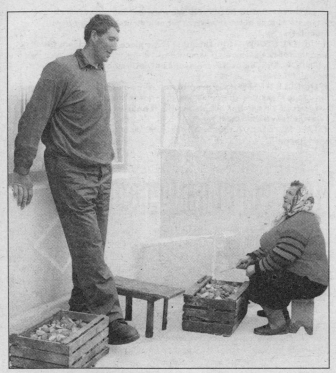

☆ **TALLEST LIVING MAN** Many people claim to be giants but will not let GWR measure their height officially. In 2006, Leonid Stadnyk (Ukraine) was measured by endocrinologist and gigantism expert Professor Michael Besser (UK) and found to be 8 ft. 5.5 in. (2.739 m) tall. GWR has accepted Besser's professional measurement but hopes to assess Stadnyk formally soon.

TALL TALE?

You can find out more about the tallest living man in the world—and about GWR's stringent rules for establishing the height of contenders for that title—on pages 103–104.

☆ **Most candles on a cake** Every year, this record gets bigger and bigger. Ten years ago, it stood at 900; now, thanks to Ashrita Furman and members of the Sri Chinmoy Centre (all U.S.A.), it stands at 27,413 lit candles,

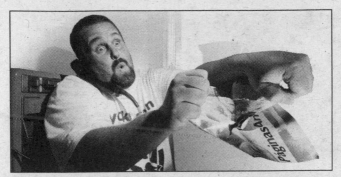

MOST PHONE BOOKS TORN IN THREE MINUTES This record has been broken eight times since 2001. The current holder is a newcomer to the event, Ed Shelton (U.S.A.), who ripped 55 telephone directories—each with 1,044 pages—from top to bottom in three minutes in Reno, Nevada, U.S.A., on November 18, 2005.

which were placed on a cake to mark the 74th anniversary of the foundation of the center in New York, U.S.A., on August 27, 2005. The cake measured 32 in. (81.28 cm) wide and 46 ft. (14.02 m) long!

☆ **Largest game of leapfrog** We have received, on average, a leapfrog record claim once a month for the past 10 years!

LONGEST ICE HOCKEY ENDURANCE MARATHON The ice hockey endurance marathon is usually beaten two or three times a year, although the last successful attempt—a 240-hour marathon staged by Brent Saik and friends (all Canada) at Saiker's Acres in Strathcona, Alberta, Canada, in February 2005—has yet to be beaten. This is the longest time that this record has remained unbroken for at least 10 years!

Most Popular Records

LONGEST DRUMMING MARATHON Multiple record holder—and GWR Hall of Fame entrant—Suresh Joachim Arulanantham (Australia) became the 13th person since 2000 to hold the solo drumming marathon record. He played for 84 hours (February 1 to 4, 2004) at the Magic Factory in Zurich, Switzerland.

The most recent successful claim came on July 4, 2006, when 1,197 participants leapfrogged at the UNESCO World Youth Festival in Stuttgart Degerloch, Germany.

Classic Claims For many years, it took claimants over three minutes to set the record for the **fastest time to eat three soda crackers.** (In 1998, for example, it was 3 min. 7 sec.) Today, Ambrose Mendy (UK) can eat three dry soda crackers in 34.78 seconds!

In 2001, the record for the **most doughnuts eaten in three minutes** stood at just three. However, in six years the record has been doubled to six, by a number of claimants!

☆**FASTEST BALLOON SCULPTING** Two men often come to "blows" over this record! John Cassidy (U.S.A., above) and Salvatore Sabbatino (Germany, inset) have been battling for years to claim this title. The current holder is John, who created 654 balloon sculptures in one hour in New York City, U.S.A., on November 21, 2005.

Eating too much? Be careful or you'll end up like Robert Earl Hughes (U.S.A., 1926–58). He had the **largest chest measurement** at 124 in., or 10 ft. 4 in. (3 m 15 cm)! Robert was so large when he died that he needed a coffin the size of a grand piano case!

CLAIMS WE *DON'T* WANT TO SEE

"I can lick my elbow"—we don't care: it's not a record.

"Fattest cat"—it's cruel, so please don't overfeed your pets.

"Fastest surgery"—no, please take your time when operating, doctor—it's not a race.

"Longest french fry" and **"Largest potato chip"**—there's no merit in these claims, so thanks but NO!

SPACE

CONTENTS

DEEP SPACE

★**Smallest stellar disc** Observations by NASA's Spitzer Space Telescope have revealed a disc of material surrounding the brown dwarf star OTS 44 that has a mass just 15 times that of Jupiter (4,770 times that of Earth, or 0.01 times the mass of the Sun).

Over millions of years, this will eventually form a miniature planetary system containing perhaps one small gas giant and a few small rocky planets.

Smallest stars First discovered in 1967, neutron stars are the remnants of stars that have self-destructed in a spectacular explosion known as a supernova. They may have a mass of up to three times that of the Sun, but diameters of only 6–19 miles (10–30 km).

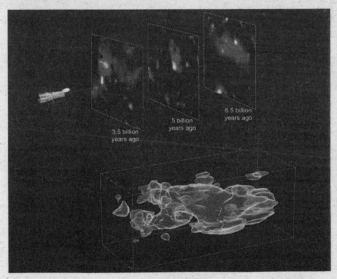

★**MOST COMMON FORM OF MATTER** Observations of the way that galaxies of stars move through space suggest that some 80–85% of the total mass of the universe is actually invisible and does not even interact with light and radiation in the way that stars and planets do. Many scientists believe that this "dark matter" may be made up of a new type of undiscovered Weakly Interacting Massive Particle—or WIMP.

The image above shows the first ever 3D map of the distribution of dark matter in the universe, based on observations by the Hubble Space Telescope.

★ **LARGEST NEARBY GALAXY** The largest galaxy in our galaxy cluster, the Local Group, is the Andromeda spiral galaxy M31. Results announced in January 2007 suggest Andromeda is five times larger than previously thought, with the discovery of stars orbiting its center from a distance of at least 500,000 light-years (compare image above top with more recent photograph, above bottom).

At 2.2 million light-years from Earth, Andromeda is also the **most distant object visible to the naked eye.**

The top photograph of the Andromeda Galaxy above is actually a mosaic of images taken by amateur astronomer Rob Gendler (U.S.A.), with a total exposure time of 90 hours. At 21,904 × 14,454 pixels, this constitutes the ☆ **largest image of any spiral galaxy to date**.

Neutron stars also have the distinction of being the densest stars in the universe. A sand-grain-sized piece of neutron star material would have the mass of a skyscraper.

First spiral galaxy discovered The Whirlpool Galaxy (M51) was the first celestial object ever to be identified as being a spiral. The discovery was made by William Parsons, Third Earl of Rosse (Ireland), in 1845.

★**Youngest galaxy** Observations of the galaxy I Zwicky 18, 45 million light-years away, by the Hubble Space Telescope reveal that it began forming stars only around 500 million years ago. By way of comparison, our own galaxy, the Milky Way, began star formation around 12 billion years ago.

★**Greatest gravitational influence** Our Local Group of around 30 galaxies is hurtling through space at a speed of approximately 1.2 million mph (2 million km/h), toward a huge agglomeration of mass located some 500 million light-years away.

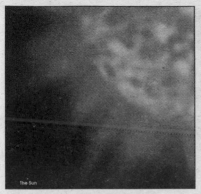

MOST LUMINOUS STAR The latest observations of LBV 1806–20, located 45,000 light-years from Earth, indicate it is between 5 million and 40 million times more luminous than the Sun. It has a mass of at least 150 times the mass of the Sun, and its diameter is at least 200 times that of the Sun.

The Sun

Hidden from view by the bulk of our own Milky Way Galaxy, this mass, dubbed The Great Attractor, is believed to be an enormous supercluster of approximately 100,000 galaxies.

Brightest supernova SN 1006, noted in April 1006 near the star Beta Lupi, flared for two years and reached a magnitude of -9.5. This titanic cosmic explosion was bright enough to be seen with the naked eye for 24 months and, at its most intense, was 1,500 times more luminous than Sirius, the brightest star in the night sky. The supernova took place around 3,260 light-years away from Earth.

★**Windiest extrasolar planet** The gas giants 51 Pegasi, HD179949b, and HD209458b are all orbiting different stars within 150 light-years of Earth. Each orbits its star within around 4.9 million miles (8 million km)—far closer than Mercury orbits the Sun. Results released in January 2007 show that the temperature difference between day and night on these planets is tiny, suggesting that supersonic winds of up to 9,000 mph (14,500 km/h.) are constantly transferring heat from their day sides to their night sides.

★**Least dense extrasolar planet** HAT-P-1b, located 450 light-years away from Earth, is a gas giant around 1.38 times the diameter of Jupiter,

---

DID YOU KNOW?

A light-year is the distance covered by light, traveling at 186,282 miles/sec. (299,792 km/sec.), in one year. It is equivalent to nearly 6 million million miles.

The Sun is located 30,000 light-years from the center of our galaxy, the Milky Way, which contains around 300 billion stars and measures approximately 100,000 light-years across.

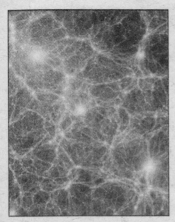

but with only half the mass. This gives HAT-P-1b a density of around one quarter that of water.

If there were an ocean large enough to accommodate it, HAT-P-1b would float in it, just as Saturn would, but at around three times higher than the famous ringed planet.

★ **Densest objects in the universe** Black holes are the remnants of stars that ended their lives as supernovas. They are characterized by a region of space in which gravity is so strong that not even light can escape. The boundary of this region is known as the "event horizon," and at the center of the black hole is the "singularity," where the mass of the dead star is compressed to a single point of zero size and infinite density. It is this singularity that generates the powerful gravitational field of a black hole.

DYNAMIC SOLAR SYSTEM

Greatest impact on Earth Most astronomers now believe that, 4.5 billion years ago, a planet the size of Mars collided with the young Earth. Some of the debris from this cataclysm went into orbit around the Earth and collected together under its own gravity to form the Moon.

Earth's entire crust would probably have been blasted off into space, leaving behind a planet whose entire surface was an ocean of molten magma.

Hottest place Although no one has visited the very center of the Sun, it is the hottest place in the solar system, with an estimated temperature of 28,080,000°F (15,600,000°C).

The pressure in the core is around 250 billion times the pressure at sea level on Earth. It is here that around 600 million metric tons of hydrogen are fused into helium every second. This ongoing nuclear reaction is what makes the Sun shine.

★**Highest clouds** In August 2006, European scientists reported their discovery of faint clouds some 55–62 miles (90–100 km) above the surface of Mars. The clouds, detected by an instrument on the European Space Agency's (ESA) *Mars Express* orbiter, are made up of carbon dioxide ice crystals.

★**Largest dust storms** Mars is the only world other than Earth where dust storms have been observed. In 1971 and 2001, dust storms grew to immense proportions, covering 100% of the planet and obscuring its surface from telescopes and spacecraft.

★**Strongest magnetic field** Generated by the liquid metallic hydrogen of its interior, Jupiter's magnetic field is around 19,000 times stronger than Earth's and extends several million miles toward the Sun and almost all the way to Saturn in the direction away from the Sun.

If it were visible to the naked eye, Jupiter's magnetic field would appear at around the same size that the full Moon does from Earth.

★**Largest DC electrical circuit** Gases spew from the volcanoes of Jupiter's moon Io, forming a huge cocoon that surrounds the planet. As Io orbits through this electrically charged gas, a massive electrical current flows between Jupiter and Io, carrying around two trillion watts of power.

This is roughly equivalent to all the man-made power produced on Earth.

Fastest winds When observed in 1989 by NASA's Voyager 2 probe, the winds on Neptune were measured at around 1,500 mph (2,400 km/h), almost five times faster than the highest known wind speed for a tornado on Earth.

Coldest observed geological activity Active geysers of frigid nitrogen gas erupt several miles high into the thin atmosphere of Neptune's moon Triton. With a surface temperature of 391°F (-235°C), Triton is so

---

DID YOU KNOW?

From July 16 to 22, 1994, over 20 fragments of comet Shoemaker-Levy 9 collided with Jupiter. The largest of these fragments was around 2 miles (3–4 km) across.

The greatest impact was caused by the "G" fragment, which exploded with the energy of roughly 600 times the world's nuclear arsenal, or around 6 million megatons of TNT. This represents the **largest recorded impact in the solar system.**

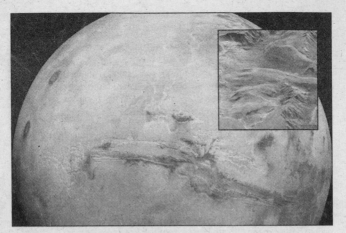

LARGEST CANYON The Valles Marineris on Mars (seen as a long "scar" on the planet's surface, above, and in detail, inset) is around 2,800 miles (4,500 km) long. At its widest, the canyon measures 370 miles (600 km) across and is up to 4.3 miles (7 km) deep. It is named after the *Mariner 9* spacecraft that first discovered it in 1971.

cold that lakes of water are frozen as hard as steel and retain impact craters that are millions of years old.

★**Largest chaotically rotating object** Saturn's misshapen moon Hyperion measures 254 × 161 × 136 miles (410 × 260 × 220 km) across and is the largest highly irregularly shaped body in the solar system (see box, page 10).

Hyperion is one of only two bodies in the solar system discovered to have chaotic rotation, meaning that it is randomly tumbling in its orbit around Saturn. The other body is the asteroid 4179 Toutatis, which measures 2.7 × 1.5 × 1.8 miles (4.5 × 2.4 × 2.9 km) across.

★**Closest moons to each other** Janus and Epimetheus share the same average orbit some 56,500 miles (91,000 km) above Saturn. As their orbital paths are only 31 miles (50 km) apart, one of the moons is always catching up with the other.

Every four years the two moons come within 6,200 miles (10,000 km) of each other and swap orbits, before drifting apart until their next encounter four years later.

The solar system is around 4.54 billion years old. It will probably last another 5 billion years.

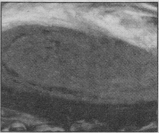

LARGEST CYCLONE The Great Red Spot on the planet Jupiter (visible as an oval shape on the planet's surface, above, and in closer detail, above right) is the largest cyclone in the solar system.

The spot varies in size, but can be up to 24,800 miles (40,000 km) long and 8,700 miles (14,000 km) wide. Three planets the size of Earth would fit along its length.

Most reflective body Saturn's small moon Enceladus reflects some 90% of the sunlight that illuminates it, making it more reflective than freshly fallen snow. Its surface is composed of icy material.

Darkest object The surface of the 5-mile-long (8-km) nucleus of Comet Borrelly reflects less than 3% of the sunlight it receives. Its low albedo (ratio of light reflected to light received) is caused by a coating of dark dust.

Borrelly has about half the albedo of the Moon, which is as dark as an asphalt parking lot. By way of comparison, Earth reflects around 30% of the sunlight it receives.

Most volcanically active body When NASA's *Voyager 1* probe passed by the giant planet Jupiter in 1979, its camera imaged the moon Io. The photographs revealed enormous volcanic eruption plumes, some reaching several hundred miles into space. Io's activity is driven by tidal energy inside it.

This tidal energy is a result of gravitational interactions between Jupiter, Io, and one of the other moons, Europa.

★**LARGEST EXTRATERRESTRIAL LAKES** In January 2004, scientists released data from the NASA/ESA Cassini mission revealing what look like lakes of liquid methane on the surface of Saturn's largest moon, Titan. Cloud-penetrating radar images show around 75 lakes, in a region near Titan's north pole, the largest of which are around 68 miles (110 km) across.

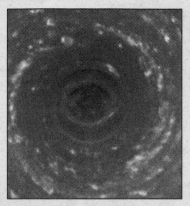

★ **TALLEST EYE-WALL CLOUDS** A massive vortex of clouds, similar to a hurricane, was discovered at Saturn's south pole in 2006. Unlike Jupiter's Great Red Spot (see page 9), this feature exhibits the classic eye wall of a hurricane on Earth.

The discovery of this south polar vortex represents the only time an eye wall has been detected on another planet. With heights of 18–46 miles (35–70 km), this cloud vortex is roughly five times higher than those in terrestrial hurricanes.

Most powerful volcano Loki, an active volcano on Jupiter's moon Io, discovered by *Voyager 1* in 1979, emits more heat than all of Earth's active volcanoes together. The volcano has an enormous caldera (volcanic crater), over 4,000 miles^2 (10,000 km^2) in area, that is regularly flooded with molten lava.

Highest mountain Located on the planet Mars, Olympus Mons is the highest mountain in the solar system. Its peak is 15 miles (25 km) above its base—making the mountain nearly three times the height of Mt. Everest.

Olympus Mons is more than 20 times wider than it is high and, despite its great height, has a very gentle slope. Because of its shape, Olympus Mons is designated a shield volcano.

SATURN'S MISSHAPEN MOON

Some scientists believe that Hyperion was involved in a large collision with a comet or asteroid millions of years ago, which broke off part of the moon and brought about its irregular shape.

PLANETS

☆ **Outermost major planet** Since the demotion of Pluto in 2006 (see page 12), Neptune is now the major planet farthest from the Sun. At 2.7 billion miles (4.5 billion km) from the Sun, it moves at around 3.39 miles/sec. (5.45 km/sec.), taking 164.79 years to complete one orbit.

HOTTEST PLANET Often referred to as the closest place to hell in the Solar System, Venus has the ★**thickest atmosphere of any planet**, with a pressure nearly 100 times that of Earth's at sea level. The gases in its atmosphere cause a greenhouse effect, and the surface temperature can reach 896°F (480°C).

☆**Smallest major planet** Since the reclassification of Pluto as a dwarf planet, Mercury is now the smallest major planet in the Solar System. At 3,032 miles (4,879 km) across, it is less than one and a half times the diameter of Earth's Moon.

Being the closest planet to the Sun, it also has the **fastest orbit,** at 30.37 miles/sec. (48.87 km/sec.).

Largest planet Jupiter has an equatorial diameter of 89,405 miles (143,884 km) and a polar diameter of 83,082 miles (133,708 km). Its mass is 318 times that of the Earth. It also has the **shortest period of rotation,** resulting in a Jovian day of only 9 hr. 55 min. 29.69 sec.

Fastest planet Mercury, which orbits the Sun at an average distance of 35.9 million miles (57.9 million km), has an orbital period of 87.968 days, giving the highest average speed in orbit of 107,030 mph (172,248 km/h.)—almost twice as fast as the Earth's orbiting speed.

Mercury is also the **closest planet to the Sun** (see page 12).

Brightest planet Viewed from Earth, the brightest of the five planets normally visible (Jupiter, Mars, Mercury, Saturn, and Venus) is Venus, which has a maximum magnitude of -4.4. Indeed, with the exception of the Sun and the Moon, Venus is the brightest object visible to us in the night sky.

★**Dwarf planet with the most moons** In 2005, two tiny moons of Pluto were discovered using the Hubble Space Telescope. Named Nix and Hydra, they are around 87 miles (140 km) and 106 miles (170 km) across, respectively.

This discovery raises the total number of Pluto's moons to three.

★**Largest dwarf planet** The icy world Eris was discovered in January 2005. It has an elliptical orbit, its distance from the Sun ranging from 9 billion miles to 7.4 billion miles, and a diameter of around 1,490 miles (2,400 km)—larger than Pluto. Before the reclassification of Pluto as a dwarf planet, Eris was regarded by many astronomers as the 10th planet.

Eris has a small moon, Dysnomia, which is approximately 217 miles (350 km) across.

VENUS Hottest surface of any planet in the Solar System, with an average temperature of around 896°F (480°C).
Diameter: 7,521 miles (12,104 km)
Mass: (Earth = 1) 0.81
Mean distance from Sun: 67,232,700 miles (108,200,600 km)
Orbital period: 224.70 days

MARS Home to Olympus Mons, the highest mountain in the Solar System, with a peak 15 miles (25 km) above base.
Diameter: 4,217 miles (6,787 km)
Mass: (Earth = 1) 0.107
Mean distance from Sun: 141,634,800 miles (227,940,000 km)
Orbital period: 686.98 days

EARTH Densest planet: average density 5.517 times that of water.
Diameter: 7,926 miles (12,756 km)
Mass: 5.976×10^{24} kg
Mean distance from Sun: 92,955,900 miles (149,600,000 km)
Orbital period: 365.25 days

MERCURY Innermost planet.
Diameter: 3,032 miles (4,879 km)
Mass: (Earth = 1) 0.055
Mean distance from Sun: 35,983,000 miles (57,910,100 km)
Orbital period: 87.97 days

JUPITER Largest major planet.
Diameter: 89,405 miles (143,884 km)
Mass: (Earth = 1) 318
Mean distance from Sun: 483,632,000 miles (778,330,000 km)
Orbital period: 11.86 years

GOODBYE, PLUTO ... HELLO, NEPTUNE On August 24, 2006, an assembly of the International Astronomical Union (IAU) in Prague, Czech Republic, voted to remove Pluto's planetary status. Henceforth, it was classified as a "dwarf planet." The Solar System now officially comprises eight major planets.

First discovered in 1930 by Clyde Tombaugh (U.S.A.), Pluto was initially thought to be larger than it actually is. (It is smaller than many moons in the Solar System.) Later research revealed objects that rivaled Pluto in size but were not classified as planets.

As a result, Neptune is now regarded as the most distant major planet.

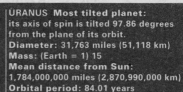

URANUS **Most tilted planet:**
its axis of spin is tilted 97.86 degrees
from the plane of its orbit.
Diameter: 31,763 miles (51,118 km)
Mass: (Earth = 1) 15
Mean distance from Sun:
1,784,000,000 miles (2,870,990,000 km)
Orbital period: 84.01 years

SATURN **Least dense planet:**
mostly hydrogen and helium, the two
lightest elements.
Diameter: 74,898 miles (120,536 km)
Mass: (Earth = 1) 95
Mean distance from Sun:
888,200,000 miles (1,429,400,000 km)
Orbital period: 29.45 years

NEPTUNE **Fastest winds in the
Solar System:** measured at around
1,500 mph (2,400 km/h.) in 1989.
Diameter: 30,775 miles (49,528 km)
Mass: (Earth = 1) 17
Mean distance from Sun:
2,800,000,000 miles (4,504,300,000 km)
Orbital period: 164.79 years

DID YOU KNOW?

Mercury and Venus are the only planets in the Solar System that do not
have moons. Earth, with its single moon, has the next fewest.
 Our Moon is actually moving away from the Earth at a rate of around
1.6 in. (4 cm) per year.

NEIL DEGRASSE TYSON

Dr. Neil DeGrasse Tyson is director of the Hayden Planetarium at the American Museum of Natural History in New York City, U.S.A. In 2001, he opened a new exhibition on the Solar System in which he controversially relegated Pluto from a planet to just one of the many small icy bodies beyond the orbit of Neptune. In August 2006, Pluto was demoted from planetary status, as Dr. Tyson explains: It's official, Pluto is no longer a planet, as voted in August 2006 by the General Assembly of the International Astronomical Union, the world body of professional astrophysicists. Pluto's planethood must now endure the modifier "dwarf."

But why is Pluto no longer deemed to be a planet? Frontier science, which is driven by data, is not normally determined, or even guided by, democratic vote. So this decision remains controversial, not only with the professional researchers but also in the hearts and minds of the general public. Yet the reasons for it are clear. According to a new criterion, a planet must have cleared its orbit of debris. Pluto fails this test—badly.

Beginning in 1992, hundreds of small icy bodies have been discovered in the outer Solar System that looked and behaved a lot like Pluto. Like the 19th-century discovery of the asteroid belt—itself a swarm of craggy chunks of rock—a new swath of populated real estate had been discovered. And this region of the Solar System contains Pluto, one of its largest members. No other planet is so crowded in its orbit.

Combine this with Pluto's other oddball properties—including its diminutive size (six moons are larger, including Earth's Moon), mass (Pluto is less than 1/20th the mass of Mercury, the next smallest planet), and its high ice content (more than half its volume)—and a new understanding of the outer Solar System emerges. We did not lose a planet. We gained perspective.

★ **MOST EARTH-LIKE PLANET** With surface temperatures ranging from 68°F to -220°F (20°C to -140°C), and a day 24.6 hours long, conditions on Mars mean that it is the planet that would be easiest for humans to colonize. Spacesuits would still be required, however, as the carbon-dioxide atmosphere is thin and poisonous.

Some scientists have suggested "terraforming" Mars—gradually changing the planet's atmosphere so that humans could survive there.

Moons

GANYMEDE The **largest satellite** is Ganymede, which is 2.017 times as heavy as the Earth's Moon and has a diameter of 3,273 miles (5,267 km). Ganymede is larger than the planet Mercury.

CALLISTO The outermost of Jupiter's four large moons, Callisto is an ancient relic whose surface is completely covered with impact craters, making it the ★ **most heavily cratered moon.**

IO The volcanoes of Io create eruption plumes reaching several hundred miles into space, making it the **most volcanically active world** in the Solar System. The moon is squeezed by tidal interactions with Jupiter and another of that planet's moons—Europa—vigorously heating its interior and causing the activity.

EUROPA Jupiter's large, icy moon Europa has the **smoothest surface of any solid body** in the Solar System. The only prominent relief on its surface are ridges a few hundred yards in height.

PLANET WITH THE MOST MOONS As of January 2006, the planet in the Solar System with the most satellites is Jupiter, with 63. Saturn comes in second with 47, and Uranus and Neptune have 27 and 13, respectively.

Of Jupiter's moons, four are large enough to be considered planets in their own right.

Most tilted planet The planet Uranus has a greater axial tilt than any of the other planets in the Solar System. Its axis of spin is tilted 97.86 degrees from the plane of its orbit. By way of comparison, the Earth has an axial tilt of only 23.45 degrees.

The reason for this extreme tilt is unknown, although one theory suggests that it was struck by an Earth-sized planet during the violent formation of the Solar System, and that the impact of the collision knocked Uranus over on its side.

☆ **PLANET WITH THE GREATEST RING SYSTEM** Jupiter, Uranus, and Neptune all have ring systems, but none is on the scale of Saturn's. This stunning image was taken by the NASA/ESA Cassini spacecraft in 2006, with the planet directly between the spacecraft and the Sun. The dark side of the planet is lit by sunlight reflecting from ring particles. These observations led to the discovery of two new faint rings, formed by micro-meteorite impacts on the tiny moons Janus, Epimetheus, and Pallene. The total mass of the ring system is estimated to be around 9×10^{19} lb. (4×10^{19} kg)—roughly equivalent to 30 million Mount Everests.

☆ **Largest moon compared to its planet** At 2,159 miles (3,474 km) across, Earth's Moon has a diameter 0.27 times that of Earth.

The Moon is the largest of the three moons in the inner Solar System and the only other world to have been visited by humans.

PLANET EARTH

CONTENTS

ATMOSPHERE

Wind speed (surface) •The **highest wind speed at a *low* altitude** was registered on March 8, 1972, at the USAF base at Thule (altitude: 145 ft.; 44 m) in Greenland, when a peak speed of 207 mph (333 km/h.) was recorded.

•The **highest surface wind speed at a *high* altitude** peaked at 231 mph (371 km/h.) on Mount Washington (altitude: 6,286 ft.; 1,916 m) in New Hampshire, U.S.A., on April 12, 1934.

Wind speed (non-surface) Scientists using the "Doppler on Wheels" mobile weather observatory, based at the University of Oklahoma, U.S.A., recorded a 302 +/-20 mph (486 +/-32 km/h.) wind speed associated with a large tornado near Bridge Creek, Oklahoma, U.S.A., on May 3, 1999.

★**Strongest microburst** On August 1, 1983, at Andrews Air Force Base in Maryland, U.S.A., a "microburst" of wind was recorded at 149.5 mph (240.5 km/h.). This rare phenomenon, characterized by a brief downdraft of hurricane-force winds, can be a threat to aircraft during takeoff or landing.

HIGHEST ATMOSPHERIC PHENOMENA Of all the phenomena visible in our skies, the very highest are the aurorae, also known as the northern and southern lights. Often visible at night from low and high latitudes, these beautiful, colored, shimmering lights are the result of charged particles from the Sun interacting with the upper atmosphere. The lowest aurorae occur at altitudes of around 62 miles (100 km), while the highest extend up to around 248 miles (400 km). Pictured is the aurora borealis at the Great Slave Lake, Northwest Territories, Canada.

LAYERS OF THE ATMOSPHERE Staring up into our atmosphere is like standing on the ocean floor, looking up through the sea. As you ascend through the atmosphere, its density decreases until it eventually merges with space, hundreds of miles above the surface. There are four distinct layers, divided by temperature: the troposphere, nearest Earth; stratosphere; mesosphere; and thermosphere, which gradually merges with space.

FASTEST ANNUAL METEOR SHOWER The Leonid meteor shower, which occurs between November 15 and 20 each year, enters Earth's atmosphere at around 44 miles (71 km) per second and begins to glow at an altitude of around 96 miles (155 km).

TROPOSPHERE: ★ MOST TURBULENT PART OF THE ATMOSPHERE The troposphere begins at ground level and reaches up to 10 miles (16 km) at the equator and 5 miles (8 km) at the poles. This region contains some 75% of the atmosphere's mass, and it is here where almost all of Earth's weather occurs. Air molecules can move from the ground right up to the top of the troposphere and back down in just a few days. Beyond the troposphere is the stratosphere, which is much more stable.

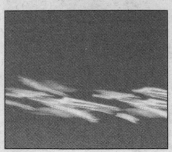

STRATOSPHERE: ★ HIGHEST OZONE CONCENTRATION O_3, or ozone, can form at ground level as a pollutant, but over 90% of the Earth's total resides in the stratosphere, where it forms the ozone layer. At around 15 miles (25 km) above the Earth, it reaches its highest concentration of just a few parts per million, but this is enough to absorb almost all the high-frequency ultraviolet light from the Sun.

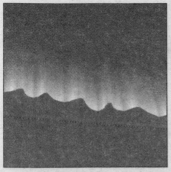

MESOSPHERE: ★ COLDEST PART OF THE ATMOSPHERE The mesosphere exists between around 30 and 50 miles (50 and 80 km) above the Earth. Here, the temperature drops with altitude, reaching a minimum of around −148°F (−100°C).

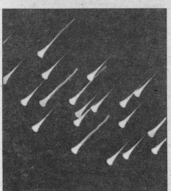

THERMOSPHERE: ★ HOTTEST PART OF THE ATMOSPHERE The thermosphere starts at around 50 miles (80 km) above the Earth and continues up to the boundary with the exosphere, at an altitude of around 310 miles (500 km). In this extremely rarified gas, the temperature rises with altitude, where it can reach 3,632°F (2,000°C) when the Sun is particularly active.

CLOUDS WITH THE GREATEST VERTICAL RANGE The cloud form with the greatest vertical range is cumulonimbus, which has been observed to reach a height of nearly 65,600 ft. (20,000 m)—nearly three times the height of Mount Everest—in the tropics.

LOWEST CLOUDS Stratus formations are patches or sheets of shapeless low gray cloud, often thin enough to see the Sun through. They give rise to light drizzle and, in winter, snow.

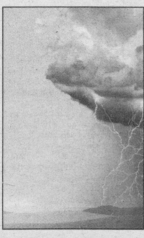

HOTTEST PLACE ON EARTH The hottest place on Earth is the air around a lightning strike. For a fraction of a second, the air is heated to around 54,032°F (30,000°C), or roughly five times hotter than the visible surface of the Sun.

Strongest jet stream The fastest jet-stream velocity ever measured is 408 mph (656 km/h.). It was recorded by instruments onboard a Skua rocket above South Uist, Outer Hebrides, UK, at an altitude of 154,200 ft. (47,000 m) on December 13, 1967.

Greatest display of solar halos On January 11, 1999, at least 24 types of solar halos were witnessed at the South Pole. Solar halos are formed by sunlight being reflected and refracted (bent) by ice crystals in the atmosphere, causing what looks like rings around the Sun and brightly colored patches in the sky.

BEAUFORT SCALE British Navy Commander Francis Beaufort devised a scale—from Force 0 to Force 12—in 1805 to quantify wind force. Force 13 to 17 were added in 1955 by the U.S. Weather Bureau, but are not in international use. Force 0 is calm, with no wind. After that, things start to get a bit blustery . . .

1. LIGHT AIR

1–3 MPH

2. LIGHT BREEZE

4–7 MPH

3. GENTLE BREEZE

8–12 MPH

4. MODERATE BREEZE

13–18 MPH

5. FRESH BREEZE

19–24 MPH

6. STRONG BREEZE

25–31 MPH

7. NEAR GALE

32–38 MPH

8. GALE

39–46 MPH

9. STRONG GALE

47–54 MPH

10. STORM

55–63 MPH

11. VIOLENT STORM

64–73 MPH

12. HURRICANE

OVER 74 MPH

★ LARGEST SOLITON CLOUD
Soliton clouds are rare, solitary forms that maintain their shape while moving at a constant velocity. The longest regular occurrence of this is known as the Morning Glory, which forms in the Gulf of Carpentaria, Australia. This backward-rolling cloud formation may be 620 miles (1,000 km) long and 3,280 ft. (1 km) high, and can travel at up to 37 mph (60 km/h.). The Morning Glory regularly attracts gliders, who catch the updraft on the leading edge of the cloud.

★ LONGEST SERIES OF CLOUD VORTICES Cloud streets are parallel rows of marine stratocumulus clouds that form along the direction of wind flow. Here the cloud street has formed a series of vortices, in the wake of Jan Mayan Island, Norway, extending for over 186 miles (around 300 km). The above image was captured by NASA's *Terra* satellite in June 2001.

★ Newest mathematical constant The study of turbulent weather and water, and other chaotic phenomena, has revealed the existence of a new universal constant, the Feigenbaum number, first calculated by Mitchell J. Feigenbaum (U.S.A.). It is approximately equal to 4.669201609102990.

EARTH

★ Thickest crust The Earth's crust is the cold, solid, outermost layer of the lithosphere, which sits above the hot, convecting asthenosphere. Its thickest point is found in the Himalaya mountains in China, at around 46 miles (75 km).

The **★ thinnest part of the Earth's crust** is just 3.7 miles (6 km) thick and occurs in parts of the Pacific Ocean. The **thinnest continental crust** is around 9 miles (15 km) thick and is located in the Great Rift Valley of northeast Africa.

★ Largest island created by volcanic eruptions The largest volcanic island is Iceland, the entirety of which was formed from volcanic eruptions

TALLEST SEA STACK The world's tallest sea stack is Ball's Pyramid (pictured left) near Lord Howe Island, Australia, in the Pacific Ocean. It is 1,843 ft. (561 m) high, but has a base axis of only 660 ft. (200 m).

from the Mid-Atlantic Ridge, upon which it sits. Measuring 39,768 miles^2 (103,000 km^2) in area, it is essentially ocean floor exposed above the ocean surface.

★**Highest mountain tabletop** Monte Roraima, on the border of Brazil, Venezuela, and Guyana, is a sandstone plateau with vertical sides measuring 9,220 ft. (2,810 m) in height. Its harsh environment has resulted in around one-third of its plant species being unique to the mountain. Monte Roraima is believed to have been the inspiration for Arthur Conan Doyle's (UK) 1912 novel *The Lost World*.

Largest island within an island Samosir in Lake Toba, Sumatra, Indonesia, has an area of 245 miles^2 (630 km^2). Formed between 30,000 and 100,000 years ago, it is the original home of the Toba Batak people.

★**LARGEST MUD VOLCANO** Azerbaijan is home to the world's largest mud volcano, measuring 0.6 miles (1 km) across at the base and reaching several hundred yards in height. Mud volcanoes are little-known relatives of the regular, magmatic variety and can be just as dynamic, if cooler. Azerbaijan is home to more than half the world's total, although the majority of mud volcanoes are small, temporary landforms.

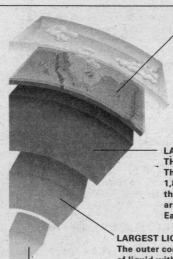

FASTEST MOVING TECTONIC PLATE The fastest moving tectonic plate is the Tonga microplate, near Samoa, which is moving at a rate of 9.4 in. (24 cm) per year.

LARGEST REGION OF THE EARTH'S INTERIOR The Earth's mantle is 1,800 miles (2,900 km) thick and makes up around 70% of the Earth's volume.

LARGEST LIQUID BODY The outer core is a layer of liquid with a thickness of 1,403 miles (2,259 km), representing 29.3% of the Earth's mass.

LARGEST CRYSTAL The Earth's inner core is a sphere of mostly iron at around 9,000–10,000°F (5,000–6,000°C). Differences in the behavior of seismic waves passing through it mean that many geologists now believe that this molten metal ball is actually a single crystal.

★ **FASTEST ROTATING PART OF THE EARTH** Precise measurements of earthquake timings have revealed that the Earth's inner core—a solid ball of iron and nickel around 1,517 miles (2,442 km) across (see artwork above)—is spinning slightly faster than the outer liquid core and the rest of the Earth. Each year, the inner core moves ahead of the Earth's surface by around 0.3–0.5 degrees—a rate of around 50,000 times the speed that the continental plates move.

★ **Lowest island** The world's lowest island is in Ye'ch'ew Hayk Lake in Ethiopia—it is 338 ft. (103 m) below sea level.

Largest island Greenland, with an area of about 840,000 miles² (2,175,000 km²), is the largest island in the world.

TALLEST MOUNTAIN FACE The Rupal face of Nanga Parbat (pictured above) in the western Himalayas, Pakistan, is a single rise of some 16,000 ft. (5,000 m) from the valley floor to the summit. Nanga Parbat—the 8th highest mountain in the world and the highest in Pakistan at 26,660 ft. (8,126 m)—is also the world's **fastest rising mountain,** growing taller at a rate of 0.27 in (7 mm) per year.

★ **Flowstone cascade with the greatest vertical extent** Flowstone cascades are sheet-like deposits of calcite that form as limestone-saturated water runs down cave walls and floors, leaving deposits that build up over time. The flowstone cascade with the greatest vertical extent is 492 ft. (150 m) in length and is located in the Neverland to Dead Sea Lechuguilla Cave in New Mexico, U.S.A.

Most remote spot from land There is a point in the South Pacific 1,600 miles (2,575 km) from the nearest land. The closest land can be found at Pitcairn Island, Ducie Island, and Peter 1 Island.

Lowest exposed body of water The Dead Sea lies at an average of 1,312 ft. (400 m) below sea level. The waters in its deepest parts are so salty and dense that they are effectively fossilized, resting on the seafloor since a few centuries after biblical times. Any fish washed into it die instantly, and no other life aside from bacteria survives in its waters.

Running along the Israeli (western) shore is the **lowest road,** at 1,290 ft. (393 m) below sea level.

LARGEST GEODE A geode discovered by geologist Javier Garcia-Guinea (Spain) near Almeria, Spain, in May 2000, forms a mineral-lined cave 26 ft. (8 m) long, 6 ft. (1.8 m) wide, and 6 ft. (1.8 m) high.

A geode is a rock cavity filled with minerals and is usually small enough to fit in the palm of a human hand.

Flattest country The country with the lowest high point is the Republic of Maldives; its loftiest peak is just 8 ft. (2.4 m) high. (Unconnected is the fact that it is also the country with the **highest divorce rate,** with 10.97 divorces per 1,000 inhabitants!)

★Least flat country From the Gangetic plain to Mount Everest, Nepal is the least flat country in the world. Within just 100 miles, the altitude of Nepal varies from 328 ft. (100 m) above sea level to 29,028 ft. (8,848 m).

Most forested country The country with the highest percentage of forested land is the Cook Islands in the South Pacific. As of 2000, a total of 95.7% of the country was covered.

In 2005, Brazil was the **most forested country by area,** with a cover of

---

HIGHEST...

• Mount Everest, in the Himalayas, has been measured to a height of 29,035 ft. (8,848 m), making it the world's *highest* mountain—that is, the peak is the highest point on Earth.

• The world's *tallest* mountain is Mauna Kea (White Mountain) on the island of Hawaii, U.S.A. Measured from its submarine base in the Hawaiian Trough to its peak, it has a combined height of 33,480 ft. (10,205 m), of which 13,796 ft. (4,205 m) is above sea level.

• Monte Pico in the Azores, Portugal, has an altitude of 7,711 ft. (2,351 m) above sea level and extends a record 20,000 ft. (6,098 m) from the surface to the seafloor, making it the **highest underwater mountain face.**

• The **highest cliffs** are the sea cliffs on the north coast of east Molokai, Hawaii, U.S.A., near Umilehi Point. They descend 3,300 ft. (1,010 m) to the sea at an average inclination of more than 55 degrees and an average gradient of more than 1 in 1.428.

• The Ojos del Salado on the border between Chile and Argentina is the world's **highest active volcano** at 22,595 ft. (6,887 m) high.

• Excluding its ice shelves, Antarctica has an average elevation of 7,198 ft. (2,194 m) above the OSU91A Geoid (similar to, and more accurate than, sea level), making it the **highest continent.**

• The Salto Angel in Venezuela, located on a branch of the Carrao River (an upper tributary of the Caroni River), is the **highest waterfall** (as opposed to vaporized "bridal veil") in the world. It has a total drop of 3,212 ft. (979 m), with the longest single drop being 2,648 ft. (807 m).

• The red sandstone Rainbow Bridge in Lake Powell National Monument, Utah, U.S.A., is the **highest natural arch.** It is only 270 ft. (82.3 m) long, but rises to a height of 290 ft. (88.4 m).

LAND MOST REMOTE FROM THE SEA The world's most distant point from open sea is in the Dzungarian Basin, which is in the Xinjiang Uygur autonomous region of far northwest China. It is at a great-circle distance of 1,645 miles (2,648 km) from the nearest open sea.

The **most remote city from the sea** is the region's capital, Urumqi (above), at about 1,500 miles (2,500 km) from the nearest coastline.

1,844,400 miles² (477,698,000 hectares), representing 57.2% of its total area. Next was the Democratic Republic of Congo, with 515,871 miles² (133,610,000 hectares)—58.9% of the country's area.

Largest tropical forest The Amazon rain forest is the largest of its kind, covering 2.5 million miles² (6.475 million km²). Served by the Amazon basin, the world's **largest river basin**, it crosses nine different countries: Brazil, Colombia, Peru, Venezuela, Ecuador, Bolivia, Guyana, Suriname, and French Guiana.

Largest tropical forest reserve The largest tropical forest reserve is the Tumucumaque National Park, in the northern Amazonian state of Amapá, Brazil. Measuring some 15,010 miles² (38,875 km²) in area—over 600 times the size of Manhattan in New York, U.S.A.—the reserve contains many endangered species of plant and animal. The creation of the park was announced on August 22, 2002, by Brazilian president Fernando Henrique Cardoso. Tumucumaque means "rock at the top of the mountain," in reference to the granite rocks rising above the forest canopy.

Largest swamp The world's largest tract of swamp is the Pantanal in the states of Mato Grosso and Mato Grosso do Sul in Brazil. It is about 42,000 miles² (109,000 km²) in area—larger than Denmark and the Netherlands combined!

MOST REMOTE ISLANDS The most remote inhabited island in the world is Tristan da Cunha (pictured with its capital, Edinburgh of the Seven Seas). It was discovered in the South Atlantic by Tristão da Cunha, a Portuguese admiral, in March 1506, and has an area of 38 miles² (98 km²). After evacuation in 1961 (owing to volcanic activity), 198 islanders returned in November 1963. The nearest inhabited land to the group is the island of St. Helena, 1,315 nautical miles (2,435 km) to the northeast.

Bouvet Island, discovered in the South Atlantic by J.B.C. Bouvet de Lozier (France) on January 1, 1739, is the most remote uninhabited island. A Norwegian dependency, it is about 1,050 miles (1,700 km) north of the nearest land—the coast of Queen Maud Land, which is also uninhabited, in Antarctica.

★LARGEST GRASSLANDS The Great Plains of North America are sandwiched between the Rockies and the Mississippi River, and run from the southern provinces of Canada through the Midwest U.S.A. to Mexico, a total area of around 1.2 million miles² (3 million km²). Bison—at up to 2,204 lb. (1 metric ton) in weight, the heaviest land animals on the North American continent—were long a common feature of these grasslands (above): their grazing still goes some way to preserving the open prairies.

★ MOST COMMON CROP In terms of global production, maize is the world's most common crop, with 600 million tons harvested annually. Rice and wheat are the next most common, at just under 600 million each. All three form the planet's primary food staples.

THE EARTH AT A GLANCE

• The Earth is **more than 4.6 billion years old.**

• The **diameter of the Earth at the equator** is 7,926.5966 miles (12,756.2726 km), but...

• The **diameter at the poles** is 7,900.0205 miles (12,713.5032 km).

• The distance between the **center of the Earth and the North Pole** is 144 ft. (44 m) *longer* than the distance from the **center to the South Pole.**

• So, the Earth is clearly **not a perfect sphere**—in fact, it has pear-shaped asymmetry.

• It has a **mass** of (deep breath!) 5,976,000,000,000,000,000,000,000 kg (that's 5.9 septillion kg).

• The mass is being added to all the time as the planet picks up about **40,000,000 kg of cosmic dust** each year.

• The **atmosphere**—the air above us—weighs 5,517,000,000,000,000,000 kg (5.517 quintillion kg).

At sea level, the weight of the air pressing down on this square inch is about 14.7 lb. (6.6 kg, or 1 kg per sq cm). At the top of Everest there is less air above you, so the atmosphere weighs about one-third of this.

• The **weight of the ocean's water** is 1,390,000,000,000,000,000,000 kg (1.39 sextillion kg).

• The **volume of the Earth** is about 259,875,300 miles³ (1,083,207,000 km³).

• The **temperature at the center of the Earth** is estimated to be 9,032–10,832°F (5,000–6,000°C).

• The **Earth's crust** is an average of 13 miles (21 km) thick, but the **deepest we've ever drilled down** is just over 7.6 miles (12 km).

LARGEST PINGO Pingos are isolated conical mounds that have a core of ice.·They form when lakes in permafrost regions drain. As the residual water in the ground under the lake freezes, it expands to push up a mound of land. Ibyuk Pingo (above), in the Tuktoyaktuk Peninsula on the western Arctic coast of Canada, is the world's largest. It measures around 160 ft. (50 m) high and 990 ft. (300 m) around its base.

★**Largest tundra** Lying along the Arctic Circle, between the northernmost tree limit and the lower fringes of the ice cap, is the tundra, a vast tract of barren, treeless land that remains frozen for most of the year. The largest swathe of tundra in the world is that found in North America—an area of permafrost (that is, land frozen for over two years) 2 million miles^2 (5.3 million km^2) across northern Alaska, U.S.A., and Canada.

ENVIRONMENT

★**Highest levels of carbon dioxide** According to the World Meteorological Organization, the atmospheric abundance of carbon dioxide, a powerful greenhouse gas, was 377.1 parts per million in 2004. This is the highest in recorded history and represents a 35% increase of CO_2 in the Earth's atmosphere since the pre-industrial era of the 18th century.

★**Largest producer of carbon dioxide (country)** In 2004, nearly 6 billion tons of carbon dioxide emissions resulted from the consumption and burning of fossil fuels in the U.S.A. China is second, with 4.7 billion, and Russia third, with 1.7 billion.

★**Largest fleet of "spy trash" (country)** In 2006, officials in the UK secretly attached "bugs" to half a million household garbage cans in order to monitor the weight of trash thrown out by British people.
  The UK has the third-worst recycling rate in Europe, and this program may eventually lead to fines for people who exceed a certain weight of garbage thrown out each week.

☆**Warmest year on record** A NASA report from January 2006 revealed that 2005 was the warmest year on record. By including data from the

★ **LARGEST ARTIFICIAL REEF** The U.S. Navy's aircraft carrier *USS Oriskany* (aka the "Mighty O," built in 1944) was decommissioned in 1976 after a long, illustrious service. It was scheduled for scrapping until it was decided to be sunk as an artificial reef in the Gulf of Mexico, 24 miles (38 km) off Pensacola, Florida, U.S.A. It was finally sunk on May 17, 2006, using 500 lb. (226 kg) of C4 explosives, taking just 37 minutes to reach the seabed. At 1,149 ft. (350.5 m) tall and 888 ft. (270 m) long, it attracts an abundance of marine life rarely seen in the northern Gulf of Mexico.

Arctic, where there are few weather stations, NASA estimates that 2005 very slightly beat 1998, when the Earth suffered an increase of 0.4°F (0.2°C). Experts have already forecasted 2007 to be even warmer.

★ **Longest surviving greenhouse gas** Of all the gases emitted by mankind that are understood to contribute to global warming, the longest surviving is the refrigerant gas tetrafluromethane, CF_4. The strong carbon-fluorine bonds mean that, once it enters the atmosphere, the gas can last in excess of 50,000 years.

☆ **Largest reforestation project** In May 2002, the Chinese State Forestry Administration announced the beginning of a 10-year reforestation project to plant an area of land the size of Sweden.

The replanted region will measure about 169,884 miles^2 (440,000 km^2),

★ **LARGEST ENVIRONMENTAL PRIZE** In February 2007, Sir Richard Branson (UK) announced a prize of $25 million to be awarded to the person or group that provides the best solution to the removal of carbon dioxide from the Earth's atmosphere. Claimants need to devise a system that will rid the atmosphere of at least 1 billion tons of carbon dioxide every year for a decade. The deadline for Branson's "Earth Challenge" is February 8, 2010.

★ LARGEST PROGRAM OF CLOUD SEEDING In order to increase the amount of rainfall over arid regions in China, around 37,000 peasants armed with rockets and antiaircraft guns regularly fire munitions containing silver iodide particles at passing clouds. These tiny particles artificially increase a cloud's likelihood of producing rain by encouraging water droplets to coalesce and pull moist air up into the clouds. Pictured are cloud-seeding aircraft bearing racks of silver iodide flares that are dropped into clouds as the aircraft flies through.

representing 5% of China's landmass. It is hoped that this audacious program will offset some of the environmental problems caused by excessive logging in China over the past century.

Greatest distance covered by campaign vessels *Rainbow Warrior 1* and *Rainbow Warrior 2*, the flagships of environmental interest group Greenpeace, are estimated to have covered 500,000 nautical miles (926,592 km). *Rainbow Warrior 2* covered 104,428 nautical miles (193,400 km) from 1996

DID YOU KNOW?

The top 10 highest ranking countries in the Environmental Performance Index 2006 are:

1. NZ 88.0

2. Sweden 87.8

3. Finland 87.0

4. Czech Rep. 86.0

5. UK 85.6

6. Austria 85.2

7. Denmark 84.2

8. Canada 84.0

9. =Malaysia 83.3

9. =Ireland 83.3

★ **HIGHEST AND LOWEST ENVIRONMENTAL PERFORMANCE** According to Environmental Performance Index (EPI) research findings presented to the World Economic Forum in January 2006 by scientists from Yale and Columbia universities in the U.S.A., the country (out of 133 investigated using 16 key indicators) with the ★ **best environmental performance** was New Zealand (above right), with a score of 88.0. The country with the ★ **worst environmental performance** was Niger (above left), with 25.7.

to 1999. Greenpeace, founded in 1971, is also the **longest running environmental campaign group.**

Largest ocean "landfill" site The North Pacific Central Gyre is a huge vortex of slowly revolving ocean water, which naturally concentrates floating litter in its center. In 2002, environmental studies revealed that the center of the Gyre contained around 13 lb. (6 kg) of waste plastic for every 2.2 lb. (1 kg) of plankton.

DEFORESTATION

• Of the 44 countries that, combined, represent 90% of the world's forests, Indonesia has the ☆ **highest annual rate of deforestation**, with 4,447,896 acres (1.8 million ha) of forest lost annually between 2000 and 2005. This equates to 2% of the country's forest per year.

• The ☆ **largest deforestation by area** occurred in Brazil, which contains 14% of the world's forests, and where 5,705,663 acres (2,309,000 ha) of tropical forest were lost in 1990–2000. In 2004 alone, Brazilian ranchers, soybean farmers, and loggers cut down 10,088 miles^2 (26,127 km^2) of rain forest.

• The ★ **earliest deforestation disaster caused by humans** occurred when Polynesians first settled Easter Island in the Pacific, around AD 700. The islanders' obsession with building huge stone figures required the use of trees for their transportation. By 1722, no tree was left standing on the 7 × 14-mile (11 × 22-km) island. This deforestation, along with the introduction of diseases and slavery, is ultimately believed to have caused the end of the original Easter Island civilization.

★ **LARGEST LIGHTBULB BAN** On February 20, 2007, Australia announced that incandescent lightbulbs would be banned by 2009 to help cut an estimated 800,000 tons of greenhouse gas emissions.

Worst river pollution On November 1, 1986, firemen fighting a blaze at the Sandoz chemical factory in Basel, Switzerland, flushed 66,150 lb. (30 tons) of agrochemicals into the Rhine River, killing half a million fish.

☆ **LARGEST HOLE IN THE OZONE LAYER** On October 2, 2006, the European Space Agency (ESA) revealed that the hole in the ozone layer above Antarctica was large enough to hold 88 billion lb. (40 million tons) of ozone.

The image (left) has been created from satellite data, with the dark colors showing the areas of least ozone in the atmosphere.

FRIGID EARTH

Coldest desert The McMurdo Dry Valleys in Antarctica receive less than 4 in. (100 mm) of precipitation per year and have a mean annual temperature of -4°F (-20°C). With an area of around 1,850 miles^2 (4,800 km^2), they are the largest ice-free zone on the continent. Despite the inhospitable conditions—and a complete lack of sunlight for much of the year—this polar desert can support life in the form of algae, nematode worms, phytoplankton, and bacteria.

★ **Fastest glacial surge** In 1953, the Kutiah Glacier in Pakistan advanced more than 7.4 miles (12 km) in three months—averaging some 367 ft. 5 in. (112 m) per day.

★ **Thickest ice** On January 4, 1975, a team of U.S. seismologists measured the depth of the ice at Wilkes Land in eastern Antarctica and found it to be 15,669 ft. (4,776 m)—equivalent to 10 Empire State Buildings!

LONGEST ICE CORE An ice core measuring 11,886 ft. (3,623 m) in length was drilled from the ice above the subglacial Lake Vostok in Antarctica in 1998. Drilling stopped around 500 ft. (150 m) above the surface of the lake in order to avoid contamination of its pristine environment.

Largest subglacial lake As a result of analyzing radar imagery in 1994, scientists discovered the subglacial Lake Vostok in Antarctica, buried under 2.5 miles (4 km) of the East Antarctic Ice Sheet. It is the **oldest** and **most pristine lake** on Earth, having been completely isolated from the rest of the world for at least 500,000 years and perhaps much longer. Covering an area of 5,400 miles^2 (14,000 km^2), it is the 18th largest lake in the world and has a depth of at least 330 ft. (100 m).

★Coldest liquid water droplets On August 13, 1999, Dr. Daniel Rosenfeld (Israel) and Dr. William Woodley (U.S.A.) reported their discovery of tiny water droplets that remained liquid for several minutes at temperatures as low as -35.5°F (-37.5°C) in clouds over west Texas, U.S.A. Their results were published in the journal *Nature* in May 2000.

LARGEST ICE SHELF The Ross Ice Shelf covers an area of 182,240 miles^2 (472,000 km^2) in the Ross Sea, an indentation into the western edge of Antarctica. At more than three times the area of New York State, it is the largest piece of floating ice in the world. *For a map of Antarctica, see page 171.*

★ LARGEST TROPICAL GLACIER The Quelccaya Ice Cap lies at an average elevation of 17,946 ft. (5,470 m) in the Peruvian Andes and covers an area of around 16.9 miles² (44 km²). Studies have shown that the glacier is melting and retreating by 197 ft. (60 m) per year.

Colder droplets have also been reported, but these 17-micron (0.00066-in.; 0.017-mm) droplets are the coldest ever found that remain stable for a period of minutes.

Longest glacier The Lambert Glacier was discovered by an Australian aircraft crew in the Australian Antarctic Territory in 1956–57.

Draining about a fifth of the East Antarctic Ice Sheet, it is up to 40 miles (64 km) wide and, with its seaward extension (the Amery Ice Shelf), it measures at least 440 miles (700 km) in length—longer than the state of Florida, U.S.A. It is also the **largest glacier** in the world.

★ MOST PRODUCTIVE ICE FLOE Disko Bay in Greenland, 185 miles (300 km) north of the Arctic Circle, produces an average of 20 million metric tons of ice and icebergs a day. The glacier that creates the ice advances at around 8,298 ft. (2,530 m) per day and produces icebergs from a front 6 miles (10 km) long.

☆ **COLDEST PERMANENTLY INHABITED PLACE** The Siberian village of Oymyakon (population 4,000; 63°16´N, 143°15´E) in Russia reached a temperature of -90°F (-68°C) in 1933. An unofficial figure of -98°F (-72°C) for this region has been published more recently.

LOWEST TEMPERATURE ON EARTH A record low of -128.6°F (-89.2°C) was registered at Vostok, Antarctica (altitude 11,220 ft.; 3,420 m), on July 21, 1983. The Vostok research station (pictured left) was established on December 16, 1957, by the Soviets but is now operated by American, French, and Russian scientists.

★ GLACIATED AREAS ★

REGION	AREA
South Polar Region	**4,860,250 mi.²**
Antarctic Ice Sheet	4,839,790 mi.²
Other Antarctic glaciers	20,460 mi.²
North Polar Region	**799,230 mi.²**
Greenland Ice Sheet	666,400 mi.²
Other Greenland glaciers	29,420 mi.²
Canadian archipelago	59,150 mi.²
Svalbard (Spitzbergen)	22,390 mi.²
Other Arctic islands	21,500 mi.²
Asia	**44,700 mi.²**
Alaska/Rockies	**29,690 mi.²**
South America	**10,230 mi.²**
Iceland	**4,700 mi.²**
Alpine Europe	**3,580 mi.²**
New Zealand	**390 mi.²**
Africa	**5 mi.²**

*all figures are approximate

ICE AGE Geological evidence suggests that the Earth endured several severe ice ages early in its history. The **longest ice age** was between 2.3 and 2.4 billion years ago and lasted around 70 million years. During this period, the entire planet was probably covered in ice, possibly to a depth of 0.6 miles (1 km), as illustrated in this artist's impression, above.

Largest area of sea ice The largest area of water covered by sea ice is in the Southern Ocean. During the winter, 6.5–7.7 million miles² (17–20 million km²) of this ocean is covered by sea ice, which decreases in size to around 1.1–1.5 million miles² (3–4 million km²) during the warmer summer months.

The Arctic Ocean, by comparison, is covered by 5–6 million miles² (14–16 million km²) of sea ice in the winter, decreasing to 2.7–3.5 million miles² (7–9 million km²) in the summer.

★Largest body of freshwater The Antarctic ice cap holds some 7.1 million miles³ (30 million km³) of freshwater—around 70% of the world's total. By contrast, the Caspian Sea—the world's **largest lake,** situated be-

---

DID YOU KNOW?

The -90°F (-68°C) recorded in Siberia represents the coldest temperature ever recorded outside of Antarctica.

---

tween Russia and Iran—contains only about 18,713 miles³ (78,000 km³) of freshwater.

Largest pancake ice Sea ice covers 7% of the world's oceans and is found mostly in the polar regions. This ice formation is usually seasonal, but in very cold places—such as the Weddell Sea in Antarctica—the ice can last for two, three, or more summers. When this occurs, "pancake ice" forms—large, rounded discs of ice that can range from 1 ft. (30 cm) to 10 ft. (3 m) in diameter and may grow up to 4 in. (10 cm) thick. The "pancakes" have raised edges from continually bumping into each other.

BLUE PLANET

Deadliest lake The lake responsible for the most deaths, excluding drowning, is Lake Nyos in Cameroon, west Africa, where toxic gases have claimed nearly 2,000 lives in recent decades. On just one night in August 1986, between 1,600 and 1,800 people and countless animals were killed by a large natural release of carbon-dioxide gas.

★**Oldest lake** Lake Baikal in Siberia, Russia, is between 20 and 25 million years old. It was formed by a tectonic rift in the Earth's crust, which still causes Baikal to widen by about 0.78 in. (2 cm) per year. It holds more water than all of North America's Great Lakes combined and has a wealth of biodiversity, including the world's only freshwater seal.

Smallest ocean The Arctic Ocean has an area of 3,662,000 miles² (9,485,000 km²), making it the smallest ocean in the world. It has a maximum depth of just 17,880 ft. (5,450 m). The ocean's surface waters are frozen for up to 10 months a year, with any surrounding land usually covered in snow and ice. Up to 19 in. (50 cm) of ice covers the frozen waters in the coldest months of March and April.

★**Fastest ocean current** The current of warm water that originates in the Gulf of Mexico and then crosses the Atlantic Ocean is responsible for the climate in some parts of Europe being a few degrees warmer than it would be otherwise. The southwest of England, for example, has a very mild climate. With peak speeds of up to 4.4 mph (7.2 km/h.), the current is the fastest found anywhere in the global circulation of the oceans.

★**Oldest ocean** The Pacific Ocean has the oldest of the current ocean basins, with the earliest rocks found on its floor being around 200 million years old. The world's oceans are constantly changing in size as tectonics make the great plates of the Earth's crust slowly move around. One effect of this plate movement is that the Pacific Ocean is gradually shrinking in size by a few inches each year, just as the Atlantic Ocean is gradually expanding.

★**Highest raised beach** The High Coast in Västernorrland, Sweden, has a gravel beach some 853 ft. (260 m) above sea level. Its high elevation is a result of land rising after the last ice age, when the vast weight of the icesheets was lifted. The region is still rising, at a rate of around 0.39 in. (1 cm) per year, and will continue rising for around another 10,000 years.

★ TOP 10 DEEPEST OCEAN TRENCHES ★

TRENCH	OCEAN	DEPTH (FT.)	DEPTH (M)
1. Mariana	Western Pacific	35,797	10,911
2. Tonga-Kermadec	Southern Pacific	35,702	10,882
3. Kuril-Kamchatka	Western Pacific	34,587	10,542
4. Philippine	Western Pacific	34,439	10,497
5. Idzu-Bonin	Western Pacific	32,185	9,810
6. Puerto Rico	Western Atlantic	30,249	9,220
7. New Hebrides	Southern Pacific	30,069	9,165
8. New Britain (Solomon)	Southern Pacific	29,988	9,140
9. Yap	Western Pacific	27,976	8,527
10. Japan	Western Pacific	27,599	8,412

LARGEST . . .

★**Untapped fossil fuel resource** Gas hydrates are molecules of methane that are trapped inside a lattice of water molecules, forming a solid similar to water ice. They occur as vast deposits under the sea floor, where the overlying pressure means that they are kept in the form of a stable solid.

Occasionally, undersea landslides and earthquakes can cause these hydrates to release their methane, which bubbles to the surface. The bizarre phenomenon of "burning water" happens on rare occasions when lightning ignites the methane at the ocean surface. It is estimated that around 10,000 trillion tons of gas hydrates exist globally, around twice the amount of all other fossil fuels combined.

Ocean The Pacific—named from the Latin Mare Pacificum, or "peaceful sea"—is the largest ocean (and largest body of water) in the world. Excluding adjacent seas, it represents 45.9% of the world's oceans, with an area of 64,186,000 miles^2 (166,241,700 km^2). The average depth of the Pacific is 12,925 ft. (3,940 m).

River basin Drained by the Amazon, the largest river basin in the world covers about 2,720,000 miles^2 (7,045,000 km^2)—an area roughly 13 times the size of France. Countless tributaries run from it, including the Madeira, the world's longest.

★**LARGEST MARINE RESERVE** The Northwestern Hawaiian Islands Marine National Monument covers 137,791 miles^2 (356,879 km^2) of the Pacific Ocean surrounding the northwestern Hawaiian Islands. The coral reefs are home to more than 7,000 marine species, a quarter of which are unique to the area. The region was designated a marine reserve in June 2006.

Iceberg The largest tabular iceberg ever was over 12,000 miles² (31,000 km²). It was 208 miles (335 km) long and 60 miles (97 km) wide and was sighted 150 miles (240 km) west of Scott Island in the Southern Ocean by the USS *Glacier* on November 12, 1956.

Bay Hudson Bay in Canada has a shoreline of 7,623 miles (12,268 km) and covers an area of 476,000 miles² (1,233,000 km²). The Bay of Bengal in the Indian Ocean is much larger, at 839,000 miles² (2,172,000 km²), but only if measured by area rather than shoreline length.

WATER WATER EVERYWHERE...

• The **highest wave,** dependent on weather or climate, was calculated at 112 ft. (34 m) from trough to crest. It was measured by Lt. Frederic Margraff of the U.S. Navy, from the USS *Ramapo* proceeding from Manila, Philippines, to San Diego, California, U.S.A., on the night of February 6–7, 1933, during a hurricane that reached 78 mph (126 km/h.).

• The **highest tsunami wash** ever reported was 1,719 ft. (524 m) high and occurred along the fjord-like Lituya Bay, in Alaska, U.S.A., on July 9, 1958. It was caused by a giant landslide and moved at 100 mph (160 km/h.).

• The **highest average tides** occur in the Bay of Fundy, which divides the peninsula of Nova Scotia, Canada, from the U.S. state of Maine and the Canadian province of New Brunswick. Burncoat Head in the Minas Basin, Nova Scotia, has the greatest mean spring range, with 47 ft. 6 in. (14.5 m).

• The **highest ocean temperature** recorded is 759°F (404°C) for a hydrothermal vent. It was measured by an American research submarine 300 miles (480 km) off the American west coast in 1985.

• The **deepest part of the ocean** was first pinpointed in 1951 by HM Survey Ship *Challenger* in the Mariana Trench in the Pacific Ocean. On January 23, 1960, the manned U.S. Navy bathyscaphe *Trieste* descended to the bottom of the trench for the first time. On March 24, 1995, the unmanned Japanese probe *Kaiko* also reached the bottom, recording a depth of 35,797 ft. (10,911 m), the most accurate measure of the trench ever made.

• The world's **clearest sea** is the Weddell Sea, off Antarctica. On October 13, 1986, scientists from the Alfred Wegener Institute in Bremerhaven, Germany, measured the clarity by lowering a standard Secchi disc, measuring 1 ft. (30 cm) across, into the water until it was no longer visible. In the Weddell Sea, the disc was visible until it reached a depth of 262 ft. (80 m)—which means the sea has a clarity similar to that of distilled water.

LARGEST WHIRLPOOLS There are several large, permanent whirlpools around the world, usually caused by merging tides, narrow straits, or fast-flowing water. The most powerful are the Saltstraumen and Moskstraumen whirlpools (both Norway), whose currents have been measured at 24.8 mph (40 km/h.) and 17.3 mph (28 km/h.) respectively. The "Old Sow" (U.S.A.) and Naruto (Japan, pictured) whirlpools have been measured at 17.2 mph (27.8 km/h.) and 12.4 mph (20 km/h.) respectively.

LONGEST . . .

★**River with its entire drainage system in one country** The Chang Jiang River in China measures 3,915 miles (6,300 km) long, making it the third-longest river in the world and the longest in Asia. Its entire drainage system is contained within Chinese territory. The Yangtze, as it is also known, has its headwaters in the glaciers of the Qinghai-Tibetan plateau, heads east across China, and empties into the East China Sea.

LONGEST RIVER The Nile, the longest river in the world, extends 4,160 miles (6,695 km) and has two tributaries. The White Nile flows through Lake Victoria in east-central Africa and merges with the Blue Nile in Sudan. The river then flows north, through Egypt, until it reaches the Nile Delta on the edge of the Mediterranean Sea.

★River tributary The Madeira tributary of the Amazon is the longest in the world, stretching 2,100 miles (3,380 km). It is surpassed in length by only 17 other rivers.

Estuary The world's longest estuary is that of the Ob River, in northern Russia, at 550 miles (885 km). In places it is up to 50 miles (80 km) wide. It is also the world's widest river that is able to freeze solid in winter.

Fjord The Nordvest Fjord arm of Scoresby Sund in Greenland extends inland 195 miles (313 km) from the sea.

LIFE ON EARTH

CONTENTS

NORTH AMERICA

Largest leech When fully extended, the Amazonian *Haementeria ghilianii* can attain a maximum total length of 18 in. (45.7 cm). However, in July 2003, the first of several mysterious mega-leeches that could break this record was found in New Jersey, U.S.A. The first specimen—and only the second terrestrial species of leech recorded from the U.S.A.—was maintained in a tank at Rutgers-Camden University, New Jersey, where it grew to just under 17 in. (43 cm) when fully extended. Moreover, James Parks (U.S.A.)—who in October 2004 found four more examples of this extraordinary species—had previously seen one measuring 20 in. (50.1 cm), curled up in a coil the size of a tennis ball. He did not realize at the time that it was special, so did not collect it. Studies are ongoing to uncover their zoological identity.

Largest flea Siphonapterologists (flea experts) recognize 1,830 species of fleas, of which the largest known is *Hystrichopsylla schefferi*. Females measuring up to 0.3 in. (8 mm) long—roughly the diameter of a pencil—were taken from the nest of a mountain beaver (*Aplodontia rufa*) at Puyallup, Washington, U.S.A., in 1913.

★ Fastest spider An adult female giant house spider (*Tegenaria gigantea*), which is native to North America, attained a maximum running speed of 1.18 mph (1.9 km/h.) over short distances during tests undertaken in the UK in 1970. This means that the spider covered a distance equivalent to 33 times her own body length in only 10 seconds.

SHORTEST GESTATION PERIOD FOR A MAMMAL The shortest mammalian gestation period is 12–13 days and is common in a number of species, including the Virginia opossum (*Didelphis virginiana*, pictured) of North America; the rare water opossum, or yapok (*Chironectes minimus*), of central and northern South America; and the short-nosed bandicoot (*Isoodon macrourus*) and the Eastern dasyure, or marsupial native cat (*Dasyurus viverrinus*), of Australia. (The gestation period is the time during which an embryo or fetus develops in the womb—in other words, the length of the pregnancy.)

☆ TALLEST LIVING TREE A coast redwood (*Sequoia sempervirens*) was discovered by Chris Atkins and Michael Taylor (both U.S.A.) in the Redwood National Park, California, U.S.A., on August 25, 2006, and named Hyperion, after the Greek god. The tree currently measures 379 ft. 1 in. (115.5 m)—this is approximately 2.5 times the height of the Statue of Liberty in New York City, U.S.A.

SMALLEST OWL The elf owl (*Micrathene whitneyi,* pictured) from the southwest U.S.A. and Mexico has an average height of 4.75–5.5 in. (12–14 cm) and weighs less than 1.75 oz. (50 g). This record is shared by the least pygmy owl (*Glaucidium minutissimum*) of southeast Brazil and Paraguay, measuring and weighing the same as the elf owl.

Oldest spider Bird-eating spiders are among the longest lived of all terrestrial invertebrates. A female of the tropical bird-eaters (family Theraphosidae) that was collected in Mexico in 1935 had the oldest recorded age—an estimated 26 to 28 years.

Largest starfish The very fragile brisingid *Midgardia xandaros* is one of 1,600 known starfish species. In 1968, a specimen measuring an astonishing 4 ft. 6 in. (1.38 m) from tip to tip was collected in the Gulf of Mexico.

★Fastest running flying bird The **fastest running bird** in the world is the flightless ostrich, but the fastest-running flying bird is the North American roadrunner (*Geococcyx californianus*). This predominantly ground-dwelling species of cuckoo is native to the southwestern U.S.A. When pursued by a car, the roadrunner has been clocked at a highly impressive 26 mph (42 km/h) over a short distance.

★Smallest centipede Hoffman's dwarf centipede (*Nannarrup hoffmani*) is only 0.4 in. (10.3 mm) long and has 41 pairs of legs. In 1998, researchers collected 10 of them in Central Park, New York City, U.S.A., and sent them to Richard Hoffman, curator of invertebrates at the Virginia Museum of Natural History. The centipede was named in his honor in 2002.

Greatest eater relative to weight The caterpillar of the North American silk moth (*Antheraea polyphemus*) eats more food relative to its own body weight than any other animal. Living on the leaves of oak, birch, willow, and maple, it eats up to 86,000 times its own weight during the first 56 days of its life. If a human baby weighing 7 lb. (3.2 kg) were to equal this feat, it would need to consume 601,800 lb. (273 tons) of food in the same period.

DID YOU KNOW?

To avoid extreme environmental conditions, certain species of animals enter into a dormant state during the summer months. This is called **aestivation** or summer hibernation.

HIGHEST RING COUNT A bristlecone pine (*Pinus longaeva*) known as Prometheus had a record ring count of 4,867 when it was cut down in 1963 on Mount Wheeler, Nevada, U.S.A. The tree grew at an elevation of 10,000 ft. (3,000 m) in very harsh conditions. In such a demanding environment, trees grow very slowly and often do not produce a ring for every year, so Prometheus is likely to have been closer to 5,200 years old—**the oldest tree ever documented.**

ENDANGERED ANIMALS

• The North American ivory-billed woodpecker (*Campephilus principalis*), America's biggest woodpecker, is also the world's ★ **most endangered bird**. It was believed to have been extinct since the 1940s. But in April 2005, after an intensive year-long search for this species, researchers from Cornell University's Cornell Laboratory of Ornithology and the Nature Conservancy found a single male specimen in the Cache River and White River national wildlife refuges of Arkansas, U.S.A.

• The Devil's Hole pupfish (*Cyprinodon diabolis*) numbers between 200 and 500 and is restricted entirely to an unusual system of water holes in Nevada, U.S.A., making it the **most endangered fish**. Its main threats come from the pumping of groundwater for irrigation, desert development, and the introduction of exotic fish species into their environment.

• The **rarest bird of prey** is the California condor (*Gymnogyps californianus*), of which only 49 are reported to exist in captivity.

★ **SLEEPIEST MAMMALS** The Uinta ground squirrel (*Spermophilus armatus,* pictured) begins aestivating (see page 51) in July and thereafter directly enters hibernation, not waking until late March to mid-April of the next year. Hence it sleeps for up to nine months of the year.

The Barrow ground squirrel (*Spermophilus undulatus barrowensis*) does not aestivate, but hibernates continuously for up to nine months to avoid the chilly conditions of its Arctic habitat.

Largest deer An Alaskan moose (*Alces alces gigas*) bull shot in the Yukon Territory, Canada, in September 1897, stood 7 ft. 8 in. (2.34 m) tall and weighed an estimated 1,800 lb. (800 kg).

★ **SMELLIEST MAMMAL** The striped skunk (*Mephitis mephitis*), a member of the mustelid family, ejects a truly foul-smelling liquid from its anal glands when threatened. This defensive secretion contains seven major volatile and stench-filled components. Two of these substances, both sulfur-containing thiols, are responsible for the secretion's strongly repellent odor and are known respectively as (E)-2-butene-1-thiol and 3-methul-1-butanethiol. They are so potent that they can be detected by humans at a concentration of 10 parts per billion—an incredibly low dilution that is roughly equivalent to mixing a teaspoonful with the water from an Olympic-sized swimming pool!

SOUTH AMERICA

★ Smelliest frog The vile-smelling skin secretion of the suitably named Venezuelan skunk frog (*Aromobates nocturnus*) is released for defense purposes and actually contains the same stink-producing organosulfur compound that is present in the famously foul emissions released by skunks. Yet, in spite of its awful stench, this extraordinary frog remained unknown to science until as recently as 1991, when it was finally described and named. Measuring 2.44 in. (6.2 cm) long, it is also the largest member of the poison-arrow frog family, Dendrobatidae.

★ Rarest snake Fewer than 150 Antiguan racers (*Alsophis antiguae*) are now believed to exist, including those in captivity. The snake was once common in Antigua, but disappeared from the island following the introduction of non-indigenous predators, black and brown rats (*Rattus rattus* and *R. norvegicus*), and the Asian mongoose (*Herpestes javanicus*). The racer was thought to be extinct, but was rediscovered in 1989 only on Great Bird Island off the northeast coast of Antigua. Following intense conservation programs, the species is slowly recovering but remains classified as critically endangered on the IUCN (World Conservation Union) Red List 2004.

★ Longest column of ants Army ants in the genus *Eciton,* from Central and South America (as well as driver ants in the genus *Dorylus* from Africa), have a reputation for traveling in highly organized columns. These can be up to 328 ft. (100 m) long and over 3 ft. (1 m) wide and may contain as many as 600,000 individuals, which can take several hours to pass one spot.

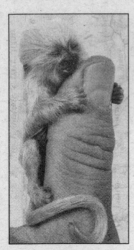

☆ Fastest bird The mean estimated ground speed recorded for a satellite-tagged grayheaded albatross (*Thalassarche chrysostoma*) in level flight was 78.9 mph (127 km/h). The speed was sustained for over eight hours while the bird was returning to its nest at Bird Island, South Georgia, in the middle of an Antarctic storm.

SMALLEST MONKEY Pygmy marmosets (*Callithrix pygmaea*) weigh a mere 0.5 oz. (15 g) at birth and commonly grow to an adult weight of just 4.2 oz. (119 g). On average, they measure 5.35 in. (136 mm) excluding the tail, which is usually longer than the body. Despite their size, they can leap up to 16 ft. 5 in. (5 m) into the air!

They are found in the upper Amazon, the forests of Peru, Ecuador, Colombia, Bolivia, and Brazil.

MOST FEROCIOUS FISH The piranha—especially those of the genera *Serrasalmus* (pictured) and *Pygocentrus,* found in the large rivers of South America—is the most ferocious fish. Attracted to blood and frantic splashing, a school of piranhas can completely strip an animal as large as a horse of its flesh within minutes, leaving only its skeleton.

★**Largest centipede** The giant centipede (*Scolopendra gigantea*) of Central and South America (also known as the Peruvian giant yellow-leg centipede) is 10 in. (26 cm) long. The jaws on its head trap and deliver venom to its prey, such as mice and frogs. A population discovered hanging from cave roofs in Venezuela feed on bats. The venom is toxic to humans (much like an insect sting) and can cause swelling and fever.

Smallest deer The smallest true deer (family Cervidae) is the southern pudu (*Pudu puda*), which is 13–15 in. (33–38 cm) tall at the shoulder and weighs 14–18 lb. (6.3–8.2 kg). It is found in Chile and Argentina.

Smallest crocodile Females of the dwarf caiman (*Paleosuchus palpebrosus*) of northern South America seldom exceed a length of 4 ft. (1.2 m). Males rarely grow to more than 4 ft. 11 in. (1.5 m).

★**SHORTEST SPECIES OF CAMEL** The vicuña (*Vicugna vicugna*) of the Andes, South America, has an average ground-to-shoulder height of 35 in. (90 cm) and weighs a maximum of 110 lb. (50 kg). The vicuña is an endangered species, as it was hunted to near-extinction in the 1970s; however, this has since prompted extensive attempts by Peru, Chile, and Argentina to conserve these animals.

NOISIEST LAND ANIMAL The fearsome screams of the howler monkey (*Alouatta*) of Central and South America have been described as a cross between the bark of a dog and the bray of a donkey increased a thousandfold! The males have an enlarged bony structure at the top of the windpipe that enables the sound to reverberate. Once in full voice, they can be heard clearly up to 3 miles (5 km) away.

Largest wingspan of a bird The South American teratorn (*Argentavis magnificens*), which lived 6–8 million years ago, had an estimated spread of 25 ft. (7.6 m).

★ **LONGEST BEETLE** The tital beetle (*Titanus giganteus,* pictured) of South America has a body length of 6 in. (15 cm)—the longest species of beetle in terms of body size alone.

LARGEST RODENT The capybara, or carpincho (*Hydrochoerus hydrochaeris*), is found in the basins of Paraná and Uruguay rivers and in the wetlands of Argentina and Brazil. It has a head-and-body length of 3 ft. 3 in.–4 ft. 3 in. (1–1.3 m) and can weigh up to 174 lb. (80 kg).

LARGEST...

• Since the early 1970s, when it was discovered as a living creature (until then it had been known only from Ice Age fossils), the world's ★ **largest species of peccary** has been the Chacoan peccary (*Catagonus wagneri*), native to the Gran Chaco region of South America. It has a head-and-body length of 3 ft.–3 ft. 7 in. (90–110 cm), a tail length of 1–4 in. (2.4–10 cm), a shoulder height of 20–27 in. (52–69 cm), and a weight of 65–88 lb. (29.5–40 kg). In 2004, however, zoologist Dr. Marc van Roosmalen (Netherlands) and wildlife cinematographer Lothar Frenz (Germany) encountered a huge, unfamiliar-looking peccary newly captured by some villagers in the Amazon region of Rio Aripuana. It was 4 ft. 3 in. (1.3 m.) long and weighed 88 lb. (40 kg), but was killed and eaten by the villagers. Some of its remains were sent for DNA analysis. The results showed that the giant peccary appears to belong to a completely separate species from the three previously known living peccaries. It is awaiting a formal description and scientific name, and is now the largest species of modern-day peccary.

• The giant water bug (*Lethocerus maximus*) is a carnivorous species that inhabits Venezuela and Brazil. Although not as heavy as some of this continent's burly terrestrial beetles and stick insects, it is still the ★ **largest aquatic insect** at 4.53 in. (11.5 cm) long.

• *Megaloprepus caeruleata* of Central and South America has been measured at up to 4.7 in. (12 cm) in length with a wingspan of up to 7.5 in. (19.1 cm)—making it the world's **largest dragonfly.**

★ **FASTEST SELF-POWERED PREDATORY STRIKE** The trap-jaw ant (*Odontomachus bauri*) of Central and South America snaps its jaws shut at speeds of 114–209 ft./sec. (35–64 m/sec.). Its jaws are employed not only to attack prey, but also to escape threat by purposely biting the ground. Its huge head muscles are used to contract its mandibles, hold them in place, and then release them with such force that it catapults itself to recorded vertical heights of 3.2 in. (8.3 cm), or horizontally through to 15.5 in. (39.6 cm)—the equivalent, in human terms, of a 5-ft. 6-in. (1.67-m) person being propeled 44 ft. (13 m) upward or 220 ft. (67 m) horizontally!

DID YOU KNOW?

The area of the world with the **highest species endemism** is the tropical Andes stretching across Venezuela, Colombia, Ecuador, Peru, Bolivia, and part of northern Argentina. So far, scientists have identified 20,000 vascular plants, 677 birds, 604 amphibians, 218 reptiles, and 68 mammals endemic to this area of 485,716 miles^2 (1,258,000 km^2).

EUROPE

Super Span The **largest prehistoric insect** was the dragonfly *Meganeura monyi*, which lived about 280 million years ago. Fossil remains discovered at Commentry, France, indicate that this dragonfly had a wing expanse of up to 27.5 in. (70 cm).

★ **Largest mammoth** The largest extinct elephant was the Steppe mammoth *Paraelephas* (=*Mammuthus*) *trogontherii*, which roamed over what is now Central Europe a million years ago. A fragmentary skeleton found in Mosbach, Germany, indicates a shoulder height of 14 ft. 9 in. (4.5 m). By way of comparison, the largest African elephant recorded had a shoulder height of 12 ft. (3.6 m).

★**LARGEST OWL** The European eagle owl (*Bubo bubo*) has an average length of 26–28 in. (66–71 cm), a weight of 3–8 lb. (1.6–4 kg), and a wingspan of more than 5 ft. (1.5 m). It is an active predator, hunting rodents and other small mammals.

Largest colony of ants

The largest recorded ant colony in the world stretches 3,700 miles (6,000 km) from northern Italy, through the south of France, to the Atlantic coast of Spain. It is home to a species of Argentine ant (*Linepithema humile*) introduced into Europe approximately 80 years ago.

Oldest fossilized animal food store

In November 2003, a team of scientists led by Dr. Carole Gee (Germany) from the University of Bonn, Germany, announced their discovery of a 17-million-year-old fossilized rodent burrow containing more than 1,200 fossilized nuts. The animal responsible was probably a hamster or a squirrel.

★Oldest spiderweb with trapped prey

The oldest known example of a spiderweb with entrapped insects has been dated back to the Early Cretaceous period of 110 million years ago; it was discovered in San Just, Spain, and reported in June 2006. The sample contains a parasitic wasp (now extinct), a beetle, a mite, and a fly trapped within 26 strands of sticky silk, and is preserved in ancient tree sap (amber).

★**Furriest fish** The extraordinary but little-known species *Mirapinna esau* ("hairy with wonderful fins") was first discovered in June 1911—when a specimen was caught at the surface in the middle of the Atlantic

MOST ENDANGERED WILDCAT The Iberian lynx (*Lynx pardinus*) is restricted to Spain and Portugal, and in 2000 it was estimated that there were only 600 survivors in an extremely fragmented population. It was once widespread across Spain, but has lost much of its territory to agriculture and urban development.

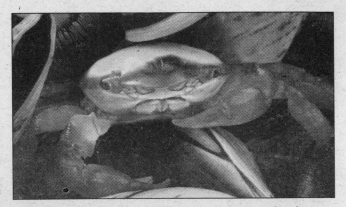

★ **FARTHEST JOURNEY BY A CRAB** In December 2006, an American Columbus crab (*Planes minutus*) was discovered washed up but still alive on a beach in Bournemouth, UK—5,000 miles (8,000 km) away from its home in the Sargasso Sea, east of Florida, U.S.A. The bright orange, 6-in. (15-cm) crab (the actual record-holder is pictured above) is believed to have made its epic journey by clinging to barnacles on a buoy for three months, surviving storms, predators, and sharp changes in sea temperature.

Ocean about 547 miles (880 km) north of the Azores—but remained undescribed and unnamed by science until 1956. *Mirapinna* measures 2.5 in. (6.35 cm) long, with a humped back and uniquely lobed fins, but its most striking characteristic of all is the fur-like covering on its body. When viewed closer, however, this "fur" is revealed to be a profuse mass of living body outgrowths, the function of which remains unknown.

★ **Newest animal phylum** A hitherto neglected genus of small flatworm-like creatures, *Xenoturbella*, was first made known to science

---

DID YOU KNOW?

The ☆ **largest extant bird egg** on record weighed 5 lb. 8 oz. (2.519 kg) and was laid by an ostrich (*Struthio camelus*) on September 19, 2006, at a farm in Borlänge, Sweden.

An average ostrich egg is 6–8 in. (150–200 mm) long, 4–6 in. (100–150 mm) in diameter, and weighs 2.4–4.2 lb. (1.1–1.9 kg)—around two dozen hen's eggs in volume. The shell, although only 0.06 in. (1.5 mm) thick, can support the weight of an adult person.

The ★ **largest duck egg** ever weighed just over 8 oz. (227 g) and was 8 in. (20 cm) in circumference and 5.5 in. (14 cm) high. It was laid by a White Pekin duck owned by Willie and Kitty Costello (Ireland).

when it was dredged up from the Baltic Sea in 1949. At the time, it was thought to be a bizarre mollusc. In November 2006, studies revealed that, in reality, its two species, *X. bocki* and *X. westbladi,* are so different from all other species of animals that they require the creation of an entirely new phylum—the highest category of animal classification—all for themselves.

★**Oldest insect** The fossilized *Rhyniognatha hirsti* lived in what is now Aberdeen, Scotland, UK, approximately 410 million years ago—making it 30 million years older than any other known insect fossil!

The specimen was first described in 1926 by entomologist Robin John Tillyard (Australia), who regarded it as unremarkable and left it to London's Natural History Museum, UK. It remained in the museum's vaults for approximately 80 years, until entomologists David Grimaldi and Michael Engel (both U.S.A.) restudied the fossil using modern microscopes and discovered the creature's classic insect features. They published the results of their research in *Nature* on February 12, 2004.

Although no wings survive, the triangular jaw structure of *R. hirsti* is similar to that of winged insects, suggesting that insect flight is 80 million years older than was previously thought.

★**Oldest tick** In April 1999, a team of American scientists unearthed a 90-million-year-old tick that had been preserved in amber. This blood-sucking parasite from the Cretaceous period was found in a vacant lot in New Jersey, U.S.A. Named *Carlos jerseyi,* the tiny insect has unusual hairs on its back, which may have been used to detect vibrations. It is a logical conclusion that many dinosaurs carried parasitic ticks, just like today's animals.

Greatest tree girth ever A European chestnut (*Castanea sativa*) known as the Tree of the Hundred Horses (*Castagno di Cento Cavalli*) was measured on Mount Etna, Sicily, Italy, in 1770 and 1780. It had a girth of 190 ft. (57.9 m).

★LONGEST BIRD LEGS While the ostrich has the longest legs of any living bird, the bird with the longest legs relative to its body size is the black-winged stilt (*Himantopus himantopus,* right), widely distributed across much of Europe, as well as Africa and Asia. Its long, pink legs measure 7–9 inch. (17–24 cm), which is up to 60% of its total 14–16 lb. (35–40 cm) body length.

LARGEST FORESTS The **largest coniferous forests** cover 1.5 million miles² (4 million km²) in northern Russia (pictured), between latitude 55°N and the Arctic Circle. By way of comparison, the **largest area of tropical forest** is the Amazon rainforest, which covers approximately 2.5 million miles² (6.5 million km²).

Largest cork tree The Whistler Tree in the Alentejo region of Portugal averages over 2,000 lb. (1 ton) of raw cork per harvest—enough to cork 100,000 wine bottles! Portugal has more cork-oak trees than any other country and is responsible for 51% of global cork production.

ASIA

Rare animals The Iriomote cat (*Felis iriomotensis*) is confined to Iriomote in the Ryukyu chain of islands, Japan, making it the ★ **rarest wild cat.** Fewer than 100 specimens are left, some in Japanese zoos.

The **rarest crocodilian** is the Chinese alligator (*Alligator sinensis*), which can grow to 6 ft. (2 m) and weight up to 88 lb. (40 kg). It is found in the lower Yangtze River, but fewer than 200 were living in the wild in 2002.

Smelliest plant Known as "the corpse flower," the *Amorphophallus titanum*—or titan arum—is believed by many to be the smelliest plant on Earth. When it blooms, it releases an extremely foul odor that smells like rotten flesh and can be detected half a mile away.

Largest leaf The largest leaves of any plant are those of the raffia palm (*Raphia farinifera = R. ruffia*) of the Mascarene Islands in the Indian Ocean,

LARGEST TREE-DWELLING MAMMAL
Bornean orangutan (*Pongo pygmaeus*) and Sumatran orangutan (*P. abelii*) males typically weigh 183 lb. (83 kg) and measure 5 ft. (1.5 m) tall. They have opposable toes on their feet and use their arm span of about 6 ft. (2 m) to swing between branches and feed off fruit, small leaves, and tree bark. Being lighter (81 lb; 37 kg), the females usually build nests in trees, whereas the adult males sleep on the ground.

and also the Amazonian bamboo palm (*R. taedigera*) of South America and Africa. Their leaf blades can measure 65 ft. (20 m) long, with petioles (the stalk by which a leaf is attached to a stem) measuring 13 ft. (4 m).

Largest bat The largest bats in the world are the flying foxes, or fruit bats (family *Pteropodidae*), particularly those living in southeast Asia. Several species in the genus *Pteropus* have a head-body length of up to 17.75 in. (45 cm), a wingspan of 5 ft. 7 in. (1.7 m), and a weight of 3 lb. 12 oz. (1.6 kg). The biggest are generally considered to be the large flying fox and the gigantic or Indian flying fox. Although certain other mammals are capable of gliding, bats are the only mammals capable of true flight.

★**Most aquatic spider** The only species of spider that lives underwater is *Argyroneta aquatica*, known as the diving bell spider or water spider. Large populations are spread

air bubble or "bell"

across northern Asia (as well as Europe and north Africa). The water spider's legs and abdomen are covered with dense hairs that trap air when it goes

---

DID YOU KNOW?

The world's **rarest seashell** is the white-toothed cowry (*Cypraea leucodon,* right). It is known from just two specimens, the second of which turned up in 1960, and is thus the most coveted species among conchologists. Its only recorded locality is the Philippines' Sulu Sea. The stomach of a fish caught here during 1960 was later found to contain that second specimen.

CARNIVOROUS PLANT WITH LARGEST PREY Of all the carnivorous plants, those of the Nepenthaceae family (genus *Nepenthes*) digest the largest prey. They are commonly found in the rainforests of Asia, in particular Borneo, Indonesia, and Malaysia. *Nepenthes villosa* (pictured), *N. rájah*, and *N. rafflesiana* are known to catch large frogs, birds, and even rats.

underwater. Although the spider makes infrequent trips to the surface to replenish the air, oxygen easily diffuses into the bubble from the surrounding water, and, conversely, carbon dioxide diffuses out.

Smallest bird of prey This record is held jointly by the black-legged falconet (*Microhierax fringillarius*) of southeast Asia and the white-fronted or Bornean falconet (*M. latifrons*) of northwestern Borneo. Both species have an average length of 5.5–6 in. (14–15 cm)—including a 2-in. (5-cm) tail—and a weight of about 1.25 oz. (35 g).

LONGEST VENOMOUS SNAKE The king cobra (*Ophiophagus hannah*), also called the hamadryad, is found in southeast Asia and India and measures 12–15 ft. (3.5–4.5 m) in length. The longest specimen caught, in Negri Sembilan (now Malaysia) in 1937, later grew to 18 ft. 9 in. (5.71 m) in London Zoo (UK). The head of the king cobra is as big as a man's hand, and it can stand tall enough to look an adult human being in the eye. The venom from a king cobra is enough to kill an elephant or 20 people.

★**LONGEST FEATHERS IN A WILD BIRD SPECIES** The central tail feathers of Reeves's pheasant (*Syrmaticus reevesii*), native to the mountains of central and northern China, sometimes exceed 8 ft. (2.4 m) in length. If thrown up in flight, they act as a brake, causing the bird to drop vertically down into the cover of trees to escape any would-be attacker.

BIG AND SMALL

• Collected from a depth of 4,675 ft. (1,425 m) in the Philippine Sea, a mature adult male of *Photocorynus spiniceps* measured only 0.24 in. (6.2 mm) in length. This is the ★ **smallest species of fish.** It also holds the record for **smallest vertebrate.**

• Mature males of the pygmy hog (*Sus salvanius*) measures 24–28 in. (61–71 cm) long; females are 21–24 in. (55–62 cm). This, the ★ **smallest species of pig,** was indigenous to the Terai region of India, Nepal, and Bhutan, but has been critically endangered since 1996. Isolated populations can still be found in Assam, India, and in wildlife sanctuaries.

• The **largest species of bee** is the king bee (*Chalicodoma pluto*). The females measure a total length of 1.5 in. (3.9 cm). The smaller males measure no more than 0.9 in. (2.4 cm) long. They are found only in the Molucca Islands of Indonesia.

• The Chinese giant salamander (*Andrias davidianus*) lives in mountain streams in northeastern, central, and southern China. One specimen measured 5 ft. 11 in. (1.8 m) in length and weighed 143 lb. (65 kg), making this the **largest amphibian** of all.

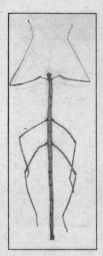

☆ **LONGEST INSECT** Two stick insects share this record, depending on how they are measured. *Pharnacia kirbyi* (pictured) is a stick insect from the rainforests of Borneo. The longest specimen known had a body length of 12.9 in. (32.8 cm) and a total length, including the legs, of 21.5 in. (54.6 cm). This makes it the longest insect in the world based on head-plus-body length. A specimen of Malaysia's *Phobaeticus serratipes* had a head-plus-body length of 10.9 in. (27.8 cm), but when its outstretched legs were included, it measured a record 21.8 in. (55.5 cm).

☆ **Oldest marsupial** The oldest known relative of all marsupials is *Sinodelphis szalayi*, a fossil discovered in China's Liaoning Province in 2001 and thought to be 125 million years old. A Sino-American research team, including Ji Qiang and Zhe Xi Luo (both China), named the fossil and concluded that it originally measured 5.9 in. (15 cm) long and weighed approximately 1.05 oz. (30 g).

★ **Most mysterious new animal** The holy goat or kting voar (*Pseudonovibos spiralis*), named in 1994 and reported by local hunters in southern Vietnam and neighboring Cambodia, is still known to scientists only as a result of the discovery, in 1993, of several pairs of horns. Each pair was around 18 in. (45 cm) in length.

Longest snake The reticulated python (*Python reticulatus*) is found in Indonesia, southeast Asia, and the Philippines. A specimen shot and measured in Celebes, Indonesia, in 1912 was 32 ft. 9 in. (10 m) long.

AFRICA

Greatest root depth A wild fig tree (*Ficus natalensis*) at Echo Caves, near Ohrigstad, Mpumalanga, South Africa, has roots penetrating a calculated 393 ft. (120 m).

Largest seed The coco-de-mer (*Lodoicea maldivica*) is a rare, very slow-growing palm that can live up to 350 years. It is found wild only in the Seychelles. The fruits can take up to six years to develop and contain one to three seeds, each measuring up to 19.6 in. (50 cm) long and weighing up to 55 lb. (25 kg).

★ **Largest pangolin** The giant pangolin (*Manis gigantea*), found from Senegal to Uganda and Angola, is the largest species of pangolin or scaly

SMALLEST CHAMELEON The tiny leaf chameleon (*Brookesia minima*, pictured) of Madagascar is acknowledged to be the smallest of its kind. Another related species, *Brookesia tuberculata*, is also extremely small, measuring an average length of 0.7 in. (18 mm) from snout to vent.

anteater. It is almost 6 ft. (2 m) long and weighs 70 lb. (32 kg); because of its size, this species is terrestrial, whereas many other pangolins are at least partly arboreal (tree dwellers).

★**Most aggressive butterfly** The world's most aggressive butterfly is *Charaxes candiope* of Uganda. This very powerful flier actively dive-bombs animals and people intruding upon its territory.

Longest survival out of water The four species of lungfish that live in Africa (*Protopterus annectens, P. aethiopicus, P. dolloi,* and *P. amphibius*) live in freshwater swamps that frequently dry out for months or even years at a time. Two of these species are considered to be the real survival experts. As the water recedes, they burrow deep into the ground and secrete mucus to form a moisture-saving cocoon around their bodies. They then build a porous mud plug at the entrance of the burrow—and wait. Abandoning gill-breathing in favor of their air-breathing lungs, they can live for up to four years in this dormant position.

Largest millipede The largest millipede in the world is a fully grown African giant black millipede (*Archispirostreptus gigas*) that measures 15.2

LOUDEST INSECT Noise intensity is measured in decibel units (dB), with silence equal to 0 dB. Rustling leaves are 10 dB, a normal conversation 60 dB, busy street traffic 70 dB, and a lawn mower 90 dB. The African cicada (*Brevisana brevis*) produces a calling song with a mean sound pressure level of 106.7 dB at a distance of 1 ft. 7.5 in. (50 cm)—almost as loud as a car horn at 110 dB! Cicada songs play a vital role in both communication and reproduction of the species.

LARGEST GAPE FOR A LAND ANIMAL The hippopotamus (*Hippopotamus amphibius*) can open its jaws to almost 180°—the greatest angle for a land animal. In a fully grown male, this gives an average gape of 4 ft. (1.2 m)!

in. (38.7 cm) in length and 2.6 in. (6.7 cm) in circumference, and has 256 legs. It is owned by Jim Klinger (U.S.A.).

★**Largest lemur ever** The largest lemur of all time was *Archaeoindris fontoynontil,* known only from incomplete fossil remains found in Madagascar's central highlands. The remains, which suggest a body size near to that of a gorilla, and an estimated weight of 330–550 lb. (150–250 kg), have been dated at 8,245 (+/- 215 years) bp (before present day).

★ LONGEST LEAF LIFE SPAN
The welwitschia (*Welwitschia mirabilis*), native to the Namib desert of Namibia and Angola, has an estimated life span of 400–1,500 years, with some specimens carbon-dated to 2,000 years old. Each plant produces two leaves per century and never sheds them. Ancient individuals sprawl out over 33 ft. (10 m) in circumference, with enough foliage to cover a 1,300-ft. (400 m) athletic field.

Greatest transient masculinization by a female mammal The only known female mammal in the world that temporarily changes sex is the juvenile female fossa (*Cryptoprocta ferox*), the largest carnivore species in Madagascar. Research carried out by Dr. Clare Hawkins and supported by Dr. Paul Racey (both UK) of Aberdeen University, UK, has shown that young, female fossas have a protrusion resembling male genitalia and secrete a substance found in male fossas. The fossas eventually outgrow this state in adulthood, when they are ready to mate and raise young.

MOST EFFICIENT SCAVENGER The spotted hyena (*Crocuta crocuta*) utilizes the carcasses of large vertebrates such as zebras and wildebeest more efficiently than any other animal. Its jaw muscles and teeth are strong enough to crush large bones—the teeth exert a pressure of 11,378 lb./in.² (800 kg/cm²)—and its powerful digestive system can break down the organic matter of bones, hooves, horns, and hides.

★ LARGEST TERMITE Queen termites of the African *Macrotermes bellicosus* species sometimes measure as much as 5.5 in. (14 cm) long and 1.4 in. (3.5 cm) across. When she reaches this size, the queen can lay up to 30,000 eggs a day. Pictured is one such queen in Okavango, Botswana, attended by her workers.

LARGEST SNAIL The largest known land gastropod is the African giant snail (*Achatina achatina*). The largest recorded specimen of this species measured 15.5 in. (39.3 cm) from snout to tail when fully extended, its shell length was 10.75 in. (27.3 cm), and it weighed exactly 2 lb. (900 g).

LONGEST FANGS The fangs of one specimen of the highly venomous gaboon viper (*Bitis gabonica*) of tropical Africa measured 2 in. (50 mm). The gaboon viper is also considered to produce more venom than any other snake. A single adult male may have enough venom to inject lethal doses into 30 adult men. Not only do they produce more venom than any other snake, but they also inject more deeply.

OCEANIA

★ **Longest gliding mammal** The yellow-bellied glider (*Petaurus australis*) of Australia can glide farther than any other species of gliding mammal (including other marsupial phalangers, as well as flying squirrels and colugos). It is able to glide up to 377 ft. (115 m) through the air and is also highly maneuverable while airborne.

★ **Largest wasp nest** A wasp nest found on a farm at Waimaukau, New Zealand, in April 1963 was composed of wood scrapings mashed up with saliva into a papier-mâché-like substance. It was so heavy that it fell from the tree in which it had been hanging, then split into two. When whole, it measured 12 ft. 2 in. (3.7 m) long, and was 5.25 ft. (1.75 m) in diameter. It had most probably been built by introduced German wasps (*Vespula germanica*).

Fastest flying insect

Modern experiments have established that the highest maintainable airspeed of any insect, including the deer bot-fly (*Cephenemyia pratti*), hawk moths (Sphingidae), horseflies (*Tabanus bovinus*), and some tropical butterflies (Hesperiidae), is 24 mph (39 km/h.). However, the Australian dragonfly (*Austrophlebia costalis*) can attain 36 mph (58 km/h.) for short bursts.

Smallest starfish

The smallest starfish is the asterinid sea star (*Patiriella parvivipara*) discovered by Wolfgang Zeidler on the west coast of the Eyre peninsula, South Australia, in 1975. It had a maximum radius of only 0.18 in. (4.7 mm) and a diameter of less than 0.35 in. (9 mm).

Most venomous mollusk

The two closely related species of blue-ringed octopus, *Hapalochlaena maculosa* and *H. lunulata,* found around

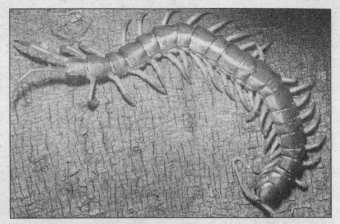

MOST VENOMOUS CENTIPEDE A peculiarly venomous form of *Scolopendra subspinipes* inhabits the Solomon Islands. The venom it injects into its victim, by a modified pair of front limbs rather than by its jaws, is so potent that human victims have been known to plunge their bitten hands into boiling water in order to mask the excruciating pain of this centipede's bite!

MOST DANGEROUS LOVE LIFE The male brown antechinus (*Antechinus stuartii*), a marsupial mouse that inhabits eastern Australia, has an insatiable sexual appetite. For two weeks every year, the entire adult male population tries to mate with as many females as possible. The heightened levels of stress from chasing females and fighting off rival males shuts down the antechinus's immune system, and the entire male population dies within a matter of days as a result of ulcers, infections, or exhaustion. Many also die of starvation, as they neglect to eat during this intense mating period!

LARGEST SPECIES OF CAMEL The dromedary, or one-humped camel (*Camelus dromedarius*), is the largest member of the Camelidae family. Although native to the Middle East, it survives today as a feral animal only in Australia and Spain and as a domestic animal elsewhere. (A feral animal or plant is one that has escaped from domestication and has returned, partly or wholly, to its wild state.)

the coasts of Australia and in parts of Southeast Asia, carry a neurotoxic venom so potent that their relatively painless bite can kill in a matter of minutes. Each individual carries sufficient venom to cause the paralysis (or even death) of 10 human adults. Fortunately, blue-ringed octopuses are not considered aggressive and normally bite only when they are taken out of the water or provoked. These mollusks have a radial spread of just 4–8 in. (100–200 mm).

Largest freshwater crustacean The largest freshwater crustacean is the Tasmanian crayfish or crawfish (*Astacopsis gouldi*), found in the streams of Tasmania, Australia. It has been measured up to 2 ft. (61 cm) in length and may weigh as much as 9 lb. (4 kg).

Most cows killed by lightning
On October 31, 2005, 68 Jersey cows sheltering under a tree at Warwick Marks' dairy farm near Dorrigo, New South Wales, Australia, were killed by a single bolt of lightning.

★**LARGEST EEL** A specimen of the yellow-edged moray eel (*Gymnothorax flavimarginatus*) found in the Coomera River in Queensland, Australia, measured 12 ft. 2 in. (3.7 m) in length and was as thick as a man's thigh. This eel is sometimes also referred to as a leopard moray eel.

SMALLEST BUTTERFLY The tiny grass blue (*Zizula hylax*) has a forewing length of 0.25 in. (6 mm). Its upper side is steely blue-gray in color with a light gray and scattered dark speckled underside.

Youngest incubator The white-rumped swiftlet (*Aerodramus spodiopygius*) lives in Australia and Papua New Guinea and is also found on several Pacific islands. The female of this species lays two eggs, several weeks apart. By the time she has laid the second one, the first has hatched and the young chick is old enough to do the incubating on the mother's behalf.

★**Thinnest lizard** The world's thinnest lizard is the Australian legless snake lizard (*Lialis burtoni*), which can measure more than 20 in. (50 cm) long, but at its mid-body is no thicker than a pencil.

GREAT GREENERY •New Zealand's tree nettle (*Urtica ferox,* above) has the most dangerous stinger. Its stinging hairs inject potent toxins into the skin that have been known to kill dogs and horses.
•The record for the longest distance traveled by a drift seed belongs to Mary's Bean (*Merremia discoidesperma*). It has the widest known drift range for any seed or tropical fruit, traveling over 15,000 miles (24,140 km) from the Marshall Islands in the north Pacific Ocean to the beaches of Norway.
•An inflorescence is a cluster of flowers on the branch of a plant. The ★**largest inflorescence** ever recorded was found on a specimen of *Furcraea gigantea* (also known as *F. foetida*)—a type of agave—measured by Elwyn Hegarty and Hans Meyer in May 2000 in Indooroopilly, Australia. The inflorescence, which took 25 years to grow, reached the remarkable height of 40 ft. (12.18 m).

Longest lizard The slender Salvadori's or Papuan monitor (*Varanus salvadorii*) of Papua New Guinea has been measured at up to 15 ft. 7 in. (4.75 m) in length, 70% of which is taken up by the tail.

AT THE POLES

★**Largest Antarctic land animal** Other than humans working in various research stations, the largest solely land animal in Antarctica is a number of species of midge (gnat-like flies) no more than 0.47 in. (12 mm) long.

★**First recorded Antarctic dinosaur** Found on Antarctica's Ross Island in 1986, the first species of Antarctic dinosaur to be discovered was *Antarctopelta oliveroi*, an ankylosaurid. Ankylosaurids were heavily armored from head to tail.

★**Most southerly bird** Few Antarctic birds nest in the continent's ice-sealed interior. The snow petrel (*Pagodroma nivea*), however, nests up to 150 miles (240 km) inland, among rocky peaks poking up through the ice, and has been spotted at the South Pole.

Deepest dive by a bird Professor Gerald Kooyman (U.S.A.) of California's Scripps Institution of Oceanography recorded a 1,751-ft. (534-m) dive by an emperor penguin (*Aptenodytes forsteri*) at Coulman Island, Antarctica, in 1993.

Southernmost plant Lichens resembling *Rhinodina frigida* were found in Moraine Canyon, at latitude 86°09′S, longitude 157°30′W, in 1971 and in the Horlick Mountain area of Antarctica, at latitude 86°09′S, longitude 131°14′W, in 1965.

The **southernmost flowering plant** is Antarctic hair grass (*Deschampsia antarctica*), found on Refuge Island, Antarctica, in 1981.

HEAVIEST BRAIN The brain of the sperm whale (*Physeter macrocephalus*, left) weighs up to 19 lb. 13 oz. (9 kg)—six times heavier than a human's. Despite its size, the whale's brain accounts for just 0.02% of its total body weight.

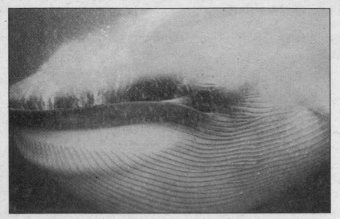

LARGEST NOSE The nose of the blue whale (*Balaenoptera musculus*, above) measures 16 ft. (5 m) long—up to 33% of its total body length. It is the largest mammalian nose, and indeed the largest nose of any animal species.

Most remote tree The nearest companion of a solitary Norwegian spruce on Campbell Island, Antarctica, is more than 137.9 miles (222 km; 119.8 nautical miles) away on the Auckland Islands.

★Lowest temperature-tolerance for insects The insect with the greatest tolerance of low temperatures is the woolly bear caterpillar of the

MOST FATTY DIET The diet of the polar bear (*Ursus maritimus*) in spring and early summer consists of recently weaned ringed seal pups, which can be up to 50% fat. From April to July, the seals are in such plentiful supply that the bears sometimes feed only on the fat below the skin and leave the rest of the carcass untouched.

Greenland tiger moth (*Gynaephora groenlandica*), native to the high Arctic. For up to 10 months of the year, its caterpillar can spend its time frozen solid at temperatures as low as −58°F (−50°C)—and possibly even lower!—and suffer no ill effects.

★**Most northerly bird** On average, the most northerly breeding range of any species of bird is that of the ivory gull (*Pagophila eburnea*). It occurs almost exclusively north of 70°N, and its principal breeding grounds can be found on Svalbard, Franz Josef Land, Novaya Zemlya, northern Canada, and northern Greenland.

★**Greatest concentration of large mammals** A herd of northern fur seals (*Callorhinus ursinus*) that breeds mostly on St. George and St. Paul (two islands in Alaska's Pribilof group) currently numbers just under one million. This herd reached a peak of approximately 2.5 million animals during the late 1950, but extensive hunting has reduced their numbers significantly.

Shortest lactation period for a mammal Hooded seals (*Cystophora cristata*) breed on ice floes, and their pups are born between mid-March and early April, weighing about 44 lb. (20 kg). Their lactation period is a mere three to five days.

LOWEST TEMPERATURE ENDURED BY A BIRD The emperor penguin (*Aptenodytes forsteri*) endures an average temperature of -4°F (-20°C) on the Antarctic sea ice, where the wind speed can vary from 16 to 47 mph (25 to 75 km/h.). Luckily, penguins have the **highest density of feathers** of all bird species—around 75 feathers per square inch in the emperor (which also has the **longest feathers of any penguin**), Adelie, yellow-eyed, and fairy penguins. The feathers have their own small muscles associated with them to allow control. On land, the feathers stay erect to trap air to insulate them; in the water, they flatten to form a watertight barrier.

NORTHERNMOST PLANT The yellow poppy (*Papaver radicatum*, pictured) and the Arctic willow (*Salix arctica*) survive at latitude 83°N, although the latter exists there in an extremely stunted form.

THE BEAR FACTS

• The **largest of all carnivores on land** is the polar bear (*Ursus maritimus*). Adult males typically weigh 800–1,320 lb. (400–600 kg)—up to twice that of a tiger—and have an average nose-to-tail length of 7 ft. 10 in.—8 ft. 6 in. (2.4–2.6 m). The **largest specimen** was a bear estimated at around 1,984 lb (900 kg)—it was shot in the Chukchi Sea, west of Kotzebue, Alaska, U.S.A., and reportedly measured 11 ft. 5 in. (3.5 m) over the body contours from nose to tail.

• A home range is the area where animals typically eat, sleep and interact. The **largest indigenous home range of any land-based mammal** belongs to the polar bear. It can typically tramp over Arctic areas of 11,500 miles² (30,000 km²)—the size of Italy—in a single year. Polar bears can also swim vast distances—up to 62 miles (100 km).

• Polar bears have the **most sensitive noses of all land mammals.** They can detect prey such as seals over 18 miles (30 km) away, often under thick ice.

• An adult male polar bear has a stomach capacity of approximately 150 lb. (68 kg), and it is known to kill animals as large as walruses weighing 1,100 lb. (500 kg) and beluga whales at 1,322 lb. (600 kg). This makes the polar bear the animal with the **largest prey.**

★ **MOST EXCLUSIVE FAMILY OF POLAR BIRDS** The sheathbills, who belong to the Chionidae family, are confined exclusively to the subantarctic-Antarctic zone. They are the only entire family of birds endemic to this faunal region, and live on or near to the shores of subantarctic Atlantic and Indian Ocean islands, often in association with penguin colonies.

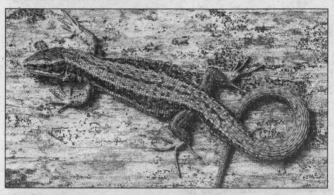

★ **MOST NORTHERLY LIZARD** The common (viviparous) lizard (*Lacerta vivipara*) lives as far north as the northern extremes of mainland Norway, and therefore high above the Arctic Circle.

★ **MOST SOUTHERLY BIRD TRACKS** The most southerly bird tracks ever recorded were those of an emperor penguin (*Aptenodytes forsteri*), discovered by chance by a team of Antarctic explorers on December 31, 1957—more than 248 miles (400 km) from the nearest sea! Pictured is an emperor on Snow Hill Island on the Antarctic peninsula.

GUINNESS WORLD RECORDS DAY 2006

U.S.A. SMALLEST WAIST Cathie Jung (U.S.A.) paid a visit to our U.S. office to have her tiny waist measured. Despite her regular height (5 ft. 8 in.; 172 m), her corseted waist is just 15 in. (38.1 cm).

CANADA ★ HIGHEST WINE CELLAR The CN Tower's Cellar in the Sky, recognized on November 8, 2006, as part of Guinness World Records Day, stands 1,151 ft. (351 m) above ground in Toronto, Ontario, Canada.

BRAZIL **TALLEST MAN** Xi Shun Bao, until recently the tallest living man at 7 ft. 8.9 in. (2.36 m), was welcomed with open arms in Brazil, where he visited Corcovado mountain and stood alongside the 125-ft.-tall (38-m) statue of Christ the Redeemer.

AUSTRALIA ★ **LARGEST UNDERWATER DANCE CLASS** An underwater dance class consisting of 74 students and instructors, who danced for 13 min. 30 sec., was held at the Sydney Olympic Park Aquatic Centre, New South Wales, Australia.

U.S.A. ☆ **MOST RATTLESNAKES HELD IN THE MOUTH** Jackie Bibby (U.S.A.) once again proved he is the most fearless snake handler on the planet by holding 10 live rattlesnakes in his mouth by their tails, without any assistance, for 10 seconds in New York City, U.S.A.!

IRELAND ★ **FASTEST ACCORDION PLAYER** Liam O'Connor (Ireland) proved he has the world's fastest fingers by playing *Tico Tico* at a speed of 11.67 notes per second on the Rick O'Shea radio show on 2FM in Dublin, Ireland.

Find out about GWR DAY 2007 at www.guinnessworldrecords.com/gwrday07.

SCOTLAND ☆ SHORTEST STREET Ebenezer Place in Wick, Caithness, Scotland, measured just 6 ft. 9 in. (2.05 m) long when verified for Guinness World Records Day. The street has a postal address (No. 1), a doorway, and a stone street sign.

CANADA ☆ LONGEST LINE OF DANCERS The record for the longest single line of dancers consisted of 1,681 participants and was organized by The Hummingbird Centre, Breakfast Television, and the Radio City Music Hall Rockettes in Toronto, Canada, on November 9, 2006, as part of Guinness World Records Day.

FRANCE ★ MOST PEOPLE KISSING SIMULTANEOUSLY A total of 594 amorous couples puckered up and kissed at an event organized by OPHA at La Défense in Paris, France.

PORTUGAL ☆ MOST WIDELY SUPPORTED FOOTBALL CLUB The most widely supported soccer club is Sport Lisboa e Benfica, Portugal, which has 160,398 paid members. The record was acknowledged on November 9, 2006, during the celebrations for Guinness World Records Day.

SWEDEN GWR AT GALLERIAN Lots of records, including the ★longest hair extensions, the most ★continuous six-step break moves, the ☆longest time controlling a soccer ball while lying down, and the ☆most yo-yos spinning simultaneously, were set at the Gallerian shopping center, in Stockholm, Sweden, as part of GWR Day.

GERMANY LONGEST SINGING MARATHON The longest singing marathon by an individual was 59 hr. 12 min. by Hartmut Timm (Germany) at Alt Waren in Waren, Müritz, Germany, between November 9 and 11, 2006, as part of Guinness World Records Day. (*This record has since been broken twice.*)

INTERNATIONAL ★ LARGEST GLOBAL NEWSPAPER A total of 71 editions of the *Metro* newspaper are published in over 100 cities, 21 countries, and 19 languages across Europe, the Americas, and Asia, attracting a daily readership of 18.5 million. Pictured is GWR Editor-in-Chief Craig Glenday (left) with *Metro*'s founder, Pelle Tornberg (Sweden).

0:10

NORWAY ☆ MOST CONCRETE BLOCKS SMASHED Narve Læret (Norway) had a smashing time on GWR Day 2006—using just his bare hands, he broke 90 concrete blocks in only a minute on the set of *Senkveld* (TV2) in Oslo, Norway.

NEW ZEALAND
☆ **FARTHEST ZORB ROLL**
The greatest distance traveled by a zorb ball in one roll is 1,870 ft. (570 m), by Steve Camp (South Africa) in Paengaroa, New Zealand. A zorb ball weighs around 198 lb. (89 kg) and keeps the "zorbonaut" inside in an air cushion about 2 ft. (60 cm) off the ground.

QATAR ☆ **LARGEST SOCCER BALL** The largest soccer ball made from artificial leather measures 29 ft. 9 in. (9.07 m). The record was set by Doha Bank, Doha, Qatar, on November 9, 2006.

★ MORE GWR DAY FUN ★

RECORD	HOLDER	DETAILS
★ Most underpants pulled on in a minute	Grant Denyer (Australia)	Denyer pulled on 19 pairs of underwear at the Sunrise TV studio (Seven Network), Sydney, Australia.
★ Most passes of a giant volleyball	Vanessa Sheridan & Paddy Bunce (both UK)	The pair made 582 passes of a giant volleyball on *Capital Breakfast with Johnny Vaughan* in London, UK.
☆ Fastest time to pop 100 balloons	Dermot O'Leary & Alan Conely (both UK)	The duo took just 25 seconds to pop them all on *The New Paul O'Grady Show* (Channel 4) in London, UK.
☆ Most skips in a minute	Philip Sutcliffe (Ireland)	Sutcliffe completed 241 skips on the set of *Ireland AM* (TV3) in Dublin, Ireland.
★ Most shoelaces tied in a minute	Andy Akinwolere (UK)	He laced up 14 shoes on the set of *Blue Peter* (BBC) in London, UK.
★ Most people sport-stacking	World Sport Stacking Association (U.S.A.)	An incredible 81,252 participants across the U.S.A. took part in a multiple-venue mass cup-stack.

ENGLAND ★ MOST SYNCHRONIZED SWIMMING BALLET LEG SWITCHES IN 1 MINUTE Members of Aquabatix (UK, above) executed 71 ballet leg switches in a minute in the Trafalgar Square fountains, in London, UK.

CHINA ☆ LARGEST GAME OF TELEPHONE The largest game of telephone involved 1,083 people from the cycling club of Chengdu City Sports Association for Oldster and was set in Chengdu City, Sichuan Province, China.

LIGHT FANTASTIC

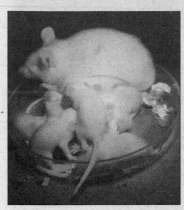

★ MICE Scientists at Advanced Cell Technology (ACTC), a pioneering biotechnology company based in Alameda, California, U.S.A., created the world's **first bioluminescent mice** by inserting a bioluminescent jellyfish gene into their DNA. Their skin, eyes, and organs glow in the dark, but their fur does not. Advanced Cell Technology has since moved on to focus exclusively on the field of human embryonic stem-cell research, to develop a new type of treatment called "regenerative medicine."

★ PIGS The world's **first bioluminescent pigs** were born in 2005, created by a scientific team from Taiwan University. They added DNA from bioluminescent jellyfish to pig embryos, which were then implanted into sows. Three male bioluminescent piglets were subsequently born. Their skin and internal organs have a greenish tinge, which becomes a torch-like glow if blue light is shone on them in the dark. Stem cells taken from them will be used to trace human diseases, as the green-glowing protein that the pigs produce can be readily observed without the need for biopsies or invasive tests.

MOST DANGEROUS GLOWING ANIMAL All scorpions glow, although none of them is bioluminescent. They are fluorescent—when ultraviolet light (invisible to the human eye) is shone upon a scorpion in the dark, visible light bounces back off of it, yielding a blue glow that humans can see. A special layer within the scorpion's cuticle, known as the hyaline layer, contains substances that change the wavelength of the ultraviolet light into visible blue light.

★LAKE Mosquito Bay on the island of Vieques in Puerto Rico, U.S.A., is the world's most bioluminescent lake, containing up to 700,000 tiny dinoflagellates per gallon of water. When agitated, these microscopic organisms (*Pyrodinium bahamense,* or "whirling fire") react by flashing a blue-green light for about one-tenth of a second. The island boasts other bioluminescent bays, but Mosquito Bay is the brightest—its narrow mouth prevents the dinoflagellates from being washed out to sea, and decaying mangrove swamps provide them with plentiful food.

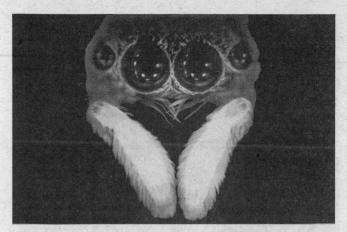

★SPIDER The male ornate jumping spider (*Cosmophasis umbratica*) uses ultraviolet fluorescence to attract a mate. Scales on the body and face reflect UV light, which sensory organs called palps, situated just below the female's eye (pictured above), react to by fluorescing bright green when stimulated, making the female the world's most **bioluminescent spider.** Biologists in Singapore and the UK have concluded that attraction between these spiders would not be possible without this sexual lightshow.

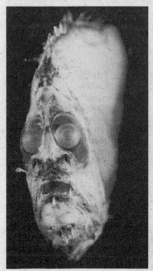

★FISH The hatchet fish (family Sternoptychidae) is the **most bioluminescent fish,** based on its brightness relative to its size. It inhabits the ocean's mesopelagic (or "twilight") zone, at depths of 650–4,900 ft. (200–1,500 m) and has ventral (belly) light organs, which may help to hide the fish's presence from would-be predators by blending it into the weak light from above.

FIREFLY The most bioluminescent insect is the firefly (*Pyrophorus noctilucus*), which has been documented as having a surface brightness of 45 millilamberts. The light emitted by fireflies (which are actually beetles, not flies) is unique as almost 100% of the energy is given off as light. In a lightbulb, for example, only 10% of the energy is light, while the other 90% is given off as heat.

★ **SQUID** The firefly squid (*Watasenia scintillans*) is the world's most bioluminescent squid and inhabits the deep waters around northern Japan. It grows to around 2.5 in. (6 cm) in length and weighs around 0.3 oz. (9 g). It emits intermittent flashes of brilliant light, which resemble those created by fireflies; hence its common name.

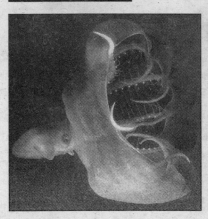

★ **OCTOPUS** The only significantly bioluminescent species of octopus is a red deepwater species from the eastern U.S.A. called *Stauroteuthis syrtensis.* When dark, a row of sucker-like structures running the length of each tentacle glows blue-green. Researchers now believe that these structures are suckers that are no longer used, but have instead evolved into light-emitting photo-lures that flash on and off to attract prey.

HIGHEST ALTITUDE BALLOON SKYWALK Mike Howard (UK) walked on a beam between two hot-air balloons at an altitude of 21,400 ft. (6,522 m) near Yeovil, Somerset, UK, on September 1, 2004, as part of a recording for the *Guinness World Records: 50 Years, 50 Records* TV show. In doing so, he broke his own record of 19,000 ft. (5,791.2 m), which he set in 1998 over Marshall, Michigan, U.S.A., without using a parachute!

★ FIRST FLIGHT WITH ROCKET-POWERED WINGS The first person to successfully achieve horizontal human flight is Yves Rossy (Switzerland), who flew for four minutes at an altitude of 5,250 ft. (1,600 m) and at a speed of 111 mph (180 km/h.) above Yverdon airfield near Lake Neuchâtel in Switzerland on June 24, 2004. The former military pilot created his "jet-man" project by adding two kerosene-powered jet engines to 10-ft.-long (3-m), foldable carbon wings.

HIGHEST COMMERCIAL DECELERATOR The highest commercial decelerator descent facility is Sky Jump at Macau Tower Convention and Entertainment Center in Macau (China)—the 10th tallest building in the world. The descent starts from level 61 of the tower, at a height of 764 ft. (233 m) from ground level, and each descent takes 17–20 seconds to complete.

The inaugural jump was completed by multiple Guinness World Record holder A. J. Hackett (New Zealand) on August 17, 2005.

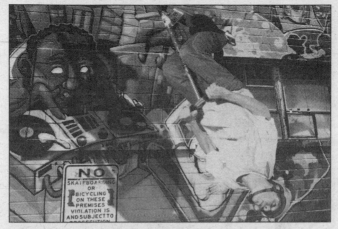

FIRST BACKFLIP ON A KICK SCOOTER Using a ramp with a height of 18 ft. (5.48 m), stuntman and action-sports expert Jarret Reid of Anaheim, California, U.S.A., performed a backflip—landing with both feet on the scooter—at Van Nuys Airport, California, U.S.A., for *Guinness World Records: Primetime* on January 21, 2001.

☆ **OLDEST PERSON TO RAPPEL DOWN A BUILDING** Doris Long (UK, b. May 18, 1914) rappeled down Millgate House—197 ft. (60 m) from the roof to the ground—in St. George's Square, Portsmouth, UK, on June 10, 2006, aged 92 years 24 days.

★ MOST BUILDINGS CLIMBED (UNASSISTED) Alain "Spiderman"
Robert (France) has climbed 70 towers, monuments, and skyscrapers
without ropes, suction devices, or safety equipment. A dedicated solo
urban climber (who suffers from vertigo), Alain uses pipes, window
frames, cables, and the gaps between brickwork to scale structures that
often measure over 1,300 ft. (400 m). He has been arrested and
imprisoned at locations all over the world for his unannounced and
illegal ascents. He is pictured here climbing the Investment Authority
building in Abu Dhabi on February 23, 2007.

LONGEST KITE SURF (FEMALE) Andreya Wharry (UK) kite-surfed 115.4 nautical miles (132.80 miles; 213.72 km) between Watergate Bay, Cornwall, UK, and Dungarven, Ireland, on September 7, 2005.

★**LARGEST VESSEL WATER-SKIED BEHIND** Dirk Gion (Germany) water-skied for five minutes at 17 knots (20 mph; 32 km/h.) behind MS *Deutschland,* a 575-ft. (175-m), oceangoing cruise liner, on June 12, 2006. Gion was brought up to speed behind the liner by a small motorboat, then jumped with his skis on, line in hand, and began waterskiing at full speed.

★**KITE BUGGY LONGEST JOURNEY** Pete Ash, Kieron Bradley, and Brian Cunningham (all UK) used a kite to propel a kite buggy 630.7 miles (1,015 km) across the Gobi Desert in China and Mongolia from September 5 to 21, 2004.

HUMAN BEINGS

CONTENTS

ANATOMICAL ANOMALIES

☆ **Most fingers and toes (polydactilism)** Pranamya Menaria (India) has 25 digits in total (12 fingers and 13 toes), as does Devendra Harne (India), who also has 12 fingers and 13 toes.

☆ **Largest appendix removed** The appendix removed from 72-year-old Safranco August (Croatia) during an autopsy at the Ljudevit Jurak University department of pathology in Zagreb, Croatia, on August 26, 2006, measured 10.2 in. (26 cm) long.

★ **Heaviest fibroid** The heaviest fibroid—a benign fibrous tumor usually found in the uterus—weighed 22 lb. 13 oz. (10.36 kg) and belonged to Indira Khetan (India). The fibroid was removed by a team of surgeons led by Dr. Archana Baser (India) at the Suyash Hospital, Indore, India, on January

☆ **HEAVIEST LIVING MAN** When work began on *Guinness World Records 2008,* Mexico's Manuel Uribe weighed an estimated 1,235 lb. (560 kg), heavier than any known living person. Uribe appeared on Mexican television making an impassioned plea for help with his extraordinary weight, which he received in the form of Italian surgeon Giancarlo De Bernardinis (Italy). He offered Uribe a gastric bypass, on condition that he lose some weight first. Uribe obliged and began a successful high-protein diet.

As we went to press, Uribe was making his first foray outdoors in five years (above, on a flatbed truck driving around Monterrey), and now weighs around 840 lb. (381 kg).

HAIRIEST FAMILY Victor "Larry" Ramos Gomez, pictured here, and his brother Gabriel "Danny" (both Mexico) suffer from a rare condition characterized by excessive facial and bodily hair. They are two of a family of 19 that spans five generations, and all suffer from congenital generalized hypertrichosis. The women are covered with a light to medium coat of hair, while the men of the family have thick hair on approximately 98% of the body, except for the hands and feet.

20, 2007. This was over three times heavier than the previous record holder, removed in an operation in India on December 25, 2000.

★ **Widest tooth extracted** Nine-year-old Shane Russell (Canada) had a tooth measuring 0.6 in. (1.52 cm) wide excised on June 28, 2000. The average width of a maxillary central incisor is 0.3 in. (0.76 mm).

The ☆ **longest tooth extracted** measured 0.997 in. (2.53 cm). It was removed from 12-year-old Philip Puszczalowski (Canada) in 1993.

☆ **Longest hair** • **Nipple** Simon Mould (UK) has a nipple hair that was measured at 4.5 in. (11.4 cm) on November 13, 2005.
☆ **Eyelash** On Jolie Matzes' (U.S.A.) right upper lid is an eyelash measuring 2.5 in. (6.4 cm) long.
☆ **Eyebrow** Ji Yang (China) had an eyebrow hair that was measured at 4.5 in. (11.5 cm) on the set of the *Guinness World Records* presentation ceremony in Beijing, China, on January 17, 2006.
☆ **Arm** Robert Starrett (U.S.A.) had an arm hair with a length of 5.3 in. (13.5 cm) when measured in Mequon, Wisconsin, U.S.A., on December 7, 2006.

LONGEST BEARD (FEMALE) Vivian Wheeler (U.S.A.) began shaving her face aged seven, but in 1993, after four marriages and the death of her mother, she finally stopped the daily trimming and grew a full beard. The longest strand from the follicle to the tip of the hair was measured at 11 in. (27.9 cm) in 2000. She prefers to tie the beard up, to allow her to continue with her day-to-day routines.

"It really helped to have a Guinness World Record," said Wheeler. "It showed me I could be proud of being me. It made me feel like I had a chance in society."

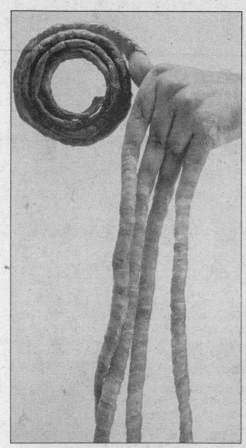

☆**LONGEST FINGERNAILS ON BOTH HANDS (MALE)** Melvin Feizel Boothe of Pontiac, Michigan, U.S.A., hasn't cut his fingernails for 25 years. As a result, he now has a total nail length of 346 in. (931 cm) for both hands—the longest nails of anyone on the planet.

For the female with the longest nails, see page 256.

DID YOU KNOW?

The discovery of Leonid Stadnyk (see page 104) leaves Guinness World Records in a quandary. Without yet having had the chance to measure him six times in a day, as our rules require, we would not normally ratify the record. The tallest man we have fully verified is Xi Shun (China), at 7 ft. 8.95 in. (2.361 m). But, because of the 7.8-in. (20-cm) difference in height between the two men, and the testimony of Professor Besser, we have accepted the claim.

☆ **TALLEST LIVING HUMAN BEING** Leonid Stadnyk (Ukraine, pictured with his mother, Galina) was measured in 2006 by endocrinologist and gigantism expert Professor Michael Besser (UK) and found to be an incredible 8 ft. 5.5 in. (2.56 m) tall. Stadnyk, a certified veterinarian in Podoliansky, Ukraine, suffers from acromegalic gigantism caused by a tumor on his pituitary gland that stimulated the overproduction of growth hormone.

LIFE STORIES

Most fetuses The highest number of fetuses in a single confinement was reported by Gennaro Montanino (Italy). On July 22, 1971, he removed the fetuses of 10 girls and five boys from a 35-year-old housewife. A fertility drug was responsible for this unique instance of quindecaplets.

Heaviest births The world's **heaviest twins,** with an aggregate weight of 27 lb. 12 oz. (12.58 kg), were born to Mary Ann Haskin (U.S.A.) on February 20, 1924.
•The **heaviest triplets,** weighing 24 lb. (10.9 kg), were born to Mary McDermott (UK) on November 18, 1914.
•The **heaviest quadruplets** (2 girls, 2 boys), weighing 22 lb. 15.75 oz. (10.426 kg), were delivered by Tina Saunders (UK) on February 7, 1989.
•Two cases have been recorded of the **heaviest quintuplets.** Both had a weight of 25 lb. (11.35 kg) and were delivered on June 7, 1953, by Liu Saulian (China) and, on December 30, 1956, by Mrs. Kamalammal (India).

Intervals between births The record for the **longest interval between the birth of twins** goes to Peggy Lynn (U.S.A.), who gave birth to a baby girl, Hanna, on November 11, 1995. She delivered the other twin, Eric, on February 2, 1996, 84 days later at the Geisinger Medical Center, Danville, Pennsylvania, U.S.A.
•The record for the ☆ **longest interval between the birth of quadruplets** goes to Jackie Iverson of Saskatoon, Canada, who gave birth normally to a boy, Christopher, on November 21, 1993, and a girl, Alexandra, eight days later on November 29, 1993. She then went on to deliver another boy and girl, Matthew and Sarah, by Cesarean section on November 30, 1993, a full nine days after the first child was born.
•The ★ **shortest interval between the birth of twins in a single confinement** is two minutes and was set by Ellen Louise Brown (UK), who gave birth to Thomas at 4:54 p.m. and Niall at 4:56 p.m. at Dryburn Hospital in Durham, UK, on July 10, 1995.

Premature births The world's **most premature twins,** Devin and Dorraine Johnson, were born on April 8, 1996, at the Elizabeth Blackwell Hospital, Riverside, Ohio, U.S.A., 119 days premature.

DID YOU KNOW?

Conjoined twins derive the name "Siamese" from the **first Siamese twins,** Chang and Eng Bunker, born in Meklong on May 11, 1811, of Chinese parents. They were joined by a cartilaginous band at the chest. Both married and fathered children, and they died within hours of each other on January 17, 1874, aged 62.

Life Stories

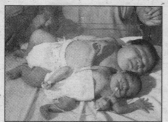 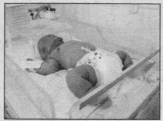

☆ **HEAVIEST NEWBORN BABIES** The heaviest baby delivered in the past 12 months was Antonio Cruz (b. January 28, 2007, pictured above left with an average newborn to show his size), who was born in Cancun, Mexico, weighing 14 lb. 1.4 oz. (6.4 kg). Despite his size, he was 2 lb. (1 kg) lighter than Ademilton dos Santos (b. January 18, 2005, above right), a boy from Salvador, Brazil who weighted 16 lb. 11 oz. (7.57 kg)! The **heaviest newborn** ever was born to Anna Bates (Canada) in Ohio, U.S.A., on January 19, 1879, and weighed 23 lb. 12 oz. (10.8 kg). He lived for only 11 hours. The **heaviest newborn to survive** was a boy weighing 22 lb. 8 oz. (10.2 kg), born in Italy in 1955.

•The **most premature triplets,** Guy, Kathryn, and Marcus Humphrey (UK), were born on February 28, 1992, at St. Mary's Hospital, Manchester, UK, 108 days early.

•The **most premature quadruplets** were delivered by Kathryn Tepper (Australia) on February 20, 1997, 15 weeks early. Ben Stewart (1 lb. 10.3 oz.; 790 g), Hannah Elise (1 lb. 6.9 oz.; 680 g), Ryan Colin (1 lb. 10 oz; 780 g) and Lisa Nicole (1 lb. 8.4 oz.; 735 g) were born at the Royal Women's Hospital, Melbourne, Australia.

Most offspring The **most children delivered at a single birth to survive** is seven, born to three women: to Bobbie McCaughey (U.S.A.), on No-

★ WORLD'S OLDEST LIVING PEOPLE ★

NAME	NATIONALITY	AGE	DATE OF BIRTH
Yoneko Minagawa (*f*)	Japan	114	Jan. 4, 1893
Edna Parker (*f*)	U.S.A.	113	Apr. 20, 1893
Maria de Jesus (*f*)	Portugal	113	Sep. 10, 1893
Helen Stetter (*f*)	U.S.A.	113	Nov. 18, 1893
Bertha Fry (*f*)	U.S.A.	113	Dec. 1, 1893
Florence Finch (*f*)	UK	113	Dec. 22, 1893
Shitsu Nikano (*f*)	Japan	113	Jan. 1, 1894
Arbella Ewing (*f*)	U.S.A.	112	Mar. 13, 1894
Marie-Simone Capony (*f*)	France	112	Mar. 14, 1894
Gertrude Baines (*f*)	U.S.A.	112	Apr. 6, 1894
Tsuneyo Toyonaga (*f*)	Japan	112	May 21, 1894

Source: Gerontology Research Group (www.grg.org) as of March 3, 2007 *f* = female

☆ **OLDEST PERSON TO GIVE BIRTH** The oldest mother is Maria del Carmen Bousada Lara (Spain, b. January 5, 1940), who gave birth by Cesarean section to twin boys, Christian and Pau, aged 66 years 358 days at the Sant Pau hospital, Barcelona, Spain on December 29, 2006.

LARGEST GATHERING OF TWINS On November 12, 1999, 3,961 pairs of twins gathered at Taipei City Hall (left) in Taiwan.

The ★ **largest gathering of opposite-sex twins,** organized by the Taipei Twins Association, was of 806 pairs of opposite-sex fraternal twins at Chung-Shan Hall, Taipei, Taiwan, on November 10, 2002.

vember 19, 1997, at Blank Children's Hospital, Des Moines, Iowa, U.S.A., and to 40-year-old Hasna Mohammed Humair (Saudi Arabia) on January 14, 1998, at Abha Obstetric Hospital, Aseer, Saudi Arabia. Eight children were born to Nikem Chukwu (U.S.A.), one on December 8, seven on December 20, 1998, at St. Luke's Hospital, Houston, Texas, U.S.A. The lightest, Odera, died on December 27, 1998.

•The greatest **officially recorded number of children born to one mother** is 69, to the wife of Feodor Vassilyev (1707–82), a peasant from Shuya, Russia. Over the course of 27 confinements, she gave birth to 16 pairs of twins, seven sets of triplets, and four sets of quadruplets.

Twins Iris Johns and Aro Campbell (b. 1914) were reunited after a record 75 years' separation!

☆ **OLDEST LIVING PERSON** Yoneko Minagawa (Japan, b. January 4, 1893) became the world's oldest living person, aged 114 years 24 days, following the death of Emma Faust Tillman (U.S.A.) on January 28, 2007.

FAMILY TREES

• The record for the **most generations born on the same day** is four, and is held by five families: Ralph Betram Williams (U.S.A., b. July 4, 1982), Veera Tuulia Tuijantÿär Kivistö (Finland, b. March 21, 1997), Maureen Werner (U.S.A., b. October 13, 1998), Jacob Camren Hildebrandt (U.S.A., b. August 23, 2001), and Mion Masuda (Japan, b. March 26, 2005) all share their birthday with a parent, grandparent, and great-grandparent.

• The Rollings family (UK) and the Taylor family (U.S.A.) have given birth to the ☆ **most consecutive generations of twins,** with four sets each.

• The **most albino siblings** were born to two families: the four eldest sons born to George and Minnie Sesler (U.S.A.), and all four children of Mario and Angie Gaulin (Canada).

• The ★ **most twin siblings born on the same day** were born to two women. Laura Shelley (U.S.A.) bore Melissa Nicole and Mark Fredrick Julian Jr. in 1990, and Kayla May and Jonathan Price Moore in 2003, all on March 25. Caroline Cargado (U.S.A.) bore Keilani Marie and Kahleah Mae in 1996, and Mikayla Anee and Malia Abigail in 2003, on May 30.

• The ☆ **tallest female twins** are Ann and Claire Recht (U.S.A., b. February 9, 1988, who, on January 10, 2007, were found to have an average overall height of 6 ft. 7 in. (2.01 m).

The **tallest male twins** are Michael and James Lanier (U.S.A., b. November 27, 1969), who have an average overall height of 7 ft. 3 in. (2.23 m).

• The record for the **youngest great-great-great-great grandmother** was set by Augusta Bunge (U.S.A., b. October 13, 1879) on January 21, 1989, at the age of 109 years 97 days, when her great-great-great-granddaughter gave birth to a son, Christopher John Bollig.

☆**LIGHTEST TWINS** The lowest combined birth weight for surviving twins is 1 lb. 13.57 oz. (847 g), recorded for Hiba and Rumaisa, born by Cesarean section to Mahajabeen Shaik (India) at Loyola University Medical Center, Maywood, Illinois, U.S.A. on September 19, 2004 (pictured).

The lightest surviving triplets—Peyton, Jackson, and Blake Coffey (all U.S.A.), born by Cesarean at the University of Virginia Hospital, Charlottesville, Virginia, U.S.A., in 1998—had a combined weight of 3 lb. 0.8 oz. (1,385 g).

MEDICAL MIRACLES

☆**Most coronary stent implants** From August 7, 2000, to March 30, 2006, Emil Lohen (U.S.A.) had a total of 34 coronary stents implanted. Until then, the most implants carried out at any one time had been six. A stent is a thin tube fed into a blood vessel in order to support or widen it.

★**Most tumors removed** The most tumors removed in one surgical procedure is eight from Kamala Devi (India), who had a total of 13 tumors in her brain. Dr. Krishan Bansal and his team (all India) performed the surgery at the Himalayan Institute Hospital Trust in Dehradun, India, on April 22, 2004.

DID YOU KNOW?

We introduced the **longest time to live with a bullet in the head** record in 2003, following a claim of 53 years from Mr. Satoru Fushiki (Japan). Each year since the record was published, a new, older claimant has stepped forward to break it.

★ **MOST KIDNEY STONES REMOVED** On January 27, 2004, it took surgeons three hours to remove 728 kidney stones from the right kidney of Mangilal Jain (India). The ☆ **most kidney stones passed naturally** is 5,704 (as of August 2006) by Donald Winfield (Canada).

Youngest heart surgery patient A team of 10 doctors at the Children's Hospital in Boston, Massachusetts, U.S.A., carried out heart surgery on a 23-week-old premature baby named Jack, who was born six weeks early in November 2001 at Boston's Brigham and Women's Hospital.

First self-contained mechanical heart implant Surgeons from the University of Louisville, Kentucky, U.S.A., performed the first self-contained mechanical heart implant on an unnamed American patient at the Louisville Jewish Hospital on July 2, 2001.

★**Youngest person to have gallstones and gallbladder removed** On April 1, 1993, Lindsay Owen (Canada, b. September 25, 1983) was admitted with abdominal pains to Saskatoon City Hospital, Saskatchewan, Canada, to have her gallbladder removed. She was aged just 9 years 189 days.

★**Greatest distance thrown in a car accident** Matt McKnight (U.S.A.), a paramedic helping at an accident scene on October 26, 2001, was struck by a car traveling at 70 mph (112.6 km/h) and thrown a distance of 118 ft. (35.9 m) along Route 376 in Monroeville, Pennsylvania, U.S.A. He broke his legs and ripped his thigh open to the bone, dislocated both shoulders, suffered a collapsed lung, and fractured his pelvis, but made a full recovery and returned to work a year later!

First separation of conjoined twins The earliest successful separation of Siamese twins was performed on xiphopagus (joined at the sternum) girls

The undiscovered twin of Hisham Ragab (Egypt) was found in 1997 . . . it had been growing inside his own abdomen for a record 16 years!

☆ **LONGEST TIME TO LIVE WITH A BULLET IN THE HEAD** William Lawlis Pace (U.S.A.) was accidentally shot in October 1917, aged eight. As of September 2006, the bullet remained lodged in the back of his head, 89 years later.

at Mount Sinai Hospital, Cleveland, Ohio, U.S.A., by Dr. Jac Geller on December 14, 1952.

★ **Largest tummy tuck operation** Surgeons at the Hospital de Cruces in Barakaldo, Spain, removed an "apron" of fat weighing 132 lb. (60 kg) from a woman in March 2006. During the nine-hour operation, small cranes were used to help remove the fat from her stomach, which hung over her

★ **FIRST BIONIC ARM RECIPIENT (FEMALE)** The first female to be equipped with a bionic arm is Claudia Mitchell (U.S.A.), who lost her left arm at the shoulder in a motorcycle accident. Her new arm was attached on September 14, 2006 and allows Mitchell to control parts of the limb by thought. She is pictured here with fellow bionic recipient Jesse Sullivan (U.S.A.).

Medical Miracles

LARGEST BLADDER STONE REMOVED
A bladder calculus—a stone formed by a buildup of mineral salts—weighing 4 lb. 2 oz. (1.9 kg) and measuring 7 × 5 × 3.7 in. (17.9 × 12.7 × 9.55 cm) was removed from José de Castro da Silva (Brazil) at the Instituto do Câncer Arnaldo Vieira de Carvalho, São Paulo City, Brazil, on August 25, 2003.

waist onto her legs. The amount of weight removed is equivalent to that of an average 17-year-old girl, and had an energy content of 462,000 calories!

☆**Most blood donated** Lionel Lewis (South Africa) donated his 376th unit of blood on August 29, 2006. Lewis has high blood pressure and so can donate every six weeks, whereas normal donation is every eight weeks.

Highest body temperature Willie Jones (U.S.A.) was admitted to the hospital on July 10, 1980, with heatstroke on a day when the temperature reached 90°F (32.2°C). His temperature was found to be 115.7°F (46.5°C).

LONGEST...

★ **Ambulance ride with patient** Ambulix Fire & Rescue (Denmark) delivered a patient a distance of 2,031 miles (3,269 km) in a Mercedes Benz Sprinter 312 Diesel ambulance from Lisbon (Portugal) to Copenhagen (Denmark) on October 14–16, 2004.

• **Ectopic pregnancy** Marina Hoey (UK) gave birth to Sam on May 22, 2002, at the Royal Jubilee Maternity Service, Belfast, after an ectopic pregnancy lasting a record 233 days (33rd week).

• **Iron-lung patient** June Middleton (Australia) has relied on an iron lung to keep her alive since contracting polio in April 1949.

• **Stay in the hospital** Martha Nelson (U.S.A.) was admitted to the Columbus State Institute for the Feeble-Minded in Ohio, U.S.A., in 1875. She died in January 1975 at the age of 103 years 6 months in the Orient State Institution, Ohio, U.S.A., after spending more than 99 years in various hospitals.

★ **Kidney dialysis** Brian Tocher (UK) began hemodialysis on June 13, 1966, and continues to be dialysed three times a week. He has undergone two kidney transplants during this time, but they were successful for only a few years at a time. In total, he has received dialysis for a record total of 33 years.

• **Porcine (pig) aortic valve replacement** As of May 11, 2007, Harry Driver (UK) was the oldest survivor of a porcine aortic valve replacement, at the age of 76 years 214 days.

☆**LARGEST OBJECT REMOVED FROM THE SKULL** On August 15, 2003, construction worker Ron Hunt (U.S.A.) fell off a ladder and landed face first on a still-revolving 18-in.-long (46-cm) drill bit. It passed through his right eye and exited through his skull above his right ear. Surgeons at Washoe Medical Center in Nevada, U.S.A., found that it had pushed his brain tissue aside rather than penetrating it, therefore saving his life.

The **highest dry-air temperature endured by heavily clothed men** was measured during U.S. Air Force experiments held in 1960 at 500°F (260°C). Temperatures of 284°F (140°C) can be found in saunas.

HEALTH & FITNESS

★**Longest time with ill health** On average, Mexican women spend 15.3% of their lives in ill health. The world average for women is 12%, according to the Organization for Economic Cooperation and Development (OECD).

Hungarian males are ill for 13.8% of their lives, on average. The world average is 9.8%.

Health budgets According to a World Health Organization (WHO) report, the U.S.A. has the ☆**highest health budget.** On average, each U.S. citizen received $5,274 of health care in 2002.

North Korea has the ☆**lowest health budget**; on average, its citizens received the equivalent of just $0.30 of care in the same year.

HIGHEST LIFE EXPECTANCY The country with the highest life expectancy in 2005—the most recent year for which figures have been recorded—is Andorra, with an average of 83.51 years: 80.6 years for males and 86.6 years for females.

Patient-doctor ratios On average, there are 71,958 patients for every doctor in Kinshasa, Congo, the ☆ **highest patient-to-doctor ratio.** African nations dominate the chart of patient-doctor ratios, holding the top 13 places.

By contrast, the ☆ **lowest ratio of patients to doctors** is in Cuba, where there are just 170 patients per doctor.

Death rates Swaziland has the ☆ **highest rate of death** of any country, with 31.2 deaths per 1,000 population per year, as of 2005. The United Arab Emirates has the ☆ **lowest rate of death,** with 1.3 per 1,000.

Population increases The country with the **highest natural population increase** (births minus deaths) is Somalia, with an estimated increase of 32 per 1,000 people in 2002. The world average for the same year was 12 per 1,000 people.

The countries with the **lowest natural population increase** (i.e., the fastest rate of a decreasing population) were Latvia and Ukraine, both with a change of -6 per 1,000 people in 2002.

☆ **LOWEST LIFE EXPECTANCY** Life expectancy in Swaziland has fallen in recent years owing to a combination of poverty and HIV. The average is just 30.8 years, for both men and women.

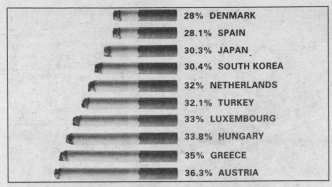

28%	DENMARK
28.1%	SPAIN
30.3%	JAPAN
30.4%	SOUTH KOREA
32%	NETHERLANDS
32.1%	TURKEY
33%	LUXEMBOURG
33.8%	HUNGARY
35%	GREECE
36.3%	AUSTRIA

WORLD'S HEAVIEST SMOKERS This chart is taken from figures published in the OECD's *Health Data 2005* report and shows the top 10 heaviest-smoking nations, based on the number of people who smoke at least one cigarette a day. Austria has the highest number of smokers, with 36.3% of the population—more than 1 in 3.

The world's **largest consumer of cigarettes,** however, is China, where 1,690,000,000,000 are sold every year—one third of all cigarettes consumed annually!

Fertility rates The country with the **highest fertility rate**—measured in terms of most children per woman—is Niger, with eight in 2004.

Niger is expected to have the world's fastest-growing population later this century, with a predicted increase of 41 million from 12 million (2004) to 53 million (2050).

Hong Kong (China) has the **lowest fertility rate,** with one baby per mother in 2004.

Infant mortality rates Sierra Leone has the ☆ **highest infant mortality rate,** with 159.8 deaths per 1,000 live births, as of 2005.

Singapore has the ☆ **lowest infant mortality rate,** with just three deaths per 1,000 live births.

★Highest rate of abortions In Russia, there were 1.6 million registered legal abortions in 2004. Not only is this the highest figure for any country, and the highest figure per capita, it is also higher than the number of live

---

AGING POPULATION

The country with the ★ **largest population of centenarians** (people aged 100 years or above) is Japan, with 25,606 centenarians by the end of September 2005. Evidence suggests that it will extend to 1 million by 2050.

★ MOST PROSTHETICS DONATED The Prostheses Foundation (Thailand) donated and attached 664 artificial legs, the most donated by a single organization, in Sanamluang, Bangkok, Thailand, from July 16 to 26, 2006. The charity was set up in 1992 with a brief to provide free artificial limbs to the poor, regardless of their nationality or religion.

births in Russia in the same year (1.5 million). According to the federal Statistics Service, Russia's population could plummet dramatically—to just 77 million—by the middle of the 21st century.

★ HIGHEST RATE OF OBESITY The South Pacific island nation of Nauru (population 13,287) has more obese people per capita than any other country, with 80.2% of men and 78.6% of women registering a body mass index greater than 30. Neighboring islands Tonga and Samoa have the next largest populations of obese citizens.

★ **HAPPIEST COUNTRY** In a poll by the World Values Survey to establish levels of happiness around the world, people were asked, "Would you say you are very happy, quite happy, not very happy, or not at all happy?" The results showed that the **world's happiest country** was Venezuela—55% of Venezuelans questioned said they were "very happy." By contrast, just 3% of Latvians thought themselves "very happy," making Latvia the world's ★ **unhappiest country**.

★ **Highest rate of death from heart disease** The country with the most deaths from heart disease is Ukraine, where 686 deaths per 100,000 population are associated with the illness.

WHO CONSUMES THE MOST...?

Calories On average, US citizens consume 3,774.1 calories every day, the highest in the world. The recommended daily requirement for men is 2,700, and for women it is 2,500.

Protein Israel consumes more protein than any other country, according to the United Nations, with every Israeli eating 4.53 oz. (128.6 g) every day on average. The world average for protein consumption is 2.65 oz. (75.3 g).

Alcohol The country that drinks the highest amount of alcohol per capita is Luxembourg. In 2003, each citizen consumed an average of 2.8 gal. (12.6 liters) of pure alcohol. Russia has the **highest consumption of liquor per person,** with every Russian drinking on average 1.4 gal. (6.2 liters) of pure alcohol in 2003.

Food Each citizen of Argentina eats, on average, 183% of the UN Food and Agriculture Organization (FAO) minimum daily recommendation.

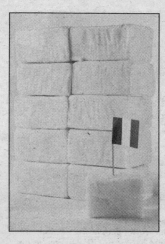

GREATEST CONSUMERS OF FAT
The French have the highest average consumption of fat. On average, each person eats 6 oz. (170.8 g) daily—the equivalent of more than 10 blocks of lard (pictured) every month!

★**Highest rate of death from HIV/AIDS** In Swaziland in 2005, HIV/AIDS was responsible for killing 1,455 people per 100,000 of the population.

Highest rate of death from cancer A 2004 OECD report lists the Netherlands as the country with the highest rate of cancer death, with 433 deaths per 100,000.

★**Highest incidence of diabetes** The country with the most type-2 diabetes in the population is the United Arab Emirates, where 20% of people aged 20 to 79 years are affected. Two other Gulf states are in the top 10: Kuwait (12.8%) and Oman (11.4%). Tied for second place are Cuba and Puerto Rico (13.2%).

Highest incidence of breast cancer According to the WHO, Iceland has the highest incidence of breast cancer, with 39.4 women out of 100,000 undergoing treatment.

FANTASTIC FEATS

CONTENTS

YOUNG ACHIEVERS

YOUNGEST . . .

☆ **Hole-in-one golfer (female)** Rhiannon Linacre (UK) was 9 years 75 days old when she scored a hole-in-one on the par-3 17th hole at Coxmoor Golf Club, Sutton-in-Ashfield, Nottinghamshire, UK, on June 18, 2006.

★ **Football referee** Aged 10 years 358 days, Martin Milkovski (U.S.A.) officiated at a football game between Avanza and Orchard Valley in Redwood City, California, U.S.A., on June 3, 2006.

★ **Top-flight national league soccer player** The youngest person to play in a top-flight national league is Nicholás Millán (Chile, b. November 17, 1991), who competed in Chile's leading division aged 14 years 297 days. He came on as a substitute (in the 79th minute) for his Colo Colo teammate, Felipe Mella (Chile), in their game against the Santiago Wanderers on September 10, 2006.

☆ **Ocean rower (on a team)** The youngest person to row across an ocean is Martin Adkin (UK, b. January 7, 1986) who rowed the craft *All Relative* across the Atlantic (east to west) with teammates Justin Adkin, Robert Adkin, and James Green (all UK). Martin was aged 19 years 327 days when he left the Canary Islands on November 30, 2005; he and his crewmates finished in Antigua on January 8, 2006.

★ **Ocean rowers (team)** The crew of *All Relative* (see above) also set a record for the youngest team of four to row any ocean. Justin Adkin (UK, b. May 28, 1979), James Green (UK, b. February 16, 1981), Robert Adkin (UK, b. June 4, 1982), and Martin Adkin (UK, b. January 7, 1986) rowed the Atlantic east to west from November 30, 2005, to January 8, 2006, with a combined age of 94 years 249 days at the start.

GAMEKEEPER On November 9, 2005, at the age of 11 years 312 days, Robert Mandry (UK, b. January 1, 1994) led his first professional shoot at his family's estate on Holdshott Farm, Hampshire, UK. Mandry dedicates most after-school evenings and weekends to gamekeeping, including rearing young birds, controling vermin, and preparing for the next season's shoots.

☆ **MOVIE DIRECTOR** The youngest director of a professionally made feature-length movie is Kishan Shrikanth (India, b. January 6, 1996), who directed *C/o Footpath* (India, 2006)—a movie about an orphaned boy who wants to go to school—when he was nine years old.

☆ **Traveler to every continent** The youngest person to have traveled to all seven continents is Imogen Grace Barnes (Australia, b. May 25, 2004), who completed her journey at the age of 1 year 240 days on January 20, 2006, in Bangkok, Thailand. She was accompanied by her parents Gregory and Katherine Barnes (both Australia).

Astronauts Major Gherman Stepanovich Titov (USSR, b. September 11, 1935) was aged 25 years 329 days when he was launched into orbit in *Vostok 2* on August 6, 1961.

The **youngest woman in space** was Valentina Tereshkova (USSR, b. March 6, 1937) who was 26 years 102 days old when she became the **first woman in space** on June 16, 1963, in *Vostok 6*.

Authors The **youngest commercially published author** is Dorothy Straight (U.S.A., b. May 25, 1958), who wrote *How the World Began* in 1962, aged four. Her book was published in August 1964.

Adauto Kovalski da Silva (Brazil) is the ☆ **youngest commercially published male author.** His book *Aprender é Fácil* was released on October 15, 2005, when the author was 5 years 302 days old.

Judge At the age of 18 years 11 months, John Payton of Plano, Texas, U.S.A., was elected as a justice of the peace. He assumed the post in January 1991.

☆ **YOUNGEST PERSON TO VISIT THE NORTH POLE** Alicia Hempleman-Adams (UK, b. November 8, 1989) stood at the geographic North Pole at the age of 8 years 173 days on May 1, 1998, the youngest person ever to have done so. She flew to the pole to meet her father, the well-known adventurer David Hempleman-Adams (UK), at the end of his successful trek to the pole.

★ LAURENCE OLIVIER AWARD WINNER On February 26, 2006, Liam Mower (UK, b. May 30, 1992, above right) became the youngest person to win a Laurence Olivier Award for his performance as Billy Elliot in *Billy Elliot the Musical,* aged 13 years 272 days. Mower shared the award for Best Actor in a Musical with the other two actors who rotated in the role: 15-year-olds James Lomas (above left) and George Maguire (center); it was the first time that such an accolade has been shared. The musical is based on the movie *Billy Elliot* (UK, 2000) about a young boy learning ballet.

Skier on every continent Timothy Turner Hayes (U.S.A., b. July 29, 1991) started skiing at the age of two in Stratton, Vermont, U.S.A. By the age of 13 years 205 days, he had skied on all seven continents: North America (Stratton, Vermont, U.S.A.) at the age of two; Europe (Courmayer, Italy) at 10; Oceania (Thredbo, New South Wales, Australia), Antarctica (Argentine Station), and Africa (Oukaimeden, Morocco) at 12; South America (Chile) and Asia (Nagano, Japan) at 13.

★ ATLANTIC SAILOR (SOLO) Michael Perham (UK, b. March 16, 1992) left Gibraltar in his boat *Cheeky Monkey* on November 18, 2006, aged 14 years 247 days, and sailed via the Canary Islands and Cape Verde, before heading west, arriving in Nelson's Dockyard, Antigua, on January 3, 2007.

(For more about his amazing trip, see next page)

MICHAEL MAKES WAVES! Fourteen-year-old Michael Perham spent six weeks sailing the Atlantic and, when not battling the elements, kept himself busy by catching up on his school homework.

At one point during the journey, rope became entangled in the boat's steering mechanism and he had to jump overboard with a knife between his teeth to clear the obstruction!

His father, Peter—an experienced yachtsman—sailed 2 miles (3.2 km) behind his son throughout the crossing and kept in regular radio contact. They spent Christmas apart, but each released flares to celebrate the occasion.

ENDURANCE MARATHONS

★**Board-gaming** Marcus Stahl, Sascha Walner, Leszek Bajorski, and Frank Riemenschneider (all Germany) played the board game Carcassonne for 42 hr. 48 min. from September 8 to 10, 2006, in Herne, Germany.

☆**Body-piercing** Charlie Wilson and Kam Ma (both UK) underwent a total of 1,015 body piercings in 7 hr. 55 min. at Sunderland Body Art, Sunderland, Tyne and Wear, UK, on March 4, 2006.

★**Inflatable-castle** On July 7–8, 2006, a team of seven members of the executive committee of the Newman Trust charity carried out a marathon "bouncy castle" session that lasted for 19 hr. 45 min. at Priory Woods School, Middlebrough, UK.

☆**Canoeing (24 hours)** The greatest distance canoed (or kayaked) on flat water in 24 hours is 150.34 miles (241.95 km) by Carter Johnson (U.S.A.) on Lake Merced in San Francisco, California, U.S.A., on April 29–30, 2006.

☆**Card-playing** Hiebaum Klaus, Arno Krautner, Mellacher Franz, Flucher Friedrich, Finster Ferdinand, and Zmugg Manfred (all Austria) played the card game Bauernschnapsen for 109 hr. 20 min. in Feldkirchen bei Graz, Austria, from October 25 to 29, 2006.

★**Carrom-playing** On July 30–31, 2005, Atul Kharecha, Narayan Paranjape, Prakash Kagal, and Pramod Shah (all U.S.A.) played the board game Carrom for a total of 32 hr. 45 min. at the Indian Association Office, Richardson, Texas, U.S.A.

★**Cello-playing** The longest cello marathon lasted 24 hours and was performed by Shamita Achenbach-König (Austria) in Dachau, Munich, Germany, on November 5–6, 2005.

During her record-breaking achievement, Achenbach-König played a selection of music by Indian composer Sri Chinmoy Kumar.

☆**Concerts (24 hours)** N. Karthik (India) performed an unprecedented 50 concerts in a 24-hour period at venues in and around Bangalore, India, on November 29–30, 2005.

Kym Coberly's (U.S.A.) record-breaking **hula-hoop marathon** lasted 72 hours, from October 17 to 20, 1984.

LADDER CLIMBING On December 3–4, 2005, 10 people from The Professional Firefighters of New Zealand recorded the ☆**farthest distance climbed on a ladder by a team in 24 hours,** with a distance of 68.1 miles (109.5 km). On the same date, Shaun Cowan (New Zealand), from the same organization, climbed 7.9 miles (12.8 km) on a ladder, the ★**farthest distance climbed on a ladder in 24 hours by a man.** The ★**farthest distance climbed on a ladder in 24 hours by a woman** is 7.1 miles (11.5 km) by Barbara Nustrini (New Zealand), also from the same organization, on the same date. All record breakers achieved their feats in Auckland, New Zealand.

☆**Cricket** The longest cricket marathon lasted 33 hr. 30 min., and was set by Citipointe Church/Global Care (Australia) at Griffith University, Brisbane, Queensland, Australia, on June 10–11, 2006.

☆**Full-body ice-contact** Gilberto da Silva Cruz (Brazil) spent a bone-chilling 1 hr. 9 min. in direct, full-body contact with ice on the set of *Funniest Video Awards* at the Fuji Television Studios, Tokyo, Japan, on February 4, 2006.

☆**Karaoke (multiple participants)** A group karaoke session lasted for 142 hours at an event organized by Karaoke Club Austria. The session ended on Vienna World Records Day, in Austria, on September 16, 2006.

☆**Keyboard** Charles Brunner (Trinidad and Tobago) played piano for 64 hours at the Hilton Hotel in Port of Spain, Trinidad and Tobago, from December 7 to 9, 2006.

★**Lacrosse** The Orange and Green teams from MetroLacrosse (U.S.A.) played a lacrosse game that lasted 8 hr. 16 min. at Saunders Stadium, Boston, Massachusetts, U.S.A., on June 26, 2005.

★**Marbles** Michael Gray and Jenna Gray (both Australia) played a 26-hour game of marbles at First Fleet Park, The Rocks, Sydney, Australia, on February 11–12, 2006.

Pedal-boating Kenichi Horie (Japan) pedaled a boat 4,660 miles (7,500 km) across the Pacific Ocean between Honolulu, Hawaii, U.S.A., and Naha, Okinawa, Japan, from October 30, 1992, to February 17, 1993. This journey is the **greatest distance covered in a pedal-powered boat.**

On May 7, 2005, the Trieste Waterbike Team (Italy) pedaled a boat a distance of 110.2 miles (177.3 km) in Trieste, Italy, the ★**greatest distance covered in a pedal-powered boat in 24 hours.**

☆ **YOUNGEST WOMAN TO COMPLETE A MARATHON ON EACH CONTINENT** On February 26, 2006, aged 26 years 244 days, Karen Zacharias (U.S.A.) became the youngest person to complete a marathon on all seven continents.

☆ **Roller coaster** Stefan Seemann (Germany) rode the Boomerang roller coaster at Freizeit-Land Geiselwind in Geiselwind, Germany, for 221 hr. 21 min. from August 10 to 19, 2006.

☆ **Scuba-submergence** The longest scuba submergence in a controlled environment is 220 hours by Khoo Swee Chiow (Singapore) at Tampines Central, Singapore, from December 16 to 25, 2005.

★ **Treadmill in 48 hours (female)** Martina Schmit (Austria) covered 192.5 miles (309.8 km) in 48 hours on a treadmill at the Fitness Company, Gitty City, Stockerau, Austria, from March 10 to 12, 2006.

☆ **TATTOO SESSION** Stephen Grady and Melanie Grieveson (both Australia) underwent a tattoo session that lasted for a total of 43 hr. 50 min., between August 26 and 28, 2006.

The marathon skin-inking was staged at the Twin City Tattoo And Body Piercing, Wodonga, Victoria, Australia.

☆**LONGEST SKATEBOARD JOURNEY** Dave Cornthwaite (UK) left Perth, Australia, in late August 2006 and arrived in South Bank, Brisbane, Australia, on January 22, 2007, having completed an epic 3,618-mile (5,823-km) trip on his skateboard *Elsa*.

☆**TABLE SOCCER** Paul Pickering, Patrick Polius, Edward Polius, and Luke Smith (all UK, pictured) played table soccer for 36 hours at Harpars Bar in Horncastle, Lincolnshire, UK, on August 26–27, 2006.

The record equaled that of Jens Rödel, Kalle Krenzer, Steffen Krenzer, and Raphael Schroiff (all Germany), who had also achieved a time of 36 hours for a table-soccer marathon at the YMCA building in Bielefeld, Germany on May 25–26, 2006.

SUPERHUMAN STRENGTH

Greatest weight balanced on the head The greatest weight ever balanced on the head and held for 10 seconds is 416 lb. (188.7 kg), by John Evans (UK) using 101 bricks at BBC Television Centre, London, UK, on December 24, 1997.

★**Heaviest milk-crate stack balanced on the chin** On June 16, 2006, Ashrita Furman (U.S.A.) balanced 17 milk crates—stacked on top of each other and with a total weight of 93 lb. 7 oz. (42.4 kg)—on his chin for 11.23 seconds in New York City, U.S.A.

★**Greatest weight supported on the shoulders** Franz Müllner (Austria) supported an average of 1,212 lb. (550 kg) on his shoulders for 30 seconds while a helicopter landed on a frame which he was partly lifting.

FASTEST IRON BAR BENDING
On July 17, 2004, Les Davis (U.S.A.) managed to bend a 19-ft. 8-in.-long (6-m) iron bar with a diameter of 0.47 in. (12 mm) and fit it into a suitcase with dimensions 19.6 × 27.5 × 7.8 in. (50 × 70 × 20 cm). He achieved this incredible feat of strength in a record 29 seconds in Dothan, Alabama, U.S.A.

The record was achieved during Vienna World Records Day in Vienna, Austria, on September 16, 2006.

☆ **Heaviest concrete block break on a bed of nails** Chad Netherland (U.S.A.) had 26 concrete blocks weighing a total of 848 lb. (384.65 kg) placed on his chest and then broken with a 16-lb. (7.25-kg) sledgehammer while he lay on a bed of nails in St. Louis, Missouri, U.S.A., on July 14, 2006.

★ **Heaviest dead lift with the little finger** On July 11, 2006, Lu Zhonghao (China) lifted 201 lb. 14 oz. (91.6 kg) with his little finger in the Tanggu district of Tianjin, China.

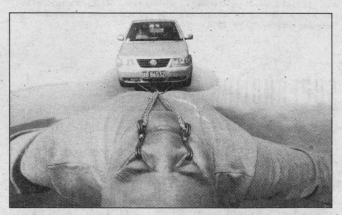

★ **HEAVIEST EYELID PULL** On September 26, 2006, Dong Changsheng (China) pulled a 3,300-lb. (1.5-ton) car for about 32 ft. (10 m) using ropes hooked on to his lower eyelids. Dong pulled off this feat in a park in Changchun, Jilin Province, China, and attributed his success to Qigong (pronounced "chi-kong," which means "energy cultivation"), a system of deep-breathing exercises.

☆ **MOST CONCRETE BLOCKS BROKEN IN A SINGLE STACK** On January 20, 2007, Narve Læret (Norway) smashed a stack of 21 concrete blocks by hand in Oslo, Norway.

★ **Longest time to restrain two cars** On October 10, 2006, Tomi Lotta (Finland) succeeded in restraining two cars for a time of 17.36 seconds on the set of *La Nuit Des Records,* Paris, France.

☆ **Vehicle pushing** Ashrita Furman (U.S.A.) pushed a van weighing 4,460 lb. (2,023 kg) a distance of one mile (1.6 km) in 21 min. 8 sec. in Long Island, New York, U.S.A., on October 5, 2006, the ☆ **fastest time for an individual to push a car for a mile.**

Krunoslav Budiselic and Mario Mlinaric (both Croatia) hold the record for the ☆ **greatest distance to push a car in 24 hours by a pair.** They pushed a 2,138-lb. 7-oz. (970-kg) Citroën a distance of 50.33 miles (81 km) around a track at RŠC Jarun, Zagreb, Croatia, on September 24–25, 2006.

★ **Heaviest vehicle pulled by rice bowl suction on the stomach** By pressing a rice bowl on his abdominal muscles, Zhang Xingquan (China) was able to create enough suction to pull a 7,287-lb. (3,305.5-kg) vehicle for

★ **MOST PANES OF SAFETY GLASS RUN THROUGH** Martin Latka (Germany) ran through a total of 10 panes of safety glass in one minute on September 9, 2006. He set this record on the set of *Guinness World Records: Die größten Weltrekorde* (RTL, Germany) in Cologne, Germany.

☆ **GREATEST DISTANCE FIRE-WALKED** Scott Bell (UK) walked 328 ft. (100 m) over embers with a temperature of 1,209–1,241°F (653–671°C) at Wuxi City, Jiangsu Province, China, on November 28, 2006.

32 ft. (10 m) on the set of *Zheng Da Zong Yi—Guinness World Records Special* in Beijing, China, on December 16, 2006.

☆**Most pine boards broken (one minute)** Glenn Coxon (Australia) broke 359 pine boards on the set of *Guinness World Records* at Seven Network Studios, Sydney, New South Wales, Australia, on August 16, 2005.

☆**Most knee bends on a Swiss ball** Ashrita Furman (U.S.A.) performed 30 knee bends in one minute while standing on a Swiss ball at the Sound One Corporation recording studio in New York City, U.S.A., on September 11, 2006.

★**Farthest washing-machine throw** Bill Lyndon (Australia) tossed a washing machine weighing 99 lb. 12 oz. (45.3 kg) a distance of 11 ft. (3.36 m) at the studios of *Guinness World Records,* Sydney, New South Wales, Australia, on June 26, 2005.

★**Most weight squat-lifted in one hour** Stuart Burrell (UK) squat-lifted 18,519 lb. (8,400 kg) in one hour at George's Gym in Rayleigh, Essex, UK, on May 29, 2005.

★ PUSH-UPS ★

MOST PUSH-UPS	NUMBER	HOLDER	DATE
One year	1,500,230	Paddy Doyle (UK)	Oct. 1988–Oct. 1989
Five hours (one arm)	8,794	Paddy Doyle (UK)	Feb. 12, 1996
Five hours (fingertips)	8,200	Terry Cole (UK)	May 11, 1996
One hour	3,416	Roy Berger (Canada)	Aug. 30, 1998
☆One hour (one arm)	1,868	Paddy Doyle (UK)	Nov. 27, 1993
☆One hour (back of hands)	1,781	Doug Pruden (Canada)	Jul. 8, 2005
☆One hour (one arm, back of hand)	677	Doug Pruden (Canada)	Nov. 9, 2006
☆One minute (one arm)	126	Jeremiah Gould (U.S.A.)	Mar. 30, 2006
Consecutive, one finger	124	Paul Lynch (UK)	Apr. 21, 1992
☆One minute (back of hands)	123	John Morrow (U.S.A.)	May 5, 2006

FITNESS FANATIC The GWR Multi-Discipline Fitness Challenge requires you to complete as many repetitions as you can of four different exercises, within a time limit of 15 minutes per discipline. Strongman Paddy Doyle (UK), who set the record on April 10, 1994, remains unbeaten with:
- 429 one-arm push-ups
- 400 squat thrusts
- 323 burpees
- 592 alternative squat thrusts.

☆ **Most watermelons crushed by forehead** In one minute, John Allwood (Australia) smashed 40 watermelons with his head in Chinchilla, Queensland, Australia, on February 17, 2007.

SURVIVAL INSTINCT

Highest g-force endured (non-voluntary) Race car driver David Purley (UK) survived a drop from 108 mph (173 km/h) to zero in 26 in. (66 cm) in a crash at the Silverstone Circuit in Northamptonshire, UK, on July 13, 1977. He endured 179.8 g—along with 29 fractures, three dislocations, and six heart stoppages.

HIGHEST FALL SURVIVED . . .

WITHOUT A PARACHUTE On January 26, 1972, Vesna Vulovic (Yugoslavia) was working as a stewardess when the DC-9 she was aboard blew up. She fell inside part of the tail section, which helped her to survive a drop of 33,333 ft. (10,160 m; 6.3 miles) over Srbská, Kamenice, Czechoslovakia (now Czech Republic). She broke numerous bones, spent 27 days in a coma, and was hospitalized for 16 months.

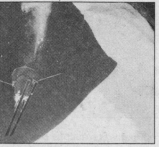

WHILE SKIING In April 1997, at the World Extreme Skiing Championships in Valdez, Alaska, U.S.A., Bridget Mead (New Zealand) fell a vertical distance of 1,312 ft. (400 m), incurring only bruises and a concussion.

DOWN AN ELEVATOR SHAFT Betty Lou Oliver (U.S.A.) survived a fall of 75 stories (over 1,000 ft.) in an elevator at the Empire State Building in New York City, U.S.A., on July 28, 1945, after an American B-25 bomber crashed into the building in thick fog.

Highest percentage of burns survived David Chapman (UK) became the first person to survive burns over 90% of his body after a fuel can exploded and drenched him with gasoline on July 2, 1996. He was taken to St. Andrew's Hospital in Essex, UK, where surgeons spent 36 hours removing dead skin. After having skin grafts for nine months in a UK hospital, the 16-year-old flew to Texas, U.S.A., for special treatment.

MOST LIGHTNING STRIKES SURVIVED The only person to survive being struck by lightning seven times was ex-park ranger Roy C. Sullivan (U.S.A.), the "human lightning conductor."

The history of his lightning liaisons runs as follows: 1942, lost big toe nail; 1969, lost eyebrows; July 1970, left shoulder seared; April 16, 1972, hair set on fire; August 7, 1973, new hair re-singed and legs seared; June 5, 1976, ankle injured; June 25, 1977, chest and stomach burned.

Sullivan died in 1993—not killed by lightning, but by his own hand, reportedly rejected in love.

Fastest motorcycle crash survived Ron Cook (U.S.A.) crashed a 1,325cc Kawasaki at 200 mph (322 km/h) on July 12, 1998, during time trials at El Mirage Dry Lake in California, U.S.A.

Youngest car accident survivor On February 25, 1999, Virginia Rivero from Misiones, Argentina, went into labor at her home and walked to a nearby road in order to hitchhike to a hospital. She was offered a lift by two men, but so advanced was her pregnancy that before long she gave birth to a baby girl on the backseat.

When Rivero told the men she was about to have a second baby, the driver overtook the car in front, only to collide with another vehicle. Rivero and her newborn daughter were ejected through the back door of the car, suffering minor injuries, but she was able to stand up and flag down another car, which took them to the hospital. Once there, she gave birth to a baby boy.

Youngest *Titanic* survivor Millvina Dean (UK, b. February 2, 1912) was just 69 days old when she sailed on the cruise liner *Titanic* with her parents and 18-month-old brother. Along with her mother and brother, she survived when the ship sank on April 14, 1912, but her father perished.

★**FASTEST CAR CRASH SURVIVED** In September 1960, during speed trials at Bonneville Salt Flats, Utah, U.S.A., Donald Campbell (UK) crashed his car *Bluebird* while traveling at a speed of 360 mph (579 km/h).

The vehicle rolled over and Campbell fractured his skull, yet against all the odds he survived.

Longest cardiac arrest Fisherman Jan Egil Refsdahl (Norway) fell into the icy waters off Bergen, Norway, on December 7, 1987, and suffered a four-hour cardiac arrest. He was rushed to nearby Haukeland Hospital after his body temperature fell to 75°F (24°C) and his heart stopped. He later made a full recovery.

MOST . . .

☆**Assassination attempts survived** In 2006, Fabian Escalante (Cuba), a bodyguard assigned to protect Cuba's president Fidel Castro, announced that there had been 638 assassination attempts on the communist leader.

Hangings survived Joseph Samuel (Australia) was due to hang for murder in Sydney, Australia, on September 26, 1803, but at the first attempt the rope broke. A second attempt failed when the rope stretched and the victim's feet touched the ground. On the third try, the rope broke again. Samuel was then reprieved.

OUT OF HELL

Having been taught by her father that settlements may be found by trekking along a water source, Juliane Koepcke (see next page) followed a stream until she stumbled on a canoe and shelter that belonged to some local lumbermen. When the men returned and discovered Koepcke, they treated her injuries as best they could before taking her downriver to Tournavista, Peru. From there she was flown to a hospital in Pucallpa, where she was reunited with her father.

John Lee (UK) also survived three hangings in Exeter, Devon, UK, in 1885. On each occasion, the trapdoor failed to open. The government of the time commuted the sentence to life imprisonment.

LONGEST SURVIVAL . . .

★At sea in a rowboat The longest collective time spent at sea in an ocean rowboat is 940 days, covering 21,275 miles (34,238 km), by Peter Bird (UK) during his rows across the Atlantic (east to west), the Pacific (east to west), and the Pacific (west to east) between 1974 and 1996.

The **longest known time that anyone has survived adrift at sea** is approximately 484 days, by Captain Oguri Jukichi and one of his sailors, Otokichi (both Japan). After their ship was damaged in a storm off the Japanese coast in October 1813, they drifted in the Pacific before being rescued off California, U.S.A., on March 24, 1815.

Without a pulse The longest time anyone has survived without a pulse in their vascular system is three days. Julie Mills (UK) was at the point of death due to severe heart failure and viral myocarditis when, on August 14, 1998, cardiac surgeons at the John Radcliffe Hospital, Oxford, UK, used a blood pump to support her for one week, while her heart recovered.

With heart outside the body Christopher Wall (U.S.A., b. August 19, 1975) is the longest known survivor of the condition *ectopia cordis*, in which the heart is not located within the chest cavity—in Wall's case, his heart lies outside his body. Most people with this condition do not live beyond 48 hours. Wall now wears a chest guard to protect his heart from potentially fatal knocks.

☆**HIGHEST DEATH TOLL FROM A LIGHTNING STRIKE** Few survival stories are more dramatic than that of Juliane Koepcke (Germany, left), the sole survivor out of 92 passengers after LANSA Flight 508 was struck by lightning and crashed in the Amazon rain forest on Christmas Eve 1971. Several passengers survived the 2-mile (3-km) fall to earth, but only Koepcke was able to leave the crash site to seek help.

Her story was later told in the movie *Wings of Hope* (Germany, 2000), directed by Werner Herzog (Germany), who had almost caught the ill-fated flight himself.

LONGEST TIME TO HOLD ONE'S BREATH On January 5, 2006, Tom Sietas (Germany) held his breath for 14 min. 12 sec. under 10 ft. (3.05 m) of water in Milan, Italy.

MOST . . .

☆**Apples cut in the air by sword** Kenneth Lee (U.S.A.) cut 23 apples in half while they were in the air, in one minute, using a samurai sword, on the set of *Live with Regis and Kelly* in New York City, U.S.A., on September 14, 2006.

☆ **MOST BRAS UNDONE IN ONE MINUTE** Thomas Vogel (Germany) unfastened 56 bras—using just one hand, as per the rules—in one minute on the set of *Guinness World Records: Die größten Weltrekorde* (RTL, Germany) in Cologne on September 9, 2006. He beat the previous record by 24!

★HIGHEST JUMP ON A POGO STICK On March 9, 2006, Brian Spencer (U.S.A.) achieved a jump of 6 ft. (182.88 cm) in Mission Viejo, California, U.S.A., using a pneumatically driven "Vurtego Pro" pogo stick.

★Grapes caught by mouth in one minute On June 21, 2006, in Jamaica, New York, U.S.A., Ashrita Furman (U.S.A.) caught 77 grapes in his mouth in a minute at a distance of 15 ft. (4.57 m).

☆Arrows caught by hand in two minutes Standing at a distance of 26 ft. (8 m) from two archers, Anthony Kelly (Australia) caught 36 arrows in two minutes in Beijing, China, on December 15, 2006.

☆Balls juggled Tim Nolan (U.S.A.) juggled 11 balls simultaneously at the Old Dominion University Fieldhouse in Norfolk, Virginia, U.S.A., on March 11, 2006.

★Hula hoop spins in one minute Leah Black (UK) completed 162 hula

MOST MILK CRATES BALANCED ON THE CHIN Frank Salvatore (U.S.A.) balanced 18 milk crates stacked on top of each other, with a total weight of 89 lb. (40.3 kg), on his chin for 11.53 seconds at Wells Fargo Arena, Tempe, Arizona, U.S.A., on January 5, 2003.

revolutions in one minute in London, UK, on April 10, 2006. The **most spins of a giant hula hoop in one minute** is 62 by Laura Rico Rodriguez (Spain) using an 11-ft. 6-in.-wide (3.5 m) hoop.

★**Nails balanced on the head of one nail** Daniel Urlings (Luxembourg) balanced 216 nails on the head of a single nail in Walferdange, Luxembourg, on April 26, 2006.

☆**Random objects memorized** Nischal Narayanam (India) recalled 225 random items in the order that they were read to him at the Hotel Taj Krishna, Hyderabad, India, on August 20, 2006.

★**Yo-yos spun at once** Eric Lindeen (Sweden) kept nine yo-yos spinning simultaneously, on hooks, at the Gallerian shopping center in Stockholm, Sweden, on November 4, 2006.

☆**Tennis balls held in the hand** Arnaud Deschamps (France) held 19 tennis balls in his left hand for 10 seconds in Epône, France, on October 22, 2005.

FASTEST . . .

☆**Egg-and-spoon mile** Jonathan Kehoe (U.S.A.) ran a mile in 7 min. 30 sec. while balancing an egg on a spoon in Summerville, South Carolina, U.S.A., on November 4, 2006.

★**Metal detectorist** Sergei Teplyakov (U.S.A.) achieved a National Metal Detecting League (NMDL) score of 11 (20 tokens found in 30 minutes) during the 2002 championships in Connecticut, U.S.A.

★**Time to bend 10 nails** Chad Netherland (U.S.A.) bent 10 nails by hand in 21.13 seconds at the Millennium Hotel and Convention Center in St. Louis, Missouri, U.S.A., on July 14, 2006.

☆**SMS message** Ben Cook (U.S.A.) typed a 160-character SMS message (see box, below) on his cell phone in 42.22 seconds in Denver, Colorado, U.S.A., on July 29, 2006.

The ★**fastest SMS sent blindfolded**—again, using 160 characters—

DID YOU KNOW?

The message used in the **fastest sms message** record is: The razor-toothed piranhas of the genera Serrasalmus and Pygocentrus are the most ferocious freshwater fish in the world. In reality they seldom attack a human.

★FASTEST TIME TO PLACE SIX EGGS IN EGGCUPS USING THE FEET
Contortionist Leslie Tipton (U.S.A.) managed to transfer six eggs into
six eggcups using her feet in 57 seconds, a feat achieved on the set of
Guinness World Records—El Show de los Récords in Madrid, Spain, on
June 11, 2006.

took Andrea Fantoni (Italy) 1 min. 23.5 sec. in Milano Marittima, Italy, on
September 2, 2006.

☆**Time to walk 50 m on stilts made from string and cans** Walking
on a pair of stilts made from only cans and string, Ashrita Furman (U.S.A.)
covered 164 ft. (50 m) in just 17.78 seconds. The record was set at the Plaza
Mayor in Tikal National Park, Guatemala, on August 6, 2006.

★**Time to complete the GWR throwing accuracy challenge**
Robert Lambert (UK) completed the Guinness World Records throwing accuracy challenge in 1.4 seconds at the Royal International Air Tattoo Show
in Swindon, UK, on July 16, 2006.

The challenge involves throwing objects across a distance of 10 ft. (3 m)
into holes of varying sizes.

★**Knitter** The fastest knitter is Miriam Tegels (Netherlands), who hand-
knitted 118 stitches in one minute at the Swalmen Townhall in the Netherlands on August 26, 2006.

Whistle for it! The ★**lowest note ever whistled** is the F below middle C,
and was achieved by Jennifer Davies (Canada) at the Impossibility Challenger Games in Dachau, Germany, on November 6, 2006.

Davies also holds the record for the ★**highest note ever whistled**—the
third E above middle C—which she set at the same event and on the same
date.

TRIVIAL PURSUITS

FASTEST TIME TO . . .

☆**Arrange a deck of playing cards** Zheng Taishun (China) arranged a shuffled deck of cards in order (ace through to 10, jack, queen, king for all suits), using just his hands, in 39.28 seconds in Fuzhou City, Fujian Province, China, on June 10, 2006.

★**Cover 50 m as a human wheelbarrow** Basil and Kerwin Miller (both Barbados) completed 50 m (164 ft.) in 15.56 seconds as a human wheelbarrow during the Barbados World Record Festival at the Barbados National Stadium, St. Michael, Barbados, on March 25, 2006.

★**Paint 10-m² wall** Wilhelm Probst (Austria) painted a 10-m² (107-ft.²) wall in 4 min. 40 sec. on Vienna World Records Day, in Vienna, Austria, on September 16, 2006, in an event organized by bauMax AG.

★**Paper aircraft accuracy** Jon Lewis and Fraser Greenhalgh (both UK) each flew three consecutive paper aircraft into a bucket from a distance of 9 ft. 10 in. (3 m) at RAF Fairford, Gloucestershire, UK, on July 17, 2004.

☆**Cover a duvet** Damien Fletcher (UK) put a duvet into its cover—and secured all the closures in order—in 1 min. 2 sec. at the Daily Mirror Studios, London, UK, on October 4, 2006.

★**Tie a Windsor knot** Zvi Dubin (U.S.A.) tied a Windsor knot with a necktie, in a professional manner, in 32 seconds, in Teaneck, New Jersey, U.S.A., on August 20, 2006.

FASTEST TIME TO TYPE ONE TO ONE MILLION Les Stewart (Australia) has typed the numbers one to one million manually, in words, on 19,990 quarto sheets. Stewart began his marathon type-athon in 1982. His target to become a "millionaire" became a reality on December 7, 1998.

Partially paralyzed after a tour of duty in Vietnam, he typed with just one finger.

FARTHEST DISTANCE TO SQUIRT MILK FROM THE EYE Ilker Yilmaz (Turkey) squirted milk from his eye to a distance of 9 ft. 2 in. (279.5 cm) at the Armada Hotel, Istanbul, Turkey, on September 1, 2004. The choice of milk is important to Yilmaz—full-fat milk clogs the tear ducts, so he uses reduced-fat or skim!

MOST . . .

★**Birth dates memorized** Biswaroop Roy Chowdhury (India) memorized 14 birth dates at the Le Meridian Hotel in New Delhi, India, on July 20, 2006.

☆**Cartwheels performed in one hour** Don Claps (U.S.A.) carried out a total of 1,297 cartwheels in one hour outside the set of ABC's *Live With Regis & Kelly* in New York City, U.S.A., on September 13, 2006.

★**Coconuts smashed in one minute** On August 13, 2005, Muhamed Kahrimanovic (Bosnia and Herzegovina) smashed a grand total of 65 coconuts in one minute, using only his hands. The attempt took place at the Tummelum Festival in Flensburg, Germany.

☆**Kicks to the head in one minute (self)** The most consecutive kicks to one's own head in one minute is held by Cody Warden (U.S.A.), who kicked himself in the forehead 77 times in succession at Bonifay, Florida, U.S.A., on November 29, 2006. Warden's record is an impressive 20 kicks greater than the record attained by the previous holder!

Thomas Schuster (Germany) snapped 81 bananas in one minute in Flensburg, Germany, on August 13, 2005.

★ **MOST SNAILS ON THE FACE**
Thomas Vincent (UK) managed to keep seven snails on his face at one time on the set of *Guinness World Records: A Few Records More* (ITV2, UK) at the London Television Studios, London, UK, on September 11, 2004.

★ **Origami cranes made in five minutes** The greatest number of origami cranes created in five minutes is six and was achieved by Eng Tze Hwee (Singapore) at the National University of Singapore on August 22, 2006.

☆ **People tossing pancakes** A total of 108 members of the Scout Association tossed pancakes simultaneously on *Blue Peter* for Pancake Day on February 20, 2007. The record attempt took place at the BBC Studios, London, UK.

★ **Rock 'n' roll windmill spins in one minute** David Felipe Verche and Monica Martinez Chust (both Spain) performed 49 rock 'n' roll "windmills" in one minute on the set of *Guinness World Records—El Show de Los Récords* in Madrid, Spain, on June 4, 2006.

★ **Sheets of glass pierced with needles in one minute** Jiang Zhan (China) pierced 21 sheets of glass with needles in one minute on the set of *Zheng Da Zong Yi—Guinness World Records Special* in Beijing, China, on December 15, 2006.

★ **MOST EGGS BALANCED BY AN INDIVIDUAL** Ashrita Furman (U.S.A.) balanced 700 eggs, vertically on one end, at the Rhode Island School of Design, Providence, U.S.A., on October 29, 2006.

★**LONGEST SOCK LINE** A line of socks measuring 0.8 miles (1.3 km) was organized by Wolfgang Zwerger (Germany) in Hechingen, Germany, on May 27, 2006.

★**Soap bubbles blown inside one large bubble** Sam Sam (aka Sam Heath, UK), from Bubble, Inc., blew 49 bubbles inside a larger soap bubble on the set of *Blue Peter* at the BBC Studios, London, UK, on May 23, 2006.

★**LARGEST BALL OF ADHESIVE TAPE** The largest adhesive-tape ball weighed 1,862 lb. (844.59 kg) and had a 23-ft. 9-in. (7.23-m) circumference.

It was made by Tim and Ryan Funk (both Canada) and measured in the city of Langley, British Columbia, Canada, on June 18, 2006. The used tape with which the pair created the ball was collected from various ice-hockey teams across the country.

DID YOU KNOW?

The ☆ **greatest number of socks worn on one foot** is 74, by Alastair Galpin (New Zealand). He performed his superlative sock-stuffing on Guinness World Records Day, November 7, 2006, in Auckland, New Zealand.

EXCEPTIONAL EXPLOITS

Fastest time to push an orange 1 mile using only the nose
Ashrita Furman (U.S.A.) pushed an orange with his nose for 1 mile (1.6 km) in 24 min. 36 sec. in Terminal 4 of JFK airport, New York, U.S.A., on August 12, 2004. He used one green, unripe orange for the attempt, as it was perfectly round and rolled far better than a ripe orange.

Heaviest mantle of bees On July 21, 1998, in Fair Oaks, California, U.S.A., Mark Biancaniello (U.S.A.) was covered by a mantle of bees weighing 87 lb. 6 oz. (39.6 kg) and comprising an estimated 350,000 bees.

★**Largest game of Head, Shoulders, Knees, and Toes** To raise money for The Rainbow Trust Children's Charity, 255 participants from Emap Advertising (all Spain) took part in a game of Head, Shoulders, Knees, and Toes on May 5, 2006.

★**Largest free-floating soap bubble** The largest free-floating soap bubble had a volume of 105.4 ft.^{3} (2.98 m^3) and was made using a wand. It was produced by XTREME Bubbles LLC in Farmington, Minnesota, U.S.A., on October 9, 2005.

☆**Longest gum-wrapper chain** Gary Duschl (U.S.A.) has been making a gum-wrapper chain since 1965. It now measures 50,905 ft. (15,515 m) long and features 1,192,492 wrappers.

★**HEAVIEST VEHICLE PULLED BY HOOKS THROUGH THE SKIN** Using two hooks inserted through the skin in the small of his back, Hannibal Helmurto (Germany) pulled an 8,818-lb. (4-ton) van a distance of 300 ft. (91.4 m) in Croydon, UK, on October 24, 2006. Quite a contrast to his previous job as a tax inspector!

LARGEST SCORPION HELD IN THE MOUTH In August 2006, Guinness World Records traveled to Castaic, California, U.S.A., to meet Dean Sheldon (U.S.A.), who held a scorpion measuring 7 in. (17.78 cm) in his mouth for a record-breaking 18 seconds!

The journey to the photoshoot was . . . eventful, shall we say. En route, the emperor scorpion (*Pandinus imperator*) you see here escaped, and began scuttling around inside the car—at which point everyone went very quiet. Luckily, it was soon recaptured, so there's no sting in this tale.

Most consecutive jumps on a pogo stick Gary Stewart (U.S.A.) managed 177,737 consecutive pogo jumps in Huntington Beach, California, U.S.A., on May 25–26, 1990.

GREATEST ALTITUDE REACHED USING HELIUM-FILLED PARTY BALLOONS Using 1,400 helium-filled toy balloons, Mike Howard (UK, pictured) and Steve Davis (U.S.A.) rose to a height of 18,300 ft. (5,580 m) near Albuquerque, New Mexico, U.S.A., on August 4, 2001.

FARTHEST...

★ **LONGEST DISTANCE WALKING OVER HOT PLATES** Rolf Iven (Germany) walked 62 ft. 8 in. (19.1 m) over hot plates while barefoot on the set of *Guinness World Records: Die größten Weltrekorde* (RTL, Germany) in Cologne, Germany, on September 9, 2006.

★ **Distance by waterslide in four hours** On July 23, 2005, Doug Mercer (U.S.A.) covered 68,400 ft. (20,848 m) in four hours on a waterslide at Surf Coaster U.S.A. water park, New Hampshire, U.S.A.

★ **Distance moonwalked in one hour** On September 10, 2006, Krunoslav Budiselic (Croatia) moonwalked for 3.265 miles (5.255 km) at the Athletic Stadium Mladost, Zagreb, Croatia.

The **farthest distance moonwalked in 24 hours** is 30.60 miles (49.252 km), by Arulanantham Suresh Joachim (Australia) at The Fregata Restaurant & Night Club, Ontario, Canada, on January 11, 2006.

★ **FARTHEST DISTANCE TO BLOW A MALT BALL WITH A STRAW** Using a straw, Wayne Iles (UK) blew a malt ball 11 ft. 0.2 in. (336 cm) on May 5, 2006. The feat took place as part of an event in support of The Rainbow Trust Children's Charity in Barcelona, Spain.

MOST . . .

★**Aircraft flown in as a passenger** Edwin A. Shackleton (UK) had flown in 841 different types of aircraft as of January 2007. Shackleton made his first flight in 1943 in a De Havilland DH 89 Dominie and has subsequently traveled in balloons, airships, helicopters, and microlights.

★**Books typed backward** Using a computer and four keyboards, Michele Santelia (Italy) typed 57 books in reverse in their original languages (a total of 3,194,024 words)—without looking at the screen—beginning in 1992.

The titles Santelia typed include *The Odyssey, Macbeth, The Vulgate Bible,* and the 2002 edition of *Guinness World Records.*

Bowling balls stacked Dave Kremer (U.S.A.) stacked 10 bowling balls vertically on the set of *Guinness World Records: Primetime,* in Los Angeles, California, U.S.A., on November 19, 1998.

Cherry stems knotted in three minutes Al Gliniecki (U.S.A.) knotted 39 cherry stems in three minutes, using only his tongue at the Guinness World Records Experience in Orlando, Florida, U.S.A., on January 26, 1999.

Gliniecki also holds the record for the **most cherry stems knotted in one hour,** with 911, a feat he achieved on the set of *The Ricki Lake Show* on September 4, 1997.

☆**Custard pies thrown in one minute (two people)** Kelly Ripa (U.S.A.) threw 24 custard pies at Wilma Valderrama (U.S.A.), star of *That 70s Show,* on the set of *Live with Regis and Kelly* (ABC) in New York City, U.S.A., on September 25, 2006.

★**Fastest time to crawl one mile** Ashrita Furman (U.S.A.)—the man who holds the most Guinness World Records, with 54 as of March 2007—crawled a mile (1.6 km) in 24 min. 44 sec. at Beardsley Park in Bridgeport, Connecticut, U.S.A., on October 18, 2006.

★**Fish snorted in one minute** In fish snorting, the participant sucks a fish up through the back of the mouth and ejects it from a nostril. India's

---

KILLER SNAKE

Jackie Bibby (next page) was not alone in his record-breaking attempt. At the same time, Rosie Reynolds-McCasland (U.S.A.) also sat in a bathtub with 75 live western diamondback rattlesnakes (*Crotalus atrox*), which can grow to 6 ft. 6 in. (1.98 m). The snake's venom can kill small mammals in minutes.

SHARING A BATHTUB WITH THE MOST RATTLESNAKES Jackie Bibby (U.S.A.) shared his tub with 75 live western diamondback rattlesnakes on September 24, 1999, in Los Angeles, California, U.S.A. The western diamondback is one of the more aggressive species found in North America and has a toxic venom.

G. P. Vijayakumar is a yoga instructor who honed his fish-snorting skills by practicing with peas before graduating to small fish. On July 21, 2005, he managed to snort eight fish in one minute at the Town Hall in Cuddalore, India.

Vijayakumar also holds the record for ★ **most fish snorted in one hour,** with 509.

★ **Kites flown at once (individual)** Ma Qinghua (China) flew 43 kites off a single string in Weifang City, Shandong Province, China, on November 7, 2006.

☆ **People skipping on the same rope** On February 26, 2006, 292 participants skipped on the same rope at the College of Engineering, Pune, India.

★ **Pogo-stick jumps in a minute** Ashrita Furman (U.S.A.) performed a total of 234 jumps on a pogo stick in one minute at Chelsea Piers, New York City, U.S.A., on March 28, 2006.

TEAMWORK

★ **Largest underwater dance class** A group of 74 students and their instructors conducted an underwater dance class (while wearing weighted scuba equipment) for 13 min. 30 sec. at the Sydney Olympic Park Aquatic Centre in Sydney, New South Wales, Australia, on October 27, 2006.

☆**LARGEST COCONUT ORCHESTRA** To celebrate St. George (the patron saint of England) and the first anniversary of the UK production of *Spamalot*—the musical "ripped off" from *Monty Python and the Holy Grail* (UK, 1975)—5,567 fans formed a coconut "orchestra" in London on April 23, 2007, to accompany "Always Look on the Bright Side of Life." Above is the show's cast with Python's Terry Jones (left of certificate) and Terry Gilliam (right).

★**Largest snowball** Rolled by students of Michigan Technological University in Houghton, Michigan, U.S.A., the world's largest snowball measured 21 ft. 3 in. (6.48 m) in circumference on February 10, 2006.

★**Largest urban scavenger hunt** The largest scavenger hunt game consisted of 116 participants at The Great Gator Hunt, Gainesville, Florida, U.S.A., on November 19, 2005.

★**Largest clapper board** A movie clapper board measuring 10 ft. 2 in. × 13 ft. 1 in. (3.11 m × 4.00 m) was created by a team of 10 people for *Une Semaine Chrono* in Vendôme, France, on July 29, 2006.

SPEED FREAKS

The ★**fastest time to hang three stips of wall-paper by a team of two** is 2 min. 34 sec., and was achieved by Del Dervish and Pas Tullio (both UK) at the BBC Studios, London, on April 12, 2006.

The ★**fastest time to run 100 miles on a treadmill by a team** (of 12) is 9 hr. 47 min. 15 sec. The record was set at the Fitness First health club in Luton, UK, on February 4, 2006.

On the same day, and at the same venue, the record for the ★**fastest time to run 100 km on a treadmill by a team** (of 12) was set, with a time of 6 hr. 4 min. 30 sec.

★**Tallest stack of poppadoms** A team from Manchester Confidential, UK—Andrew Mullet, Jayne Robinson, Georgina Hague, Tristan Welch (all UK)—stacked poppadoms to a height of 4 ft. 6 in. (1.37 m) at an event organized by Scope in Albert Square, Manchester, UK, on October 13, 2006.

☆**Longest cigar** A cigar measuring 135 ft. 2 in. (41.2 m)—about the length of 515 regular cigarettes—was hand-rolled by Patricio Peña (Puerto Rico) and his team from Don Ray Cigars in Fort Buchanan, Puerto Rico, between February 13 and 15, 2007.

LONGEST . . .

☆**Bra chain** On April 30, 2006, the Cyprus Cancer Patients Support Group in Paphos Harbour, Cyprus, created a bra chain that included 114,782 bras fastened together, which stretched for 68.9 miles (111 km).

★**Distance spinning on static cycles by 100 teams in 24 hours** The record for the farthest distance covered spinning on static cycles by 100 teams in 24 hours stands at 40,093.27 miles (64,524 km), and was set during the CentrO Festival in Oberhausen, Germany, from September 30 to October 1, 2006.

★**Human teddy-bear chain** A total of 431 people and 430 teddy bears linked hands and paws at an event organized by Unilever GmbH during the Vienna World Records Day in Vienna, Austria, on September 16, 2006.

★**LONGEST IN-LINE SKATING CHAIN** A chain of 280 participants in Padang, Singapore, skated at an event organized by Samsung Asia Pte Ltd. (Singapore) on August 6, 2006.

★ LONGEST FOOSBALL TABLE Made by workers of the sheltered workshop at the St. John of God's Establishment in Gremsdorf, Germany, the longest foosball game table measures 40 ft. 2 in. (12.26 m) long and can accommodate 40 participants The game, displayed on June 8, 2006, has 80 poles, 234 soccer figures, and 30 balls.

★ Journey on an electric mobility vehicle (team) John Duckworth, Simon Parrott, David Benham, and Geoff West (all UK) traveled from Land's End counterclockwise around the UK and back to Land's End on a Horizon Mayan electric mobility scooter from May 5 to August 5, 2004, covering a distance of 3,412 miles (5,491 km).

☆ **Concert by multiple artists** Over 700 solo and group musicians, organized by piano teacher Kuniko Teramura (Japan), took turns playing live music for a total of 184 hours in Hikone, Shiga, Japan, from March 23 to 31, 2007.

☆ **Straw chain** Made up of 50,000 drinking straws, the longest straw chain measured 28,158 ft. (8,582.59 m). The chain was made by Brad Mottashed, Evgueni Venkov, and 18 fellow students (all Canada) of Waterloo University, Ontario, Canada, on April 1, 2006.

MOST . . .

☆ **People inside a soap bubble** Ana Yang (Canada) managed to fit 26 people inside a soap bubble on the set of *Zheng Da Zong Yi* in Beijing, China, on December 16, 2006.

RULES FOR MASS RECORDS

• Attendance numbers must be accurately confirmed.

• The two overall independent witnesses must confirm the final figure of total participants.

• Sufficient stewards must be involved to ratify that all the contestants fully participate in the attempt.

☆ **MOST PEOPLE CRAMMED INTO A MINI** On June 17, 2006, 21 students of INTI College Subang Jaya in Selangor, Malaysia, crammed into an "old style" Mini (above).

The record for the ☆ **most people crammed into a "new style" Mini** is 22. It was organized by Ignacio Sáchez Diaz-Calderón for 22 of his friends (all Spain) on the set of *Guinness World Records—El Show de los Records* in Madrid, Spain, on June 11, 2006.

☆ **Dominoes toppled** It took a team of 90 builders about two months to set up 4,400,000 dominoes for Domino Day 2006 in Leeuwarden, the Netherlands, on November 17. In all, a record 4,079,381 "stones" fell.

☆ **Siblings to complete a marathon** The 12 Irwin siblings—Frank, Martin, Barry, Margaret, Maria, Geraldine, Patricia, Katrina, Josephine, Veronica, Cecilia, and Rosemary (all Ireland)—ran the Dublin City Marathon on October 31, 2005. All completed the marathon in under eight hours.

☆ **Faces painted in an hour (team)** A team of five painted a total of 405 different faces, using a minimum of three colors per face, as part of The Rainbow Trust Children's Charity "Day of 1,000 Lions" event held at Longleat House, Wiltshire, UK, on June 3, 2006.

On November 17, 2006, five face painters drew a total of 1,071 different faces, using a minimum of three colors per face, as part of a Children in Need fundraiser held at BBC Birmingham, The Mailbox, Birmingham, UK. This represents the ★ **greatest number of faces painted in four hours by a team.**

☆ **Heads shaved in an hour (team)** The greatest number of heads shaved in one hour by a team of 10 barbers was 229 at the "Short Cut to the Cure" event at Drill Hall in Wetaskiwin, Alberta, Canada, on June 17, 2006.

☆ **Most people fire-breathing** To celebrate the 2006 Burning Man festival in Black Rock City, Nevada, U.S.A., a total of 82 fire-breathers amassed to form "Ocean of Fire II"—the largest simultaneous breathing of fire. The gathering, on August 31, beat the previous attempt—held at Stonehenge in the UK in 2004—by 12 fire-breathers.

MASS PARTICIPATION

MOST PEOPLE . . .

★**Nordic walking** On September 22, 2006, 1,026 people Nordic-walked a minimum of 1.8 miles (3 m) in Lidingöloppet, Sweden.

☆**Scuba diving** On February 25, 2006, 958 people scuba dived at Sunlight Thila in Male, Maldives.

★**Shaking hands** A total of 596 couples shook hands for 30 seconds at Lincoln Way High School, New Lenox, Illinois, U.S.A., on September 30, 2005.

☆**Toasting (single venue)** A total of 13,500 participants toasted in the New Year on December 31, 2005, at the Fremont Street Experience, Las Vegas, Nevada, U.S.A., at an event organized by Beaulieu Vineyard (U.S.A.).

☆**Wearing balloon hats** On August 16, 2006, 1,876 people wore balloon hats at an event organized by United Way and Intel Oregon as part of a Celebrate Hillsboro event in Hillsboro, Oregon, U.S.A.

☆**Wearing Groucho Marx glasses** The most people simultaneously weairng Groucho Marx–style glasses, nose, and mustache at one location was 1,463 by visitors to the Gorham, Maine Family Festival in Maine, U.S.A., on July 30, 2006.

★**MOST WOMEN BREAST-FEEDING SIMULTANEOUSLY** At an event organized by Children for Breastfeeding, Inc. and the City of Manila in partnership with Nurturers of the Earth, a total of 3,541 women breastfed their infants in Manila, Philippines, on May 4, 2006.

☆ **MOST PEOPLE BRUSHING TEETH SIMULTANEOUSLY** A total of 33,628 people gathered for the Aquafresh Minty Mouth Challenge as part of the BT Giant Sleepover in over 1,000 locations around the world on June 18, 2006. The record for the ☆ **most people brushing their teeth at a single venue** is 13,380, at the Cuscatlán Stadium (pictured), City of San Salvador, El Salvador, on November 5, 2005.

LARGEST . . .

★ **Car horn ensemble** A cacophony of 19 cars tooted and honked in time during the Vienna World Records Day in Vienna, Austria, on September 16, 2006.

☆ **Cheerleading cheer** A group of 884 cheerleaders performed a cheer in Baltimore, Maryland, U.S.A., on November 7, 2004.

☆ **Group hug** On September 25, 2005, a total of 6,623 people gathered in Juárez, Mexico, for a group hug.

★ **Language lesson** Thomas Bug and Bastian Sick (both Germany) taught 6,287 participants at the Kölnarena in Cologne, Germany, on March 13, 2006.

★ **Mass handstand** At an event organized by the Braderie Comity of Wevelgem in Wevelgem, Belgium, on September 17, 2006, 399 people stood on their hands.

★ **Mass headstand** On March 12, 2006, 159 people performed a simultaneous, unassisted headstand in Mechelen, Belgium.

★ **LARGEST GAME OF BINGO** As part of their 20th anniversary celebrations, the San Manuel Indian Bingo and Casino organized a game of bingo with 53,991 players—all of them spectators at Dodger Stadium in Los Angeles, U.S.A.—on July 7, 2006. The stadium was turned into a temporary open-air bingo hall and everyone in attendance received a bingo card to play for three prizes of $10,000, $6,000, and $4,000.

Fantastic Feats

LARGEST SMURF GATHERING On May 21, 2006, the Bay to Breakers Foot Race in San Francisco, California, U.S.A., was overrun with 290 people dressed as Smurfs. Each Smurf had a blue-painted face and white hat, as per official Guinness World Records rules.

★**Parade of bicycles** In total, 641 people cycled together for 2.17 miles (3.5 km) in Leiden, the Netherlands, on March 29, 2006.

★**Pub crawl** A pub crawl of 2,237 "crawlers" visited 17 pubs in Maryborough, Queensland, Australia, on June 11, 2006, in an event arranged by the World's Greatest Pub Crawl Committee (Australia).

★**Stand-up (multiple venue)** On October 15–16, 2006, a staggering 23,542,614 participants in 11,646 events around the globe took part in the United Nations' Millennium Campaign "Stand Up Against Poverty."

★**Tugboat flotilla** A flotilla of 68 tugboats assembled for the ITS Tug Parade in Rotterdam, the Netherlands, on April 26, 2006.

★**LONGEST LINE OF FLOATING AIR-BEDS** A continuous line of 863 air-beds—each with a participant on board—was assembled as part of the Coogee Arts Festival at Coogee Beach, Sydney, Australia, on January 26, 2006.

★ LATEST GREATEST GATHERINGS ★

EVENT	PARTICIPANTS	COUNTRY	DATE
☆ Tree planting (24 hours) (total planted: 254,464) (*picture 1*)	300	India	Oct. 1–2, 2005
★ 5-km run (*2*)	101,246	UK	Jun. 4, 2006
☆ Longest drawing (*3*) (length: 12,595 ft.; 3,839 m)	900	Japan	Oct. 1, 2005
★ Pumpkin carving (*4*)	118	U.S.A.	Oct. 28, 2006
☆ Golf cart parade (*5*)	3,321	U.S.A.	Sep. 4, 2005
★ Skipping (*6*)	7,632	UK	Mar. 24, 2006
☆ Snow angels (*7*)	8,962	U.S.A.	Feb. 17, 2007
☆ Drum ensemble (*8*)	7,951	India	Oct. 28, 2006
★ Bunny hop (*9*)	1,879	U.S.A.	Apr. 15, 2006
☆ Music lesson (*10*)	539	Switzerland	May 12, 2006
☆ Sing-along	293,978	UK	Dec. 9, 2005
★ Champagne cork-popping	410	Germany	Jul. 16, 2005
★ Game of musical bumps	137	UK	Sep. 17, 2006
★ Game of musical statues	265	Spain	May 5, 2006
☆ Quiz	1,263	Australia	Jun. 14, 2006
☆ Hora dance	13,828	Romania	Jan. 24, 2006
☆ Didgeridoo ensemble	238	UK	Aug. 5, 2006
☆ Longest line of footprints (length: 14,711 ft.; 4,484 m)	15,200 prints	Australia	Dec. 10, 2005
★ Longest line of handprints (length: 116,478 ft.; 35,502.5 m)	119,537 prints	Germany	Oct. 6, 2005

EPIC ENDEAVORS

CONTENTS

CROSSING THE SEAS

★First mother-and-daughter team to row across any ocean
Sarah and Sally Kettle (both UK) rowed across the Atlantic east to west in
Calderdale–Yorkshire Challenger between January 20 and May 5, 2004.

First person to row an ocean twice in a year Michael Perrens (UK)
crossed the Atlantic east to west in *Carpe Diem* between January 20 and
March 8, 2004, and again in *Britannia Endeavour* between November 12
and December 23, 2004.

★Smallest rowing boat to cross an ocean The smallest ocean rowing boat to successfully cross any ocean is *Alison May,* which measured 16
ft. (4.87 m) long, and was rowed by Matthew Boreham (UK) across the Atlantic east to west solo between January 20 and April 13, 2004.

First woman to row any ocean Sylvia Cook rowed the Pacific east to
west along with John Fairfax (both UK) in *Britannia II* between April 26,
1971, and April 22, 1972, becoming the **first woman ever to row across the
Pacific.**

★Oldest female to row an ocean The oldest female ocean rower—
and the first British woman to row any ocean solo—is Diana Hoff (UK,
b. May 1, 1944), who rowed the Atlantic east to west solo in *Star Atlantic II*
between September 13, 1999, and January 5, 2000. She was 55 years 152 days
old at the outset.

Fastest rowing across the Atlantic •The **fastest row ever recorded
for crossing the Atlantic in any direction land to land** is 35 days 8 hr. 30
min., a record held by the 11-man crew of *La Mondiale.* The French team
rowed east to west from Santa Cruz de la Palma in the Canary Islands to
Martinique, West Indies, between March 25 and April 29, 1992.
•The **★fastest Ocean Four to row across the Atlantic west to east from
Canada** was the crew of *Naturally Best*—George Rock, Robert Munslow,
Nigel Morris, and Steve Dawson (all UK)—in a time of 39 days 22 hr. 10

**FIRST MOTHER-AND-SON
TEAM TO ROW ACROSS
ANY OCEAN Between
October 12, 1997, and
January 21, 1998, Jan Meek
and Daniel Byles (both UK)
rowed the Atlantic east to
west. They started their
journey in Los Gigantes in
the Canary Islands and
rowed to Barbados, West
Indies, in *Carpe Diem.***

★ **FIRST OCEAN FOUR TO ROW THE ATLANTIC WEST TO EAST** The first Ocean Four to row the Atlantic west to east from the U.S.A. was the crew of *Vopak Victory*: Gijs Groeneveld, Robert Hoeve, Jaap Koomen, and Maarten Staarinnk (all Netherlands). They achieved this feat on June 27, 2005, and in doing so achieved the **fastest recorded time** for this route: 60 days 16 hr. 19 min.

min. 30 sec. between May 31 and July 10, 2005. They were also the ★ **first Ocean Four to row the Atlantic west to east from Canada.**

• The ★ **first** and ★ **fastest Ocean Four to row across the Atlantic east to west** were Shaun Barker, Jason Hart, Phil Langman, and Yorkie Lomas (all UK) on *Queensgate,* in 36 days 59 min. between January 20 and February 26, 2004.

• The **first person to row across the Atlantic west to east solo from U.S.A. land to land** is Oliver Hicks (UK), who rowed *Miss Olive, Virgin Atlantic* between May 27 and September 28, 2005, aged 23 years 175 days (at the start). He rowed from Atlantic Highlands, New Jersey, U.S.A. to St. Mary's, Isles of Scilly, UK, in 123 days 22 hr. 8 min. Hicks, pictured right, is also the **youngest person to row any ocean solo.**

• The **youngest person to row across the Atlantic east to west solo** is Sam Knight (UK, b. June 19, 1980), who rowed *Pacific Pete TNT,* leaving La

★ SOLO OCEAN ROWERS ★

FIRST PERSON TO ROW...	RECORD HOLDER	DATE
Any ocean (Atlantic east to west)	John Fairfax (UK)	Jan. 20–Jul. 9, 1969
Pacific east to west	Peter Bird (UK)	Aug. 23, 1982–Jun. 14, 1983
Pacific west to east	Gerard d'Aboville (France)	Jul. 11–Nov. 21, 1991
Atlantic west to east from U.S.A.	Gerard d'Aboville (France)	Jul. 10–Sep. 20, 1980
Atlantic west to east from U.S.A. land to land	Oliver Hicks (UK, pictured above)	May 27–Sep. 28, 2005
★ Atlantic west to east from Canada land to land	Robert Munslow (UK)	Jun. 27–Aug. 30, 2006
★ Atlantic east to west, Europe to South America	Stein Hoff (Norway)	Aug. 10–Nov. 14, 2002
★ Atlantic east to west, Spain to West Indies	Leven Brown (UK)	Aug. 26, 2005–Jan. 26, 2006

★FARTHEST MONOHULL SAILING IN A DAY *ABN Amro Two,* skippered by Sebastien Josse (France), sailed 562.96 nautical miles (647.8 miles; 1,042.6 km) in 24 hours at an average speed of 23.45 knots during the second leg (Cape Town to Melbourne) of the Volvo Ocean Race in the Southern Ocean on January 11, 2006.

Gomera, Canary Islands, on January 20, 2004, aged 23 years 214 days, and arriving in Barbados on March 19, 2004.

•The **first Ocean Four to row the Atlantic west to east from the U.S.A. land to land,** from Liberty Island, New York, U.S.A., to Port Pendennis Marina, Falmouth, UK, were Jordan Hanssen, Dylan Le Valley, Brad Vickers, and Greg Spooner (all U.S.A., right), between June 10 and August 20, 2006, in a time of 71 days 3 hr. 22 min. 35 sec.

☆FASTEST OVERALL TRANSATLANTIC SAILING Bruno Peyron (France) and the crew of *Orange II* crossed the Atlantic in 4 days 8 hr. 23 min. 54 sec., reaching Lizard Point, Cornwall, UK, from Ambrose Light Tower, New York City, U.S.A., on July 7, 2006. *Orange II* also set a new 24-hour sailing record of 766 nautical miles (882 miles; 1,420 km).

OCEAN ROWING SOCIETY

Guinness World Records accepts only ocean-rowing records ratified by the Ocean Rowing Society. Prior to this, we were indebted to Squadron Leader D. H. "Nobby" Clark, DFC, AFC, who began ratifying rowing records for the founders of the book, Ross and Norris McWhirter, in 1967.

Today, Nobby's accumulated facts and statistics on ocean rowing can be found on the ORS's website, www.oceanrowing.com, which continues to monitor attempts at crossing the oceans by rowing boat.

At the time of going to press, at least 21 ocean-rowing attempts were under way or planned for 2007—look out for potential new records from a team of four British police officers attempting the fastest row across the Atlantic; the first American to row solo from the U.S.A. to Europe; the first woman to row solo across the Pacific; and the British women's record for rowing across the Atlantic. Good luck from everyone at Guinness World Records!

★ **FASTEST SOLO ROW ACROSS THE ATLANTIC WEST TO EAST**
Emmanuel Coindre (France) rowed from Cape Cod, Massachusetts,
U.S.A., to Île d'Ouessant, France, in 62 days 19 hr. 48 min. between July
9 and September 10, 2004—a distance of around 3,400 nautical miles
(3,900 miles; 6,300 km).

LONGEST SWIM UNDER ICE WITH BREATH HELD The ultimate subzero
swimming champion is Wim Hof (Netherlands). Without using any
special equipment, and wearing only bathing trunks and goggles, Hof
has managed to swim 188 ft. 7-in. (57.5 m) under ice in just 1 min. 1 sec.
To do so, he endured a "bracing" water temperature of 21.2°F (-6°C).

REACHING THE POLES

SOUTH POLE

First person to reach the South Pole A Norwegian party of five men led by Roald Engebereth Gravning Amundsen reached the pole at 11 a.m. on December 14, 1911, after a 53-day march with dog sleds.

★First solo journey At the age of 29, Erling Kagge (Norway) became the first person to reach the South Pole after a solo and unsupported trek, on January 7, 1993. His 870-mile (1,400-km) journey from Berkner Island took 50 days.

First crossing of the Antarctic continent A party of 12 led by Sir Vivian Ernest Fuchs (UK) completed a crossing of the surface of the Antarctic continent at 1:47 p.m. on March 2, 1958, after a trek of 2,158 miles (3,473 km), lasting 99 days from November 24, 1957. The crossing was from Shackleton Base to Scott Base via the pole.

Fastest solo kite-assisted journey The fastest unsupported journey to the pole (solo) was made by explorer Børge Ousland (Norway), who skied—with assistance from a parafoil kite—in 34 days from November 15 to December 19, 1996. The journey was unsupported—i.e., he received no outside assistance. Ousland also achieved the **fastest** and **first solo and unaided crossing of Antarctica** from November 15, 1996, to January 18, 1997.

First balloon flight over the South Pole Balloonist and adventurer Ivan André Trifonov (Austria) floated over the South Pole at an altitude of 15,000 ft. (4,571 m) on January 8, 2000.

★FIRST MARRIED COUPLE TO REACH BOTH POLES UNASSISTED After setting out from Ward Hunt Island, Canada, on March 22, 2002, Thomas and Tina Sjögren (Sweden) walked unassisted to the North Pole, arriving there on May 29, 2002. Only a few weeks earlier, on February 1, 2002, they had also arrived unaided at the South Pole.

★ **MOST POLAR EXPEDITIONS** Paul Landry (Canada) has completed seven successful treks to the North and South poles: he visited the magnetic North Pole in April 1998, and the geographic North Pole in April 2000, April 2001, and April 2002. He reached the geographic South Pole in January 2002, January 2003, and January 2005. At the time of going to press (April 2007), he was on his fourth trip to the geographic North Pole.

☆ **FASTEST OVERLAND JOURNEY TO THE SOUTH POLE** The fastest overland journey to the South Pole from Patriot Hills on the Antarctic coastline took 69 hr. 21 min. on December 9–12, 2005, by a team of five drivers—Jason De Carteret, Andrew Regan, Richard Griffiths, Andrew Moon (all UK), and Gunni Eglis (Iceland)—using a modified 6×6 vehicle.

DID YOU KNOW?

The vehicle above had air suspension (metal gets too cold and brittle) and was equipped with huge 44-in. (111-cm) tires that create as much contact with the ground as possible.

☆**FASTEST SOLO UNSUPPORTED TREK TO THE SOUTH POLE** Hannah McKeand (UK) skied her way to the South Pole from the Hercules Inlet at the edge of the Antarctic continent in 39 days 10 hr. 33 min. between November 19 and December 28, 2006. The former marketing manager made the journey—in 24-hour sunshine—without resupplies. She ate noodles for breakfast and freeze-dried meals for dinner, and snacked throughout the day on chocolate, salami, and the explorer's favorite: Kendal mint cake.

NORTH POLE

First to reach the North Pole Explorer Robert Peary (U.S.A.) is widely regarded as the first person to have reached the North Pole. Peary set off from Ellesmere Island, Canada, on March 1, 1909, with his close associate Matt Henson (U.S.A.), and on April 6 made observations indicating that he had reached his destination. Although rival explorer Frederick Cook (U.S.A.) challenged his claim and asserted that he had reached the pole first earlier that month, the U.S. Congress acknowledged Peary's achievement in 1911.

★**First undisputed surface journey to the North Pole** Expedition leader Ralph Plaisted (U.S.A.), accompanied by a team of three, reached the North Pole across the sea ice on April 19, 1968, after a 42-day snowmobile trek.

Fastest ski journey to the North Pole (female) Catherine Hartley and Fiona Thornewill (both UK) skied to the North Pole (supported) in 55 days from March 11 to May 5, 2001, after setting out from Ward Hunt Island, Northwest Territories, Canada.

☆**Most northerly marathon** The North Pole Marathon has been held annually since 2002, and the course at the geographic North Pole has been certified by the Association of International Marathons and Road Races.

FIRST MOTHER AND SON TO REACH A POLE At 9:15 p.m. local time (GMT 5 a.m.) on May 2, 2007, Daniel Byles and his mother, Jan Meek (both UK), reached the magnetic North Pole (N 78° 35.724′, W 104° 11.940′) following a 24-day trek on foot and skis from Resolute Bay in Canada—a journey of around 350 miles (560 km). *Read about the pair's ocean-rowing record on page 163.*

The fastest men's completion time to date is 3 hr. 36 min. 10 sec. by Thomas Maguire (Ireland) in the 2007 marathon, and the fastest woman is Susan Holliday (UK) in 6 hr. 17 min. 40 sec., also in 2007.

Pole to pole Marek Kamiński (Poland) completed a solo, unsupported walk to the North Pole on May 23, 1995, and an unsupported walk to the South Pole on December 27, 1995, the ★ **first person to trek to both poles unsupported.**

Thomas and Tina Sjögren (Sweden) reached the South Pole on February 1, 2002, and the North Pole by May 29, 2002—the ★ **shortest time between walking to both poles.**

The **first person to walk to both poles** was Robert Swan (UK). His team reached the South Pole on January 11, 1986; he arrived at the North Pole three years later on May 14, 1989.

★ **YOUNGEST PERSON TO WALK TO THE NORTH POLE** On April 10, 2006, 14-year-old Jordan Maguire (UK, b. August 23, 1991) set out on foot from the Borneo air base in Russia and walked 111 miles (178 km) to the North Pole, arriving 10 days later.

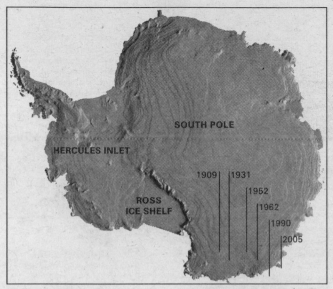

MAGNETIC POLES The Earth's magnetic poles are the places toward (and from) which a compass points and are located a considerable distance from the geographic poles. The magnetic poles "wander" slowly over the years, constantly changing position. (See above for how the poles have shifted since 1909.)

SCALING THE HEIGHTS

Murderous mountain On July 13, 1990, 43 people were killed in a huge ice and snow avalanche on Peak Lenin on the border between Tajikistan and Kyrgyzstan. Only two climbers survived this, the **worst mountaineering disaster** ever.

EVEREST

First ascent Mount Everest (29,028 ft.; 8,848 m) was first climbed at 11:30 a.m. on May 29, 1953, when the summit was reached by Edmund Percival Hillary (New Zealand) and Sherpa Tenzing Norgay (Nepal). The successful expedition was led by Col. (later Hon. Brigadier) Henry Cecil John Hunt (UK).

★ **MOST CONQUESTS OF EVEREST** Apa Sherpa (Nepal, center) reached the summit of Mount Everest for the 16th time on May 19, 2006, the most times anyone has ever successfully climbed the world's highest mountain, at 29,028 ft. (8,848 m).

First ascent without oxygen Reinhold Messner (Italy) and Peter Habeler (Austria) made the first successful ascent of Mount Everest without supplemental oxygen on May 8, 1978. This feat is regarded by some purist mountaineers as the first "true" ascent of Everest, since overcoming the effects of altitude (i.e., the low oxygen content of the air) is the greatest challenge facing high-altitude climbers.

First solo summit Reinhold Messner (Italy) was the first to successfully climb Mount Everest solo, reaching the summit on August 20, 1980. It took him three days to make the ascent from his

☆ **OLDEST EVEREST CLIMBER** Takao Arayama (Japan, b. October 4, 1935) reached the 29,028-ft.-high (8,848-m) summit of Everest on May 17, 2006, aged 70 years 225 days. Arayama was only three days older than the previous record-holder.

base camp at 21,325 ft. (6,500 m), and the climb was made all the more difficult by the fact that he did not use bottled oxygen.

Longest stay on summit Babu Chhiri Sherpa of Nepal completed a stay of 21 hours at the summit of Mount Everest without the use of bottled oxygen in May 1999.

KILIMANJARO

Fastest ascent Sean Burch (U.S.A.) ran the 21.1 miles (34 km) from the base to the summit of Mount Kilimanjaro, Tanzania (altitude 19,340 ft.; 5,895 m), in 5 hr. 28 min. 48 sec. on June 7, 2005, the fastest anyone has climbed Africa's highest peak.

Walking backward From July 20 to 23, 1997, Jurgen Gessau (South Africa) climbed to the summit of Mount Kilimanjaro in 72 hours, walking backward from Marangu Gate to Ulhuru Peak.

K2

First ascent K2 is situated in the Karakoram mountain range on the border between Pakistan and China. At 28,251 ft. (8,611 m), it is the world's second-highest mountain. The first successful ascent of K2 was achieved by Achille Compagnoni and Lino Lacedelli (both Italy) on July 31, 1954. They were members of an Italian expedition led by Ardito Desio (Italy).

First ascent by a woman Wanda Rutkiewicz (Poland) reached the summit of K2 on June 23, 1986, becoming the first woman to do so.

★**FASTEST CLIMB OF EVEREST AND K2 WITHOUT OXYGEN** In 2004, Karl Unterkircher (Italy) became the first mountaineer ever to summit the world's two highest mountains, Mount Everest and K2 (pictured), in the same season without bottled oxygen. He repeated this feat between May 24 and July 26, 2006—a record of 63 days.

OTHER PEAKS

Peaks over 8,000 m When Reinhold Messner (Italy) summited Lhotse (27,890 ft.; 8,501 m) on the Nepal-Tibet border on October 16, 1986, he became the **first person to climb the world's 14 peaks over 8,000 m** (26,246 ft.). His quest had started in June 1970. The difficulty of this feat is illustrated by the fact that by the second half of 2005, only 12 people had achieved it.

Jerzy Kukuczka (Poland) climbed the 14 peaks higher than 8,000 m (26,246 ft.) in 7 years 11 months 16 days, starting on October 4, 1979, and finishing on September 18, 1987. This is the **fastest ascent** ever of these peaks.

Canadian high points Jack Bennet (Canada) climbed the highest points in each of the 13 Canadian provinces and territories, including the new Inuit territory of Nunavut, which is 520 miles (837 km) from the North Pole. It took 5 years 361 days to complete all the climbs, with the final summit reached on June 15, 1998.

European high points Rob Baber (UK) reached the highest point in each of the 47 European countries in the 835 days between May 2, 1998, and August 14, 2000. He began with Iceland's highest point, Hvannadalshnúkur, and finished with Mount Ararat, Turkey.

★Largest simultaneous climb During the Big Event on September 10, 2000, a record 600 people simultaneously scaled 112 mountains in the UK and Ireland.

★YOUNGEST CLIMBER OF EL CAPITAN At 3,593 ft. (1,095 m) tall, El Capitan in Yosemite National Park, California, U.S.A., is the **tallest granite monolith in the world.** A prow between its two faces, known as the Nose, is the most popular choice for climbers wishing to summit "El Cap." On September 8–9, 2001, Scott Cory (U.S.A.) became the youngest person to climb the Nose, aged 11 years 110 days. On October 2, 2001, he tackled El Cap again and became the ★**youngest to ascend in one day,** aged 11 years 133 days. Pictured is Cory in March 2006, bouldering in Red Rock, Nevada, U.S.A.

FASTEST SEVEN SUMMITS BY A WOMAN Joanne Gambi (UK, pictured here with her husband, Rob) climbed the highest peak on each continent in 799 days, starting with Mt. McKinley, Alaska (North America), on June 12, 2003, and finishing at Puncak Jaya, Indonesia (Oceania), on August 19, 2005.

The first person to successfully climb the Seven Summits was Patrick Morrow (Canada), who completed the last, Ngga Pulu, Indonesia (Oceania), on May 7, 1986.

CIRCUMNAVIGATING THE GLOBE

LAND

Fastest by car The record for the first and fastest man and woman to have circumnavigated the Earth by car covering six continents under the rules applicable in 1989 and 1991 embracing more than an equator's length of driving (24,901 road miles; 40,075 km), is held by Saloo Choudhury and his wife Neena Choudhury (both India). The journey took 69 days 19 hr. 5 min. from September 9 to November 17, 1989. The couple drove a 1989 Hindustan "Contessa Classic" starting and finishing in Delhi, India.

Fastest by bicycle Steven Strange (UK) cycled around the world in a time of 276 days 19 hr. 15 min. between May 9, 2004, and February 13, 2005, having cycled a total of 18,424 miles (29,651 km) and traveled over 24,800 miles in total (including transfers). His journey started and finished in Vancouver, Canada.

Lowest fuel consumption Starting on January 17, 2006, John and Helen Taylor (UK and Australia, respectively) drove an unmodified Volkswagen Golf FSI a minimum distance of 18,000 miles (28,970 km) in 78 days. The couple used just 286 gallons (1,303 liters) of gas, which works out at an incredibly low fuel-consumption rate of 63 miles per gallon (22.2 km per liter).

AIR

Fastest by helicopter (female) Jennifer Murray (UK) piloted her Robinson R44 helicopter around the world in 99 days from May 31 to September

FASTEST BY MICROLIGHT Colin Bodill (UK) circumnavigated the globe in his Mainair Blade 912 Flexwing microlight aircraft (above) in 99 days from May 31 to September 6, 2000, starting and landing at Brooklands airfield, Weybridge, Surrey, UK. Bodill flew alongside Jennifer Murray on her successful solo helicopter circumnavigation (see page 175). The pair covered approximately 21,750 miles (35,000 km), across 30 countries.

6, 2000, at an average speed of 10.55 mph (16.99 km/h). The journey started and finished at Brooklands airfield in Surrey, UK, and crossed 30 countries.

Fastest by scheduled flights The fastest time to fly around the world on scheduled flights, according to the FAI definition, is 44 hr. 6 min. by David J. Springbett (UK). His 23,068-mile (37,124-km) route took him from Los Angeles, U.S.A., eastabout via London, Bahrain, Singapore, Bangkok, Manila, Tokyo, and Honolulu on January 8–10, 1980.

Fastest by airplane via both poles The fastest aerial circumnavigation of the Earth via both geographical poles is 54 hr. 7 min. 12 sec. (including refueling stops) by a Boeing 747 SP piloted by Captain Walter H. Mullikin (U.S.A.) between October 28 and 31, 1977. The journey started and finished in San Francisco, U.S.A., stopping off in Cape Town, South Africa, and Auckland, New Zealand.

★Fastest by scheduled flights with a single airline Between November 21 and 24, 2006, Brother Michael Bartlett (UK) circumnavigated the globe on scheduled Air New Zealand flights, taking just 59 hr. 58 min.

The only person to circumnavigate the globe solo in a balloon is Steve Fossett (U.S.A.)—it took him 13 days 8 hours in 2002.

SEA

First ever The first ever world circumnavigation was accomplished when *Vittoria,* under the command of navigator Juan Sebastian de Elcano (Spain), sailed into Seville, Spain, on September 9, 1522. The ship had set out along with four others as part of an expedition led by Ferdinand Magellan (Portugal) in 1519. *Vittoria* was the only ship to survive—of the 239 Europeans who set out, only 17 returned. Magellan had been killed in a squabble in the Philippines in 1521.

☆**Youngest solo sailor** The youngest person to circumnavigate the globe, sailing solo, nonstop, and unsupported, is Jesse Martin (Australia, b. August 26, 1980), who sailed in *Lionheart* from New South Wales, Australia, on December 8, 1998, aged 18 years 104 days. He returned on October 31, 1999, taking 327 days 12 hr. 52 min.

Fastest (crew) A crew of 14 captained by Bruno Peyron (France) sailed around the world in 50 days 16 hr. 20 min. 4 sec. in *Orange II* from January 24 to March 16, 2005. The journey started and finished in Ushant, France.

FASTEST SOLO SAILOR
Ellen MacArthur (UK, left) sailed solo and nonstop around the world in 71 days 14 hr. 18 min. from November 28, 2004, to February 7, 2005, in the trimaran *B&Q.* She set sail from Ushant, France, rounded the Cape of Good Hope, sailed south of Australia, and rounded Cape Horn before heading back up to Ushant.

★FASTEST NONSTOP WESTBOUND SAIL (SOLO FEMALE) The fastest female to sail around the world westbound, nonstop, solo, and unsupported is Dee Caffari (UK) in *Aviva,* a 72-ft. (22-m) monohull. She took 178 days 3 hr. 5 min. 34 sec. to sail back to her starting point in Portsmouth, UK, between November 20, 2005, and May 18, 2006.

★FASTEST NONSTOP WESTBOUND SAIL (SOLO MALE) Sailing nonstop, solo, and unsupported, Jean-Luc Van Den Heede (France) set off in *Adrien* on November 7, 2003. It took 122 days 14 hr. 3 min. 49 sec. for him to cross the Lizard Point–Ushant finishing line on March 9, 2004.

★ **DEEPEST WAVE-PIERCING POWERBOAT** The world's most efficient wave-piercing powerboat—one that cuts through waves rather than riding over the top—is *Earthrace,* a 78-ft.-long (24-m) trimaran that can submarine through waves at record depths of 23 ft. (7-m). Skippered by Pete Bethune (New Zealand), *Earthrace* set out to break the powerboat circumnavigation world record (using only renewable fuels) on March 10, 2007.

☆ **FASTEST MONOHULL (SOLO MALE)** Vincent Riou (France) circumnavigated the globe in 87 days 10 hr. 47 min. 55 sec. during the 2004 Vendée Globe single-handed yacht race, starting and finishing at Les Sables d'Olonne, France. He covered a distance of 21,760 nautical miles (25,040 miles; 40,299 km) in his yacht *PRB* from November 7, 2004, to February 2, 2005.

PROBING THE DEPTHS

☆**Largest underwater press conference** A group of 21 journalists dived to a depth of 16 ft. (5 m) to attend the press conference held by Leo Ochsenbauer and Klaus M. Schremser for the release of their new book *Zero-Time, Sex, and Depth Intoxication: 333 Answers to Divers' Questions* in Lake Traunsee, Austria, on June 17, 2006.

DEEPEST . . .

Manned ocean descent On January 23, 1960, Dr. Jacques Piccard (Switzerland) and Lt. Donald Walsh (U.S.A.) piloted the Swiss-built U.S.

DEEPEST SCUBA DIVE BY A DOG Dwane Folsom (U.S.A.) regularly takes his dog, Shadow, scuba diving off the coast of Grand Cayman Island. The pair usually descend to around 13 ft. (4 m). When diving, Shadow wears a specially adapted diving suit made up of a helmet, weighted dog jacket, and breathing tube connected to his owner's air tank.

Navy bathyscaphe *Trieste* to a depth of 35,797 ft. (10,911 m) in the Challenger Deep section of the Mariana Trench—the deepest known point on Earth.

Descent into an ice cave In 1998, the glacier explorer Janot Lamberton (France) descended to a depth of 662 ft. (202 m) in a cave in a glacier in Greenland.

Underwater escape without equipment The greatest depth from which an escape has been made without any equipment is 225 ft. (68.6 m), by Richard A. Slater (U.S.A.) from the rammed submersible *Nekton Beta* off Catalina Island, California, U.S.A., on September 28, 1970.

Underwater rescue Roger R. Chapman and Roger Mallinson (both UK) were trapped in the mini-sub *Pisces III* for 76 hours after it sank to 1,575 ft. (480 m), a distance of 150 miles (241 km) southeast of Cork, Ireland, on August 29, 1973.

DEEPEST DIVING SUBMARINE IN SERVICE On August 11, 1989, the Japanese research submarine *Shinkai 6500* (above left) reached a depth of 21,414 ft. (6,526 m) in the Japan Trench off Sanriku, Japan.
Shown above right is Masanobu Yanagitani, one of the two pilots who steer this deep submergence research vehicle (DSRV) to the bottom of the sea. He is seen sitting inside the cockpit of *Shinkai 6500*.

☆ **DEEPEST UNDERWATER CYCLING** Vittorio Innocente (Italy) cycled at a depth of 196 ft. (60 m) on the seafloor off Genoa, Italy, on July 13, 2005. He made minor modifications to his standard mountain bike, such as adding small lead weights and a plastic wing behind the seat and flooding the tires to reduce buoyancy.

It was hauled to the surface on September 1, by the cable ship *John Cabot* after work by *Pisces V*, *Pisces II*, and the remote-control recovery vessel *Curv* (Controlled underwater recovery vehicle).

Recovery The greatest depth at which a salvage operation has been carried out is 17,251 ft. (5,258 m), to recover a helicopter that had crashed into the Pacific Ocean in August 1991.

The crew of the USS *Salvor* and personnel from Eastport International raised the wreckage to the surface on February 27, 1992, so that the cause of the accident could be investigated.

Half-marathon The deepest half-marathon race took place at a depth of 695 ft. (212 m) in the Bochnia salt mine, Poland, on March 4, 2004.

The track was 7,998 ft. (2,438 m) long, and the 11 runners made approximately 8.5 circuits, covering a total distance of 69,215 ft. (21,097 m).

DEEPEST SEAWATER SCUBA DIVE Nuno Gomes (South Africa) dived to a depth of 1,044 ft. (318.25 m) in the Red Sea off Dahab, Egypt, on June 10, 2005.

While the descent was accomplished in a matter of minutes, the ascent took more than 12 hours, to allow for decompression.

Underwater mailbox The world's deepest underwater mailbox is located 32 ft. (10 m) beneath the waters of Susami Bay, Japan. Sports divers can send mail from the box, which is officially part of the Susami post office, and the mail is collected daily.

The mailbox is opened only by authorized employees using post office keys, and the divers use special waterproof plastic postcards. More than 4,273 items of undersea mail were collected in the mailbox's first year of operation.

Live Internet broadcast On July 24, 2001, live footage of HMS *Hood* was broadcast over the Internet from a depth of 9,200 ft. (2,800 m) at the bottom of the Denmark Strait, where the ship sank in 1941. The broadcast, from a remotely operated vehicle (ROV), followed the discovery of the wreck by David Mearns (UK) of Blue Water Recoveries Ltd. (UK), in an expedition organized by ITN Factual for Channel 4 (UK).

Live TV broadcast The world's deepest live TV broadcast was hosted by Alastair Fothergill (UK) at an underwater depth of 1.5 miles (2.4 km) on *Abyss Live* (BBC, UK).

The dive was broadcast on September 29, 2002, from inside a MIR submersible, along the Mid-Atlantic Ridge off the east coast of the U.S.A.

Live radio broadcast CBC Radio Points North (Canada) performed the deepest underground live radio broadcast, at a depth of 7,680 ft. (2,340 m), on May 24, 2005. The broadcast was carried out in Creighton Mine, Sudbury, Ontario, Canada.

Scuba dive (female) Verna van Schaik (South Africa) dived to a depth of 725 ft. (221 m) in the Boesmansgat Cave in South Africa's Northern Cape province on October 25, 2004. The dive lasted 5 hr. 34 min., of which only 12 minutes were spent descending.

Freshwater scuba cave-dive On August 23, 1996, Nuno Gomes (South Africa) scuba dived to a depth of 926 ft. (282.6 m) at the Boesmansgat Cave in the Northern Cape province of South Africa. Essentially a very deep sinkhole, the cave, at the surface, resembles a small lake with vertical sides.

And Gomes breaks records in salt water too—see bottom page 181 ...

MODERN SOCIETY

CONTENTS

MAN'S BEST FRIEND

★**Country with the highest rate of pet ownership** The country with the highest rate of pet ownership per household, as of 2003, is Australia, with 66% of households having at least one animal as a companion (typically a cat or dog) and 83% of Australians having owned a pet at some point in their life.

☆**Fastest dog weaving** The record for the fastest time for a dog to weave between 60 poles is 12.14 seconds by Zinzan, a German shepherd owned by Kobus Engelbrecht (UK), at the Wallingford agility show in Newbury, Berkshire, UK, on April 23, 2006.

★FIRST CLONED DOG The first cloned dog to survive birth is Snuppy, an Afghan hound "created" by Hwang Woo-Suk (South Korea) and his team of scientists at Seoul National University (SNU) in South Korea, after which the dog was named. He was born on April 24, 2005.

HIGHEST JUMP BY A DOG
Cinderella May a Holly Grey, a greyhound owned by Kate Long and Kathleen Conroy (both U.S.A.), jumped a record height of 68 in. (172.7 cm). The record was set at the Purina Incredible Dog Challenge National Finals, Gray Summit, Missouri, U.S.A., on October 7, 2006.

★**Largest obedience lesson** The largest dog obedience lesson involved 257 dogs with handlers at Nestlé Purina PetCare's BonzOmerspelen in Arnhem, the Netherlands, on May 16, 2004.

☆**Longest dog tunnel** Aidee, a border collie owned by Lynn van Beers (New Zealand), successfully ran through a "tunnel" of legs formed by 457 volunteers standing astride. The record was achieved on October 27, 2006, in conjunction with the Otago Canine Training Club (New Zealand) and Anderson's Bay School in Dunedin, New Zealand.

☆**Largest dog walk** The Butcher's Great North Dog

★**MOST STAIRS CLIMBED WHILE BALANCING WATER ON THE NOSE** Sweet Pea, a border collie–Australian-Alsatian cross owned by Alex Rothacker (U.S.A.), is able to walk up and down 15 stairs with a glass of water balanced on her nose. She can perform the trick without spilling a drop.

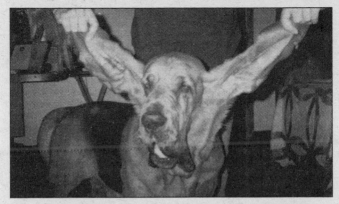

☆ **LONGEST DOG EARS** Tigger, a bloodhound owned by Bryan and Christina Flessner of St. Joseph, Illinois, U.S.A., has a right ear that measured 13.75 in. (34.9 cm) and a left ear that measured 13.5 in. (34.2 cm) on September 29, 2004.

Walk, organized by Anthony Carlisle (UK), involved 7,766 dogs going for a walk together in South Shields, Tyne and Wear, UK, on June 18, 2006.

★ **Longest dog living** Mon Ami von der Oelmühle, owned by Jürgen Rösner and Joachim and Elke Müller (Germany), is an Irish wolfhound measuring 91 in. (232 cm) from nose to tail tip.

★ **LARGEST DOG WEDDING CEREMONY** On February 12, 2006, in Hilversum, the Netherlands, 27 pairs of dogs were "married" in a ceremony organized by Nestlé Purina PetCare Nederland B.V. The dogs had all met during a speed-dating session prior to the mass wedding and were issued with certificates to celebrate the happy day.

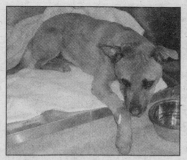

★HARDIEST DOG On April 15, 2003, a mixed-breed dog named Dosha slipped out of her owner's home in Clearlake, California, U.S.A., only to be run over by a car. Concerned police officers decided to end her pain and shot her in the head; she was then sealed in a bag and placed in a freezer at an animal center. She was discovered two hours later by staff—alive and sitting upright!

The **longest dog ever** was Aicama Zorba of La-Susa, an 8-ft. 3-in.-long (2.544-m) Old English mastiff, last measured in 1987.

Tallest dog ever Gibson, a harlequin Great Dane, measured 42.2 in. (107 cm) tall on August 31, 2004. Milleniums' *[sic]* Rockydane Gibson Meistersinger—as he is more formally known—is owned by Sandy Hall (U.S.A.) and works as a therapy dog. When standing on his hind legs, the 170-lb. (77-kg) pooch measures more than 7 ft. (2 m) tall. By comparison, the smallest dog ever was a dwarf Yorkshire terrier that measured just 2.8 in. (7.11 cm) to the shoulder!

★**Largest dog breed** According to the American Kennel Club, the largest dog breed is the Irish wolfhound, which weighs 105–125 lb. (47–56 kg) and stands 30–35 in. (76–88 cm) at the shoulder.

The ★**smallest breed of dog** is the chihuahua, which weighs just 2–6 lb. (1–3 kg) and stands 6–9 in. (15–23 cm) at the shoulder.

GUIDE DOGS

• The **longest period of active service for a guide dog** is 14 years 8 months (August 1972–March 1987) in the case of a Labrador retriever named Cindi-Cleo, owned by Aron Barr of Tel Aviv, Israel. The dog died on April 10, 1987.

• The **longest serving hearing guide dog** was Donna, owned by John Hogan of Pyrmont Point, New South Wales, Australia. She completed 10 years of active service in Australia up to 1995—and eight years of service prior to that in New Zealand—before her death on May 6, 1995, at the age of 20 years, 2 months.

• The Guide Dogs for the Blind Association is the world's **largest breeder and trainer of working dogs.** Around 1,200 would-be guide dogs are born every year in Warwickshire, UK, to breeding stock specially chosen for their intelligence and temperament.

★Most dogs washed by a team in eight hours A team of 12 people managed to wash 848 dogs in an eight-hour period. Australia's Biggest Dog Wash was organized by The Veterinary Science Foundation of the University of Sydney and held on September 14, 2003, in Sydney, Australia.

★Most skips by a dog in one minute Sweet Pea (see bottom, page 186) also achieved an incredible 65 skipping-rope jumps in one minute. She performed the trick on the set of the TV show *La Nuit Des Records* filmed in Paris, France, on October 10, 2006.

★First pet movie star A border collie named Jean, owned by movie director Larry Trimble (U.S.A.), became the first doggie star when he appeared in the 1910 feature *Jean and the Calico Doll.* He went on to star in a number of movies, including *Jean and the Waif* and *Jean Goes Fishing.*

Most successful police dog Trepp (short for Intrepid)—a golden retriever owned by Tom Kazo (U.S.A.)—has been credited with over 100 arrests and the recovery of illegal drugs worth over $63 million.

★First animal whose evidence is admissible in court Essentially a nose with a dog attached, the bloodhound is the first animal whose evidence is legally admissible in court.

A typical bloodhound's nose is lined with 230 million scent receptors—around 40 times more than the human nose—which are used in court to match scene-of-crime evidence to criminals.

★MOST POPULAR BREED OF DOG According to yearly statistics gathered by the American Kennel Club (AKC), out of 153 breeds acknowledged by the AKC for 2006, the most popular purebreed in the U.S.A. was the Labrador retriever, with 123,760 dogs registered in 2006. The breed has held the U.S. top spot since 1991 and was also the most popular in Canada and the UK.

FOOD & DRINK

LARGEST

☆**Bowl of soup** Residents of Salonta in Romania cooked up a 1,109-gallon (5,045-liter) goulash soup at their town hall on June 3, 2006.

☆**Ice-cream cake** An ice-cream cake made by Beijing Allied Faxi Food Co., Ltd., for Beijing Children's Art Theater Co., Ltd., weighed in at 19,290 lb. (8,750 kg) and was displayed in Beijing, China, on January 16, 2006.

The ★**largest ice-cream cup** weighed 8,865 lb. (4,021 kg) and was made on September 13, 2005, by Baskin-Robbins at its headquarters in Canton, Massachusetts, U.S.A.

☆**Kebob skewer** On February 16, 2007, the company Chih'ua Tacos y Cortes of Chihuahua, Mexico, served up a kebob that weighed 8,258 lb. (3,745.8 kg).

☆**Piñata** A piñata is a brittle, hollow sculpture that is filled with confectionery and usually smashed to pieces by blindfolded children as a party game. The world's largest piñata measured 39 ft. 8 in. (12 m) high with a diameter of 42 ft. 6 in. (12.95 m) and was made at the Cincy-Cinco Latino Festival and displayed in Cincinnati, Ohio, U.S.A., on May 5, 2006.

☆**Stir-fry** A stir-fry weighing 2,319 lb. (1,052 kg) was prepared by the Wesvalia High School in Klerksdorp, South Africa, on October 22, 2005.

☆**Gingerbread man** The Gingerbread House in Rochester, Minnesota, U.S.A., baked a cookie child weighing 466 lb. 6 oz. (211.5 kg) on February 21, 2006. Those with a sweet tooth beware: this works out at something like 750,000 calories!

☆**LARGEST BURGER** The largest commercially available burger is Big Bob's Texas Belt Buster—a 78-lb. 8-oz. (35.6-kg) monster available at Bob's BBQ and Grill at Pattaya Beach in Chonburi, Thailand, as of July 31, 2006. It costs $23.95 and anyone who can finish the entire thing within three hours receives a refund, together with their name on a plaque and a gift certificate to use for a future visit. To date, no one has achieved this: the fastest finishing so far is eight hours!

★ **LARGEST CHOCOLATE IGLOO** Marco Fanti (Italy) and his team of builders used a total of 330 chocolate bricks, and worked for 23 hours, to make a chocolate igloo weighing 6,613 lb. (3 tons) in Perugia, Italy, on October 17, 2006.

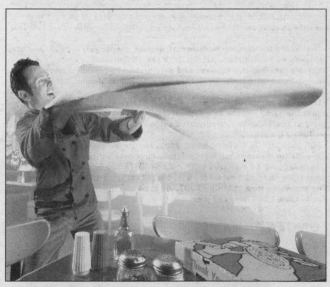

★ **LARGEST SPUN PIZZA CRUST** Tony Gemignani (U.S.A., above) spun 17.6 oz. (500 g) of dough for two minutes to form a pizza crust measuring 33.2 in. (84.33 cm) wide at the Mall of America in Minneapolis, Minnesota, U.S.A., on April 20, 2006, during the filming of *Guinness World Records Week* for the Food Network channel.

On the same day, at the same event, Joe Carlucci (U.S.A.) set a new record for the ★ **highest pizza-crust toss** using 20 oz. (567 g) of dough, achieving a height of 21 ft. 5 in. (6.52 m).

'NORMOUS NOSH If the last few years are anything to go by, the record-breaking public hasn't lost its appetite for creating titanic treats and fantastic feasts:

• The record for ☆ **most number of dishes displayed** is 2007, and was achieved by His Holiness Sri Sri Sri Vasanth Gurudev Shakthipeetadhipathi (above) and Sri Parshva Padmavathi Seva Trust at Sri Parshva Padmavathi Shakthipeet Temple, Krishnagiri, India, on March 3, 2007.

• The world's **largest meatball** tips the scales at 43 lb. 3 oz. (19.6 kg)—about the same weight as a typical five-year-old boy—it was made by chefs at the SANS Bergmannskroa restaurant in Løkken Verk, Norway, on June 24, 2006.

• Still peckish? On November 19, 2005, the Juniorchamber Veenendaal-Rijnvallei in Veenendaal, Netherlands, completed their record for the ☆ **largest bag of cookies** with a 7,054-lb. (3,200-kg) package measuring 18 ft. (5.5 m) wide, 6 ft. 6 in. (2 m) tall and 10 ft. (3 m) deep. The supersize sack contained 207,860 cookies; filling it with the baked goods took 3,600 hours of work!

LONGEST

★**Chili-pepper string** James Johnson (U.S.A.) made a chili-pepper string measuring 1,039 ft. (316.69 m) long and consisting of 20,150 chili pods.

☆**Damper bread** Scouts from the Glimåkra Scout Troop baked a damper bread measuring 410 ft. (125 m) in Glimåkra, Sweden, on September 9, 2006.

☆**Drinks-can line** The longest line of drinks cans consisted of 84,498 cans in an event organized by Bridge FM Radio and Bridgend County Council in Bridgend, UK, on October 26–27, 2006.

★LONGEST BARBECUE A barbecue measuring 4,232 ft. (1,290 m) long was built and fired up by the residents of Hermosillo, Mexico, on November 20, 2006. Over 11,000 lb. (5,000 kg) of meat and potatoes were served to a 20,736-strong crowd.

☆**Garlic string** A garlic string measuring 407 ft. (124.2 m) long was made for the Garlic Festival in Borgholm, Sweden, by a team led by Gunnar Kvarnbäck (Sweden) on September 25, 2005.

★Gingerbread The record for the longest gingerbread is 75.9 ft. (23.14 m) and was achieved by a team of chefs employed at the Langham Place Hotel in Mongkok, Hong Kong, on December 3, 2005.

☆**Loaf of bread** A loaf of bread stretching for 3,975 ft. (1,211.6 m) was baked during the Bread and Bakers' Party in Vagos, Portugal, on July 10, 2005.

☆**Pasta strand** On September 10, 2005, Ristorante Hammermühle in Ober-Darmstadt, Germany, created a single strand of pasta measuring 1,492 ft. 9 in. (455 m)—in other words, longer than six jumbo jets!

☆**Salami** Salumificio Manuelli, s.r.l., made a 1,853-ft. 3-in.-long (564.88-m) salami in Varallo, Vericelli, Italy, on August 14, 2005.

★Sausage roll A 364-ft. (111-m) sausage roll was made by King Pie in Faerie Glen, South Africa, on June 25, 2005.

DID YOU KNOW?

The white truffle (*Tuber magnum pico*) is the world's **most expensive edible fungus,** usually fetching $3,000 per kilo. They can be found only in the Italian regions of Piedmont, Emilia-Romagna, Tuscany, and Marches, and because they grow up to 12 in. (30 cm) underground, they can only be located with the help of sows or trained dogs.

MOST EXPENSIVE PIE A pie sold at the Fence Gate Inn in Lancashire, UK, will cost you £8,195 ($14,260) or £1,024 ($1,781) per slice when ordered by eight guests. (Head chef and pricey-pie creator Spencer Burge, UK, is pictured.) The pie's expensive ingredients include:
• $870-worth of Japanese wagyu beef fillet (from cattle that are massaged by hand);
• Chinese matsutake mushrooms ($420 per lb.)—so precious, they are harvested under guard;
• Bluefoot mushrooms ($175 per lb.);
• gravy made from two bottles of vintage 1982 Château Mouton Rothschild wine ($1,740 each);
• edible gold leaf costing $174 per sheet.

GROSS GASTRONOMY

TABASCO SAUCE Most drunk in 30
sec.: 4.2 fl. oz. (120 ml)
Andrew Hajinikitas (Australia)
May 8, 2005

MILKSHAKE Fastest time to drink
17 oz. (500 ml) by straw: 9.8 sec.
Osi Anyanwu (UK)
November 9, 2005

★GARLIC Most eaten in 1 min.:
4 cloves
Alastair Galpin (Australia)
November 9, 2006

OYSTERS Most eaten in 3 min.: 187
Rune Naeri (Norway)
September 6, 2003

M&M'S Most eaten in 3 min. using
chopsticks: 170
Kathryn Ratcliffe (UK)
November 24, 2004

RICE Most eaten with chopsticks in
3 min.: 64 grains
Tae Wah Gooding (South Korea)
November 7, 2000

DOUGHNUTS (POWDERED) Most
eaten in 3 min.: 4
Shared: Simon Krischer, Jay
Weisberger, Adam Fenton, Anthony
Albelo (all U.S.A.)
June 12, 2002

☆JELL-O Most eaten in 1 min. with
chopsticks: 6.34 oz. (180 g)
Damien Fletcher (UK)
October 4, 2006

SWEET CORN (CANNED) Most eaten
with cocktail stick in 3 min.: 236
kernels
Ian Richard Purvis (UK)
August 27, 2003

PEAS (CANNED) Most eaten with
cocktail stick in 3 min.: 211
Mat Hand (UK)
November 8, 2001

★FERRERO ROCHER Most
unwrapped and eaten in 1 min.: 5
Matthew Winn (UK)
June 3, 2006

JELLY DOUGHNUTS Most eaten in
3 min. (without licking lips): 6
Steve McHugh (UK)
June 28, 2002

ALE Fastest time to drink a yard of
ale (1.42 liters; 3 U.S. pints): 5 sec.
Peter Dowdeswell (UK)
May 4, 1975

★BANANAS Most peeled and eaten
in 1 min.: 2
Steve Payne (UK)
May 5, 2006

★ MEGA MEALS ★

LARGEST...	RECORD	WHO	WHEN
Breakfast (uncooked)	27,854 diners	Nutella, Gelsenkirchen, Germany	May 29, 2005
Breakfast (cooked)	18,941 diners	Cowboy Breakfast Foundation, San Antonio, Texas, U.S.A.	Jan. 26, 2001
★Risotto	16,556 lb. (7.5 tons)	Ricegrowers Assoc. of Australia, Sydney, Australia	Nov. 26, 2004
★Chili con carne	1,438 lb. (652.4 kg)	Keystone Aquatic Club, Harrisburg, Pennsylvania, U.S.A.	Jul. 19, 2003
☆Fish and chips	77 lb. 12 oz. (35.26 kg)	Icelandic, U.S.A., Inc., Boston, Massachusetts, U.S.A.	Mar. 15, 2004
☆Guacamole	3,368.44 lb. (1,527.9 kg)	Festival, Con Sabor A Mexico, Dallas, Texas, U.S.A.	Oct. 15, 2005
★Hummus	800 lb. (362 kg)	Sabra Mediterranean, New York, U.S.A.	Mar. 6, 2006

HOT DOGS Most eaten (with buns and condiments) in 3 min.: 4
Peter Dowdeswell (UK)
July 27, 2001

BAKED BEANS Most eaten with cocktail stick in 3 min.: 136
Nick Thompson (UK)
August 18, 2005

KETCHUP Fastest time to drink a 14-oz. (396-g) bottle of ketchup by straw: 33 sec.
Dustin Phillips (U.S.A.)
September 23, 1999

MINCE PIES Fastest time to eat three: 1 min. 26 sec.
David Cole (UK)
December 20, 2005

GRAPES Most eaten using a teaspoon in 3 min.: 133
Mat Hand (UK)
November 8, 2001

JALAPEÑO CHILES Most eaten in 1 min.: 16
Alfredo Hernandes (U.S.A.)
September 17, 2006

SAUSAGES Most eaten in 1 min.: 8
Stefan Paladin (New Zealand)
July 22, 2001
Most swallowed whole in 1 min.: 8
Cecil Walker (U.S.A.)
March 13, 2003

SHRIMP Most eaten in 3 min.: 9.6 oz. (272.1 g)
William E. Silver (U.S.A.)
February 26, 2003

STOUT Fastest time to drink 1 British pint: 2.1 sec.
Peter Dowdeswell (UK)
April 24, 2001
Fastest time to drink 2 British pints: 6.1 sec.
Ken Robinson (UK)
December 8, 2004

TOWERING TREATS

• The ☆ **tallest Champagne fountain** was constructed by Luuk Broos (Germany) and his team during the CentrO Festival in Oberhausen, Germany, on September 9, 2006. The phenomenal fizzy fountain consisted of 61 stories.

• The ★ **tallest chocolate sculpture**, created by Hyatt Regency Chicago pastry chef Alain Roby (France), was a replica of the Rockefeller Center, the Empire State Building, and the Chrysler Building. The skyscraping confectionery, measuring 20 ft. 8 in. (6.2 m), was unveiled at the FAO Schwarz toy store in New York City, U.S.A., on October 10, 2006.

• The ★ **tallest cooked sugar sculpture** measured 12 ft. 10.4 in. (3.91 m). It was made in 11 hours by Alain Roby (France) at Mall of America, Minneapolis, Minnesota, U.S.A., on April 21, 2006. As with Roby's record-breaking chocolate sculpture (see above), it was created during the filming of *Guinness World Records Week* for the Food Network channel.

• The record for the ★ **tallest pyramid of cookies** is 4 ft. 10.7 in. (1.49 m) and was achieved by Jan Vinzenz Krause (Germany) and members of the diocese Essen using 12,180 Leibniz butter cookies at the CentrO shopping center in Oberhausen, Germany, on September 16, 2006.

BEER Fastest time to drink...
2 British pints: 2.3 sec.
Peter Dowdeswell (UK), June 11, 1975
1 British pint upside down: 3 sec.
Peter Dowdeswell (UK), February 16, 1988
1 liter: 1.3 sec.
Steven Petrosino (U.S.A.), June 22, 1977
2 liters: 6 sec.
Peter Dowdeswell (UK), February 7, 1975

BRUSSELS SPROUTS (COOKED)
Most eaten in 1 min: 21
Liam McCormack (Ireland)
February 17, 2007

CRACKERS Fastest time to eat three: 34.78 sec.
Ambrose Mendy (UK)
May 9, 2005

MEATBALLS Most eaten using a cocktail stick in 1 min.: 27
Nick Marshall (UK)
November 18, 2002

MILK Fastest time to drink 2 UK pints: 3.2 sec.
Peter Dowdeswell (UK)
May 31, 1975

GAMES & PUZZLES

SCRABBLE

★**Highest scores** •**Tournament** In a qualifying round of the 1986 British National Championships, Joyce Cansfield (UK) finished with a score of 855 points.

•The highest score in a tournament game using the *Official Scrabble Words International* (OSWI) rules is 785, achieved by Jackie McLeod (UK) in 2002.

•**Club** Under the *U.S. Official Tournament and Club Word List, Second Edition* (OWL2) rules, Michael Cresta (U.S.A.) scored 830 points on October 12, 2006.

•Under UK rules, governed by the *Official Scrabble Words* (OSW) book, the highest score achieved was 793 by Peter Preston (UK) in 1993.

★**Highest combined scores** •**Tournament** A game played on June 13, 1993, between Mark Landsberg and Alan Stern (both U.S.A.), ended 770–338—a combined record total of 1,108.

TRY ME!

You can attempt some puzzles on these pages—and maybe even set some new Guinness World Records along the way. Just make a photocopy of this spread and grab a pencil and stopwatch. If you think you can break a record, find out how to register it with us on p. xvi.

★ **HIGHEST THEORETICAL SINGLE-WORD SCRABBLE SCORE** Which word, according to the World Scrabble Championships website, is the longest feasible word in the game? The board below is set up in such a way that, if you play all the tiles in the rack (HRBYSCZ), you would score 1,790 points. *Note: the word, a 15-letter chemical name, could not be used in a club- or tournament-level game, as it relies on proper nouns, contrary to conventional matchplay practice.* *

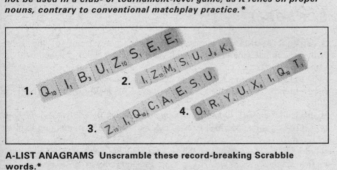

A-LIST ANAGRAMS Unscramble these record-breaking Scrabble words.*
1. ★ **Highest scoring opening word**, 124 points, Sam Kantimathi (U.S.A.), 1993: *Noun*, a card game.
2. ★ **Highest possible score for an opening word**, 128 points: *Noun* (plural), Russian peasants.
3. ★ **Highest scoring single word**, 392 points, Karl Khoshnaw (Germany), 1982: *Noun* (plural), tribal chiefs in the Americas.
4. ★ **Highest scoring single word (U.S. rules)**, 365 points, Michael Cresta (U.S.A.), 2006: *Noun*, romantic chivalry.

•**Club** A game played at club level between Michael Cresta and Wayne Yorra (both U.S.A.) resulted in a final score of 1,320 (830–490). Cresta's score of 830 is also an individual world record (see above).

*Answer at bottom of p. 199.

Very Easy

1	7				6		8	
	8	9		3	4	2		
			5					
7		5		4		1		
		1		9		7		6
				7				
	7	8	9			2	3	
6		3				9		5

Easy

2								3
		1	4				9	5
				7	8	1		
			7	3	5	6	8	
6	5						4	2
		3	4	2	8	7		
			5	7	9			
	4	2					6	9
8								1

★ **FASTEST TIME TO COMPLETE A "VERY EASY" SUDOKU GRID** The rules of sudoku are simple: every column, every row, and every block of nine must contain the numbers 1–9. But how fast can you complete a grid? On the left is a "Very Easy" puzzle—can you solve it faster than the record holder? ★ **The fastest time to complete a "Very Easy" sudoku puzzle** is 1 min. 23.93 sec. by Thomas Snyder (U.S.A.) at BookExpo America, Washington DC, U.S.A., on May 20, 2006. He also holds the record for ★ **fastest "Easy" sudoku puzzle,** at 2 min. 8.53 sec. (right).

★ **Largest puzzle world championships** The World Puzzle Championships, organized by the World Puzzle Federation, is the largest event of its kind on the planet. The 15th annual competition was held in 2006 in Borovets, Bulgaria, and attracted a record 200 competitors from 20 countries. Among the challenges set each year are sudokus, logic puzzles, and spot-the-differences.

★ **Highest losing score** A losing score of 545 was suffered by Kevin Rickhoff (U.S.A.) against Mark Milan's (U.S.A.) 558 in the 18th round of the 2006 U.S. Open, under *Tournament World List* 2006 (TWL06) rules.

★ **Lowest winning score** Rod Nivison (U.S.A.) won a game at the 1990 Midwest Invitational in the U.S.A. by a score of -8 to -10. This bizarre result was achieved after he and his opponent repeatedly passed turns or changed tiles, and the only word to be placed on the board (DORMINE) was challenged off!

★**Most points scored with one tile** In a tournament game in 1999, Tom Kelly (U.S.A.) scored 99 by laying an S to form QUIRKS and SMOTHERED.

CROSSWORDS

☆**Most crosswords compiled in a lifetime** Roger F. Squires (UK) compiles an average of 31 puzzles a week. By December 2005, he had compiled 65,000 published crosswords.

★**Largest arrow-word puzzle** An arrow-word puzzle measuring 4 ft. 3 in. × 11 ft. 3 in. (1.03 × 3.45 m) and containing 16,000 blocks with 3,200 clues was published by Revistas Coquetel (Brazil) in Rio de Janeiro, Brazil, in March 2006.

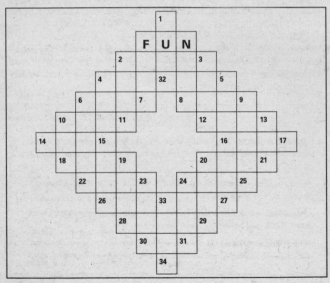

FIRST CROSSWORD The first crossword puzzle appeared in the Sunday "Fun" section of U.S. newspaper *New York World* on December 21, 1913. Created by journalist Arthur Wynne (UK), it was based on a diamond-shaped grid, had no blacked-out squares, and featured simple, non-cryptic clues. Try completing the crossword for yourself—the clues are listed in the panel on p. 201. Solution on p. 602.

CROSSWORD CLUES Here are the clues to the crossword on page 200. The solution is given on p. 602.

ACROSS		DOWN	
2–3	What bargain hunters enjoy	10–18	The fiber of the gomuti palm
4–5	A written acknowledgement	6–22	What we all should be
6–7	Such and nothing more	4–26	A daydream
8–9	To cultivate	2–11	A talon
10–11	A bird	19–28	A pigeon
12–13	A bar of wood or iron	F-7	Part of your head
14–15	Opposed to less	23–30	A river in Russia
16–17	What artists learn to do	1–32	To govern
18–19	What this puzzle is	33–34	An aromatic plant
20–21	Fastened	N-8	A fist
22–23	An animal of prey	24–31	To agree with
24–25	Found on the seashore	3–12	Part of a ship
26–27	The close of day	20–29	One
28–29	To elude	5–27	Exchanging
30–31	The plural of is	9–25	To sink in mud
		13–21	A boy

Largest published crossword In July 1982, Robert Turcot (Canada) compiled a crossword comprising 82,951 squares. It contained 12,489 clues across, 13,125 down, and covered 38.21 ft.^{2} (3.55 m^2).

Longest word in a crossword The Welsh town name Llanfairpwll-gwyngyllgogerychwyrndrobwllllantysiliogogogoch is the longest word ever used in a cryptic crossword. Roger F. Squires (UK) used it in the July 1979 edition of the *Telford Wrekin News*.

DID YOU KNOW?

• The word "sudoku" is an abbreviation of the Japanese phrase "suji wa dokushin ni kagiru" ("the numbers must be alone"—i.e., appear only once).

• Mathematicians proved that 6,670,903,752,021,072,936,960 different Sudoku boards are possible.

• The ★ **first sudoku TV show,** *Sudoku Live,* was broadcast in the UK on July 1, 2005, and hosted by Carol Vorderman.

• The ★ **first sudoku world championships** were held in Lucca, Italy, on March 10–12, 2006. The winner was Jana Tylová (Czech Republic).

COLLECTIONS

Autographed books Michael Silverbrooke and Pat Tonkin (both Canada) have collected 722 books, each signed by their original authors.

☆**Barbie dolls** Bettina Dorfmann (Germany) has 2,500 different Barbie dolls.

Board games Since 1992, Linda Ivey (U.S.A.) has put together a collection of 868 different board games.

★**Bookmarks** Frank Divendal (Netherlands) owns 71,235 bookmarks that he has collected from all over the world. He began his collection in 1982.

★**Cat-related items** Florence Groff (France) has a collection of 11,717 cat-related items, including 2,118 different cat figurines.

Cigarette cards (museum) Edward Wharton-Tigar (UK, 1913–95) amassed over 1 million cigarette and trade cards in some 45,000 sets. The collection was given to the British Museum, London, UK, after his death.

COLLECTING GUIDELINES

•Preference goes to items accumulated personally, over time, rather than those made on behalf of a third party, such as a newspaper appeal.

•The record is based on the number of items of the same type in the collection. Duplicates do not count. For paired items, such as earrings or cuff links, the number of *pairs* should be given.

•Claims are to be submitted by the owner with a brief history of when and why the collection began. Also of interest is where the collection is housed and if there is a favorite item, and why.

•It is essential that a total count of the items claimed be taken by some accurate method of counting.

•The number of items in the collection must be included in any witness statements.

•A concise inventory should be submitted for all claims.

•One of the signed statements of authentication should come from a recognized society specializing in collections of the type submitted, if possible.

•Failure to include the required documentation will delay the outcome of a claim or lead to its rejection.

Modern Society

GNOMES AND PIXIES Since 1979, artist Ann Fawssett-Atkin (UK) has collected a total of 2,032 garden gnomes and pixies, all of which have gone to live with her in her 4-acre (1.6-ha) Gnome Reserve and Wild Flower Garden in West Putford, Devon, UK. Visitors to the Gnome Garden and Museum are issued with pointy hats when they enter, "so as not to embarrass the gnomes that live there."

☆**Coffeepots** Irma Goth (Germany) started her collection some 20 years ago; she now owns 3,028 different coffeepots.

☆**Coins from different countries** Justin Gilbert Lopez (India) has a collection of 255 coins representing 255 different countries. He has been collecting coins since 1986.

★*Dragonball* **memorabilia** Since 1996, Michael Nilsen (U.S.A.) has collected 5,065 unique items of memorabilia relating to *Dragonball,* a popular Japanese animation series.

DICE Kevin Cook (U.S.A.) has a collection of 11,097 dice that he has amassed since 1977. A member of the Dice Maniacs Club (aka the Random Fandom), Kevin began collecting dice from gaming shops after taking up Dungeons & Dragons. Since 1998, about 80% of his dice have come from eBay, the online auction company.

★**Earrings** Carol McFadden (U.S.A.) has 37,706 different pairs of earrings, which she has been collecting since 1952.

Footballs (soccer) Roberto A. Fuglini (Argentina) has 861 different soccer balls, which he has collected since 1995.

★**Hats** The record for the largest collection of hats belongs to Roger Buckey Legried (U.S.A.). The collection is made up of 82,792 different items that Buckey has accumulated from all over the world. He has been collecting since 1970.

★**Magic sets** Manfred Klaghofer (Austria) has 2,017 different magic sets from all over the world. He started collecting them in 1995, and his oldest set dates back to the 19th century.

★ COLLECTIONS A–Z ★

COLLECTION	NUMBER	HOLDER (NATIONALITY)
★Armored vehicles (*picture 1*)	229	Jacques Littlefield (U.S.A.)
Bar towels (*picture 2*)	2,372	Robert Begley (U.S.A.)
★Cigarette cases	1,351	Colin Grey (UK)
Dinosaur eggs	10,008	Heyuan Museum (China)
Erasers	19,571	Petra Engels (Germany)
Four-leaf clovers (*picture 3*)	72,928	George J. Kaminski (U.S.A.)
Golf clubs	4,393	Robert Lantsoght (Spain)
Handcuffs	843	Stan Willis (U.S.A.)
Ice-lolly (popsicle) sticks	449	Poul Lykke Jepsen (Denmark)
Jet fighters	110	Michel Pont (France)
Key chains	41,418	Brent Dixon (U.S.A.)
Letter openers	1,365	Bengt Olsson (Sweden)
Mickey Mouse memorabilia (*picture 4*)	2,143	Janet Esteves (U.S.A.)
★Napkins (*picture 5*)	21,000	Antónia Kozáková (Slovakia)
Owls	18,055	Dianne Turner (U.S.A.)
Penguin-related items	2,520	Birgit Berends (Germany)
There are no collections beginning with Q in the Guinness World Records database		
Radios (*picture 6*)	625	M. Prakash (India)
★Spoon rests	635	Frank Cassa (U.S.A.)
★Teapots	3,950	Sue Blazye (UK)
Uncut banknotes	123 sheets	Leigh Follestad (Canada)
Vintage lawn mowers	790	Andrew Hall and Michael Duck (both UK)
Whisky bottles	10,500	Alfredo Gonçalves (Portugal)
There are no collections beginning with X in the Guinness World Records database		
Yo-yos	4,251	John Meisenheimer (U.S.A.)
There are no collections beginning with Z in the Guinness World Records database		

Do you have a collection of quilts, xylophones, or Zippo lighters? Guinness World Records currently has no collections beginning with Q, X, or Z, so if you collect anything that starts with these letters, get in touch to see if you can set a new world record. Find out how to register your claim on p. xvi.

★**Model trucks** The largest collection of model trucks belongs to Peter and Jens Pittack (both Germany). They have amassed 2,169 different trucks since they began collecting in 1997.

Nutcrackers Uwe and Jürgen Löschner (Germany) have collected 4,334 nutcrackers, all of which are housed at the Nut Cracker Museum in the town of Neuhausen, Germany.

★**Policemen's patches** Ross Kaiser (U.S.A.) has 3,271 policemen's patches, which he started collecting in 2001.

LARGEST COLLECTION?

Compiled by Ed Brassard (U.S.A.), the largest collection of items currently listed on the *Guinness World Records* database contains a staggering 3,159,119 individual matchbook covers.

Royal memorabilia Ronny Bragança (Portugal) has collected 2,950 pieces of memorabilia celebrating Diana, Princess of Wales, since 1991.

★ **Salt and pepper packets** Tim Leigh (UK) has 100 matching pairs of salt and pepper packets in his collection, each with a different company logo. He has been collecting the packets since 1998.

★ **Shoe-related items** Darlene Flynn (U.S.A.) has 7,765 different shoe-related items, which she has been collecting since 2000.

★ **Stamps from different countries** Jose Gilbert J. (India) has amassed a total of 192 stamps representing 192 different countries.

Teddy bears Jackie Miley (U.S.A.) has a collection of 4,190 different teddy bears that she has amassed since 2002.

★ **Tribal and ethnic footwear** William Habraken (Netherlands) has 2,322 different pairs of footwear, originating from 155 countries, which he has been collecting since 1968.

★ **Watches** Franciscus Hendricus Maria Salari (Netherlands) has amassed a collection of 1,366 different watches, depicting various logos, businesses, and products.

PLAYTIME

★ **Cartwheeling** **The greatest distance traveled in 24 hours by a team doing cartwheels** is 31 miles (50 km) by 10 gymnasts from Beausejour Gymnos (Canada) at the track in Memramcook, New Brunswick, Canada, from September 8 to 9, 2006.

Ducks and drakes Kurt Steiner (U.S.A.) achieved 40 consecutive skips of a stone on water (aka "ducks and drakes") at the Pennsylvania Qualifying Stone Skipping Tournament held at Riverfront Park, Franklin, Pennsylvania, U.S.A., on September 14, 2002.

Egg-and-spoon racing •The record for the **largest egg-and-spoon race (single venue)** was set by 859 students from Raynes Park High School in Raynes Park, London, UK on October 24, 2003.
•The **largest simultaneous egg-and-spoon race (multi-venue)** involved 1,277 racers at various venues around Herefordshire, UK, in an event organized by Ready Steady Win, UK, on March 30, 2004.
•On April 23, 1990, Dale Lyons (UK) ran the London Marathon (26 miles 385 yd.; 42.195 km) carrying a spoon with a fresh egg on it, in 3 hr. 47 min., the **fastest marathon run with an egg and spoon.**

★ **LARGEST GAME OF TUNNEL BALL** In tunnel ball, teams line up and pass a ball along their length, alternately through the legs and over the head. The player at the end then goes to the front and the process repeats. The winner is the first team to get its front player back to the start.

The largest tunnel ball game involved 80 children from Berwick Lodge Primary School, Victoria, Australia, on April 19, 2006. The game took 2 hr. 23 min. to complete.

★ **Hula dance** On June 4, 2005, 122 dancers performed the largest hula dance at an event sponsored by Hicks Lumber (Canada) to support the Help a Child Smile charity at the annual Rose Festival in Welland, Ontario, Canada.

★ **LARGEST ROCK, PAPER, SCISSORS CONTEST** The fifth Rock Paper Scissors world championships—organized by the World Rock Paper Scissors Society (RPS)—was staged at the Steam Whistle Brewery in Toronto, Canada, on November 11, 2006, and attracted 500 competitors. Bob Cooper (UK, above left) took the title of world champion, along with a gold medal and CAN$7,000 ($6,000) in prize money.

★ MOST LEAPFROG JUMPS IN ONE MINUTE The greatest number of leapfrog jumps performed in a minute is 48. The feat was achieved by James Fryer and Nick Jenkins (both UK) from Emap Advertising to raise money for The Rainbow Trust Children's Charity, and was staged in Barcelona, Spain, on May 5, 2006.

Sack race competition On October 11, 2002, a group of 2,095 students from Agnieton College and primary-school pupils from Zwolle, Wezep, and Hattem took part in the largest sack race competition. The race was staged in Zwolle, the Netherlands.

☆ LARGEST EASTER EGG HUNT On April 1, 2007, an Easter egg hunt featuring 501,000 eggs was staged at the Cypress Gardens Adventure Park in Winter Haven, Florida, U.S.A.
    In total, 9,753 children took part in the hunt for the eggs, accompanied by their parents.

FASTEST 10-KM SACK RACE Ashrita Furman (U.S.A.) set the record for the fastest sack race over 10 km (6.2 miles) with a time of 1 hr. 22 min. 2 sec. in Montauk, New York, U.S.A., on August 23, 2001.

★**Secret Santa** The largest game of Secret Santa involved a total of 618 participants and was staged at St. Oliver's National School in Killarney, County Kerry, Ireland, on December 19, 2006.

☆**Simon Says** On April 22, 2006, 1,169 participants played the largest ever game of Simon Says at Victoria Park in Glasgow, UK.

☆**Surfing** A record-breaking 44 surfers rode the same wave simultaneously in Lahinch, Ireland, on May 13, 2006.

☆**Table-soccer tournament** The largest table-soccer contest took place at the Veltins-Arena, Gelsenkirchen, Germany, on May 7, 2006.

It was organized by PV Autoteile and FC Schalke 04 and involved 1,564 players.

☆**Tea party** On October 8, 2006, the city of Nishio, Japan, and the chamber of commerce and industry of Nishio arranged the largest tea party in one venue: 14,718 people drank matcha (powdered green tea) in a traditional Japanese tea ceremony in Nishio City, Aichi, Japan.

SKIP IT!

• Alain Trottier (U.S.A.) completed a 100-m (328-ft.) sprint in 15.3 seconds while skipping rope at Calvary Chapel School in Santa Ana, California, U.S.A., on October 25, 2003, the ★ **fastest time to skip 100 m with a rope**.

• The **fastest time to skip 10 miles with a rope** (16 km) is 58 minutes and was achieved by Vadivelu Karunakáren (India) in Madras, India, on February 1, 1990.

• The record for the ★ **most skips in 30 seconds** is 152 and was achieved by Megumi Suzuki (Japan) at the Japanese Rope-Skipping Championships in Saitama Prefecture, Japan, on September 10, 2006.

• The **longest skipping marathon (with a rope)** lasted 27 hours and was set by Jed Goodfellow (Australia) at Oasis Shopping Mall, Broadbeach, Queensland, Australia, on December 5–6, 2003.

★MOST PAPER AIRCRAFT LAUNCHED SIMULTANEOUSLY On December 17, 2006, 1,665 paper aircraft were launched simultaneously—and successfully flew a distance of 16 ft. 4 in. (5 m) or more—at an event organized by The Boys' & Girls' Clubs Association of Hong Kong, in Wan Chai, Hong Kong, China.

DID YOU KNOW?

The **largest flyable paper aircraft** had a wingspan of 45 ft. 10 in. (13.97 m). It was built by students from the faculty of aerospace engineering at Delft University of Technology, the Netherlands, and underwent its maiden flight on May 16, 1995.

GARDEN GIANTS

Longest beet A beet grown by Richard Hope (UK) measured 20 ft. 2 in. (6.14 m) on September 27, 2003, at the Llanharry Giant Vegetable Championships in Rhondda Cynon Taff, Wales, UK. In the same year, at the same show, Richard also presented the ☆ **longest parsnip**, a "Gladiator" measuring 17 ft. 1 in. (5.2 m).

☆ **Longest carrot** A carrot grown by Peter Glazebrook (UK) and showcased on BBC TV's *The Great British Village Show* at Highgrove, UK, on October 2, 2006, measured 17 ft. 3 in. (5.25 m).

Longest zucchini In 2005, Gurdial Singh Kanwal (India) grew a zucchini measuring 7 ft. 10.3 in. (2.39 m) long in Brampton, Ontario, Canada.

☆ **LONGEST CUCUMBER**
A cucumber grown by Alfred J. Cobb (UK) and presented at the UK National Giant Vegetables Championships in September 2006 measured 35.1 in. (89.2 cm). The "big veg" contest forms part of *Amateur Gardening* magazine's annual National Show at the Bath & West Showground in Shepton Mallet, Somerset, UK.

Cobb also produced the heaviest cucumber—a 27-lb. 5-oz. (12.4-kg) specimen—for the 2003 championships.

GREAT GARDENS

• The **largest garden** in the world is that created by André Le Nôtre (France) at Versailles, France, in the late 17th century for King Louis XIV. The magnificent formal gardens and parkland were created in what had been a marshland. They cover more than 15,000 acres (6,070 ha)— about the size of 10 football fields—of which the famous formal garden covers 247 acres (100 ha).

• Monsieur Le Nôtre would have no doubt made good use of the world's ★ **largest garden spade.** The titanic tool measures 10 ft. 4 in. (3.16 m) tall, with a blade 21.1 in. (53.8 cm) wide, and was made by employees of Joseph Bentley in Barton upon Humber, Lincolnshire, UK. It was measured on May 11, 2005.

• Fans of topiary—the art of sculpting hedges—should pay a visit to Levens Hall in Cumbria, UK, home of the world's **oldest topiary garden.** Initial planting and training was carried out in the 1690s, and some of the designs are over 300 years old.

• The **oldest surviving hedge maze** is located at Hampton Court Palace in Surrey, UK, and was built for King William III and Mary II of England in 1690 using hornbeam (*Carpinus betulus*).

☆**Largest bouquet** A bouquet made from 156,940 roses was created by NordWestZentrum shopping mall in Frankfurt am Main, Germany, on September 29, 2005.

★ HEAVIEST FRUIT & VEGETABLES ★

FRUIT/VEGETABLE	WEIGHT	NAME	YEAR
Apple	4 lb. 1 oz. (1.84 kg)	Chisato Iwasaki (Japan)	2005
Avocado	4 lb. 6 oz. (1.99 kg)	Anthony Llanos (Australia)	1992
Beet	156 lb. 10 oz. (71.05 kg)	Piet de Goede (Netherlands)	2005
Blueberry	0.24 oz. (7 g)	Brian Carlick (UK)	2005
Broccoli	35 lb. (15.87 kg)	John & Mary Evans (both U.S.A.)	1993
Brussels sprout	18 lb. 3 oz. (8.3 kg)	Bernard Lavery (UK)	1992
Cabbage	124 lb. (56.24 kg)	Bernard Lavery (UK)	1989
Cabbage (red)	42 lb. (19.05 kg)	R. Straw (UK)	1925
Cantaloupe	64 lb. 13 oz. (29.4 kg)	Scott & Mardie Robb (both U.S.A.)	2004
Carrot	18 lb. 13 oz. (8.61 kg)	John Evans (U.S.A.)	1998
Cauliflower	54 lb. 3 oz. (24.6 kg)	Alan Hattersley (UK)	1999
Celery	63 lb. 4 oz. (28.7 kg)	Scott & Mardie Robb (both U.S.A.)	2003
Cherry	0.76 oz. (21.69 g)	Gerardo Maggipinto (Italy)	2003
Cucumber	27 lb. 5 oz. (12.4 kg)	Alfred J. Cobb (UK)	2003
Garlic head	2 lb. 10 oz. (1.19 kg)	Robert Kirkpatrick (U.S.A.)	1985
Gooseberry	2 oz. (61.04 g)	K. Archer (UK)	1993
Gourd	94 lb. 5 oz. (42.8 kg)	Robert Weber (Australia)	2001
Grapefruit	6 lb. 12 oz. (3.06 kg)	Debbie Hazelton (Australia)	1995
Jackfruit	76 lb. 4 oz. (34.6 kg)	George & Margaret Schattauer (both U.S.A.)	2003
Kale	58 lb. 9 oz. (26.58 kg)	David Iles (U.S.A.)	2006
Kohlrabi	96 lb. 15 oz. (43.98 kg)	Scott Robb (U.S.A.)	2006
Leek	17 lb. 13 oz. (8.1 kg)	Fred Charlton (UK)	2002
Lemon	11 lb. 9 oz. (5.26 kg)	Aharon Shemoel (Israel)	2003
Mango	6 lb. 13 oz. (3.1 kg)	Tai Mok Lim (Malaysia)	2006
Marrow	136 lb. 9 oz. (62 kg)	Mark Baggs (UK)	2005
Nectarine	12 oz. (360 g)	Tony Slattery (New Zealand)	1998
Onion	16 lb. 8 oz. (7.49 kg)	John Sifford (UK)	2005
Parsnip	10 lb. 8 oz. (4.78 kg)	Colin Moore (UK)	1980
Peach	25 oz. (725 g)	Paul Friday (U.S.A.)	2002
Pear	4 lb. 8 oz. (2.1 kg)	Warren Yeoman (Australia)	1999
Pineapple	17 lb. 12 oz. (8.06 kg)	E. Kamuk (Papua New Guinea)	1994
Pomegranate	2 lb. 3 oz. (1.04 kg)	Katherine Murphey (U.S.A.)	2001
Potato	7 lb. 11 oz. (3.5 kg)	K. Sloane (UK)	1994
Potato (sweet)	81 lb. 9 oz. (37 kg)	Manuel Pérez Pérez (Spain)	2004
Pummelo	10 lb. 11 oz. (4.86 kg)	Seiji Sonoda (Japan)	2005
Pumpkin	1,502 lb. (681.3 kg)	Ron Wallace (U.S.A.)	2006
Quince	5 lb. 2 oz. (2.34 kg)	Edward Harold McKinney (U.S.A.)	2002
Radish	68 lb. 9 oz. (31.1 kg)	Manabu Oono (Japan)	2003
Zucchini (Courgette)	64 lb. 8 oz. (29.25 kg)	Bernard Lavery (UK)	1990

☆ HEAVIEST PUMPKIN The heaviest pumpkin weighed 1,502 lb. (681.3 kg) when it was presented by Ron Wallace (U.S.A., left) at the Southern New England Giant Pumpkin Growers Weigh-off, held in Warren, Rhode Island, U.S.A., on October 7, 2006.

HEAVIEST APPLE On October 24, 2005, Chisato Iwasaki (Japan) picked an apple weighing 4 lb. 1 oz. (1.84 kg) that he had grown on his apple farm in Hirosaki City, Japan. Chisato may want to consider using his giant fruit to beat the record for the **longest unbroken apple peel.** Kathy Wafler (U.S.A.) peeled an apple in 11 hr. 30 min. with a peel length of 172 ft. 4 in. (52.51 m), at Long Ridge Mall in Rochester, New York, U.S.A., on October 16, 1976.

☆ TALLEST COTTON PLANT D. M. Williams (U.S.A.) grew a cotton plant (*Gossypium hirsutum*) that was 27 ft. 1 in. (8.25 m) tall when measured in August 2006.

★**Longest flower box** Edgar Ehrenfels made a 1,059-ft. 9-in.-long (323 m) flower box using flowers from Ralf Plawky (both Germany). It is situated on the bridge between Karlstadt and Karlburg in Germany.

★ TALLEST PLANTS ★

PLANT	HEIGHT	NAME	YEAR
Amaranthus	15 ft. 1 in. (4.61 m)	David Brenner (U.S.A.)	2004
Bean plant	46 ft. 3 in. (14.1 m)	Staton Rorie (U.S.A.)	2003
Brussels sprout	9 ft. 3 in. (2.8 m)	Patrice & Steve Allison (both U.S.A.)	2001
Cactus (homegrown)	70 ft. (21.3 m)	Pandit S. Munji (India)	2004
Celery	9 ft. (2.74 m)	John Priednieks (UK)	1998
Chrysanthemum	14 ft. 3 in. (4.34 m)	Bernard Lavery (UK)	1995
Coleus	8 ft. 4 in. (2.5 m)	Nancy Lee Spilove (U.S.A.)	2004
Collard	9 ft. 2 in. (2.79 m)	Reggie Kirkman (U.S.A.)	1999
Cosmos	12 ft. 3 in. (3.75 m)	Cosmos Executive Committee, Okayama, Japan	2003
Cotton	27 ft. 1 in. (8.25 m)	D. M. Williams (U.S.A.)	2006
Daffodil	5 ft. 1 in. (1.55 m)	M. Lowe (UK)	1979
Dandelion	3 ft. 3 in. (1 m)	Ragnar Gille & Marcus Hamring (both Sweden)	2003
Eggplant (Aubergine)	18 ft. (5.5 m)	Abdul Masfoor (India)	1998
Fuchsia (climbing)	37 ft. 5 in. (11.40 m)	Reinhard Biehler (Germany)	2005
Herba cistanches	6 ft. 4 in. (1.95 m)	Yongmao Chen (China)	2006
Papaya tree	44 ft. (13.4 m)	Prasanta Mal (India)	2003
Parsley	4 ft. 7 in. (1.39 m)	Danielle, Gabrielle, & Michelle Kassatly (all U.S.A.)	2003
Pepper	16 ft. (4.87 m)	Laura Liang (U.S.A.)	1999
Periwinkle	7 ft. 2 in. (2.19 m)	Arvind, Rekha, Ashish, & Rashmi Nema (all India)	2003
Petunia	19 ft. 1 in. (5.8 m)	Bernard Lavery (UK)	1994
Rosebush (self-supported)	13 ft. 3 in. (4.03 m)	Paul & Sharon Palumbo (both U.S.A.)	2005
Rose (climbing)	91 ft. (27.7 m)	Anne & Charles Grant (both U.S.A.)	2004
Sugarcane	31 ft. (9.5 m)	M. Venkatesh Gowda (India)	2005
Sunflower	25 ft. 5 in. (7.76 m)	M. Heijms (Netherlands)	1986
Sweet corn (maize)	31 ft. (9.4 m)	D. Radda (U.S.A.)	1946
Texas bluebonnet	5 ft. 5 in. (1.64 m)	Margaret Lipscome & Arthur Cash (both U.S.A.)	2005
Tomato	65 ft. (19.8 m)	Nutriculture Ltd., Lancashire, UK	2000
Umbrella	27 ft. (8.22 m)	Konstantinos Xytakis & Sara Guterbock (both U.S.A.)	2002
Zinnia	12 ft. 6 in. (3.81 m)	Everett Wallace Jr. & Melody Wagner (both U.S.A.)	2004

WORK & EMPLOYMENT

Longest career Shigechiyo Izumi (Japan) began work goading draft animals at a sugar mill in Tokunoshima, Japan, in 1872. He retired as a sugarcane farmer in 1970—98 years later—aged 105.

☆**Longest career in one company** Lester J. Nichols (U.S.A.) started work as a shipping clerk for Malleable Iron Fittings in Connecticut, U.S.A., in 1866. He retired in 1945 having been secretary, assistant, treasurer, and director of the company!

Greatest distance walked in a career Stanley E. Rychlicki (U.S.A.) spent 37 years as a pipeline inspector and walked a distance of 136,887 miles (220,288 km), sometimes covering over 20 miles (32 km) per day across Pennsylvania and New York, U.S.A.

☆**Hardest working industrialized nation** According to the Organization for Economic Cooperation and Development (OECD), the industrialized country with the hardest-working citizens in 2006 was South Korea, whose working population (excluding self-employed labor) clocked up 2,423 hours per employee for 2004.

Highest unemployment According to 2003 estimates, the country with the highest rate of unemployment is Liberia, with 85% of its labor force not in paid work.

★**Longest serving chief of police** Thomas E. Hawley (U.S.A.) served as the chief of police in Green Bay, Wisconsin, U.S.A., from August 17, 1897, to June 1, 1946—a total of 49 years.

☆**Longest career—recording artist** Kasper Delmar "Stranger" Malone (U.S.A.) released recorded music over eight consecutive decades. His

☆**FASTEST OFFICE** The fastest office is a street-legal desk that can attain a maximum speed of 87 mph (140 km/h.). It was created by Edd China (UK) and driven across Westminster Bridge into the city of London, UK, on November 9, 2006, as part of international Guinness World Records Day.

OLDEST SOCCER PLAYER Tércio Mariano de Rezende (Brazil, b. December 31, 1921) plays regularly as a right-winger for Goiandira Esporte Clube in Goiandira, Goiás, Brazil. The 87-year-old is registered with the Catalao Levindo da Fonseca Soccer League.

first song—"Let Me Call You Sweetheart"—was recorded in 1926; his last was in 2003. Throughout his varied career, he played cornet, clarinet, flute, double bass (including a 10-year spell with the Tucson Symphony Orchestra), and guitar.

He died in 2005, aged 95.

★**Longest career—music teacher** Charles Wright (U.S.A., b. May 24, 1912) began teaching piano professionally in 1931 and continues to do so.

★ LONGEST WORKING CAREERS ★

CAREER	HOLDER (NATIONALITY)	WORKING SPAN	YEARS
Accountant	Harilal D. Maniar (India)	1929–present	78
Actor	Curt Bois (Germany)	1908–87	79
Actress	Maxine Elliott Hicks (U.S.A.)	1914–92	78
Bartender	Angelo Cammarata (U.S.A.)	1933–present	74
Butler	Horace Mortiboy (UK)	1937–40, 1945–70, 1987–present	51
Cartoon voice-over	Jack Mercer (U.S.A.)	1934–79	45
Clown	Charlie Rivel (Spain)	1899–1981	82
Construction worker	Edward William Beard (UK)	1896–1981	85
Dance teacher	Tommy Moss (UK)	1929–present	78
Movie director	King Vidor (U.S.A.)	1913–80	67
Newspaper boy	Velmore Smith (Canada)	1958–2002	44
Opera singer	Danshi Toyotake (Japan)	1898–1979	81
Pilot	Clarence Cornish (U.S.A.)	1918–95	77
Radio DJ	Ray Cordeiro (Hong Kong)	1949–present	58
Santa Claus	Dayton C. Fouts (U.S.A.)	1937–97	60
Teacher	Medarda de Jesus Leon de Uzcategui (aka La Maestra Chucha, Venezuela)	1911–present	96
TV naturalist	Sir David Attenborough (UK)	1954–present	53

LARGEST EMPLOYER The world's largest commercial or utility employer is Indian Railways, with 1.65 million regular employees as of 2000. This state-owned company is one of the busiest in the world, transporting over six billion people and around 750 million tons of freight and cargo every year, covering the entire length and breadth of the country.

MOST CRASH TESTS As of March 2007, W. R. "Rusty" Haight (U.S.A.) had driven in 846 crash tests as a "human crash-test dummy." During the tests (left), conducted for research purposes, Rusty and the vehicle are equipped with an array of sensors (accelerometers) for gathering data, which is used by his Collision Safety Institute and others to improve motor vehicle safety.

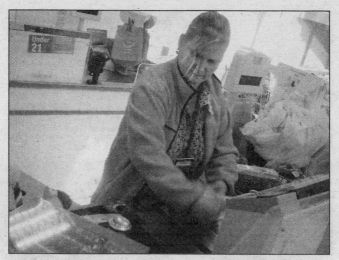

★FASTEST TIME TO SCAN AND BAG 50 SHOPPING ITEMS In just 3 min. 31 sec., checkout operator Debbie O'Brien (UK) scanned and bagged 50 shopping items at the ASDA store in Clapham Junction, London, UK, on November 9, 2006, as part of Guinness World Records Day.

☆ **Longest career—conductor** Juan Garcés Queralt (Spain) has been a conductor in Valencia, Spain, for 67 years. He started leading bands in 1939 and continues to do so at the age of 92.

Longest serving executioner William Calcraft (GB, 1800–79) served as public executioner for 45 years. He officiated at nearly every hanging at Newgate Prison, London, UK.

WORST JOBS

•**Most feet and armpits sniffed** Madeline Albrecht (U.S.A.) was employed for 15 years at the Hill Top Research Laboratories in Cincinnati, Ohio, U.S.A., where she tested products for hygiene company Dr. Scholl. She had the unenviable task of sniffing feet and armpits, and smelled approximately 5,600 feet and an indeterminate number of armpits.

•**Longest working grave digger** It is recorded that Johann Heinrich Karl Thieme, sexton of Aldenburg, Germany, dug 23,311 graves during a 50-year career. After his death in 1826, his understudy dug *his* grave!

OLDEST ASTRONAUT
The oldest astronaut was John Glenn, Jr. (U.S.A.), who was 77 years 103 days old when he was launched into space as part of the crew of *Discovery STS-95* on October 29, 1998.

The **oldest female astronaut** is Shannon Lucid (U.S.A., pictured), who was 53 years 67 days old at the launch of the space shuttle mission *STS-76 Atlantis* on March 22, 1996.

★**Longest serving blooper-show host** Denis Norden (UK, b. February 6, 1922) has hosted a TV blooper (outtakes) show for 29 years. He started with *It'll be Alright on the Night* in 1977 and hosted his last show—*All the Best from Denis Norden*—in 2006.

CULTS, FANS & FOLLOWERS

LONGEST STANDOFF WITH A CULT In 1993, law-enforcement agencies engaged in a standoff with the Branch Davidians, a religious sect led by David Koresh (U.S.A., above right), for 51 days at the Mount Carmel Compound in Waco, Texas, U.S.A.

Hostilities began on February 28, when federal agents tried to enter the compound, and ended on April 19, when police stormed the main building and fire broke out. In all, 82 Davidians died.

★ **LARGEST GATHERING OF ZOMBIES (OKAY . . . PEOPLE *DRESSED AS ZOMBIES*)** On October 29, 2006, unsuspecting shoppers at the Monroeville Mall in Pennsylvania, U.S.A., would have been horrified to behold a record-breaking gathering of 894 zombies shuffling through the shopping center.

Longest civil disobedience march In March and April 1930, Mohandas Karamchand Gandhi (India) led 78 followers on a 241-mile (387-km) march between the Gujurat towns of Sabarmati Ashram and Dandi to protest British India's levy of salt tax.

The protest became known as the Dandi Salt March. Gandhi addressed crowds en route, attracting increasing numbers to the march.

☆ **Largest mass suicides** In July 1944, Japanese troops were defeated by U.S. soldiers during the Battle of Saipan Island in the Pacific Ocean. About 5,000 islanders jumped off cliffs into shark-infested waters or blew themselves up with grenades rather than face the torture that they thought they would suffer at the hands of their American captors. **Ancient:** As reported by the historian Flavius Josephus, some 960 Jewish zealots killed themselves by cutting each other's throats at Masada, Israel, in AD 73, as the palace was being besieged by Romans.

★ MODERN MASS SUICIDES ★

GROUP	DEATHS	LOCATION	DATE
The Movement for the Restoration of the Ten Commandments of God	924	Uganda	Mar.–Apr. 2000
People's Temple	913	Guyana	Nov. 1978
Branch Davidians	82	U.S.A.	Apr. 1993
Order of the Solar Temple	74	Switzerland, Canada, and France	Sep. 1994–Mar. 1997
Heaven's Gate	39	U.S.A.	Mar. 1997
The Move	11	U.S.A.	May 1985
Simbionese Liberation Army	6	U.S.A.	May 1974

Source: Cult Information Center

★ **MOST ENDURING CARGO CULTS** The oldest so-called cargo cults appeared in the late 19th century, typically in Melanesia and New Guinea, but many have now died out. The most enduring, though, are those associated with "John Frum"—they worship a mythical World War II American GI of that name (possibly derived from the words "John from America")—and the nearby Yaohnanen tribe (pictured), who, for reasons that remain unclear, worship Britain's Prince Philip, Duke of Edinburgh, as a divine being. *Find out more in box below.*

FANS & FAN CLUBS

Loudest scream by a crowd (indoors) On September 6, 2001, 10,500 fans screamed, cheered, and whistled in Wembley Arena for the first London performance of UK group Hear'say's national tour, generating a sound-level reading of 128.8 dBA.

☆ **Largest human national flag** A "human" flag made up of 18,788 women was organized by Realizar Impact Marketing (Portugal) and unveiled at the National Stadium of Jamor, in Lisbon, Portugal, on May 20,

---

CARGO CULTS

The term "cargo cults" was coined in 1945 to describe remote tribes—found mostly in Melanesia—that pray for the return of the various goods that appeared, seemingly miraculously, during occupation of their islands by colonialists.

The two key phases of this occupation were the turn of the 20th century and World War II, during the Allied forces' Pacific campaign. The **earliest known cargo cult**—Fiji's Tuka Movement—is thought to date back to 1885.

★ **LARGEST FURRY FAN CLUB** Furry fandom is a club genre for a subculture that enjoys dressing up as animals. "Furries," as they are known, meet at con*fur*ences and share their love of animal anthropomorphism—that is, the depiction of animals with human characteristics, such as the rabbits in Richard Adams' novel *Watership Down.* The largest annual furry gathering occurs at Anthrocon in Pittsburgh, Pennsylvania, U.S.A., and on June 18, 2006, a record 2,489 furries attended. Among the trivial "fursuits" on offer were a furries parade, various guests of honor, and a charity auction.

2006. The national flag was formed to highlight the support for the national soccer team by Portuguese women in the run-up to the soccer world cup.

Most fan mail Although fan mail is traditionally associated with movie stars, no actor or actress has received the 3.5 million letters delivered to Charles Lindbergh (U.S.A.) following his solo, nonstop, transatlantic flight in May 1927.

Most fan mail received in a year The highest confirmed volume of mail received by any private citizen in one year is 900,000 letters by the baseball star Hank Aaron (U.S.A.), as reported by the U.S. Postal Service in June 1974.

Approximately one-third of these were hate letters received after Aaron broke Babe Ruth's career record for home runs.

Most fan clubs for a singer As of March 2000, there were more than 613 Elvis Presley fan clubs worldwide, with a total membership of 510,489. The oldest is the French *La Voix d'Elvis,* founded in 1956.

★ **Longest parades** •**Fiats** The Fiat 500 Club Italia organized a parade of 500 Fiat cars and their fans from Villanova d'Albenga to Garlenda, Italy, on July 9, 2006.

☆ **LARGEST ELVIS GATHERING** The largest gathering of Elvis impersonators (or should that be Elvi, plural?) was organized by 109 employees of Maris Interiors (UK), who collectively performed the song "Suspicious Minds" at Gatwick Airport, UK, on December 3, 2006 (pictured). **The longest Elvis singing marathon** lasted 43 hr. 11 min. 11 sec. and was carried out by Thomas "Curtis" Gäthje (Germany) at Modehaus Böttcher, Heide, Germany, on June 24–26, 2004.

•**Steamrollers** The Great Dorset Road Builders arranged for 32 vintage steamrollers to pass over a length of new road at the Great Dorset Steam Fair, UK, on August 31, 2003.

DID YOU KNOW?

The **largest science fiction fan club** is Starfleet, the International *Star Trek* Fan Association. Founded in 1974 and based in Independence, Missouri, U.S.A., the organization boasts over 4,100 members dedicated to the ideals of the *Star Trek* TV series.

FESTIVALS

Easter •The **largest Easter egg** on record weighed 10,483 lb. (4.76 tons) and was made by staff of the Cadbury Red Tulip factory in Ringwood, Victoria, Australia, on April 9, 1992.

NEW YEAR'S The 2007 New Year's celebrations on the island of Madeira were dominated by the world's ★ **largest fireworks display** (above). In just eight minutes, a total of 66,326 fireworks were launched from over 40 sites.
•Incidentally, the ★ **most fireworks launched in 30 seconds** is 56,405, by Dr. Roy Lowry (UK) at the 10th British Firework Championship in Plymouth, UK, on August 16, 2006.
•Rod Stewart's free gig at Copacabana Beach in Rio de Janeiro, Brazil, on New Year's Eve 1994, attracted the **largest free concert** audience of 3.5 million.

•The world's ★ **largest decorated Easter egg** was created by Meisterstammtisch Oberneukirchen, Austria. It measured 26 ft. 7 in. (8.1 m) long and 17 ft. 8 in. (5.39 m) in diameter in April 2004.

Food & drink The **largest beer festival** in the world is Munich's Oktoberfest. The busiest year was 1999, when 7 million visitors consumed a record 1.2 million gallons (5.8 million liters) of beer in 11 beer tents on a site as large as 50 football fields.
•The Fellsmere Frog Leg Festival in Fellsmere, Florida, U.S.A., is the **largest frog-leg festival** in the world. From January 18 to 21, 2001, it attracted 75,000 visitors with a taste for amphibians' appendages.
•The three-day Gilroy Garlic Festival, held each summer in Gilroy, California, U.S.A., is the **largest garlic festival**, attracting 130,000 people to try garlic-flavored food from meat to ice cream.
•The Rock Creek Lodge Testicle Festival in Clinton, Montana, U.S.A., is the ★ **largest testicle festival** in the world. Every year, around 5,600 lb. (2.5 tons) of bull testicles (aka "Rocky Mountain oysters") are served to an average of 15,000 visitors.
•The Elmira Maple Syrup Festival held in Elmira, Ontario, Canada, is the world's **largest maple syrup festival.** The busiest event to date was on April 1, 2000, when 66,529 people attended the 36th annual event.

Music & dance The Festival de Dança de Joinville in Santa Catarina, Brazil, is the **largest dance festival** in the world. First produced in 1983, the

CHRISTMAS ☆ LARGEST SANTA GATHERING The Liverpool Santa Dash on December 4, 2005, involved 3,921 people dressed as Mr. and Mrs. Claus running through the streets of Liverpool city center (left) in the UK.

• The ★ **largest area covered with artificial snow** was 134,148 ft.^{2} (12,462.78 m^2) of Bond Street in London, UK. Snow Business (UK) showered the street with fake snow to celebrate the switching on of the Christmas lights in November 2006.

• The ☆ **largest Christmas stocking** measured 63 ft. 2 in. (19.25 m) long and 27 ft. (8.23 m) wide (heel to toe) on January 11, 2006, and was made by shoppers and staff of the MetroCentre, Gateshead, UK.

• The record for the ☆ **most letters to Santa collected** was 410 in an event organized by the Rainbow Trust charity at the Trocadero in London, UK, on December 16, 2006.

• The ☆ **longest Christmas cracker**—207 ft. (63.1 m) long— was made by parents of children at Ley Hill School, Chesham, UK, on December 20, 2001.

• A tree adorned with 140,000 lights for the RTL-ChariTree 2005 set the record for the ★ **most lights on a Christmas tree**. The feat was achieved by RTL Television on November 26, 2005, at Cologne Cathedral, Germany.

• The world's **tallest Christmas tree** was a 221-ft. (67-m) Douglas fir (*Pseudotsga menziesii*) erected and decorated at Northgate Shopping Center, Seattle, Washington, U.S.A., in December 1950.

festival is held over a minimum of 10 days and is attended by 4,000 dancers from 140 amateur and professional dance groups, and watched by more than 200,000 people annually.

• The **largest rock festival attendance** was 670,000 at Steve Wozniak's 1983 U.S. Festival in Devore, California.

HALLOWEEN •The most pumpkins carved in one hour is 42 by Stephen Clarke (U.S.A., left) for the Halloween celebrations of *The Early Show* (CBS, U.S.A.) on October 31, 2002, in New York City, U.S.A. •Clarke also carved 2,000 lb. of pumpkins in 4 hr. 17 min. 26 sec. at SeaWorld, Orlando, Florida, U.S.A., on October 29, 2005. •Classroom assistant Jill Drake (UK) registered the loudest scream—129 decibels—during the Halloween festivities in the Millennium Dome, London, UK, in October 2000.

•The **largest international music festival** is WOMAD (World of Music, Arts, and Dance), which has presented more than 90 events in 20 different countries since 1982.

•The world's **largest jazz festival** is the Festival International de Jazz de Montreal in Quebec, Canada, which attracted a record 1,913,868 people for its 25th anniversary in July 2004.

Arts •The Edinburgh Arts Festival in Scotland, UK, is the **largest arts festival** on the planet. Its record year was 2003, when 12,940 artists gave 21,594 performances.

•The world's **longest film festival** is the 25-day-long Fort Lauderdale International Film Festival (FLIFF) held in Fort Lauderdale, Florida, U.S.A.

•The **largest film festival** is the Festival international du film de Cannes held in the south of France. The annual event—arguably the most glamorous in the movie calendar—attracts between 40,000 and 50,000 movie industry workers each year, and countless cinephiles flock to the area to catch a glimpse of their favorite stars.

DID YOU KNOW?

The **largest gay festival** is the annual MiX Brasil: Festival of Sexual Diversity in São Paulo, Brazil. In its record year, 2005, the festival was attended by 1.8 million people.

•The **largest carnival** is the Rio de Janeiro annual festival in Brazil, normally held during the first week of March. It attracts approximately two million people each day. In 2004, a record 400,000 foreign visitors attended.

RELIGIOUS RITUALS The **largest religious crowd**—and the greatest recorded number of people assembled with a common purpose—was an estimated 20 million at the Hindu festival of Kumbh Mela, held at the confluence of the Jamuna, Ganges, and mythical "Saraswati" rivers in Allahabad (Prayag), Uttar Pradesh, India, on January 30, 2001. Pictured here is the Ardh (half) Khumn of 2007, a smaller gathering that occurs every six years.

• The **largest annual gathering of women** takes place in February or March each year, when over one million amass at the Attukal Bhagavathy Temple in Kerala, India, for the Pongala offering. The women, from all religions, gather with cooking pots to perform a ritual for health and prosperity. The highest attendance recorded was 1.5 million women on February 23, 1997.

LARGEST GATHERING OF...

Centenarians A total of 21 centenarians (people aged over 100) flew on one aircraft between Antwerp, Belgium, and London City Airport, UK, on August 15, 1997.

Clowns In 1991, in Bognor Regis, UK, 850 clowns, including 430 from North America, gathered for their annual convention.

Dancing dragons A total of 40 dragons, with 10 dancers per dragon, amassed at the Taman Jurong Community Club in Taman Jurong, Singapore, on March 5, 2005.

Giant papier-mâché puppets A total of 215 papier-mâché giants made by 88 organizations gathered in Solsona, Catalonia, Spain, on July 6, 2003.

Religious leaders The Millennium World Peace Summit of Religious and Spiritual Leaders involved 1,000 people at the United Nations in New York City, U.S.A., in August 2000.

Test-tube children A group of 579 children born as a result of artificial insemination gathered at the Iscare IVF Assisted Reproduction Center in Prague, Czech Republic, on September 6, 2003.

BUSINESS & FINANCE

LARGEST . . .

★**Annual trade surplus (country)** For 2005, boosted by Christmas sales of products in the West, China had a trade surplus of 823 billion Chinese yuan ($102 billion). A country's trade surplus is the difference in value between what it exports and what it imports.

☆**National debt** The largest debtor nation in history is the United States of America. As of March 28, 2007 (at 2 p.m. GMT), the U.S. national debt stood at $8,845,127,059,284.86. With the U.S. population numbering just over 300 million, each person's share of the debt is $29,357.26.

★**Stock market crash** Stock markets across the world saw their largest ever drop during October 1987, starting with "Black Monday" on the 19th. By the end of the month, the U.S. stock market had dropped 22.68% (the equivalent of $500 billion lost), the Canadian stock market 22.5%, and the UK stock market 26.4%. Asian markets fared even worse, with the Hong Kong and Australian markets dropping 45.8% and 41.8%, respectively, in the same period.

Some of the causes of the decline have been attributed to over-valuation and market psychology at the time. However, no exact explanation has ever been found.

★**Tax scam** On March 3, 2005, U.S. entrepreneur Walter Anderson was charged with failing to pay more than $200 million in personal income taxes. Eighteen months later, in September 2006, Anderson admitted to two counts of evading taxes and one of fraud, and was sentenced to 10 years' imprisonment. He further pleaded guilty to hiding $365 million of income by using aliases, shell companies, offshore tax havens, and secret accounts.

★**Tax dispute** On September 11, 2006, a dispute between the U.S. Internal Revenue Service (IRS) and pharmaceutical giant GlaxoSmithKline (GSK) was finally settled. GSK agreed to pay $3.1 billion in taxes and interest payments after tax accounts dating back 16 years were disputed by the IRS.

PAY UP!

The ★ **largest payout by an insurer** amounted to $50 billion. It followed the damage by the twin strikes of hurricanes Katrina and Rita in August and September 2005 in the U.S.A. In 1992, Hurricane Andrew had caused $22 billion worth of damage.

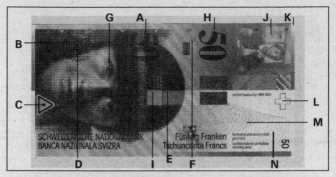

★ **MOST SECURE BANKNOTE** Swiss franc notes have up to 18 security features to deter counterfeiting, 14 of which are visible on the front of the bill (see above). In addition, the "paper" is made from the by-products of the cotton-making process, and the bills are printed with special inks that are resistant to 18 different chemicals and machine-washable at high temperatures.

A. CHAMELEON DIGIT Optically variable ink (OVI) changes color as light hits it from different angles

B. TILTING DIGIT Denomination printed in such a way that it can be seen only from an unusual angle

C. SYMBOL FOR VISUALLY HANDICAPPED A raised symbol used to help the blind determine denomination

D. GLITTERING DIGIT Denomination printed in metal

E. INTAGLIO DIGITS Denomination of bill etched into the paper; feels rough to the touch

F. MICROPERF® DIGITS Denomination punched into bill as tiny perforations

G. ULTRAVIOLET DIGIT Denomination appears only under UV light

H. KINEGRAM® DIGIT Moving image of the bill's denomination created in foil

I. MICROTEXT Text so tiny that it can be read only by magnifying glass

J. WATERMARK DIGITS Denomination of bill printed as a traditional watermark

K. IRIODIN® DIGITS Denomination of bill printed in a shimmering, transparent ink that can be seen only from a particular angle

L. TRANSPARENT REGISTER A cross printed on each side, one smaller than the other

M. GUILLOCHES Fine, entwined lines that change color as the light changes

N. WATERMARK PORTRAIT Repeat of main portrait

★ **Leveraged buyout** A leveraged buyout involves taking over a company by purchasing a controlling amount of the equity.

On February 25, 2007, a deal was agreed for the leveraged buyout of energy provider TXU Corporation (U.S.A.) by a group led by private-equity firms Texas Pacific Group and Kohlberg Kravis Roberts & Co. The deal was valued at $43.8 billion.

☆ **MOST EXPENSIVE OFFICE SPACE** According to real estate managers C. B. Richard Ellis, London, UK (above), is the priciest location for office space. As of June 2006, the cost per square meter per month including rent, taxes, and service charges in London's West End was £107 ($201).

☆ **Media corporation** In 2006–07, Time Warner (U.S.A.) recorded assets of $131.67 billion, according to *The Forbes Global 2000.*

☆ **Public companies** •**By profit:** Oil and gas giant Exxon-Mobil (U.S.A.) made $39.5 billion in profit in 2006–07.
•**By assets:** British bank Barclays currently owns the equivalent of $1,949.17 billion in assets. Source: *The Forbes Global 2000.*

OLDEST . . .

Family business Houshi Ryokan (Japan) dates back to AD 717 and is a family business spanning 46 generations. (A ryokan is a traditional Japanese inn.)

★ **Record shop** Spillers Records (Cardiff, UK) was founded in 1894 to sell phonographs, wax cylinders, and shellac discs. It has been running as a music and record store nonstop ever since.

FIRST PAPER MONEY The use of paper currency can be traced back to the Song Dynasty (960–1279) in China, when it was utilized by a group of wealthy merchants and businessmen in Sichuan, the same place where printing was invented. Each bill issued had pictures of houses, trees, and people printed on it. The seals of the issuing banks were then applied and confidential marks were made on each bill in order to prevent counterfeiting.

☆ **LARGEST RETAILER BY SALES REVENUE** Sam Walton opened the first Wal-Mart store in 1962. During the fiscal year 2006–07, Wal-Mart Stores, Inc. of Bentonville, Arkansas, U.S.A., had a total sales revenue of $348.65 billion.

SMALLEST BANKNOTE The smallest national currency note ever issued was the 10-bani bill of the ministry of finance in Romania in 1917. Its printed area measured 1.08 × 1.49 in. (27.5 × 38 mm). This is roughly one-tenth the size of a $1 bill.

COLOSSAL COMPANIES

Below is a list of the world's largest companies by sector, based on market value at the end of the 2006–07 fiscal year:

- **Banking:** Citigroup (U.S.A.), $247.42 billion

- **Conglomerates:** General Electric (U.S.A.), $358.98 billion

- **Consumer durables:** Toyota (Japan), $217.69 billion

- **Household and personal products:** Procter & Gamble (U.S.A.), $200.34 billion

- **Media:** Time Warner (U.S.A.), $77.99 billion

- **Oil and Gas:** ExxonMobil (U.S.A.), $410.65 billion

- **Pharmaceuticals:** Pfizers (U.S.A.), $192.05 billion

- **Retail:** Wal-Mart (U.S.A.), $201.36 billion

- **Software:** Microsoft (U.S.A.), $275.85 billion

- **Telecommunications:** AT&T (U.S.A.), $229.78 billion

LARGEST CHECK The greatest amount paid by a single check in the history of banking was £2,474,655,000 ($3,971,821,324). Issued on March 30, 1995, and signed by Nicholas Morris, company secretary of Glaxo plc (UK), the check represented a payment by Glaxo to Wellcome Trust Nominees Ltd. The Lloyds Bank Registrars (UK) computer system could not generate a check this large, so it was completed by a Lloyds employee using a typewriter. The typist was so overawed by the responsibility that it took three attempts to produce the check, numbered 020503.

A check for $4,176,969,623.57 was drawn on June 30, 1954, although this was an internal U.S. Treasury check.

SUPER RICH

★**Country with the most billionaires** As of February 2004, the country with the most dollar billionaires is the U.S.A., with 276 according to *Forbes'* Rich List.

Youngest billionaire Aged just 24, his Serene Highness 12th Prince Albert von Thurn und Taxis (Germany, b. June 24, 1983) has an estimated net worth of $2.1 billion.

☆**Highest annual earners** •**Author:** *The Da Vinci Code* novelist Dan Brown (U.S.A.) earned $88 million in 2005–06.
•**Band:** The Eagles earned an estimated $45 million in 2005–06.

LARGEST . . .

☆ **Bar of gold** On June 11, 2005, the Mitsubishi Materials Corporation manufactured a pure gold bar weighing 551 lb. (250 kg) at the Naoshima Smelter & Refinery, Kagawa Prefecture, Japan.

☆ **National lottery jackpot** The U.S.A.'s Powerball jackpot stood at $365 million when drawn on February 18, 2006. It was claimed by eight workers in a meat-processing plant who bought their lucky ticket in Lincoln, Nebraska, U.S.A.

★ **Bank (assets)** The Bank of Tokyo-Mitsubishi UFJ opened in Tokyo, Japan, on January 1, 2006. The result of a merger between Mitsubishi Tokyo Financial Group and UFJ Holdings, Inc. on October 1, 2005, the combined estimated assets totaled ¥162,714 billion ($1,440 billion).

☆ **LARGEST PRIVATELY OWNED YACHT** *Golden Star,* which measures 524 ft. 10 in. (160 m) long, is owned by Sheikh Mohammed bin Rashid al-Maktoum, the ruler of Dubai, United Arab Emirates (UAE). The yacht was commissioned in 1996 and launched for sea trials in April 2005; it is presently moored at the Jebel Ali Docks, Dubai. Although precise figures are unobtainable, the price of this "megayacht" is estimated at $300 million.

J. K. ROWLING

J. K. Rowling's success story began with the tale of a 10-year-old wizard with a lightning-bolt scar. To date, her Harry Potter books have sold a staggering 325 million copies worldwide, giving her the record for the highest annual earnings by a children's author. She talked to us about her achievements.

Of all the things you have been able to buy, which is your favorite?

My favorite material thing is our house in the north of Scotland, where it's very peaceful and we have a lot of fun with family and friends. Probably the very best thing my earnings have given me, though, is absence of worry. I have not forgotten what it feels like to worry about whether you'll have enough money to pay the bills. Not to have to think about that any more is the biggest luxury in the world.

Given your fame, how do you keep yourself and your family grounded?

It's one of my top priorities. We try to lead a pretty normal life. We go to stores like anyone else, and walk around town like anyone else. Aside from very special events like premieres or fund-raisers, I tend to keep a fairly low profile and carry on like any other regular person.

Faced with a number of rejections from publishers and having a young daughter to raise, did you ever think of giving up on Harry?

I didn't! Because I really believed in—and really loved—the story. Iris Murdoch, a British writer, once said, "Writing a novel is a lot like getting married. You should never commit yourself until you can't believe your luck." I really couldn't believe my luck having had this idea, and I was determined to press on with it until the last publisher had rejected it, which—at one point—looked likely. What would I be doing if I had given up writing? I'd be teaching!

How do you feel about the series coming to an end?

On the one hand, I think I'm going to feel sad. Harry's been an enormous part of my life, and it's been quite a turbulent phase of my life as well...so there will be a sense of bereavement. But there will also be a sense of liberation, because there are pressures involved in writing something so popular. I think that there will.also be a certain freedom in escaping that particular part of writing *Harry Potter*.

LARGEST DIAMOND PENDANT
The largest nonreligious pendant is the "Crunk Ain't Dead" design owned by hip-hop artist Lil' Jon (U.S.A.). With 3,576 white diamonds, alone it weighs 34.4 oz. (977.6 g), with its gold chain 5 lb. (2.3 kg). On December 13, 2006, it was valued at $500,000.

MOST EXPENSIVE . . .

★**Cell phone** The most expensive handset commercially available is the Signature Vertu (a subsidiary of Nokia), launched in Paris, France, on January 21, 2002. There is a choice of nine different metal finishes, ranging from stainless steel to platinum diamond (decorated with a 0.25-carat solitaire diamond and costing $46,650). Each handset features a sapphire crystal face.

★**Kidney stone** On January 18, 2006, *Star Trek* actor William Shatner (U.S.A.) sold a kidney stone for $25,000 to online casino Golden Palace.com. He donated the money from the sale to charity.

RICH LIST

• U.S. oil baron John D. Rockefeller was the **richest person ever,** with an estimated wealth of $900 million in 1913, equivalent to $189.6 billion today.

• William H. Gates III (U.S.A.), chairman and chief software architect of Microsoft Corporation, is the **richest living person** according to *Forbes* magazine, which estimated his wealth at $50.1 billion in March 2005.

• According to *Forbes,* the **richest woman** is Liliane Bettencourt (France), heiress to the L'Oréal cosmetics fortune, who in 2005 had an estimated net worth of $16 billion.

• The **richest monarch** in the world, as of 2005, is Prince Alwaleed bin Talal Alsaud of Saudi Arabia, with an estimated personal wealth of $20 billion.

• The **youngest uninherited millionaire** was the American child actor Jackie Coogan (1914–84). In 1923–24, he was earning $22,000 per week and retained approximately 60% of his movies' profits. He was a millionaire in his own right by the age of 13.

☆ **MOST EXPENSIVE COCKTAIL** The Trader Vic's Original Mai Tai costs £750 ($1,425) and is featured on the menu of The Bar at the Merchant Hotel, Belfast, Northern Ireland, UK. The high price is due to one particular ingredient: the rare 17-year-old Wray and Nephew Jamaican rum.

★**MP3 player** The Presidential MP3 by Douglas J. is available in a choice of white or yellow gold casing, studded with diamonds. Launched in November 2005 by Meng Duo Ltd., London, UK, it is priced at £25,000 ($43,000).

★**Wall calendar** "To Touch an Angel's Wings," a calendar designed for the Muir Maxwell Trust epilepsy charity, was sold at auction for £15,000 ($26,100) to Stephen Winyard (UK) on December 10, 2005.

MOST VALUABLE . . .

★**Fortune cookie** A fortune cookie sold for £10,000 ($17,473) at an auction during the Chinese New Year Gala Dinner in aid of the charity Kids, at the Banqueting House, Whitehall, London, UK, on February 8, 2006.

MOST VALUABLE POTATO An exclusive variety of potato—Bonnottes de Noirmoutier, grown on the island of Noirmoutier, France—was sold at auction for £2000 ($3,050) in April 1996. The bidder took 10 lb. (4.5 kg) of potatoes home, worth approximately £33 ($56) each.

★ MOST DIAMONDS SET IN ONE RING
The "Dance of the Angel" ring, made by the Lobortas & Karpova jewelry house in Kiev, Ukraine, in 2006, is set with a record 837 diamonds and weighs 5.57 carats.

☆ **Telephone number** The most money paid for a telephone number is 10 million QAR ($2.75 million), by an anonymous Qatari bidder, for the cellular number 666–6666 during a charity auction hosted by Qatar Telecom on May 23, 2006.

☆ **Truffle** Three white truffles weighing a total of 3 lb. 5 oz. (1.51 kg) sold at auction for €125,000 ($160,572) in Hong Kong, China, on November 12, 2006.

☆ **Tooth** The upper-right canine tooth extracted from the mouth of Napoleon Bonaparte (Napoleon I of France) in 1817 sold for £11,000 ($19,140) at a British auction on November 10, 2005. The tooth is believed to have been extracted in 1816 because of scurvy infection.

POLITICS

Country with the youngest voting age Universal suffrage—that is, the right of men and women to vote in political elections—is set at 15 years of age in Iran.

First country to pass women's suffrage The 1893 Women's Suffrage Petition led to New Zealand becoming the first self-governing nation in the world to grant women the right to vote. Governor Glasgow signed the Electoral Bill in September 1893.

☆ **Most corrupt country** As of 2006, the title of most corrupt country is held by the former French Caribbean colony of Haiti, which scored a record low of 1.8 on Transparency International's Corruption Perceptions Index (CPI). The CPI compares the misuse of public office for private gain in more than 160 countries, as perceived by business and political analysts.

★ Most countries to be head of state simultaneously The greatest number of independent nations for which the same person is lawfully head of state, at the same time, is 16. The record belongs to Her Majesty, Queen Elizabeth II (UK). While the queen's role is nominal and ceremonial, over 128 million people in 15 Commonwealth states (plus the UK) recognize her as their monarch.

★ MOST POLITICAL DEMONSTRATIONS IN 24 HOURS To highlight flaws in the Serious and Organized Crime and Police Act (SOCPA) UK, Mark Thomas (UK) staged 20 demonstrations on October 9, 2006. Ironically, Thomas first had to inform the authorities as, under SOCPA laws, it is illegal to demonstrate outside British Parliament buildings without police permission!

★ **Most votes for a pharmaceutical product in a political campaign** A brand of foot hygiene powder won a mayoral election in the small Ecuadorian town of Picoazà (population 4,000) in 1967. The pharmaceutical company behind the Pulvapies brand of powder ran a series of election-inspired ads, such as "Vote for any candidate, but if you want well-being and hygiene, vote for Pulvapies." The advertising campaign coincided with an

★ **MOST VOTES FOR MR. POTATO HEAD IN A POLITICAL CAMPAIGN** In 1985, Mr. Potato Head received four postal votes in the mayoral election in Boise, Idaho, U.S.A. However, he failed to win the election—which is a good thing, as Mr. Potato Head is a toy manufactured by Hasbro (U.S.A.).

LONGEST SERVING UK LABOUR PRIME MINISTER In 1994, at the age of 41, Tony Blair (UK) became the youngest ever head of the British Labour party when he was elected as its leader. In 1997, aged 44 (top left), he became the youngest person to serve as British prime minister since Lord Liverpool in 1812. On his 2,838th day in office, on February 6, 2005 (middle left), he became the longest serving Labour PM.

actual municipal election, and the foot powder was voted in by the electorate on the strength of receiving the most postal votes!

Most votes for a chimpanzee in a political campaign

In the 1988 mayoral election campaign in Rio de Janeiro, Brazil, the anti-establishment "Brazilian Banana Party" presented a chimp called Tião as its candidate. The chimpanzee came in third out of 12 candidates, taking just over 400,000 votes. Known for his moody temper, his campaign slogan was "Vote monkey—get monkey." Tião passed away in December 1996, aged 33, at his cage in Rio zoo.

★ **NEWEST INDEPENDENT COUNTRY** In a national referendum held on May 21, 2006, the people of Montenegro—a Balkan nation of 630,548 people—voted for independence from Serbia, thus creating the world's newest state. It will now apply to the European Union, the United Nations, and other international institutions in its own right.

★ **SMALLEST AREA TO CLAIM NATION STATUS** Founded in international waters 6 miles (10 km) off the Suffolk coast, UK, the Principality (or Duchy) of Sealand is a former World War II sea fort that remained derelict until 1966, when it was declared an independent state by Paddy Roy Bates (UK). Prince Roy I and his family declared themselves hereditary royal rulers and government officials, and have spent years struggling to have their claim recognized. They argue that most major European states and international lawyers have declared that Sealand has fulfilled all the legal requirements for a state.

☆ **Most handshakes by a politician in eight hours** As part of his campaign to become governor of New Mexico, U.S.A., Bill Richardson (U.S.A.) shook hands with 13,392 visitors to the New Mexico State Fair in Albuquerque on September 14, 2002. It was clearly worth the trouble—he won the seat!

☆ **Highest population of prisoners (documented)** With more than 2.1 million people (approximately 25% of the world's prison population) in

---

SEALAND FACTS

- Sealand is just 13,990 ft.^{2} (1,300 m^2).

- The Sealanders have produced their own constitution, flag, national anthem, currency—the Sealand dollar—and passports (above).

- It's a tax-free zone, and there are no gaming restrictions or customs duties.

- A dramatic takeover was staged in 1978 by the prime minister, but Prince Roy launched a helicopter assault and retook Sealand.

---

jail in the United States at any one time, the U.S. prison system is the largest in the world. Its incarceration rate is 737 per 100,000 people; the average rate in most Western nations is around 100 per 100,000 people.

★ **Newest NATO Force** The most recent establishment of a force under NATO (North Atlantic Treaty Organization) is the NATO Response Force, or NRF—a technologically advanced force that can be deployed rapidly wherever needed. Its objectives range from combat missions, crisis response, and peacekeeping to counterterrorist and noncombatant evacuation. It reached its full operational capability of some 25,000 troops in late 2006.

Youngest serving prime minister Representing the Dominica Labour party, the Hon. Roosevelt Skerritt (b. June 8, 1972) was appointed prime minister of Dominica on January 8, 2004.

KINGS & QUEENS

• The king of Thailand, Bhumibol Adulyadej (Rama IX, b. December 5, 1927), is currently the world's **longest reigning living monarch**, having succeeded to the throne following the death of his older brother on June 9, 1946.

• The country with the **youngest reigning monarch** is Swaziland, where King Mswati III was crowned on April 25, 1986, aged 18 years 6 days. He was born Makhosetive, the 67th son of King Sobhuza II.

• The **longest reign of any monarch** is that of Phiops II (also known as Pepi II or Neferkare), a Sixth Dynasty pharaoh of Ancient Egypt. His reign began ca. 2281 BC, when he was six years of age, and is believed to have lasted about 94 years.

TERRORISM & CONFLICT

Most bombed country Between May 1964 and February 26, 1973, some 5 billion lb. (2.26 million metric tons) of bombs of all kinds were dropped on Laos along the north to south Ho Chi Minh Trail supply route to South Vietnam.

Most recent malicious use of nerve gas The nerve gas sarin was released with the intention to kill on March 20, 1995, in Tokyo, Japan. Members of the Aum Shinrikyo sect, a Buddhist splinter group, released the gas at several points in the subway system, killing 12 people and injuring more than 5,000.

☆ **COUNTRY WITH MOST TROOPS DEPLOYED OVERSEAS** As of May 2005, the country with the highest number of military personnel serving their country overseas is the U.S.A., with approximately 350,000 personnel on active duty. This figure includes those forces normally present in Germany, Italy, the UK, and Japan, except when bases at those locations are actively supporting a combat operation.

☆ **Most recent nuclear bomb test** On October 9, 2006, a nuclear test explosion occurred underground near Kilchu, North Korea. Estimates of the bomb's size range from 1.2 to 33 million lb. (550 to 15,000 metric tons) of TNT. As a comparison, the first nuclear bomb used during conflict—at Hiroshima, Japan, during World War II—had an explosive force of around 27 million lb. of TNT.

★ **Largest organization for regional security** The Organization for Security and Cooperation in Europe (OSCE) has a membership of 56 states from Europe, central Asia, and North America. It spans an area from Vancouver in Canada to Vladivostok in Russia and employs around 450 people in its various institutions and a further 3,000 in its field operations.

☆ **Oldest living World War I veteran** Henry Allingham (UK), the oldest man in the UK, was born in London, UK, on June 6, 1896. He is the oldest surviving member of the armed forces, having served in both world wars.

DID YOU KNOW?

The country with the **highest military spending per capita** is Israel. In 2005, the Israeli military cost its citizens $1,429.03 each. The country with the **lowest military spending per capita** is Iceland, with $0 spent as of 2005!

BLODDIEST ANCIENT BATTLE
Roman losses at the Battle of
Cannae in 216 bc, as portrayed in
Hans Burgkmair's painting (left),
have been estimated at 48,000 to
50,000 dead and 4,500 prisoners
out of a force of about 80,000 men.
The losses among the opposing
forces under Hannibal have been
estimated at 5,700. Cannae is
considered the greatest battle of
annihilation in history.

★**Oldest person to receive a service medal** Commander William
Leslie King (UK) received the Arctic Emblem at the age of 96 on board
HMS *Belfast* in London, UK, on October 10, 2006. The medal, introduced
in March 2005, is given in recognition of sailors who served in the Arctic
convoys supplying vital aid to the Soviet Union between 1941 and 1945.

★ BLOODIEST BATTLES IN WORLD HISTORY ★

BATTLE	DATE	FATALITIES
Brusilov Offensive WWI	Jun. 4–Sep. 20, 1916	2,000,000
Battle of Stalingrad WWII (above)	Aug. 21, 1942–Feb. 2, 1943	750,000–1,800,000
Siege of Leningrad WWII	Sep. 8, 1941–Jan. 27, 1944	850,000–1,500,000
Merv massacre	AD 1221	1,300,000
Urgench massacre	AD 1220	1,200,000
Battle of Moscow WWII	Oct. 2, 1941–Jan. 7, 1942	719,000–900,000
Battle of Kiev WWII	Aug.–Sep. 26, 1941	400,000–678,000
Siege of Betar	AD 135	580,000
Battle of Gallipoli WWI	Feb. 19, 1915–Jan. 9, 1916	115,000–552,000
Battle of Smolensk WWII	Jul. 10–Sep. 10, 1941	500,000–535,000

★ **LARGEST PEACEKEEPING FORCE** The global deployment of United Nations peacekeeping representatives reached a historic high at the end of October 2006, with 80,976 military and police personnel and 15,000 civilians serving in peace operations around the world—the largest present-day peacekeeping force deployed on multiple operations. Pictured is the former UN Secretary-General Kofi Annan (Ghana, center) and French Forces commander General Alain Pellegrini (right) on August 29, 2006, at the UN peacekeeping base in Naqura, Lebanon.

FIRSTS

• In August 2003, NATO (North Atlantic Treaty Organization) took over command and coordination of the International Security Assistance Force (ISAF) in Afghanistan, and in doing so commenced the ★ **first international NATO operation** outside its former Euro-Atlantic area. In Afghanistan, NATO's role includes working closely with UN organizations and the Afghan authorities to prevent Afghanistan from falling into the hands of warlords and insurgents.

• Ergot is a type of fungus blight, and ingestion can cause delusions, paranoia, seizures, and cardiovascular problems that can lead to death. In the 6th century BC, the Assyrians, who lived in present-day Iraq, used rye ergot to poison enemy wells—the **first incidence of biological warfare.**

• The **first aerial bombardment by airplane** occurred on November 1, 1911, during the Italo-Turkish War. Second Lieutenant Giulio Gavotti of the Italian Air Flotilla threw four small 4.5-lb. (2-kg) Cipelli grenades over a Turkish camp stationed in Ain Zara, Libya, from his Taube monoplane, which was flying at an altitude of 600 ft. (185 m).

★ **MOST WANTED TERRORIST**
Osama bin Laden (Saudi Arabia), leader of the global terrorist organization Al-Qaeda, is the only terrorist on the U.S. Federal Bureau of Investigation (FBI) list of the Ten Most Wanted, and is sought by other nations for his terrorist activities. A reward for his capture of up to $25 million is being offered by the Rewards for Justice Program of the U.S. Department of State, and a further $2 million is being funded by the Airline Pilots Association and the Air Transport Association.

★ **HIGHEST BOUNTY ON A DOG** In 2004, a bounty of $10,000 was placed on Agata, a female golden labrador who is one of Colombia's top drug-sniffer dogs. The bounty was raised by drug traffickers following a very successful string of detections. Luckily, Agata has a 24-hour bodyguard who checks her food for poison.

WEAPONS

★ **Most powerful trebuchet** A siege trebuchet at Warwick Castle, Warwickshire, UK, gained the record as the ★ **most powerful trebuchet** when, on August 26, 2006, it hurled a 29-lb. (13.2-kg) projectile over a distance of 817 ft. (249 m). The power output of the trebucet was 23,773.4 lb./ft. (3,286.8 kg/m). It is also the world's ★ **largest trebuchet,** measuring 59 ft. (18 m) tall, weighing 48,500 lb. (22 metric tons), and able to slingshot 44-lb.

HEAVIEST NUCLEAR BOMB The MK 17, which was carried by U.S. B-36 bombers in the mid-1950s, weighed 41,998 lb. (19,050 kg) and was 24 ft. 6 in. (7.49 m) long. It had a maximum yield of 20 megatons, equivalent to a thousand of the bombs dropped on Hiroshima on August 6, 1945.

(20-kg) projectiles up to 82 ft. (25 m) high and over a range of 984 ft. (300 m).

☆ **Highest death toll from an atomic bombing raid** On August 6, 1945, an atomic bomb was used for the first time against an enemy in war. The bomb, named "Little Boy," was dropped by the U.S.A. from a B-29 Superfortress bomber, the *Enola Gay,* on the Japanese city of Hiroshima. In 1986, the number of identified victims of the explosion was given on the cenotaph memorial in Hiroshima as 138,890, the **highest death toll from a nuclear explosion** ever.

☆ **Largest non-nuclear conventional weapon in existence** The Boeing Massive Ordnance Penetrator (MOP) weighs a huge 30,000 lb. (13,600 kg), including 6,000 lb. (2,270 kg) of explosives. The weapon can be used to penetrate targets that might normally be resistant to attack, such as nuclear facilities and weapons bunkers hidden to depths of 200 ft. (61 m)—even those buried beneath 26 ft. (8 m) of reinforced concrete could be "penetrated" by the device.

The U.S. Air Force is expecting to take delivery of the weapon sometime in 2007, after testing of it was completed in 2006.

Smallest nuclear weapon The W54 fission bomb, deployed by the U.S.A. in Europe between 1961 and 1971, is the smallest nuclear weapon ever made. With a warhead weigh-

★ **FIRST HEAT-RAY WEAPON** The Active Denial System projects a high-energy microwave beam within a 1,640-ft. (500-m) range. On being struck by the beam, human targets feel a burning sensation as the microwave penetrates skin to a depth of 0.015 in. (0.5 mm), raising the temperature to 122°F (50°C). The nonlethal beam is designed to disperse hostile crowds.

★ **FIRST TESTS CONDUCTED WITH PILOTLESS FLYING BOMBS** The first flight of the Kettering Aerial Torpedo (later known as the "Kettering Bug") was conducted in the U.S.A. on October 2, 1918, during World War I. The bomb was intended to have a range of 50 miles (80 km), but project funding was withdrawn when the war ended. This early form of cruise missile was never used operationally.

ing just 51 lb. (23.13 kg), the weapon had a yield of 0.1 kilotons and a maximum range of only 2.5 miles (4 km).

Most accurate human-portable antiaircraft missile The U.S.-made Stinger missile, introduced in the early 1980s, is 5 ft. (1.5 m) long and weighs

---

HIGHEST CALIBER

• The **largest caliber ship guns** were the nine 18-in. (45.7-cm) guns installed on the Japanese battleships *Yamato* and *Musashi*. The shells weighed 3,200 lb. (1,452 kg) and had a range of 27 miles (43.5 km).

• The **highest caliber cannon** ever constructed is the Tsar Pushka ("Emperor of Cannons"), now housed in the Kremlin, Moscow, Russia, and built in the 16th century. It has a bore of 35 in. (89 cm) and a barrel 17 ft. 6 in. (5.34 m) long.

• The world's **largest bore for a piece of artillery** measures 36 in. (91.4 cm) in diameter and belongs to the Mallet mortar, which was designed by Robert Mallet (Ireland) and completed in March 1857.

• The **largest caliber mortars** ever constructed are Mallet's mortar and the "Little David" of World War II, made in the U.S.A. Each had a caliber of 36 in. (91.4 cm), but neither was ever used in action.

★ **FIRST LASER WEAPON TO SHOOT DOWN A ROCKET** The U.S. Army and the Israeli defense department destroyed a Katyusha rocket carrying a live warhead using the High Energy Laser/Advance Concept Technology Demonstrator in New Mexico, U.S.A., on June 7, 2000.

22 lb. (9.9 kg). It has a range of about 3 miles (4.8 km) and a top speed of about 1,300 mph (2,000 km/h). The Stinger's cryogenically cooled infrared seeker can distinguish between an aircraft's infrared signature and counter-measures that are normally used to disguise an aircraft, such as flares.

★ **Smallest working cannon** A fully operational cannon made from wood, brass, iron, and steel by Joseph Brooks (U.S.A.) measures just 1.25 in. (3.175 cm) in length, 0.86 in. (2.2 cm) in width, and 0.62 in. (1.6 cm) in height—an overall scale to the real thing of 1:48. The cannon was fired for the first time ever in Okeechobee, Florida, U.S.A., on October 22, 2006.

★ **Most synchronized two-hand rifle spins in one minute** Constantine Wilson, Abraham Robbins, Patrick Reed, and Valentino Cuba (all U.S.A.) completed a total of 168 synchronized two-hand spins—84 cycles—

★ **LARGEST CONTRACT TO EXPORT AN AMRAAM WEAPONS SYSTEM** The largest contract for advanced medium-range air-to-air missiles (AMRAAM) is the $284-million deal by U.S. manufacturer Raytheon to supply the Pakistan Air Force with 200 Sidewinder AIM–9M–8/9 and 500 AIM–120C5 AMRAAM missiles. The contract was announced in January 2007.

★ SMALLEST REVOLVER The smallest working revolver is the C1ST made by SwissMiniGun (Switzerland), with a caliber of 2.34 mm. It measures 2.2 in. (5.5 cm) long, 1.4 in. (3.5 cm) high, and 0.4 in. (1 cm) wide, and weighs just 0.7 oz. (19.8 g). It fires the smallest live and blank rimfire ammunition.

in one minute at the Navy and Marine Reserve Center, Anacostia Naval Base, Washington, D.C., U.S.A., on January 28, 2006.

On the same day and at the same location, the four men also set the record for the ★ **most underhand inline rifle exchanges in one minute.** Standing in a line formation, they completed 26 exchanges.

FIND OUT MORE

For more about weapons and military hardware, see pages 392–397.

ANIMALS & MAN

★ **LARGEST MOVIEGOERS** On June 6, 2006, Asian elephants and their handlers (mahouts) were invited to attend a special open-air screening being held in the Ayuthaya Province of Thailand. The main feature was the Thai animated film *Kan Kluay* (2006) which tells the story of a young elephant who grows up to be a war hero and assistant to the king of Thailand, set 400 years ago. Asian elephants (*Elephas maximus*) can measure up to 10 ft. (3 m) in height, with males weighing up to 11,000 lb. (5 tons).

★ **OLDEST PENGUIN IN CAPTIVITY**
The oldest ever penguin in captivity was Rocky, one of six rockhopper penguins (*Eudyptes chrysocome*) that arrived at Bergen Aquarium, Norway, in 1974. He lived there until his death in October 2003, aged 29 years 4 months.

TALLEST LIVING HORSE Radar, a Belgian draft horse, measured 19 hands 3.5 in. (79.5 in.; 202 cm), without shoes, on July 27, 2004, at the North American Belgian Championship in London, Ontario, Canada. Radar is owned by Priefert Manufacturing, Inc., Mount Pleasant, Texas, U.S.A. As of July 7, 2006, the record for the **smallest living horse** was held by Thumbelina, a miniature sorrel brown mare that measures 17.5 in. (44.5 cm) to the withers and is owned by Kay and Paul Goessling (both U.S.A.), who live in St. Louis, Missouri, U.S.A. The two horses were united for the first time by Guinness World Records for this photo shoot on September 3, 2006.

★ OLDEST ANIMALS IN CAPTIVITY ★

ANIMAL	LOCATION	AGE
★ Salamander	Artis Zoo, Amsterdam, Netherlands	52
★ Gray seal	National Seal Sanctuary, Gweek, Cornwall, Uk	43
★ Water buffalo	Tal-Khed, Maharashtra, India	43
☆ Kinkajou	Honolulu Zoo, Hawaii, U.S.A.	40
★ Polar bear	Assiniboine Park Zoo, Winnipeg, Canada	40
★ Panda	Wuhan, Hubei Province, China	37
☆ Koala	Lone Pine Sanctuary, Queensland, Australia	23

★LONGEST JUMP RIDING A LION Performing for the Russian State Circus Company on July 28, 2006, Askold (pictured) and Edgard Zapashny (Russia) made a jump of 7 ft. 6 in. (2.3 m) while riding a lion called Michael.

★LARGEST PROSTHETIC LEG After losing her front left foot in a land mine accident in 1999, Motala was operated on by 30 vets at the Hang Chat Elephant Hospital in Lampang, Thailand—the most vets involved in one operation. In September 2006, Motala received a silicon/fiberglass limb big and strong enough to sustain the weight of a typical Asian elephant (6,500–11,000 lb.; 3–5 tons).

★ SMALLEST POLICE DOG The smallest dog used for law enforcement is Midge, a chihuahua–rat terrier cross measuring 11 in. (28 cm) tall and 23 in. (58 cm) long. Midge works as an official "Police K9" with her owner, Sheriff Dan McClelland (U.S.A.), at Geauga County Sheriff's Office in Chardon, Ohio, U.S.A.

FASTEST ROBOT JOCKEY Kamel is a robot jockey designed by K-Team (Switzerland) for racing camels in the Arabian Gulf states. Traditional to the region, the sport has attracted human rights groups who fear for the lives of the jockeys, some as young as four years old, who are forced—often after starvation to keep weight down—to race. To combat this, the ruling sheiks of Qatar are calling for all camel races to be ridden by robot jockeys by the end of 2007. Weighing 60 lb. (27 kg), Kamel comes with in-built GPS and shock absorbers, and can be controlled remotely by joystick. The fastest time recorded to date is 25 mph (40 km/h).

★ LARGEST PANDA CUB
The largest panda cub born in captivity weighed 7.6 oz. (218 g) shortly after its birth at the Wolong Giant Panda Research Center in Chengdu, Sichuan Province, China, on August 7, 2006. The cub is the first offspring of Zhang Ka, who was in labor for 34 hours, itself the **★ longest recorded labor for a captive panda.** The average weight of newborn pandas is 3–6.7 oz. (83–190 g).

PANDA FACT FILE

• The giant panda (*Ailuropoda melanoleuca*) is the **★ most costly of all zoo species.** The entire captive giant panda population is indigenous to and owned by China. Four zoos in the U.S.A. (San Diego, Atlanta, Memphis, and Washington) each pay an annual leasing fee of $1 million to the Chinese government for a pair of these creatures. If cubs are born, a one-time payment of $600,000 per offspring must also be made. A panda's upkeep (including bamboo production and security) makes them five times more costly than elephants.

• The **★ oldest panda ever in captivity** was Dudu, who was born in 1962 and lived for most of her life in Wuhan Zoo, Chengdu, China, until her death on July 22, 1999, aged 37 years.
A male giant panda called Bao Bao was born in China in September 1978, but went to live at Berlin Zoo, Germany, in 1980, at the age of two. He has remained there ever since—the **★ oldest panda living in captivity.**

• The **★ longest recorded pregnancy** for a giant panda lasted 200 days for Shu Lan, who gave birth to a healthy male cub on October 21, 2004, at Chengdu research center for giant pandas, Sichuan Province, China. The average pregnancy for a panda is 95 to 160 days.

★ **HIGHEST DEATH TOLL FROM LION ATTACKS** A total of 563 people were killed by lions across Tanzania from 1990 to 2005, including eight fatalities and 16 serious injuries in the region of Sudi and Mingoyo in Lindi, Tanzania, by a pack of four lions from 2001 to 2004 alone. Pictured above is Hassan Dadi (Tanzania), who lost his arm in a lion attack in the village of Usuru, Tanzania.

Another major period of attacks occurred from 1932 to 1947. During these 15 years, 1,500 people were killed by lions (*Panthera leo*) roaming an area of 150 miles² (388.5 km²) in Njombe, Tanzania. This equates to an average of 100 people per year. Lions typically attack humans only when their normal prey and/or habitat is severely compromised by human development.

★ ANIMAL ATTACKS ON HUMANS ★

KILLER ANIMAL	LOCATION & DATE	FATALITIES
Long saltwater crocodiles (Crocodylus porosus)	Ramree, Burma February 19–20, 1945	980 Japanese soldiers
Tiger	Champawat district, India 1902–07	436 people
Pack of wolves	Darovskoye district, Russia 1948	40 children
"Beast of Gévaudan" (possibly a wolf)	Lazère, France 1764–66	Dozens of children and adults

AWESOME ANATOMY

★MOST NEEDLES IN THE HEAD The record for the most acupuncture needles in the head and face is 1,790 and was achieved by Wei Shengchu (China) in Nanning City, China, on March 23, 2004. Wei is a medical aesthetics and cosmetology doctor in Nanning City, Guangxin Zhuang Autonomous Region, China.

MOST SWORDS SWALLOWED Natasha Veruschka (U.S.A.) swallowed 13 swords, each at least 15 in. (38.1 cm) long, at the Third Annual Sideshow Gathering and Sword Swallowers Convention, in Wilkes-Barre, Pennsylvania, U.S.A., on September 3, 2004. She is shown here swallowing a neon strip light as part of her jaw-dropping stage act.

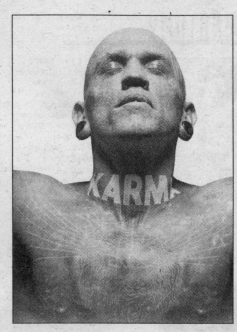

MOST TATTOOED PERSON Lucky Diamond Rich (Australia) has endured over 1,000 hours of tatooing. His all-over covering includes eyelids, the delicate skin between the toes, down into the ears, and even his gums. With multiple layers of tattoos, his total covering is in excess of 200%.

LONGEST FINGERNAILS ON A PAIR OF HANDS Lee Redmond (U.S.A.), who hasn't cut her nails since 1979, has grown and carefully manicured them to reach a total length of 24 ft. 7.8 in. (7 m 51.3 cm).

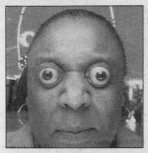

FARTHEST EYEBALL POP Kim Goodman (U.S.A.) can pop her eyeballs to a protrusion of 0.43 in. (11 mm) beyond her eye sockets. She first discovered her startling talent when she was hit on the head with a hockey mask and one of her eyeballs popped out much farther than normal. Ever since, Kim's eyes would protrude out of her head every time she yawned, and she has now taught herself to pop her eyes out on cue.

STRANGEST DIET For nearly 50 years (beginning in 1959) Michel Lotito (France) of Grenoble, France—known as Monsieur Mangetout—adhered to a diet that included metal and glass. Gastroenterologists who had X-rayed his stomach described his ability to consume 2 lb. (900 g) of metal per day as unique.

Since 1966, he has consumed, among other unconventional culinary delights, 18 bicycles, 15 supermarket carts, seven TV sets, six chandeliers, two beds, a pair of skis, a low-calorie Cessna light aircraft, and a computer. He is said to have provided the only example in history of a coffin (handles and all) ending up *inside* a man.

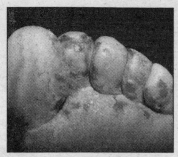

MOST COMMON SKIN INFECTION *Tinea pedis,* usually called "athlete's foot," is the most common skin infection in humans. The fungus afflicts up to 70% of the world's population.

STRETCHIEST SKIN Garry Turner (UK) is able to stretch the skin of his stomach to a distended length of 6.25 in. (15.8 cm), because of a rare medical condition called Ehlers-Danlos Syndrome, a disorder of the connective tissues affecting the skin, ligaments, and internal organs. With this condition, the collagen that strengthens the skin and determines its elasticity becomes defective, resulting in, among other things, a loosening of the skin and the "hypermobility" of the joints.

OLYMPIC HALL OF FAME

BIRGIT FISCHER Birgit Fischer (GDR/Germany, left) won four consecutive canoeing golds from the South Korean Olympics in 1988 through to the Sydney Olympics in 2000, the most consecutive Olympic gold medals won by a woman.

JACKIE JOYNER-KERSEE The most Olympic heptathlon golds won by an athlete is two, by Jackie Joyner-Kersee (U.S.A.) in 1988 and 1992. She also took gold in the 1988 long jump.

ED MOSES The most Olympic gold medals in the men's 400 m hurdles event won by an individual athlete is two by Ed Moses (U.S.A., left), in 1976 and 1984, and Glenn Davis (U.S.A.), in 1960 and 1964.

X-REF

• Turn to our sports reference section on page 528 for a wealth of stats from all your favorite sports.

• You'll find all the latest track and field records on pages 413–423.

• Crazy about swimming and other water sports? Then dive into page 504.

• If you like your sports to be a little more radical, check out X Games on page 522.

DALEY THOMPSON At the 1984 Games, Daley Thompson (UK) scored 8,847 points, which remained the **most points scored in the men's Olympic decathlon** for an incredible 20 years. The current record holder is Roman Šebrle (Czech Republic), with 9,026 points.

★ MOST OLYMPIC MEDALS [ATHLETE] ★

ATHLETE (COUNTRY)	SPORT	GOLD	SILVER	BRONZE	TOTAL
1 Larissa Latynina (USSR, above)	Gymnastics	9	5	4	18
2 Nikolai Andrianov (USSR)	Gymnastics	7	5	3	15
3 Edoardo Mangiarotti (Italy)	Fencing	6	5	2	13
= Takashi Ono (Japan)	Gymnastics	5	4	4	13
= Boris Shakhlin (USSR)	Gymnastics	7	4	2	13
6 Paavo Nurmi (Finland)	Track & field	9	3	0	12
= Birgit Fischer (Germany/ East Germany)	Canoeing/ Kayaking	8	4	0	12
= Sawao Kato (Japan)	Gymnastics	8	3	1	12
= Jenny Thompson (U.S.A.)	Swimming	8	3	1	12
= Alexei Nemov (Russia)	Gymnastics	4	2	6	12

CARL LEWIS Olympic great Carl Lewis (U.S.A.) shares the record for **most men's Olympic gold medals,** with nine: four in 1984 (100 m, 200 m, 4 × 100 m, and long jump); two in 1988 (100 m and long jump); two in 1992 (4 × 100 m and long jump); and one in 1996 (long jump). Only two other men have won the same number of Olympic golds: Paavo Nurmi (Finland) and Mark Spitz (U.S.A.).

OLYMPIAN FEATS

• The **earliest celebration of the ancient Olympic Games,** of which there is a definite record, is that of July 776 BC, when Coroibos, a cook from Elis, won the foot race. It is possible, however, that they date back to *ca.* 1370 BC.

• The total spectator attendance at the Olympic Games held in Los Angeles, California, U.S.A., in 1984 was given as 5,797,923 people, representing the **greatest attendance at an Olympic Games.**

• A total of 201 countries participated in the Summer Olympic Games held in Athens, Greece, from August 13 to 29, 2004. This unprecedented number constitutes the **most countries to attend a Summer Games.**

• A total of 10,651 athletes, of whom 4,069 were women, participated in the Summer Olympic Games celebration held in Sydney, Australia, in 2000. This represents the **most participants at a Summer Games.**

• The U.S.A. won 2,215 medals in the Summer Games, 1896 to 2004, the **most Olympic medals won by a country.**
  The Winter Olympic Games were first held in 1924. The **most medals won by a country in the Winter Games** is 280, by Norway.

• The U.S.A. won 907 gold medals in the Summer Olympic Games, from 1896 to 2004, making it the **country with the most gold medals in the Summer Games.**
  The U.S.A. also holds the record for the **most gold medals won at a single Summer Olympics,** with a record 83 at the XXIII Olympic Games held in Los Angeles, California, U.S.A., in 1984.

• The **youngest Olympic champion** was Kim Yun-mi (South Korea; b. December 1, 1980), at the age of 13 years 85 days, in the 1994 women's 3,000 m short-track speedskating relay event.
  Oscar Swahn (Sweden) was in the winning Running Deer shooting team at the 1912 Olympic Games in Stockholm, Sweden, aged 64 years 258 days, making him the **oldest Olympic gold medalist.**

HEIKE DRECHSLER The greatest number of Olympic gold medals won in the women's long-jump event is two by Heike Drechsler (Germany) in 1992 and 2000.

★ MOST OLYMPIC MEDALS [COUNTRY] ★

COUNTRY	GOLD	SILVER	BRONZE	TOTAL
U.S.A.	897	691	603	2,191
USSR*	395	319	296	1,010
GB	188	242	237	667
France	184	196	216	596
Italy	182	147	164	493
Germany**	147	153	189	489
Sweden	142	154	171	467
Hungary	156	136	157	449
Germany (East)	153	129	127	409
Australia	117	122	147	386

*1952–92
**1896–1936, 1956–64, 1992–present

GREG LOUGANIS Two divers share the record for **most diving medals,** with five each. Greg Louganis (U.S.A.) won four golds and one silver in 1976, 1984, and 1988. He is seen here in a famous incident in 1988, when his head hit the board mid-dive. Klaus Dibiasi (Italy) also won five diving medals, from 1964 to 1976.

MICHAEL JOHNSON Michael Johnson (U.S.A.) ran the **fastest men's 200 m sprint** in 19.32 seconds in Atlanta, Georgia, U.S.A., on August 1, 1996. In the same Games, he became the **first man to complete the 200 m and 400 m "double"** in Olympic history.

JESSE OWENS One of the greatest Olympians of all time, Jesse Owens (left) was a member of the U.S. quartet that set a time of 39.8 seconds for the fastest 4 × 100 m relay, on August 9, 1936, in Berlin, Germany, known to many as the "Hitler Olympics." German premier Adolf Hitler had intended to use the event to prove to the rest of the world the superiority of the "Aryan" race and was visibly annoyed as he watched Owens win four gold medals.

The current record of 37.4 seconds is shared by the U.S. 4 × 100 m teams who competed in Spain, in 1992, and Germany, in 1993.

RAYMOND CLARENCE EWRY The greatest number of gold medals won in a men's individual event is eight, by Raymond Clarence Ewry (U.S.A.). He took gold in the standing long, triple, and high jumps in 1900 and 1904, and the standing long and high jumps in 1908. (Ewry also won two golds at the 1906 Intercalated Games, but the International Olympic Committee does not officially recognize that event.)

SIR STEVE REDGRAVE The most Olympic rowing gold medals won by a man is five, by Steve Redgrave (UK), in the coxed fours (1984), coxless pairs (1988, 1992, and 1996), and coxless fours (2000).

SCIENCE & TECHNOLOGY

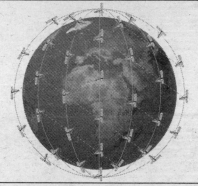

CONTENTS

CUTTING-EDGE SCIENCE

Computers In November 2006, IBM's BlueGene/L System, the world's ☆ **fastest computer,** retained its number-one spot on the list of top 500 computers with a performance of 280.6 teraflops (trillions of floating-point operations, or calculations) per second.

The world's ★ **smallest external hard drive** is the 4 GB MF-DU204G made by Elecom Japan, at 2.6 in. × 1.1 in. × 0.5 in. (68 mm × 30 mm × 13 mm).

The ★ **smallest USB flash drive** is ATP Taiwan's Petito, released in March 2006. It measures 0.37 in. × 0.69 in. × 1.42 in. (9.4 mm × 17.6 mm × 36.6 mm).

★ **Largest flexible LCD** Samsung (Korea) has created a 7-in.-thick (17.78-cm) flexible liquid crystal display (LCD) that maintains its thickness when bent, keeping picture quality stable. The high-resolution LCD is sandwiched between two sheets of high-end flexible plastic that are much thinner and less brittle than current screens.

★ **Biggest award in science and technology** The €1,000,000 ($1,331,345) Millennium Technology Prize is awarded every two years in recognition of outstanding contributions to world science and technology. The 2006 winner was Professor Shuji Nakamura (Japan) at the University of California, U.S.A. His scientific achievements included the invention of blue-light-emitting diodes and the blue-laser diode.

★ **Thinnest chip** On February 5, 2006, Hitachi Ltd. (Japan) announced it had developed and verified operation of the world's smallest and thinnest chip, measuring 0.0002 in.^{2} (0.15 mm^2) in area, and 7.5 μm (microns, or millionths of a meter) thick. The chip is thinner than paper (which is typically 80–100 microns thick), so one application could be used as an "intelligent" watermark in paper currency.

★ **Oldest human DNA** A team of French and Belgian researchers have extracted DNA from the tooth of a Neanderthal child who lived in the Meuse Basin, Belgium, around 100,000 years

★ SHARPEST MAN-MADE OBJECT Scientists at the National Institute for Nanotechnology and the University of Alberta (both Canada) have created a tungsten needle that tapers to a thickness of just one atom. The breakthrough, announced in May 2006, should allow the construction of better super high-resolution electron microscopes. Pictured is the tip imaged by a field ion microscope.

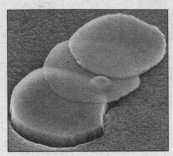

ago. The analysis of the DNA, released in June 2006, shows that Neanderthals had a greater genetic diversity 100,000 years ago than they did by the time modern humans arrived in Europe around 35,000 years ago.

Highest intensity focused laser The Vulcan laser at the Rutherford Appleton Laboratory, Oxfordshire, UK, is the highest intensity focused laser in the world. Following its upgrade, which was completed in 2002, it is

---

MAN-MADE SUBSTANCES

• **Most bitter**... The most bitter-tasting substances are based on the denatonium cation and have been produced commercially as benzoate and saccharide. Taste-detection levels are as low as one part in 500 million, and a dilution of one part in 100 million will leave a lingering taste.

• **Sweetest**... Thaumatin, also known as Talin—obtained from the arils (appendages found on certain seeds) of the katemfe plant (*Thaumatococcus daniellii*) discovered in West Africa—is 1,600 times as sweet as sucrose.

• **Darkest**... An alloy of nickel and phosphorus around 25 times less reflective than conventional black paint reflects just 0.16% of visible light. The principle was first developed by researchers in the U.S.A. and India in 1980. In 1990, Anritsu (Japan) further refined this method to produce the darkest version so far. In 2002, the National Physical Laboratory, UK, developed a new technique for the commercial manufacturing of this coating.

• **Stinkiest**... The stinkiest substances on Earth are the man-made "Who-Me?" and "U.S. Government Standard Bathroom Malodor," which have five and eight chemical ingredients, respectively. Bathroom Malodor smells primarily of human feces and becomes incredibly repellent to people at just two parts per million. It was originally created to test the power of deodorizing products.

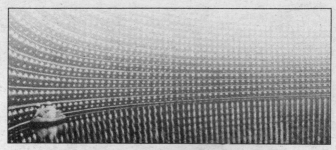

☆ **LARGEST UNDERGROUND NEUTRINO OBSERVATORY** Super-Kamiokande is a joint U.S.-Japanese research facility located 3,280 ft. (1,000 m) below ground in the Kamioka silver mine in Japan. It consists of a vast cylinder measuring 131 ft. (40 m) in height and 131 ft. (40 m) in diameter, which is filled with ultra-pure water. The interior is covered with 13,000 sensitive light detectors called photomultiplier tubes, which watch the water for Cerenkov light—the telltale sign that a particle has passed through the water. The men in the boat pictured above left are inspecting and cleaning the tubes.

now capable of producing a laser beam with an irradiance (focused intensity) of 10^{21} watts per square inch.

★**Largest digital graphic** A digital graphic measuring over 10,000 ft.^{2} (929 m^2) has been featured on the six bay doors of the Boeing Company in Washington, DC, U.S.A., since February 15, 2006.

☆ **LARGEST HDTV SCREEN** Mitsubishi Electric (Japan) has installed a high-definition television (HDTV) screen measuring 37 × 218 ft. (11.2 × 66.4 m) at the Tokyo Racecourse in Tokyo, Japan, at a cost of ¥3.2 billion ($27.2 million). The LED screen has a surface area of 8,000 ft.^{2} (744 m^2)—equivalent in size to three tennis courts or 1,550 32-in. television sets!

★ **LARGEST FLEXIBLE E-PAPER** In 2006 in Korea, LG.Philips LCD, in cooperation with E-ink, unveiled a sheet of WXGA (wide extended graphics display) flexible E-paper with a diagonal measurement of 14.1 in. (35.8 cm) and a resolution of 1,280 × 800 dpi. One possible application of such technology will be reducing the size of newspapers to a single sheet.

★ **Smallest transistor** Scientists at the University of Manchester, UK, have created prototype transistors using graphene, the world's thinnest material (see page 270). Measuring just one atom thick by less than 50 atoms wide, the transistors could eventually render the silicon chip obsolete and allow the development of a brand-new type of super-fast computer chip. Their achievement was announced in March 2007.

★ **Most advanced cloaking device** In October 2006, a team of U.S. and UK scientists announced the creation of a device that could partially "cloak" an object from view in the microwave region of the electromagnetic spectrum. It consists of an array of 10 fiberglass rings coated with copper elements that change the direction of electromagnetic waves striking them. Placed around a copper cylinder, the cloaking device was able to deflect incoming microwaves and partially channel them around the cylinder, as if they had passed through it unaffected. This work could one day lead to technology that would hide an object from human eyes in visible wavelengths of light.

SCIENCE

★**Hardest metallic element** With a Mohs' value of 8.5, chromium is the hardest of the metallic elements. It is responsible for the red color in rubies. The ★ **softest metallic element** is cesium, with a value of just 0.2. It is soft enough to be cut with a butter knife, melts at 82°F (28°C), and explodes when dropped in water.

★**Longest half-life** Half-life is the measure of how long it takes an unstable element to decay. A half-life of a day means that it would take a day for half the atomic nuclei in a sample to decay into a more stable element. In 2003, scientists discovered that bismuth-209—previously believed to be stable—in fact gradually decayed with a half-life of around 20 billion billion years—more than a billion times the age of the Universe!

☆**MOST POWERFUL PARTICLE ACCELERATOR** The Large Hadron Collider (LHC) is an international project designed to study matter by emulating conditions just a few billionths of a second after the big bang. It is located in a 16.7-mile-long (27-km) circular tunnel (pictured) at the CERN laboratory in Geneva, Switzerland, that previously housed the Large Electron Positron Collider.

The 38,000-ton collider will accelerate two beams of matter in opposite directions around the tunnel. Once traveling at nearly the speed of light, the two streams of particles will be allowed to collide, producing showers of exotic subatomic particles that will be detected by instruments in the tunnel.

The LHC is due for completion in November 2007 and will require 120 MW of power and 91 tons of liquid helium to operate. One principle aim of the LHC is to find the theorized but as yet unseen Higgs boson particle—often nicknamed the God Particle.

★ **LONGEST LINEAR ACCELERATOR** The Stanford Linear Accelerator Center (SLAC) in California, U.S.A., is a particle accelerator some 2 miles (3.2 km) long. Since beginning operations in 1966, its key achievements include the discovery of the charm quark and tau lepton subatomic particles.

The accelerator is located underground and is, according to administrators, among the world's longest, straightest objects (left). Pictured above is the earthquake-proof Mark II Detector into which the electrons and protons are propelled in order to release subatomic particles.

★ **Heaviest gas** Radon (atomic number 222) is inert and non-reactive. At room temperature and pressure, a cubic meter of radon weighs 21.4 lb. (9.73 kg)—100 times heavier than a cubic meter of hydrogen.

★ **Heaviest non-elemental gas** Tungsten hexafluoride has a density of 0.81 lb./ft.^{3} (13.1 kg/m^3)—more than 10 times heavier than air and 76 times lighter than water. It is also nearly seven times heavier than the **lightest man-made solid,** aerogel.

· **Most accurate value for π (pi)** As part of a long-running project, Yasumasa Kanada (Japan) of the University of Tokyo calculated π (pi) to 1,241,100,000,000 decimal places. He broke his record of 206 billion places in December 2002 after 400 hours of computation power using a Hitachi SR8000/MPP supercomputer.

Elements with the lowest melting and boiling points Helium (He) cannot be obtained as a solid at atmospheric pressure, the minimum pressure required being 2.532 MPa (24.985 atmospheres) at -458.275°F (-272.375°C). Helium also has the lowest boiling point of any element at -452.070°F (-268.928°C). For metallic elements, mercury (see page 276) has the lowest melting and boiling points.

★ **First wildfire** The earliest wildfire smoldered 419 million years ago, when oxygen levels may have been considerably higher than today. Scientists from Cardiff University, UK, found evidence of a low-intensity burn, probably started by a lightning strike, while studying charred fossils of small plants found in rocks near Ludlow, UK, in April 2004.

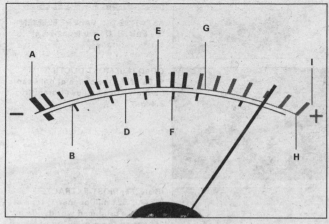

RECORD-BREAKING SOUNDS

A. -9.4 DB QUIETEST PLACE ON EARTH Anechoic Test Chamber at Orfield Laboratories, Minneapolis, Minnesota, U.S.A.

B. 93 DB LOUDEST SNORING Kåre Walkert (Sweden), Örebro Regional Hospital, Sweden, on May 24, 1993

C. 100 DB LOUDEST APPLAUSE BBC's Big Bash, at the NEC, Birmingham, West Midlands, UK, on October 24–27, 1997

D. 104.9 DB LOUDEST BURP Paul Hunn (UK), London, UK, on July 20, 2004

E. 108 DB LOUDEST FINGER SNAP Bob Hatch (U.S.A.), Pasadena, California, U.S.A., on May 17, 2000

F. 110.44 DB LOUDEST CLAP Alastair Galpin, Acoustics Testing Service, University of Auckland, New Zealand, on July 18, 2005

G. 125 DB LOUDEST WHISTLE Marco Ferrera (U.S.A.) from 8 ft. 3 in. (2.5 m), Santa Monica, California, U.S.A., on March 5, 2004

H. 188 DB LOUDEST ANIMAL SOUND Blue whales (*Balaenoptera musculus*) and fin whales (*B. physalus*)

I. UNKNOWN DB LOUDEST NOISE Eruption of Krakatoa, Indonesia, on August 27, 1883; 26 times the power of the largest ever H-bomb test; the sound was heard 3,100 miles (5,000 km) away

DID YOU KNOW?

The diamond allotrope of carbon is the **hardest element** on Earth, with a maximum score of 10 on the Mohs' scale of hardness. They are formed at least 93 miles (150 km) beneath the Earth's surface, where the pressures and temperatures are great enough to force the carbon atoms to adopt the diamond structure.

RECORD-BREAKING ELEMENTS

ASTATINE (At) RAREST ELEMENT ON EARTH Only 0.9 oz. (25 g) exists naturally

GOLD (Au) MOST DUCTILE ELEMENT One ounce of gold can be drawn to 43 miles (1 gram to 2.4 km)

IRON (Fe) MOST EXTRACTED METAL 521 million metric tons of iron were produced worldwide in 1999 from the processing of mined iron ore

LITHIUM (Li) LEAST DENSE METAL At room temperature, lithium has a density of just 0.5334 g/cm³

MERCURY (Hg) LOWEST MELTING AND BOILING POINTS (METAL) -37.892°F (-38.829°C) and 673.92°F (356.62°C), respectively

☆**Largest known prime number** A prime number is one that can be divided only by itself and the number one—the number 13 is a "prime" example. On December 15, 2005, a team led by Professors Curtis Cooper and Steven Boone (both U.S.A.) were able to generate a prime number that ran to a length of 9,152,052 digits, making it the longest ever recorded prime number.

RECORD-BREAKING TEMPERATURES

∞—HIGHEST TEMPERATURE EVER At the very instant of the big bang, 13.7 billion years ago, the Universe is thought to have had infinite temperature

3.6 BILLION°F (2 BILLION°C)—HIGHEST MAN-MADE TEMPERATURE Achieved using the Z-Machine at the Sandia National Laboratories, Albuquerque, New Mexico, U.S.A.

28,080,000°F (15,600,000°C)—CENTER OF THE SUN

360,000°F (200,000°C)—HOTTEST WHITE DWARF According to Klaus Werner (Germany) of the Universität Tübingen, the glowing remnant of the dead star H1504+65 is roughly 30 times hotter than the surface of the Sun

6,177°F (3,414°C)—HIGHEST MELTING POINT AND 10,557°F (5,847°C)—HIGHEST BOILING POINT Tungsten has the highest melting and boiling points of any element

896°F (480°C)—HOTTEST PLANET Venus has the hottest surface of any planet in the solar system—hot enough to melt lead!

120.5°F (49.2°C)—HIGHEST TEMPERATURE ON EARTH Marble Bar, Western Australia, peaked during the period between October 31, 1923, and April 7, 1924

59°F (15°C)—MEAN TEMPERATURE ON EARTH

57.5°F (14.2°C)—LOWEST BODY TEMPERATURE On February 23, 1994, Karlee Kosolofski (Canada), then aged two, survived being accidentally locked outside her home for six hours in a temperature of -8°F (-22°C)

-35.5°F (-37.5°C)—COLDEST WATER DROPLETS Aircraft measurements of clouds over west Texas on August 13, 1999, revealed tiny water droplets that remained liquid for several minutes

-128.6°F (-89.2°C)—LOWEST TEMPERATURE ON EARTH Occurred at Vostok, Antarctica, on July 21, 1983

450 PICOKELVIN—COLDEST MAN-MADE TEMPERATURE Achieved by a team at MIT, Cambridge, Massachusetts, U.S.A., led by Aaron Leanhardt (U.S.A.). A picokelvin is one million-millionth of a kelvin

-273.15°C (-459.67°F)—LOWEST POSSIBLE TEMPERATURE The coldest that any substance can theoretically be is when there is no vibration in its atoms; aka zero kelvin. This has never been achieved

°C

FORENSIC SCIENCE

★**First use of DNA profiling to clear a criminal suspect** The world's first DNA-based manhunt took place from 1986 to 1988 in Enderby, Leicestershire, UK, during the investigation of a double rape-murder—that of Linda Mann (UK) in 1983 and Dawn Ashworth (UK) in 1986. The prime suspect, a local boy named Richard Buckland (UK), confessed to the second killing, but deoxyribonucleic acid (DNA) profiling of the victims revealed that the killer's DNA and that of Buckland did not match. Buckland thus became the first suspect exonerated using DNA profiling. In 1988, after further DNA testing, the real killer, Colin Pitchfork (UK), was sentenced to life imprisonment.

★**First use of forensic entomology** According to forensic biologist Mark Benecke (Germany), the study of insects taken from crime scenes dates back to a 13th-century textbook—*Hsi Yuan Lu* ("The Washing Away of Wrongs")—by Sung Tz'u (China). Called upon to investigate a fatal stabbing. Tz'u asked workers to lay down their sickles; blowflies were drawn to one sickle covered in invisible blood traces, forcing its owner to confess to the crime. (It is now known that certain blowflies lay their eggs in fresh blood.)

★**Largest forensic science training program** Competition is extremely tough for the 16 places on a 10-week course at the National Forensic Academy in Knoxville, Tennessee, U.S.A. Only candidates who are already employed by a law-enforcement agency can apply for a position. Three sessions are run each year: in January, May, and September.

Longest running body farm The "Body Farm," Knoxville, Tennessee, U.S.A., was founded in 1971. It is a 3-acre (1.2-ha) plot of land where human bodies are allowed to decompose, under a variety of conditions, in order for scientists to study how the decay happens.

★**Largest database of the human skeleton** FORDISC—or FORensic DISCrimination—is the world's most complete database relating to the human skeleton. It was established as part of the research undertaken at the University of Tennessee's "Body Farm," and allows data obtained from decomposing bodies to be analyzed by forensic anthropologists. As a result, it

X-REF

• Check out more cutting-edge science on page 269.

• Wild about weaponry? Then turn back to page 245.

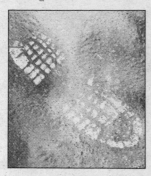

is now possible to calculate the size, height, and possibly sex and age of a victim from a single bone.

★ **Most common cause of homicide** Death by "penetrating trauma"—i.e., by stabbing or shooting—is the most common cause of murder.

★ **People most likely to commit murder** According to the U.S. Department of Justice, the people most likely to commit murder are males aged 17–30 years. Almost 90% of murders are committed by young males—in 74.6% of cases, killing another young male.

★ **LARGEST BRAIN BANK** The Harvard Brain Tissue Resource Center at the McLean Hospital in Belmont, Massachusetts, U.S.A., holds 3,000 brains, which are redistributed internationally for research. The bank has stored over 6,000 specimens since it opened in 1978, and each year typically receives 30 "healthy" brains and 240 diseased brains from patients who have suffered from neurodegenerative diseases and neuropsychiatric disorders.

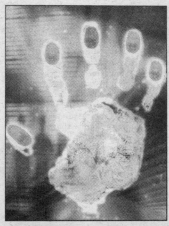

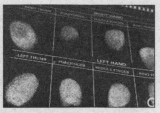

FIRST SYSTEM OF FINGERPRINTS
The earliest effective system of identification by fingerprints—the science of dactylography—was instituted in 1896 by Edward Henry (UK), an inspector-general of police in British India, who eventually became commissioner of the Metropolitan Police in London, UK.

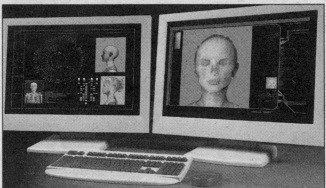

★ **FIRST USE OF FORENSIC FACIAL RECOGNITION** Modern forensic anthropology arguably began with the work of Wilton M. Krogman (U.S.A.), who popularized the use of facial reconstructions in forensic criminal investigations. By mapping tissue of varying thicknesses to cranial (skull) remains, Krogman could build a clay model closely resembling the deceased. His 1939 work *Guide to the Identification of Human Skeletal Material* helped found the discipline.

Today, computer-generated reconstructions (see above) continue the tradition.

☆ **MOST CRIMINALS IDENTIFIED FROM ONE ARTIST'S COMPOSITES** Since 1982, 523 criminals have been positively identified in Texas, U.S.A., as a result of the detailed composites drawn by forensic artist Lois Gibson (U.S.A., left). Shown above center is an "age-progression" sketch that she created based on a photo of a suspected murderer (above left) as a younger man, which helped lead to his capture. Above right, the criminal is shown in later life.

MORE FORENSIC FIRSTS

• In January 2000, scientists revealed that they had extracted DNA from a bone belonging to a 60,000-year-old ancestor of modern humans, thereby setting a record for the **oldest extracted human DNA**.

• The ★ **first use of DNA profiling to secure a conviction** involved a case against Robert Melias (UK), who was found guilty of rape on November 13, 1988, by DNA evidence.

• Gary Dotson (U.S.A.) was accused of raping Cathleen Crowell (UK), found guilty in July 1979, and sentenced to 25–50 years for rape and the same again for aggravated kidnapping. In 1988, DNA tests (not previously available) were conducted, proving that Dotson was innocent. He was exonerated on August 14, 1988, having served eight years, in a case that marked the ★ **first use of DNA profiling to overturn a conviction**.

• The ★ **first use of fingerprints from a postmortem for a conviction** occurred in 1978. Police used black magnetic powder to lift fingerprints from the left ankle of a deceased female suspected of being assaulted in North Miami Beach, Florida, U.S.A. The prints were matched to those of Stephen William Beattie (U.S.A.), who was found guilty on the basis of the fingerprint evidence and given three consecutive death sentences on February 1, 1979.

★ **OBJECT MOST FREQUENTLY FOUND AT A CRIME SCENE** According to the National Forensic Academy, the object most commonly found at a crime scene is a cigarette butt. However, it has been estimated that up to 30% of butts recovered are left by police attending the scene!

SPACE TECHNOLOGY

★ **FIRST FEMALE SPACE TOURIST** Anousheh Ansari (Iran) became the first female space tourist on September 18, 2006, when the *Soyuz TMA-9* capsule blasted off for a 10-day visit to the *International Space Station*. Businesswoman Ansari has had a lifelong fascination with space and is thought to have paid $20 million for the experience.

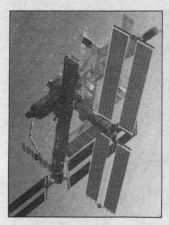

☆ **MOST REMOTE MAN-MADE OBJECT** *Voyager 1,* launched from Cape Canaveral, Florida, U.S.A., on September 5, 1977, is the farthest man-made object from Earth. On February 17, 1998, it surpassed the slower *Pioneer 10,* which was launched on March 2, 1972. As of August 2007, *Voyager 1* is more than 9.61 billion miles (15.47 billion km) from the Sun. (See box at bottom of page for more *Voyager 1* facts.)

Largest room in space The largest single habitable volume lifted into space was the NASA space station *Skylab,* which was launched in May 1973. Its main body consisted of a converted third-stage booster from a Saturn V rocket launcher. This cylindrical space station had internal dimensions of 48 ft. 1.2 in. (14.66 m) long by 22 ft. (6.70 m) in diameter, giving a habitable volume of 10,426 ft.³ (295.23 m³).

☆ **Longest time survived on Mars by a Rover** The twin Mars Exploration Rovers *Spirit* and *Opportunity* touched down successfully on Mars on January 4 and 25, 2004, respectively. Since then, they have each traveled across the Martian surface, taking scientific images and measurements. As of March 2007, both Rovers are still operational. In February 2007, the *Opportunity* Rover had traveled a total of 32,808 ft. (10,000 m) across the surface—some six times the distance for which it was originally designed.

Greatest spacecraft collision On June 25, 1997, an unmanned supply vehicle weighing 15,000 lb. (7 metric tons) collided with the Russian *Mir* space station. *Mir*'s Vasily Tsibliev and Alexander Lazutkin had to work quickly to seal a breach in the hull of *Mir*'s *Spektr* module, while astronaut Michael Foale prepared *Mir*'s *Soyuz* capsule for a possible evacuation. Loss

---

***VOYAGER 1:* ITS ONGOING MISSION . . .**

Voyager 1 is now in the region of the solar system known as the heliosheath—where the sun's influence begins to wane. The spacecraft, traveling at around 1 million miles per day (1,000 km per minute), is expected to pass beyond the heliosheath within the next 10 years and become the first man-made object to leave the solar system.

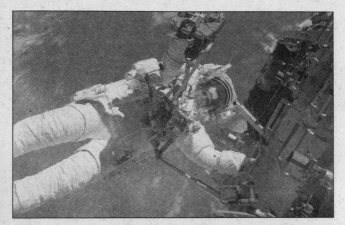

☆ **LARGEST SPACE STATION** The *International Space Station* (ISS) has been under construction since its first component, the Zarya module, was launched in 1998. The latest element to be added was the P5 truss, on December 12, 2006, bringing the total mass of the ISS to 471,442 lb. (213,843 kg). Pictured is Christer Fuglesang (Sweden), the first and only Swedish astronaut, during a space walk on December 14, 2006.

of life was avoided, but the station was left low on power and oxygen and temporarily tumbling out of control.

★ **Most powerful camera to leave earth orbit** The High Resolution Imaging Science Experiment (HiRiSE) is a camera on NASA's Mars Reconnaissance Orbiter (MRO). It is capable of taking digital images of the planet measuring 40,000 × 20,000 pixels. From its orbit 158–200 miles (255–320 km) above Mars, it can take images of the landscape showing details as small as 3 ft. (1 m) across. MRO launched on August 12, 2005, and arrived in orbit on March 10, 2006.

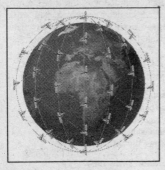

★ **LARGEST PRIVATE SATELLITE CONSTELLATION** A fleet of 66 satellites in cross-linked low-Earth orbits (illustrated left) is privately owned and operated by Iridium Satellite LLC (U.S.A.). The satellite fleet, which orbits at an altitude of 485 miles (780 km), provides global communication coverage, allowing the use of satellite telephones—and various handheld devices—anywhere on Earth, even at the poles and in the middle of the oceans.

FASTEST EARTH DEPARTURE SPEED The fastest speed at which a spacecraft has ever departed from Earth is 36,250 mph (58,338 km/h). It was achieved by NASA's *New Horizons* spacecraft, which was launched from Cape Canaveral, Florida, U.S.A., on January 19, 2006, beginning a nine-year flight to Pluto and its moons. Pluto—recently downgraded to the status of a dwarf planet—is yet to be surveyed by a spacecraft.

☆ **MOST REUSED SPACECRAFT** NASA's space shuttle *Discovery* was launched on December 10, 2006, at 1:47 UCT (Universal Coordinated Time), to make its 32nd trip into space. (Pictured is the launch from Kennedy Space Station in Florida.) Its mission (STS-116) was to deliver the *International Space Station*'s third port truss segment and to exchange crew. The flight also carried Sweden's first astronaut, Christer Fuglesang (see page 284). It was the first night flight for NASA in four years. *Discovery* has been in operation since 1984.

★FIRST SUCCESSFUL SOLAR SAIL DEPLOYMENT In August 2004, the Japanese space agency JAXA launched a rocket that successfully deployed two prototype solar sails in space at altitudes of 75 miles (122 km) and 105 miles (169 km) above the Earth. Solar sails are a potential new means of providing propulsion for spacecraft, using the pressure of sunlight on extremely thin reflective membranes (artist's impression left).

CONSUMER TECHNOLOGY

★Smallest TV tuner box In October 2005, Compro Technology announced the launch of the VideoMate U900, a full-function USB 2.0 TV box shorter in length than a credit card. Despite its size of just 2.9 × 2.1 × 0.5 in. (7.6 × 5.4 × 1.4 cm), it allows a PC to be used for watching TV, recording in MPEG1, 2, and 4 formats, and video/audio capture via its USB port.

Largest DMB TV screen With its 10-in. (25.4-cm) screen, the Samsung R7 is the world's largest digital multimedia broadcasting (DMB) television. DMB is the system used to access TV and high-quality CD sound on mobile devices such as cell phones and laptops—effectively, mobile digital television. The R7 has an aspect ratio of 16:9.

Most TV sets The country with the most televisions is China, which had an estimated 400 million sets in 1997.

Highest definition screen on a TV wristwatch With 130,338 pixels, the sharpest picture achieved on a wearable television screen is the NHJ TV Wristwatch. The 1.5-in. (3.8-cm) color

☆HIGHEST RESOLUTION CELLULAR PHONE CAMERA In March 2006, Samsung unveiled the SCH-B600, the cellular phone with the highest resolution camera, at 10 megapixels—higher than many digital cameras. The LCD can reproduce 16 million colors, and users can also watch live TV through a satellite DMB (digital multimedia broadcasting) function.

★ SMALLEST CAMCORDER Sony's HandyCam DCR-PC55 is, across its longest length, just 3.8 in. (99 mm) and weighs 0.79 lb. (360 g).

TV screen relies on TFT (Thin Film Transistor) technology to deliver such a high-resolution picture and retails for around $200.

Smallest instant camera The Polaroid PopShot, the world's **first disposable instant camera,** measures 6.5 × 4.25 × 2.5 in. (16.51 × 10.79 × 6.35 cm) and weighs 9 oz. (255 g). The PopShot camera can take 10 4.4 × 2.5 in. (11.17 × 6.35 cm) color photographs and comes with a postage-free mailing envelope that makes for easy recycling.

★ Thinnest computer keyboard The eMark Super Mobile Keyboard manufactured by Kimura Metal (Japan) is a silicone-vinyl sheet between just 0.03 and 0.2 in. (1 and 5 mm) thick.

The keyboard is also spill-resistant and is so thin that it can be rolled up into a tube.

Fastest growing consumer entertainment product According to Understanding & Solutions, the DVD player is the fastest growing consumer electronics product in history. Since its launch in 1997, over 627 million units have been sold worldwide.

★ Most successful technology manufacturer Hewlett-Packard Co. (U.S.A.) enjoyed sales revenues of $94.08 billion and profits of $6.52 billion as of April 2007. The company has a workforce of around 156,000 people.

★ Deepest diving watch The deepest diving watch, the CX Swiss Military's 12,000-feet model, can function at 12,000 ft. (3,657 m; 2,000

☆ **SMALLEST MULTIMEDIA PLAYER** In August 2005, MPIO (UK) launched the MPIO-One, a 1.2-oz. (34-g) media player measuring just 1.2 × 2.1 in. (3.2 × 5.4 cm). It can play MPEG4, WMV, AVI, and Div-X video files (as well as MP3, WMA, and OGG audio files), and has a 1.04-in. (2.64-cm) OLED screen capable of displaying up to 26,000 colors.

★ **FASTEST HOVER SCOOTER** In January 2006, Hammacher Schlemmer & Company, Inc. (U.S.A.) announced the release of the Levitating Hover Scooter. It hovers approximately 4 in. (10 cm) above the ground and has a top speed of 15 mph (24 km/h). Riders control their direction by transferring their weight and modify the engine/fan speed by levers on the airboard's handlebars.

fathoms). It was made by Montres Charmex SA of Switzerland in 2006. The mechanical chronograph is a limited edition of only 365 pieces.

★ **Most expensive watch** The Super Ice Cube by Chopard, Switzerland, retailed at $1,130,620 as of 2005. It has 66.16 carats of diamonds, which includes 288 trapeze cut diamonds, 16 center stones, and 1,897 brilliant cut diamonds.

★ **MOST POWERFUL SUBWOOFER** The most powerful home audio subwoofer is Eminent Technology's Model 17. It can efficiently reach frequencies as low as 1 hertz, compared with the usual lowest frequencies of around 20 hertz for regular subwoofers. The Model 17 has to be professionally fitted in an attic or basement, which effectively becomes a giant speaker.

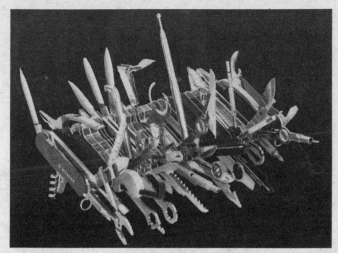

★ **MOST FUNCTIONS ON A PENKNIFE** The "Giant Knife Version 1.0" is made by Wenger, the makers of the Swiss Army Knife. It weighs 2 lb. 11 oz. (0.95 kg), is 8.75 in. (22.22 cm) long, and features 85 tools—including a laser pointer, flashlight, whistle, and cigar cutter. It retails for €900 ($1,200) through the company.

RING THE CHANGES...

• Korean technology giant Samsung Electronics has developed a combination portable TV/cellular phone unit measuring $3.6 \times 2 \times 1.4$ in. $(9.2 \times 5.1 \times 3.6$ cm), the **smallest cellular phone TV.** The SCH-M220 provides up to 200 minutes of continuous TV viewing time.

• Currently, the world's ☆ **thinnest cellular phone** is the Samsung Ultra Edition II (right), just 0.2 in. (5.9 mm) thick. The handset has a 3-megapixel camera and 11 hours of music play time.

• The ☆ **most expensive cellular phone** was designed by GoldVish of Geneva, Switzerland, and was sold for €1,000,000 ($1,320,270) at the Millionaire Fair in Cannes, France, on September 2, 2006.

• Samsung's (Korea) Ultra Edition 8.4 is the world's ★ **thinnest 3G cellular phone,** featuring a 2-megapixel camera mounted in a body just 0.3 in. (8.4 mm) thick.

• The **most powerful cellular phone gun** is a .22 caliber pistol, disguised as a cell phone, which can fire a (close-range) lethal round of four bullets when numbers 5, 6, 7, 8 are pressed in quick succession.

世界最大 103v型

☆ **LARGEST PLASMA SCREEN** A prototype of Panasonic's 103-in. plasma display, measuring over 8 ft. 6 in. (2.6 m) in width, was revealed at the 2006 International Consumer Electronics Show in Las Vegas, Nevada, U.S.A., on January 5–8, 2006. It retails at around $70,000.

ROBOTS

★**Oldest android design** There is sufficient evidence to suggest that Leonardo da Vinci (Italy) planned and sketched out a humanoid robot design around 1495. Although his sketches of the finished model have never been found, other da Vinci drawings show a mechanical knight with anatomically correct joints operated by cables and pulleys. A full-sized working replica was built by roboticist Mark Rosheim (U.S.A.) in the late 1990s to show how the "Robot Knight" worked.

★**SMALLEST BIPEDAL HUMANOID ROBOT** Omnibot2007 i-SOBOT measures 6.5 in. (165 mm) high and is able to walk, stand up from a lying-down position, and balance on one foot. It was manufactured by Takara Tomy (Japan) and demonstrated at the Toy Forum 2007 on January 23 in Tokyo, Japan.

Science & Technology

★FIRST TRUE ANDROID AVATAR Geminoid HI-1 (above left) is a humanoid doppelgänger built by Hiroshi Ishiguro (Japan). Its innards are covered with a silicone mold of Ishiguro himself, and it can be used as his avatar—that is, using motion-capture and voice-relay systems, Ishiguro can have his robot double duplicate his movements remotely, allowing him to teach a class without needing to be there in person. Pressurized air and tiny motors are used to give Geminoid micromovements such as blinking and fidgeting, and the chest even moves up and down as he "breathes."

Pictured above right is Ishiguro's female robot Actroid Repliee demonstrating its abilities at the Prototype Robot Exhibition in Aichi, Japan, on June 9, 2005.

★**First robot reference** The word "robot" was introduced as a word by novelist and playwright Karel Čapek (Austria-Hungary, now Czech Republic, 1890–1938) in his play *R.U.R.* (*Rossum's Universal Robots*), which premiered in Prague in 1921. The play features "artificial people" built in a factory and designed to enjoy laborious work, and it explores the issue of whether or not such robots have rights. The word "robot" was suggested to Čapek by his brother Josef, and derives from the Czech word "robota," meaning slave labor.

Highest jumping robot Sandia National Laboratories, U.S.A., has developed "hopper" robots that use combustion-driven pistons to jump to heights of 30 ft. (9 m). They have potential applications in planetary exploration, where hoppers could be released by a probe to survey a landscape.

Fastest running humanoid robot ASIMO (Advanced Step in Innovative Mobility) has been developed and refined by Honda (Japan) since 2000. In December 2005, Honda announced that ASIMO had been improved in order to allow it to run at a speed of 3.7 mph (6 km/h).

☆**Largest robot competition** A total of 646 engineers, 466 robots, and 13 countries took part in the 2006 RoboGames (formerly the ROBOlympics) held in San Francisco, California, U.S.A. Events included soccer with reprogrammed AIBO robot dogs, robo sumo wrestling, bipedal racing, and musical artistry. The U.S.A. won 28 gold, 31 silver, and 21 bronze medals.

★FIRST ROBOT-STAFFED RESTAURANT Robot Kitchen in Hong Kong, China, opened in July 2006. It has two robot staff members capable of taking orders from customers and delivering their meals to them. A third robot is being constructed that should be able to perform simple culinary tasks, such as preparing omelettes and flipping burgers.

ROBOT HISTORY

- **350 BC** Greek mathematician Archytas of Tarentum builds a steam-driven mechanical bird.

- **1738** Jacques de Vaucanson (France) builds three lifelike automata.

- **1801** Joseph Jacquard (France) builds an automated loom that is controlled by punch cards.

- **1921** Karel Čapek (Austria-Hungary) introduces the word "robot" in his play *R.U.R.* (*Rossum's Universal Robots*).

- **1962** First robotic industrial arm introduced.

- **1966** ELIZA, the first artificial-intelligence program, created.

- **1989** "Genghis," the first walking robot, developed at the Massachusetts Institute of Technology (MIT), U.S.A.

- **1999** Sony releases the AIBO robotic pet dog.

- **2000** Honda unveils ASIMO, the humanoid robot.

- **2001** Cyberknife, a robotic surgeon, is cleared for use in American hospitals.

- **2005** Researchers at Cornell University, U.S.A., build a self-replicating robot.

Longest distance between patient and surgeon Madeleine Schaal (France) had her gallbladder removed by a robot in an operating room in Strasbourg, France, while her surgeons—Jacques Marescaux (France) and Michel Gagner (U.S.A.)—remotely operated the ZEUS robotic surgical arms on a secured fiber-optic line from New York, U.S.A., a total distance of 3,866 miles (6,222 km) away, on September 7, 2001. The operation lasted 55 minutes and Madeleine went home after 48 hours.

★**Most advanced medical minirobot** In March 2007, researchers from Japan's Ritsumeikan University unveiled a prototype robot (pictured right) measuring just 0.78 in. (2 cm) long and 0.39 in. (1 cm) wide, with a mass of only 0.17 oz. (5 g). It is designed to be implanted into a person, after which it can travel inside the body equipped with various tools such as arms, a camera, and a device to deliver medication to specific parts of the body. Previous medical mini-robots only carried cameras.

Cheapest robot Walkman, a 5-in.-tall (12.7-cm) robot, was built from the remains of a Sony Walkman for just $1.75 at the Los Alamos National Laboratory in New Mexico, U.S.A., in 1996. In tests, the insect-like "junkbot," as such creations are called, struggled to get free when its legs were held—without being programmed to do so and without making the same movement twice.

★**FIRST ROBOT SOMMELIER** NEC System Technologies and Mie University, Japan, have developed a robot capable of tasting wine and recognizing the differences between a few dozen varieties. To "taste," the "winebot" fires an infrared beam through the wine and analyzes the various wavelengths of light that are absorbed. A built-in speaker is used to announce the variety of wine selected.

★MOST DEGREES OF FREEDOM ON A ROBOT ARM In December 2006, OC Robotics (UK) announced it had designed and built a snake-like robot arm with 27 degrees of freedom. It is designed to reach inside very restrictive enclosed spaces during the construction of large aircraft.

Most gender-aware robot The Intelligent Earth company has developed visual gender-recognition software for its robotic head *Doki*. Based on visual data alone, it can recognize the gender of women with an accuracy of 100%, and that of men with an accuracy of 96%.

Largest robot dog Roboscience's RS-01 Robodog measures 32 × 26 × 14 in. (82 × 67 × 37 cm) and is strong enough to lift a five-year-old child.

INTERNET

★Largest video-sharing service According to a survey by the *Wall Street Journal,* published in August 2006, the website YouTube.com contained some 6.1 million uploaded video clips, totaling around 45 terabytes of data. The video clips had been viewed a total of 1.73 billion times. *See page 297 for the most viewed viral videos.*

★Greatest broadband penetration According to Point Topic Ltd., the U.S.A. has the greatest broadband coverage with 40,876,000 users. The **highest broadband coverage per capita,** however, is in South Korea, where 24.66 per 100 people have access.

☆Most internet users On February 28, 2006, technology market research company eTForecasts released figures revealing that the U.S.A. had

668 users per 1,000 people, the world's highest rate of internet use per capita.

Country with the most internet hosts The U.S.A. has an incredible 195,138,696 web hosts, which works out at one for every 65 people.

★ Most virtual friends Model Tila Tequila (U.S.A.) had 1.6 million virtual friends on the social networking website MySpace as of December 2006. Ms. Nguyen (her real surname) has used her online fame to establish careers in advertising, acting, and singing.

☆ Largest wireless internet provider Since its launch by NTT DoCoMo in February 1999, i-Mode—a Japanese service specifically aimed at cell-phone users—had gained 45,687,117 subscribers as of January 2006.

☆ Largest online game economy According to research by Prof. Edward Castronova at Indiana University, U.S.A., in 2005, the Kingdom of Norrath in the game *Everquest* has a gross national product (GNP) per capita of

☆ MOST POPULAR ONLINE NEWS SEARCHES According to Google, the top online news searches of 2006 were:
1. Paris Hilton (U.S.A., above left)
2. Orlando Bloom (UK, above right)
3. Cancer
4. Podcasting
5. Hurricane Katrina
6. Bankruptcy
7. Martina Hingis (Switzerland)
8. Autism
9. 2006 NFL draft
10. *Celebrity Big Brother 2006*

Overall, the ☆ **most popular search term** on Google for 2006 was "bebo," the social networking site.

★ LARGEST INTERACTIVE WORLD MAP Earth Viewer was acquired by Google in 2004. Relaunched as Google Earth in 2005, it is a virtual 3-D globe of the Earth consisting of satellite data that can be browsed by home internet users. Most of the world's land area is covered at a 49 ft. (15 m) resolution, with many areas having resolutions as high as 5.9 in. (15 cm). The London, UK, offices of Guinness World Records are pictured left.

$2,266. This figure was based on a market-exchange rate between virtual Norrath gold coins sold at an online auction.

The GNP category has since been replaced by that of gross national income (GNI). Based on the latest available figures from the World Bank, for 2005, this would make Norrath the world's 125th largest economy, coming after the actual economy of Swaziland, which had a GNI per capita of $2,280.

The **most expensive virtual object** was also purchased in the game *Project Entropia. To find out the full story, turn to page 301.*

★ Longest live cheese webcam broadcast A 44-lb. (20-kg) piece of cheddar cheese maturing in Somerset, UK, has been broadcast live on a webcam continuously since January 1, 2007. As of March 2007, more than 525,000 people have logged on to cheddarvision.tv to watch the cheese gradually mature and change color. It is expected to take 12 months to mature fully, after which it will be auctioned off for charity.

First internet browser Released on April 22, 1993, NCSA Mosaic was the world's first internet browser. It was created by researchers at the National Center for Supercomputing Applications of the University of Illinois, Urbana-Champaign, Illinois, U.S.A., and was designed to allow people to retrieve data from computer networks.

First cyberclinic In March 1997, Dr. Kimberly Young (U.S.A.) established the Center for On-Line Addiction, the world's first psychiatric cyberclinic for internet addicts and those with related mental-health problems.

DID YOU KNOW?

Google Earth works by superimposing aerial satellite imagery and geographic information systems (GIS) onto a 3-D globe. Visit earth.google.com to download the software. Try to find your house. Even see the view from the peak of Everest.

★ **MOST SUCCESSFUL INTERNET TRADE** On July 12, 2005, Canadian internet blogger Kyle MacDonald traded a red paper clip for a pen online. Over the next 12 months, he traded the pen for more and more valuable items until, on July 12, 2006, he swapped a short role in a movie for a house in Kipling, Saskatchewan, Canada.

eBAY STATS

• The ★ **largest online auction house** is eBay, which had more than 210 million worldwide registered users as of October 2006, trading items worth $12.6 billion.

• Pierre Omidyar (France) launched eBay on September 4, 1995, from the U.S.A. The ★ **first eBay transaction** was made in the same month, when Omidyar sold a broken laser pointer for $14.83.

• Internet monitoring company Envisional looked at 100 companies from the FTSE-100 index and analyzed the prominence of those companies' names on a number of web pages, news sites and bulletin boards. As of April 2005, eBay was found to be the ★ **most popular online brand**.

• On December 27, 2002, Bridgeville, California, U.S.A., *almost* became the first town sold on eBay when a closing bid of $1.8 million was made. Measuring 82 acres, the town included 10 houses, four cabins, a post office and a ZIP code. The anonymous bidder backed out of the deal when he saw the work involved, and the town—which was home to 25 people—was eventually sold to Bruce Krall (U.S.A.) for $700,000 in 2003.

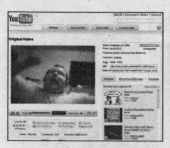

★ MOST POPULAR VIRAL VIDEO The term "viral video" refers to a video clip that is passed from one internet user to another; the clip effectively "spreads" in this way, much like a virus does. In November 2002, Ghyslain Raza (Canada, above right) filmed himself performing fighting moves with a metal golf-ball retriever, mimicking the fighting style of Darth Maul from the *Star Wars* movie *The Phantom Menace* (U.S.A., 1999). Months later, the clip was discovered and uploaded to the internet. According to The Viral Factory (UK/U.S.A.) marketing agency, over 900 million internet users had seen the video as of November 2006.

In second place was Gary Brolsma (U.S.A., above left), whose video of himself miming to the pop song "Dragostea din tei" (aka "Numa Numa") by O-Zone (Moldova) had been watched 700 million times.

★ GREATEST ONLINE BINGO WIN On April 10, 2006, Jo Collins (UK, above right) won £162,701 ($283,099) playing bingo on galabingo.co.uk. The mother-of-three, who is a driver for a special needs school and also a "Meals on Wheels" volunteer, had only been playing the game for five days before her win. She is pictured with model Nancy Sorrell, wife of British TV comedian Vic Reeves (both UK).

★**LARGEST ENCYCLOPEDIA** Launched on January 15, 2001, Wikipedia was founded by Jimmy Wales (pictured) and Larry Sanger (both U.S.A.) as a free online encyclopedia that users can add to and edit. As of March 1, 2007, it contained 6,628,781 articles in total, across all 250 versions, and 1,663,419 articles in English. Around 5,000 articles are added each day.

VIDEO GAMES

★**Youngest professional video gamer** Born on May 6, 1998, "Lil Poison" (U.S.A., aka Victor De Leon III) picked up a Dreamcast Controller at the age of two to play *NBA 2K*. He entered his first competition—a *Halo* tournament in his native New York—aged four, and competed in the Major League Games a year later.

By the age of seven, Lil Poison had won $2,000 in gaming tournaments—often competing against adult players—making him the ★**youngest video gamer to win a cash prize.**

Despite his tender years, Lil Poison has signed an exclusive deal with gaming tournament organizers Major League Gaming, who arrange endorsement deals for gamers.

★ **BEST-SELLING Wii GAME** Wii launch title *Wii Sports,* which came bundled with the console in most territories around the world, has sold over 2.89 million copies since September 2006.

★ **Highest video game score ever** J. C. Padilla (U.S.A.) scored 2,181,619,994,299,256,480 points playing *GigaWings2* for the Sega Dreamcast gaming console (Score Attack Mode—Stage 2) on May 17, 2004.

In contrast, the world record on Cinematronic's *Space Wars,* created in 1977, was only 19 points, a record that still stands.

★ **First gamer to score 1 billion points** On January 15, 1984, at the end of a 44-hour 45-minute marathon game of *Nibbler* at Twin Galaxies,

★ CLASSIC ARCADE HIGH SCORES* ★

GAME	SCORE	PLAYER	FROM	DATE
★ *1942*	13,360,960	Martin Bedard	Canada	Nov. 19, 2006
★ *Asteroids Deluxe (Tournament)*	167,790	Donavan Stepp	U.S.A.	Aug. 22, 2004
★ *Black Widow*	930,100	James Vollandt	U.S.A.	May 1, 1984
★ *Burgertime*	9,000,000	Bryan L. Wagner	U.S.A.	Jun. 2, 2006
★ *Dance Dance Revolution*	652,095,760	Takeo Ueki	Japan	May 8, 2003
★ *Discs of Tron*	418,200	David Bagenski	U.S.A.	Jun. 28, 1986
★ *Donkey Kong*	1,049,100	Steve Wiebe	U.S.A.	Mar. 23, 2007
★ *Donkey Kong 3*	473,400	Dwayne Richard	Canada	Oct. 22, 2005
★ *Gyruss (Tournament)*	1,306,100	Richard W. Marsh	U.S.A.	Jun. 22, 2004
★ *Hard Drivin'*	219,758	David Nelson	U.S.A.	May 13, 2006
★ *Star Castle*	9,833,940	Bob Mines	U.S.A.	Sep. 14, 1984
★ *Mario Bros.*	3,481,550	Perry Rodgers	U.S.A.	Jul. 2, 1985
★ *Top Skater (Hard/Expert)*	836,733	Tai Kunag Neng	Malaysia	Jul. 13, 2002
★ *Warlords*	911,875	Peter Skahill	U.S.A.	Aug. 29, 1982
★ *Sea Wolf*	10,800	Peter Skerritt Jr.	U.S.A.	Jun. 3, 2001
★ *Space Invaders Deluxe*	425,230	Matt Brass	U.S.A.	Sep. 16, 1982
★ *Stargate*	197,500	Bill Jones	U.S.A.	Mar. 24, 2005
★ *Star Trek*	123,467,525	Darren Harris	U.S.A.	Jul. 8, 1985
★ *Time Crisis II (Singles)*	1,712,400	Dennis Blechner	Germany	May 3, 2001
★ *Time Pilot (Tournament)*	1,092,800	Kelly R. Flewin	Canada	Nov. 19, 2005

Twenty of the greatest video-game scores of all time, as selected by Twin Galaxies

Ottunnwa, Iowa, U.S.A., Tim McVey (U.S.A.) had amassed an incredible 1,000,042,270 points.

The feat was made all the more remarkable as McVey had used just one quarter to achieve his record-breaking score.

★**First video game world champion** Ben Gold (U.S.A.) became the first video game world champion when he won the North American Video Game Olympics on January 8–9, 1983. The event was later seen on ABC TV's *That's Incredible.*

★**Longest video game marathon** Competitors in the Twin Galaxies' Iron Man Contest were offered a share of a $10,000 prize if they could complete 100 hours of gaming using just one quarter. James Vollandt (U.S.A.) held out the longest, with a time of 67 hr. 30 min. The contest was staged from July 5 to 8, 1983, at Johnny Zee's Family Fun Center, in Victoria, British Columbia, Canada.

Because of the attendant health risks, Twin Galaxies now sanctions very few marathons of this nature.

Most ported computer game *Tetris,* created by Alexey Pajitnov (USSR) in 1985, has been ported (translated) to more than 70 different computer-game platforms, including, most recently, the XBox and numerous cell phones.

DID YOU KNOW?

Dennis "Thresh" Fong (U.S.A., b. 1977) is regarded as the ★ **first professional gamer in history.** He won every tournament he attended over a five-year period and has earned the nickname "the Michael Jordan of gaming."

★ BEST-SELLING STAND-ALONE Wii GAME The biggest-selling stand-alone Wii title is *The Legend of Zelda: Twilight Princess,* which has sold over 1.87 million copies to date. In its first few weeks of launch, three copies of the game were sold for every four Wii purchases.

★ Most participants in a video game league in a single season
World Cyber Games (WCG) reported that there were 1.3 million contestants in the video game league for the 2006 championships. A total of 700 players, representing 70 countries, advanced to the grand final in Monza, Italy. Korea was the overall league winner, with two gold medals, one silver, and one bronze.

★ BEST-SELLING PLAYSTATION 3 GAME *Resistance: Fall of Man,* a sci-fi first-person shooter developed by Insomniac Games (U.S.A.) and released in November 2006, had sold 1.02 million copies as of March 2007. The game was hailed as the best of the launch titles for the PS3, winning seven IGN awards in 2006 in the PS3 category (Game of the Year, Best First-Person Shooter, Best Graphics, Best Original Score, Best Sound, Best Online Multiplayer, Most Innovative Design).

GUINNESS WORLD RECORDS GAMER'S EDITION 2008

Every major new game reviewed

GUINNESS WORLD RECORDS 2008: GAMER'S EDITION Video game fans—look out for the forthcoming Guinness World Records book dedicated entirely to gaming! We've teamed up with record-breaking referees **Twin Galaxies** to create the ultimate guide to **gaming records, facts and figures,** from the highest earners and best selling games to the highest-spec consoles and most powerful game engines. You'll also find all the **latest news and reviews** for all the top games. GWR 2008: Gamer's Edition—on sale **February 2008!**

The total prize money on offer at the World Cyber Games 2006 championships was $462,000.

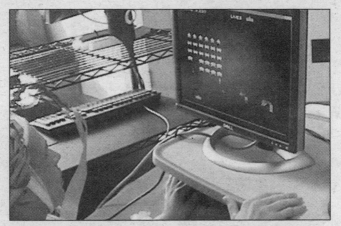

★ **HIGHEST MIND-CONTROL SCORE ON *SPACE INVADERS*** Scientists at
Washington University, St. Louis, U.S.A., have devised a hands-free
system of playing *Space Invaders* using brainpower alone. As part of
studies into brain activity, researchers attached an
electrocorticographic (ECoG) grid to the brain of a teenager suffering
from epilepsy. Engineers then adapted Atari software to react to stimuli
transmitted through this grid, so that the unnamed volunteer could
control an on-screen cursor simply by imagining the movements he
would have to make to do so.

The subject reached the third screen of the game, amassing 5,000
points. This is the highest *Space Invaders* score achieved using brain
power alone.

★ **Largest orchestra for a computer game** The PlayStation2 game
Onimusha (2001) features a sound track by Mamoura Samuragoch
(Japan)—dubbed the "Digital Age Beethoven"—that required 203 players
(the 150-piece New Japan Philharmonic Orchestra and 53 traditional Japanese instrumentalists and vocalists).

ARTS & MEDIA

CONTENTS

MOVIE STARS

☆ **Most public appearances made by a film star in 12 hours** The greatest number of public appearances by a film star at different cities in 12 hours promoting the same film is five by Jürgen Vogel and Daniel Brühl (both Germany). They walked the red carpet, signed autographs and introduced the film *Ein Freund von mir* (Germany, 2006) at cinemas in Munich, Berlin, Hamburg, Düsseldorf and Cologne, Germany, on October 22, 2006. They were accompanied by the film's director, Sebastian Schipper (Germany).

★ **First brothers to receive Best Actor Oscar nominations** River Phoenix (U.S.A., August 23, 1970—October 31, 1993) received an American Academy Award nomination for Best Actor—at the age of 17—for his role in Sidney Lumet's (U.S.A.) *Running on Empty* (U.S.A., 1988); his brother Joaquin (U.S.A., b. October 28, 1974) received his nomination for *Walk the Line* (U.S.A., 2005). Neither brother went on to win the coveted statue.

☆ **Highest basic salary for an actor** Basic salaries for a leading actor appeared to have peaked in 2000/2001 at $30 million, last earned by Arnold "Terminator" Schwarzenegger (U.S.A.) for his starring role in *Terminator 3: Rise of the Machines* (U.S.A., 2003), and Brad Pitt (U.S.A.) for *Ocean's Eleven* (U.S.A., 2001).

The **highest paid actor ever** is Bruce Willis (U.S.A.), who received $100 million for his role in *The Sixth Sense* (U.S.A., 1999) through his salary and a percentage of the film's receipts and video takings.

☆ **Highest annual earnings by an actress** Between June 2005 and June 2006, Jodie Foster (U.S.A.) earned $27 million, thanks to *Flightplan* (U.S.A., 2005) and *Inside Man* (U.S.A., 2006). Her next movie, *The Brave One* (U.S.A., 2007), will reportedly earn her $15 million.

★ **MOST CONSECUTIVE BEST ACTOR OSCAR WINS** Tom Hanks (U.S.A.) won Best Actor in a Leading Role in two consecutive years, for *Philadelphia* (U.S.A., 1993) and *Forrest Gump* (U.S.A., 1994)—a record he shares with Spencer Tracy (U.S.A.), who won Best Actor Oscars for *Captains Courageous* (U.S.A., 1937) and *Boys Town* (U.S.A., 1938).

☆ **MOST POWERFUL ACTRESSES** According to the Forbes *100 Celebrity List,* Jennifer Aniston (U.S.A., left) and Angelina Jolie (U.S.A., right) are the world's most powerful actresses, with both sharing the 35th position in the top 100. The list is based on earnings from June 2005 to June 2006, web hits, press clippings, mentions on Factiva and appearances on the cover of 26 major consumer magazines.

★ **Lowest aggregate age for Best Actor and Best Actress Oscar nominees** The lowest aggregate age for Best Actor and Best Actress Oscar nominees is 38 years 148 days for Jackie Cooper (U.S.A., b. September 15, 1922) and Norma Shearer (Canada, b. August 10, 1902), who were aged 9 years 56 days and 29 years 92 days respectively on November 10, 1931—the date of the fourth American Academy Awards (Oscar) ceremony.

★ **Most connected living actor** The University of Virginia's (U.S.A.) "Oracle of Bacon" is software—named after the actor Kevin Bacon (U.S.A.)—that maps the working relationship between 1,250,000 actors and actresses in the Internet Movie Database. According to the Oracle, the most connected living movie star—that is, the living person at the "Center of the Hollywood Universe"—is Christopher Lee (UK).

Lee is the ★ **most credited living movie actor,** with 244 acknowledged film and TV movie roles out of at least 358 screen credits. According to movie stuntman and historian Derek Ware (UK), Lee also holds the record for the ★ **most screen swordfights,** having duelled in 17 films with foils, swords, lightsabres, and billiard cues!

TRILOGIES

There were more movie trilogy final parts released in 2007 than in any other year. These were: *Spider-Man 3, Shrek the Third, Pirates of the Caribbean: At World's End, Ocean's Thirteen, The Bourne Ultimatum,* and *Rush Hour 3* (all U.S.A.).

☆**Shortest actor in a leading adult role** Indian actor Ajay Kumar, who performed in the lead role of his debut feature film, *Atbhutha Dweep* (India, 2005), measures 2 ft. 6 in. tall.

★**Most facial-motion-capture markers used by an actor at the same time** During the filming of *King Kong* (NZ/U.S.A., 2005), 132 motion-capture markers were applied to the face of Andy Serkis (UK) to help animators at Weta Digital in New Zealand record his facial expressions—actions which were then mirrored in the computer-generated character of the gorilla. Serkis spent two months studying gorillas at Regent's Park Zoo, London, UK, to assist his performance.

JOHNNY DEPP

As the flamboyant Captain Jack Sparrow, Johnny Depp (U.S.A.) has become the world's favorite pirate. We caught up with him on the set of *At World's End*, the third instalment of the *Pirates of the Caribbean* (U.S.A.) series, and asked him what he enjoyed most about filming the record-breaking trilogy: Relaxing...hanging with family and friends on my boat in The Bahamas.

The entire cast seem to be having a blast. Are there likely to be any more Pirates adventures? Audiences seem to love it so we might go beyond the three. We'll see how the third one turns out!

Jack Sparrow's become an iconic figure—why is he such a popular character? It's beyond me how such a character has taken root in people's hearts. It's an enormous surprise because, though I had pretty solid ideas about who he was and what he should be like, there were a number of people, including the better-dressed people at Disney, who thought I was nuts.

You seem drawn to pirates, whether as author J. M. Barrie in *Finding Neverland* or as Jack. Have you always had secret dreams of playing a pirate? Doesn't everybody? It seems to me that a lot of people would love to be totally irreverent and have total freedom. I've heard people saying they'd love to emulate Jack's total irreverence.

What about his trademark swagger? What inspired that? I spent lots of time in the sauna! I thought that Jack would be out on the seas for a long time exposed to the intense heat and the elements. Whenever you lock yourself in a very hot place it affects the way you move and you become uncomfortable in...erm...delicate places...so that's how the Jack Sparrow movement was born!

☆ **MOST POWERFUL ACTOR** Tom Cruise (U.S.A.) once more leads *Forbes'* Hollywood power list, unseating Johnny Depp (U.S.A.). Cruise previously held this position five years ago and has regained his top spot thanks to his earnings from *War of the Worlds* (U.S.A., 2005), his high-profile relationship with Katie Holmes (U.S.A.), and the birth of their daughter, Suri.

☆ **HIGHEST GROSSING ACTOR AT THE BOX OFFICE** The highest grossing actor is Samuel L. Jackson (U.S.A.), whose 75 movies have grossed over $7.84 billion at the global box office.

The most Oscar-nominated actor is Jack Nicholson—he was acknowledged 12 times (and won three).

☆**HIGHEST AVERAGE BOX-OFFICE GROSS** By virtue of having starred only in the four blockbusting *Harry Potter* movies, Daniel Radcliffe and Emma Watson (both UK, above) have achieved a record average box-office gross per movie of $279.8 million each.

BOX-OFFICE BLOCKBUSTERS

HIGHEST . . .

★**Average movie gross for a screenwriter** The movies of Andrew Stanton (U.S.A.)—*Toy Story* (U.S.A., 1995), *Toy Story II* (U.S.A., 1999), *A Bug's Life* (U.S.A., 1998), *Monsters, Inc.* (U.S.A., 2001), and *Finding Nemo* (U.S.A., 2003)—have grossed an average of $239.2 million each.

★**Movie gross for a composer** The 51 movies scored to date by John Williams (U.S.A.) have grossed a total of $7.93 billion.
  The highest grossing movie scored by Williams was *Star Wars IV: A New Hope* (U.S.A., 1977) at more than $460 million, followed by *E.T. the Extra-Terrestrial* (U.S.A., 1982) at more than $435 million.

★**Average movie gross for a producer** Darla K. Anderson (U.S.A.), the producer of *A Bug's Life* (U.S.A., 1998), *Monsters, Inc.* (U.S.A., 2001), and *Cars* (U.S.A., 2006), averages nearly $221 million per movie.

★**Average film gross for a director (male)** George Lucas (U.S.A.) has directed only six movies in his career—from *THX 1138* (U.S.A., 1971) to *Star Wars: Episode III—Revenge of the Sith* (U.S.A., 2005)—but their success means that Lucas is the director with the highest average box-office gross, having made $283 million per movie.

☆ **HIGHEST GROSSING MOCKUMENTARY** As of November 19, 2006, *Borat: Cultural Learnings of America for Make Benefit Glorious Nation of Kazakhstan* (UK, 2006) recorded a gross of $157,470,996. Sacha Baron Cohen (UK), the star of the movie, is pictured.

★ **Film gross for a director (male)** The 23 major motion pictures directed by Steven Spielberg (U.S.A.)—from *Sugarland Express* (U.S.A., 1974) to *Munich* (U.S.A., 2005)—have grossed a total of $4.3 billion at the box office, making him the most successful movie director of all time, based on total international ticket gross.

Spielberg's average gross per movie is just short of $150 million.

Box-office movie gross The movie with the highest earnings is *Titanic* (U.S.A.), released on December 19, 1997. Written and directed by James

★ **HIGHEST GROSSING FEMALE DIRECTOR** In terms of sole directorship, the highest grossing female director is Nancy Meyers (U.S.A., pictured above), whose movie *What Women Want* (U.S.A., 2000) earned Paramount more than $182 million.

☆ **HIGHEST BOX OFFICE MOVIE GROSS (OPENING WEEKEND)** *Spider-Man 3* (U.S.A., 2007), the third movie in the Spider-Man series, took $151.1 million at the U.S. box office during the opening weekend of May 4–6, 2007. See the table below for more *Spider-Man* records.

Cameron (Canada), it became the first movie ever to take $1 billion at the international box office, with a total gross of $1,834,165,466.

☆ **Movie gross for an animation** *Shrek 2* (U.S.A., 2004), made by DreamWorks, is the highest grossing animation ever. It has taken $920.6 million worldwide at the box office since opening on May 19, 2004.

★ **Movie gross for a producer** Kathleen Kennedy (U.S.A.), the producer behind movie series such as *Jurassic Park, Indiana Jones, Back to the Future,* and *Gremlins,* has grossed over $4.8 billion—an average of $92.3 million per movie.

☆ **Highest grossing Memorial Day weekend** *Pirates of the Caribbean: At World's End* (U.S.A., 2007), starring Johnny Depp (see page 309),

★ SPIDER-MAN 3 BOX-OFFICE BONANZA ★

☆ Highest box-office film gross—opening weekend	$151.1 million
☆ Highest box-office film gross—opening day	$59.8 million
☆ Highest box-office film gross—single day (non-opening)	$51,336,732
☆ Highest box-office film gross (international)—opening weekend	$230,544,376
☆ Fastest $100 million box-office film gross	Less than two days ($38,576 every minute)
☆ Widest film release opening day (single country)	4,252 cinemas (over 10,000 screens)

★ **MOST SUCCESSFUL BOND MOVIE** As of March 2007, *Casino Royale* (UK, 2006)—the latest installment in the James Bond series—had grossed $587,607,.184 worldwide. Daniel Craig (UK, pictured)—initially considered a controversial choice for the role—went on to become the first Bond actor to receive a best actor BAFTA nomination.

took $141.2 million over Memorial Day weekend. This U.S. holiday—the weekend that includes the last Monday in May—honors America's war dead, and is a major date in the moviegoing calendar.

The long and the short of it The ★longest full title of any Oscar-nominated movie (with 85 characters) is *Those Magnificent Men in Their Flying Machines or How I Flew from London to Paris in 25 hours 11 minutes* (UK, 1965).

•*The Lord of the Rings: The Return of the King* (U.S.A./New Zealand/ Germany, 2003) is the ★longest movie title of any movie to win a Best Picture Academy Award—if the name of the trilogy is included—at 36 characters.

★ ALL-TIME TOP 10 BLOCKBUSTERS ★

MOVIE	GROSS
1 *Gone with the Wind* (U.S.A., 1939)	$3,161,014,684
2 *Star Wars IV: A New Hope* (U.S.A., 1977)	$3,106,145,963
3 *Snow White and the Seven Dwarfs* (U.S.A., 1937)	$2,840,373,681
4 *Titanic* (U.S.A., 1997)	$2,684,157,635
5 *Jurassic Park* (U.S.A., 1993)	$1,447,498,443
6 *Bambi* (U.S.A., 1942)	$1,394,873,024
7 *The Lord of the Rings: The Return of the King* (U.S.A./New Zealand/ Germany, 2003)	$1,390,530,963
8 *Harry Potter and the Philosopher's Stone* (UK/U.S.A., 2001)	$1,261,535,853
9 *Star Wars Episode I: The Phantom Menace* (U.S.A., 1999)	$1,234,338,694
10 *The Lion King* (U.S.A., 1994)	$1,209,460,511

Inflation-adjusted box-office earnings to the end of Dec. 2006

★ **MOST SUCCESSFUL ANIMATED MOVIE SERIES** The *Shrek* series has, to date (June 1, 2007), grossed over $1.65 billion at the international box office. *Shrek* (U.S.A., 2001) grossed $484 million; *Shrek 2* (U.S.A., 2004) took almost double this, at $920.6 million; and *Shrek the Third* (U.S.A., 2007), which opened on May 18, 2007, has so far amassed $247 million.

If the title of that trilogy is excluded, the record-holders are *Around the World in Eighty Days* (UK, 1956) and *One Flew Over the Cuckoo's Nest* (U.S.A., 1975). Both titles feature 26 characters.

•The ★ **shortest title of any Oscar-nominated movie** is *Z* (Algeria/France, 1969), which won two Oscars in 1970. This also makes *Z* the ★ **shortest title of any Oscar-winning movie.**
•*Gigi* (U.S.A., 1958) has the record for the ★ **shortest title of any movie to win a Best Picture Oscar.**

WORLD CINEMA

★ **Most Best-Foreign-Language Oscars (country)** From a total tally of 27 nominations, Italy has won the American Academy Award for Best Foreign Language Film a record 10 times, the most recent being *La Vita è Bella*, aka *Life is Beautiful* (1997), on March 21, 1999.

★ **Most songs in a musical** Madan Theaters' movie *Indra Sabha* (*The Court of Lord Indra*, India, 1932), the first Indian musical in verse form, featured 71 songs in all.

★ **MOST EXPENSIVE BOLLYWOOD MOVIE** *Devdas* (India, 2000/01) cost an estimated 500 million rupees ($11.2 million) to make. The actress Madhuri Dixit (India), star of *Devdas,* is pictured.

LE FABULEUX DESTIN D'AMÉLIE POULAIN (*Amélie*) France/ Germany, 2001 $144.5 million Director: Jean-Pierre Jeunet (France)

CIDADE DE DEUS (*City of God*) Brazil/France/U.S.A., 2002 $7.5 million Director: Fernando Meirelles (Brazil)

YING XIONG (*Hero*) Hong Kong/China, 2002 $169 million Director: Yimou Zhang (China)

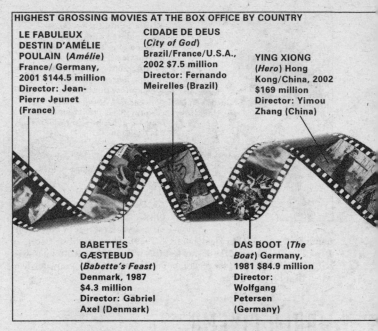

BABETTES GÆSTEBUD (*Babette's Feast*) Denmark, 1987 $4.3 million Director: Gabriel Axel (Denmark)

DAS BOOT (*The Boat*) Germany, 1981 $84.9 million Director: Wolfgang Petersen (Germany)

★**Most directors of one movie** For *Paris, je t'aime,* 21 international directors were asked to tell the story of a romantic encounter in Paris, France. Most of the directors were non-Parisians and each contribution had to be five minutes or less. The movie launched in France on June 19, 2006.

Largest studio Ramoji Film City, Hyderabad, India, measures 1,666 acres (674 ha). Comprising 47 sound stages, it has permanent sets ranging from railroad stations to temples.

★**Most Hollywood releases in one year** Hollywood released 607 movies in 2005, compared with 549 in the previous year. This growth in output corresponded to an increase in ticket sales, ending a three-year decline in U.S. movie theater attendance.

★**Largest cast of credited actors** A total of 381 actors featured in *Die Zweite Heimat—Chronik einer Jugend,* aka *The Second Homeland—Chronicle of a Youth* (Germany/UK/Spain/Sweden/France/Norway/Finland/Austria/Denmark/Australia, 1992), directed by Edgar Reitz (Germany).

Most prolific producer Dr. D. Rama Naidu (India) has produced 110 movies during his career in Indian cinema, since 1963.

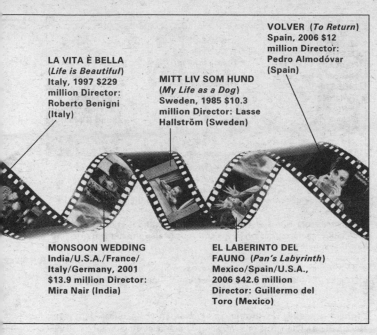

VOLVER (*To Return*) Spain, 2006 $12 million Director: Pedro Almodóvar (Spain)

LA VITA È BELLA (*Life is Beautiful*) Italy, 1997 $229 million Director: Roberto Benigni (Italy)

MITT LIV SOM HUND (*My Life as a Dog*) Sweden, 1985 $10.3 million Director: Lasse Hallström (Sweden)

MONSOON WEDDING India/U.S.A./France/ Italy/Germany, 2001 $13.9 million Director: Mira Nair (India)

EL LABERINTO DEL FAUNO (*Pan's Labyrinth*) Mexico/Spain/U.S.A., 2006 $42.6 million Director: Guillermo del Toro (Mexico)

★**Highest ranking foreign-language movie on IMDb** According to visitors to the Internet Movie Database (IMDb), the most popular foreign-language movie is *Shichinin no Samurai,* aka *The Seven Samurai* (Japan, 1954). It is ranked as the 10th greatest movie of all time, with a score of 8.8 out of 10 from 52,099 votes as of March 21, 2007.

Longest monologue in a dramatic movie In *L'Aigle à Deux Têtes* (*The Eagle Has Two Heads,* France, 1948), directed by Jean Cocteau (France), a 20-minute speech is made by the character Natasha, played by Edwige Feuillère (France, 1907–98).

★**First foreign-language movie to earn more than $100 million in the U.S.A.** *Wo hu Cang Long* (Taiwan/Hong Kong/U.S.A./China, 2000),

---

BOLLYWOOD

Bollywood is the name given to the Mumbai-based Hindustani-language movie industry in India. The name derives from Bombay (the former name for Mumbai) and Hollywood. Indian movie output is the largest in the world in terms of movies produced and tickets sold.

★HIGHEST GROSSING FOREIGN-LANGUAGE ANIMATION *Sen to Chihiro no Kamikakushi* (aka *Spirited Away,* Japan, 2001), an anime about a young girl who finds herself in a parallel universe populated with Japanese gods and spirits, grossed $259.2 million globally at the box office.

JAPANIMATION *Spirited Away* (Japan, 2001) is the first movie to gross $200 million *before* opening in the U.S.A. It is also the highest grossing non-U.S. movie ever made!

aka *Crouching Tiger, Hidden Dragon,* grossed $128,067,808 at the U.S. box office, the first foreign-language movie (it was filmed in Mandarin Chinese) to break the $100-million mark.

Highest grossing UK movie *The Full Monty* (UK), released in August 1997, earned a total gross of $256,550,122 before closing on July 17, 1998.

HIGHEST BOX-OFFICE GROSS FOR A RELIGIOUS MOVIE *The Passion of the Christ* (U.S.A., 2004), depicting the final hours of Jesus, opened on February 25, 2004, and took a total of $604.3 million at the box office worldwide before closing on July 23, 2004.

MOVIE PRODUCTION

★ **Most nominees for a Special-Effects Oscar** The year 1940 saw a record 14 movies short-listed at the American Academy Awards for achievements in special effects, including *Dr. Cyclops, The Invisible Man Returns, One Million B.C.* (all U.S.A., 1940), and the winner, *The Thief of Bagdad* (UK, 1940).

★ **Largest battle sequences** Peter Jackson's (New Zealand) *Lord of the Rings* (NZ/U.S.A., 2001–03) trilogy featured battle scenes with over 200,000 fighting characters. To achieve this, Weta Digital (New Zealand) wrote custom crowd-simulation software called "Massive," which combined digital animation with an artificial intelligence that governed how the characters interacted.

The *Lord of the Rings* trilogy also required 20,602 human extras, but the **movie with the most extras** is *Gandhi* (UK, 1982). For a 125-second funeral scene, 300,000 extras were drafted in, most of whom were paid the equivalent of 78¢ each.

Largest budget for special effects A total of $6.5 million was budgeted for effects in *2001: A Space Odyssey* (U.S.A., 1968)—over 60% of its $10.5-million production cost.

If this percentage is compared with *Star Wars: Episode I—The Phantom Menace* (U.S.A., 1999), it would be the equivalent of spending $69 million of the $115-million budget on effects!

★ **GREATEST DISTANCE WALKING IN PLACE BY A FOLEY ARTIST** It is the job of the Foley artist to record live sound effects—such as footsteps, rustling newspapers, banging doors, and so on—to synchronize with the action on screen (above left). The job is named after Jack Foley (U.S.A., above right), who performed this role at Universal Studios (U.S.A.) from the dawn of the "talkies." Foley's career in sound effects began with *Show Boat* (U.S.A., 1929), and during his 40-year career he is estimated to have walked 5,000 miles (8,000 km) in place, recording the sound of footsteps for the likes of James Cagney, Marlon Brando, and Kirk Douglas.

★ MOST COMMON SOUND EFFECT Archived sound effects are repeatedly spliced into movie sound tracks, and arguably the most common—or at least most famous—is the "Wilhelm Scream." In the postproduction of *Distant Drums* (U.S.A., 1951), a series of six short recordings were made to accompany the visuals of an unnamed soldier being bitten by an alligator (*1*). The sound was archived and used in a series of Warner Bros. movies, including *Them!* (U.S.A., 1954) and *A Star is Born* (U.S.A., 1954), before being picked up by sound-effects editor Ben Burtt (U.S.A.). Burtt dubbed it the "Wilhelm Scream," after a character in *Distant Drums* named Wilhelm, who is shot in the leg (*2*), and used it in, among others, *Star Wars* (U.S.A., 1977, *3*) and *Raiders of the Lost Ark* (U.S.A., 1981, *4*). Since then, the scream has been adopted by countless editors and used in at least 133 movies.

A close contender for this title is "Castle Thunder," recognized by horror-movie fans as the clap of thunder used first in *Frankenstein* (U.S.A., 1931).

★ **MOST CANNON ROLLS IN A CAR** Stuntman Adam Kirley (UK) achieved seven cannon rolls in an Aston Martin DBS during filming for the 21st James Bond film, *Casino Royale* (2006), at Millbrook Proving Ground in Milton Keynes, UK, in July 2006. The car was equipped with a nitrogen cannon in order to blast it into the air and begin the record-breaking roll.

★ **MOST DETAILED CGI MODEL** The 1,100-ft.-long (335-m), 234-ft.-tall (71-m) ocean liner *Poseidon,* in the movie remake of the same name (U.S.A., 2006), was created by visual-effects company ILM using computer graphics to render everything from the ship's exterior and interior—including 382 cabins, 876 portholes, 73 towels, and 681 deck chairs—to a casino with dealers, cards, chips, and gamblers, and 40 dining tables complete with five settings of food, cutlery, glasses, chairs, and flowers. In total, 181,579 individual, editable, renderable objects were created.

FIRST . . .

★ **Special-effects shot** The silent, minute-long *Execution of Mary, Queen of Scots* (U.S.A., 1895), shot at the Edison Laboratories in West Orange, New Jersey, U.S.A., was the first piece of movie footage to use

★ **FIRST USE OF MORPHING** The Ron Howard/George Lucas (both U.S.A.) movie *Willow* (U.S.A., 1988) was the first to make credible use of "morphing," in which one image is metamorphosed seamlessly into another. The software used for the effect—in which a sorceress morphs into animals—was written for Industrial Light & Magic (ILM) by Doug Smyth (U.S.A.).

stop-action, giving the impression of a beheading. So compelling was the scene that some viewers at the time believed an actress had given her life to film it!

★ **"Alan Smithee" movie** Alan Smithee is a pseudonym used when a director does not wish to be associated with a movie. It originated with *Death of a Gunslinger* (U.S.A., 1969), when Bob Totten (U.S.A.) walked off set, followed by his replacement, Don Siegel (U.S.A.). They complained to the Directors Guild of America, who credited the movie to "Alan Smithee." Other directors who have used the name include David Lynch and William Friedkin (both U.S.A.).

★ **FIRST USE OF COMPUTER-GENERATED ANIMATION** The Disney movie *Tron* (U.S.A., 1982) was the first major motion picture to fully utilize computer-generated (CG) animation. The movie's setting—inside a video game—was ideal inspiration for the fledgling CG companies; indeed, the most effective and memorable sequence in the movie is the "lightcycle" race (pictured), created by computer companies Triple-I and MAGI (both U.S.A.).

★ FIRST DIGITAL 3-D MOVIE
Chicken Little (U.S.A., 2005) was the first mainstream cinematic release to be distributed in a digital, stereographic, three-dimensional format. It was shown in 3-D at 85 U.S. theaters and—unlike earlier 3-D titles that needed a special venue, such as an IMAX theater, or a special process—it could be watched with or without polarizing glasses. Experiments and shorts aside, the first color 3-D movie was *Bwana Devil* (U.S.A., 1952), which used the red-green "anaglyph" process first demonstrated as early as 1856.

★ CG character *Young Sherlock Holmes* (U.S.A./UK, 1985) was the first full-length movie to feature a completely computer-generated character. To achieve the effect of a stained-glass knight emerging from a window, animator John Lassiter (U.S.A.), who would go on to create *Toy Story* (U.S.A., 1995), relied solely on computer graphics.

★ Dolly-zoom shot Also known as a contra-, vertigo-, Hitchcock-, or trombone-zoom, a dolly zoom involves moving (dollying) a movie camera toward the subject while zooming out, or vice versa; as the focal length changes, the background appears to fall away while the subject retains its relative size in the frame. This dizzying shot was designed by Irmin Roberts (U.S.A.) for Alfred Hitchcock's (UK) *Vertigo* (U.S.A., 1958) and has since been used countless times, most notably and effectively in *Jaws* (U.S.A., 1975) and *Goodfellas* (U.S.A., 1990).

POP CULTURE

COMICS

Fine and Dandy *The Dandy* comic has been published every week by D. C. Thomson & Co. of Dundee, UK, since December 4, 1937.

★ Largest *otaku* group *Otaku* is a Japanese honorific word meaning "home," but also a slang term for "geek" or "nerd" groups, and particularly those obsessed, often secretly, with manga and anime. A study of such consumers in 2005 revealed that the manga *otaku* in Japan is the largest of all such *otaku* groups, numbering around 350,000 and spending upward of ¥83 billion ($729 million) each year on manga-related products. Other groupings include video-game, celebrity, and computer *otaku*.

★ **LARGEST COMIC PUBLISHED** The largest comic book is the *KISS 4K* #1 Destroyer Edition at 19.8 × 30.5 in. (50.4 × 77.6 cm). Published by Platinum Studios, Los Angeles, U.S.A., the comic tells the story of how the band was transformed from "rock stars to world-protecting warrior spirits." Pictured is Platinum's Scott Mitchell Rosenberg (U.S.A.) flanked by KISS bassist/vocalist Gene Simmons (Israel, left) and guitarist Paul Stanley (U.S.A.).

★ **Largest comic-book distributors** The world's largest distributor of English-language comic books and related product lines—such as graphic novels, trading cards, models, and games—is Diamond Comic Distributors, Inc., (U.S.A.). It was founded by Steve Geppi (U.S.A.) in 1982 and now buys and sells more than 3,500 new product lines each month among over 4,000 comic-book shops around the world.

★ **Largest comic publisher** Marvel Comics has the largest market share of any comic publisher in the world, and had claimed 44.1% of the total market at the end of 2006.

DID YOU KNOW?

We're looking for fans of the role-playing game *Dungeons & Dragons* to set a new record for the most people playing at once. If you're a fan of the game, and have lots of willing friends, why not give it a try? Find out how to register on page xvi.

★ **MOST EXPENSIVE COMIC-BOOK MOVIE** With a budget estimated to have been in excess of $270 million, Bryan Singer's *Superman Returns* (U.S.A., 2006) is the most expensive movie ever made based on a comic-book character.

★ **LARGEST *STAR WARS* COSTUME GROUP** This year (2007) is the 10th anniversary of the *Star Wars* 501st Legion (U.S.A.), the world's largest *Star Wars* costume group. What was a "storm trooper fan club" in 1997 is now 3,300 strong. According to the handbook, members "celebrate the *Star Wars* movies through the wearing of costumes . . . and most importantly contribute to the local community through charity and volunteer work. . . ."

★ **MOST EXPENSIVE ANIME** The budget for Katsuhiro Otomo's *Steamboy* (Japan, 2004) anime was an estimated ¥2.4 billion ($20 million), making it the most costly animated movie in Japanese history. Set in Victorian England, *Steamboy* is a retro science-fiction saga in which a powerful new energy source is unleashed upon the steam age.

Most expensive comic The world's most expensive comic is a 1939 "pay copy" of *Marvel Comics No. 1,* which was sold to Jay Parrino (U.S.A.) for $350,000 in November 2001. It is called the "pay copy" because of notations on its pages regarding payments to the creators of each piece. It was graded for its quality by the Comics Guaranty at 9.0 (Very Fine to Near Mint).

★ **Largest manga publisher** Shueisha, Inc., founded in Tokyo in 1925, is the world's largest publisher of manga, with over $600 million in annual sales and a 30% share of the Japanese manga market (2002 figures). Titles include the world's **most popular manga magazine,** *Shonen Jump.*

★ **Best-selling** *Shōjo Fruit Baskets,* written by Natsuki Takaya (Japan) and published by Hakusensha (Japan), is the world's best-selling *Shōjo* series. There were 23 volumes from January 1999 to November 2000, while in the U.S.A., two million copies of the first 15 volumes, published by Tokyopop (Japan), were shipped in December 2006. *Shōjo,* Japanese for "little girl," is a term for manga aimed at young women.

GAMES

★ **Largest trading card game (TCG) prize** The Spoils tournament trading card game (TCG), organized by Tenacious Games (U.S.A.), has the largest single prize for a TCG. Qualifying rounds have started, but the final prize is $400,000, to be awarded in 2008.

★ **Longest TCG marathon** William Stone, Bryan Erwin, and Christopher Groetzinger (all U.S.A.) played *The Lord of the Rings* trading card

★ MOST EXPENSIVE *BATMAN* MEMORABILIA
A Batmobile used in Joel Schumacher's movie
Batman Forever (U.S.A., 1995) sold at the Kruse
International car collector's auction in Las Vegas in
September 2006 for a record $335,000 to John
O'Quinn (U.S.A.). At the same auction held the
previous year, O'Quinn—the "most successful
lawyer in Texas," who has made a fortune in multibillion-dollar tobacco
settlements—spent $690,000 on a 1975 Ford Escort GL once owned by
Pope John Paul II.

game at The Courtyard, Colorado Springs, U.S.A., for 128 hours from December 27, 2002, to January 1, 2003.

★ Most expensive role-playing-game (RPG) product In August 2004, the Alderac Entertainment Group released *World's Largest Dungeon*, a 1,000-page role-playing-game (RPG) book, containing nearly 1,000,000 words and 100 maps—**the largest RPG in a single book.** On its release, it retailed for $99.95, making it the most expensive single RPG product commercially available.

BOND CAR

A 1965 Aston Martin driven by Pierce Brosnan in the film *GoldenEye*
(U.S., 1995) sold at auction for £157,750 ($228,264) at Christie's,
London, on February 14, 2001. The car was bought by Max Reid (UK) as
a Valentine's gift for his wife.

★ **LARGEST *MONTY PYTHON* GATHERING**
Monty Python fans have been visiting
Doune Castle, Scotland, UK, since the
movie *Monty Python and the Holy Grail*
was partially filmed there in 1974. In 2004,
the Historic Scotland organization staged
Doune's first ever Monty Python Day, an
event that attracted about 1,500 fans from
all over the UK, and some from overseas.
The event has been repeated in September
each year since, though later events had to
limit the number of fans attending.

ART & SCULPTURE

☆ **Most expensive painting** The largest amount of money ever paid for
a painting is $140 million, when financier David Martinez (Mexico) bought
Jackson Pollock's *No. 5 1948* in a private sale on November 2, 2006. Previously, the largest amount paid for a painting was $135 million, when Ronald
Lauder (U.S.A.) bought Gustav Klimt's fine example of Viennese Secession
art, *Portrait of Adele Bloch-Bauer,* in a sale on June 18, 2006.

☆ **MOST RHINESTONES ON A BODY** The record for the most
rhinestones on a body is 31,680 and was achieved by body artist Mem
Bourke, who applied the fake jewels to Alastair Galpin (both New
Zealand) for Guinness World Records Day in Auckland, New Zealand,
from November 12 to 14, 2006.

★ LARGEST SPOOL ART *Reflections* is a permanent installation at the Centro Medico Train Station, San Juan, Puerto Rico. It was constructed from 60,000 spools of thread (right), which coalesce into a photo-realistic image when seen reflected in one of 23 convex mirrors mounted on an opposing wall.

★ OLDEST ICONIC SCULPTURE The oldest known iconic sculpture is presumed to be an animal head, carved into the vertebra of a woolly rhinoceros from Tolbaga, Siberia, Russia, and dated to over 35,000 years old.

One of the most notable ancient stone figurines (which lacks the features associated with sculpture), is *Tan-Tan*, a 400,000-year-old quartzite figurine found in Morocco (pictured).

MASSIVE MOSAICS

• The record for the ☆ **largest candy mosaic** is 399 ft.² (37.126 m²), achieved by the Calderdale Looked After Children Education Service in Halifax, UK, on February 4–5, 2006.

• The ★ **largest button mosaic** measured 720 ft.² (66.89 m²), contained 296,981 buttons, and was made at Maritime Square, Tsing Yi District, Hong Kong, China, for the "Springrolllll•Love•Mosaic" project, between July 23 and 28, 2006.

• The ☆ **largest can mosaic** was made by 116 students from 42,804 cans for the Month of Environmental Education, an event staged by the Hong Kong Playground Association at the Creative Arts Playground, Wong Tai Sin, Hong Kong, China, on September 24, 2006.

★LARGEST CALLIGRAPHY BRUSH The largest calligraphy brush measured 18 ft. 4 in. (5.6 m) long, 6 ft. 9 in. (2.06 m) wide, and was used by calligrapher Zhang Kesi (China) to paint the Chinese character for "long" (which means dragon) during a demonstration at the China International Horticultural Exposition in Shenyang, Liaoning Province, China, on May 6, 2006.

★MOST BALLS USED IN AN ART INSTALLATION Between May 28 and July 24, 2005, Nike Savvas (Australia) used 65,600 spray-painted polystyrene balls to create an art installation titled *Atomic: full of love, full of wonder* (2005). She displayed it for the first time at the Australian Centre for Contemporary Art in Melbourne, Australia. The balls were suspended on nylon wire and electric fans in the room were used to agitate the balls, causing them to shimmer and reverberate.

★LARGEST TEDDY BEAR MOSAIC Measuring 46.5 ft.² (4.32 m²) and consisting of 360 teddy bears, the world's largest teddy bear mosaic—essentially a huge teddy bear American flag—was created at the Chelsea Teddy Bear Factory, Michigan, U.S.A., on July 1, 2006, as part of Independence Day celebrations.

★ **LARGEST ABORIGINAL ART INSTALLATION** The largest Australian Aboriginal artwork has an area of 32,808 ft.² (10,000 m²) and was created using a method of "painting" with many different types of colored sand. It was produced by Sheila Humphries, Fatima Drayton, and Deborah Nannup (all Australia) as part of the Look Up and Smile Project on Australia Day, in New Norcia, Australia, on January 26, 2007.

☆ **LARGEST PAINTING BY ONE ARTIST** David Åberg (Sweden) created the largest painting by a single artist. It measured 87,144 ft.² (8,096 m²) when unveiled in Valhall Park, Ångelholm, Sweden, on June 19, 2006.

☆ **LARGEST PHOTOMOSAIC** Created by the Institut Municipal de Cultura and Elche Council in Elche, Spain, and measured on October 31, 2006, the world's largest photomosaic had an area of 4,878.62 ft.² (453.24 m²) and contained 60,828 individual photographs.

★ **LARGEST BEAD MOSAIC** A bead mosaic created by Abisag Ludivina Zamora Quezada (Mexico) and containing 767,602 chaquira beads measured 30.03 ft.² (2.79 m²) when assessed on September 14, 2006. The brightly colored mosaic, which depicts an ancient Aztec calendar, took two years to complete.

★**LARGEST HORSESHOE SCULPTURE** The largest horseshoe sculpture contained 1,071 horseshoes and was created by Donnie Faulk (U.S.A.) in Pulaski, Tennessee, U.S.A. The final count of the horseshoes, confirming its record-breaking status, was made on September 4, 2006.

★**LARGEST NAIL MOSAIC** Saimir Strati (Albania) created a nail mosaic that covered a total area of 86 ft.² (8 m²). It was displayed at the Arbnori International Center of Culture, Tirana, Albania, on September 4, 2006.

MUSIC

★**Slowest No. 1 climb** Tony Christie's (UK) single "(Is This The Way To) Amarillo" first made the UK charts on November 20, 1971, and reached No. 1 on March 26, 2005.

Fastest selling debut single in the UK Released on March 12, 2001, "Pure and Simple" by Hear'Say became the biggest selling debut single on the UK charts, with 549,823 sales in the first week—taking them to No. 1 in the week ending March 24, 2001.

☆**HIGHEST GROSSING MUSIC TOUR** The Rolling Stones (UK) regained their crown for the top-grossing tour when their 2006 "A Bigger Bang" concerts grossed $437 million.

★ **HIGHEST GROSSING MUSIC TOUR PER CONCERT BY A FEMALE ARTIST** Madonna (U.S.A.) broke the record for money grossed during a tour by a female entertainer when her 60-date 2006 "Confessions" tour—which was seen by 1.2 million fans—grossed an estimated $193.7 million. That works out to $3.2 million per concert!

★ **Most albums to reach No. 1 in the UK in one year** An unprecedented 34 different albums topped the UK charts in 2006.

★ **Longest time between No. 1 albums in the U.S.A.** Johnny Cash's album *American V: A Hundred Highways* topped the U.S. Pop chart on July 2, 2006. It was the late U.S. country singer's first chart-topper since *Johnny Cash at San Quentin* on August 23, 1969.

★ **Most No. 1 albums by a female artist in the UK** Madonna scored a record ninth No. 1 solo album when *Confessions on a Dance Floor* hit the top of the UK albums chart on November 26, 2005.

★ **Most albums to reach No. 1 in the U.S.A. in one year** In the calendar year of 2006, 40 albums reached No. 1 in the U.S.A.—more than in any other year.

★ GRAMMY AWARDS ★

MOST AWARDS:	NUMBER	NAME/NATIONALITY
Group	22	U2 (Ireland)
Female artist	15	Aretha Franklin (U.S.A.)
Male artist	22	Stevie Wonder (U.S.A.)
Group (single year)	8	Santana (U.S.A.), in 2000
Individual (single year)	8	Michael Jackson (U.S.A.), in 1984
Individual (lifetime)	31	Sir Georg Solti (Hungary)

★MOST ALBUMS TO REACH NO. 1 IN THE UK BY A BRITISH MALE SOLO ARTIST The most successful British male solo act is Robbie Williams. When his album *Rudebox* topped the UK charts on November 4, 2006, it gave him his eighth No. 1 as a solo artist—equaling a record set in 1993 by David Bowie (UK). But unlike Bowie, Williams also chalked up three No. 1s as a group member of Take That.

DOWNLOADS

★Highest rate of music download sales (country) In July 2006, South Korea became the first country to report that downloads represented more than 50% of its total music sales.

☆ BEST-SELLING DOWNLOAD SINGLE IN THE U.S.A. IN ONE WEEK
"Fergalicious" by Fergie (U.S.A.) sold 295,000 tracks in the week ending December 30, 2006, making it the best-selling download single in the U.S.A. in one week.

★ BEST-SELLING DOWNLOAD SINGLE IN THE UK Downloaded 418,250 times as of March 6, 2007, the best-selling download single in the UK is "Crazy" by Gnarls Barkley (U.S.A.). Performer Cee-Lo is pictured (far right) with Danger Mouse.

★Biggest selling download single in the U.S.A. The download of Gwen Stefani's (U.S.A.) "Hollaback Girl" passed the million mark on October 3, 2005. It sold 58,500 copies in its first week of release (ending May 7, 2005).

Fastest selling download in a week in the U.S.A. D4L's single "Laffy Taffy" is the fastest-selling download in the U.S.A. At its peak, 175,000 downloads of the single were selling in a week. As of February 17, 2006, the total number of downloads sold was almost 780,000.

★Most songs downloaded in one year In 2005, an estimated 420 million music tracks were legitimately downloaded around the world (with a value of over $1.1 billion). This figure was 20 times greater than that of the previous year.

☆**Most download sales in one week in the U.S.A.** In the week ending December 30, 2006, a record 30.1 million downloads were sold in the U.S.A. This total included over 1 million albums—the first time that albums had passed that mark in a week.

DID YOU KNOW?

The original "Thunder in My Heart" was a No. 22 hit in 1977; the 2006 hit was a remix by DJ Meck (real name Craig Dimech), a British DJ and producer.

★Highest percentage of music singles sold as paid downloads in the UK In 2006, 53,018,000 tracks were legally downloaded (up 100.49% on 2005), accounting for 79.26% of all UK singles sales that year.

iRecord The record for the ★**most songs downloaded from one company** belongs to iTunes, which in February 2006 became the first company to have sold over 1 billion downloaded tracks. They accomplished this figure in just three years. The billionth download was "Speed of Sound" by Coldplay.

CHART HITS

★Most places jumped on U.S. Hot 100 chart On October 14, 2006, "Smack That" by Senegal-born rapper Akon (Aliaune Thiam) and U.S. rapper Eminem (Marshall Mathers III) jumped a record 88 places from No. 95 to No. 7.

☆Most places jumped to reach No. 1 on the UK singles chart On November 29, 2003, Irish group Westlife became the only act to ever jump from the very last position on the UK Top 200 chart to the top spot with their single "Mandy."

★Most entries in the UK Top 40 chart by a duo UK duo the Pet Shop Boys (Neil Tennant and Chris Lowe) have had a record 42 singles in the UK Top 40.

★Most entries simultaneously in the U.S. Top 100 in one week Hannah Montana (played by Miley Cyrus, U.S.A.) had one reentry and six

★ MOST NO. 1 HITS ON THE U.S. MODERN ROCK CHART The Red Hot Chili Peppers topped the U.S. Modern Rock chart for the 11th time in February 2007 with the single "Snow (Hey Oh)." Four of the band's singles have topped this chart for at least 10 weeks—another record.

★ **MOST HITS FROM A SOUND TRACK IN THE U.S. CHART SIMULTANEOUSLY** On February 11, 2006, nine tracks from the Disney Channel Original Movie *High School Musical* were simultaneously in the U.S. Hot 100—a world first. These included five tracks in the Top 40, the week's four highest entries, and the biggest-ever jump in the chart when "Breaking Free" by Zac Efron (main figure in white, left), Andrew Seeley, and Vanessa Anne Hudgens (main figure, right)—all U.S.A.—rose from no. 86 to no. 4. Four tracks from the sound track also made the Top 10 on the Digital Download chart.

new singles enter the U.S. Hot 100 chart on November 11, 2006. The star of the TV series *Hannah Montana* (Disney, U.S.A.) sold 281,000 tracks that week.

★ **Most popular song title on the UK charts** A record 13 different songs with the title "Angel" have appeared in the UK Top 40—the last one was by Pharrell Williams (U.S.A.) in February 2006.

CHART BUSTERS

• Irish vocalist Daniel O'Donnell has amassed the ★ **most albums to reach the UK chart in the 21st century,** with 10.

• In the week ending December 24, 2005, UK album sales totaled 10,581,571—the ★ **most albums sold in one week in the UK.**

• On February 24, 2007, American George Strait scored his 42nd U.S. country music No. 1 single with "It Just Comes Natural." With his 41st chart-topper, "Give it Away," he took the record for the ★ **most entries at No. 1 on the U.S. country chart.**

★LONGEST CAREER ON THE U.S. R&B CHARTS The late Ray Charles (U.S.A.) began his career as leader of the Maxine Trio with the single "Confession Blues" in April 1949. Charles's most recent album, *Ray Sings, Basie Swings,* was released on October 21, 2006.

☆ MOST CONSECUTIVE TOP 5 ENTRIES ON THE UK CHART Irish group Westlife achieved a record 21 successive Top 5 singles in the UK between May 1999 and November 2006, when "The Rose" became their 14th No. 1.

☆ MOST ENTRIES AT NO. 1 ON U.S. ALBUMS CHART BY A RAP ARTIST Rapper Jay-Z (Shawn Carter, U.S.A.) has entered the U.S. pop albums chart at No. 1 a record nine times. The last entry was *Kingdom Come* on December 9, 2006.

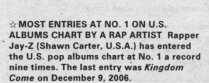

★MOST CONSECUTIVE TOP 10 ENTRIES IN THE UK BY A GROUP (FEMALE) Girls Aloud, winners of the 2002 UK reality TV show *Popstars: The Rivals,* tallied their 17th Top 10 entry in a row in March 2007 with "Walk This Way."

★LONGEST TIME TO RETURN TO NO. 1 ON THE UK SINGLES CHART UK singer Leo Sayer returned to the top of the UK chart on February 18, 2006, with "Thunder in My Heart Again." The newly recorded hit came 29 years after his only other No. 1, "When I Need You," on February 19, 1977.

BEST-SELLING . . .

☆**Album in the UK** *Greatest Hits* by UK rock band Queen is the top-selling album of all time in the UK, with sales of 5.41 million.

★**Single in the UK chart in one week by an artist (female)** "A Moment Like This" by Leona Lewis (UK) sold 571,253 copies in the week after its release on December 17, 2006.

★**Ringtone oldie** Lynyrd Skynyrd's (U.S.A.) "Sweet Home Alabama" is the top-selling "oldie" available as a ringtone, with sales to the end of 2006 of over 1.2 million.

Debut album in the U.S.A. *Boston* by Boston (U.S.A.), released in 1976, has sold over 17 million copies worldwide.

The ☆**best-selling debut album in the UK** is *Back to Bedlam* (2005) by James Blunt (UK), which had sold 3.01 million copies by mid-January 2007.

Biggest selling album in the U.S.A. by a group *Their Greatest Hits 1971–75* by the Eagles (U.S.A.) has sold an estimated 29 million copies to date.

The **biggest selling album on the UK chart** is *Sgt. Pepper's Lonely Hearts Club Band* by the Beatles (UK), with a reported 4.8 million sales since its release in June 1967.

Biggest selling single in the world "White Christmas" was written by Irving Berlin and recorded by Bing Crosby (both U.S.A.) on May 29, 1942. It has been reissued annually ever since and is also the **best-selling Christmas song.** Sales are now estimated to have exceeded 50 million, although there are no exact figures available.

BIGGEST SELLING ALBUM EVER This year (2007) marks the 25th anniversary of the first release of Michael Jackson's (U.S.A.) *Thriller.* Estimates from Sony and the Recording Industry Association of America (RIAA) put sales at over 55 million copies, although Jackson's management claims that international sales have pushed the total global figure to over 100 million. While it is impossible to verify the final global sales, there is no doubt that it remains the biggest selling album of all time.

★ **BEST-SELLING ALBUM SERIES BY AN ARTIST** The most successful album series by one act is Meat Loaf's *Bat Out of Hell* (1977), *Bat Out of Hell II* (1993), *Bat Out of Hell Live* (2004), and *Bat Out of Hell III* (2006), with world sales in excess of 50 million.

OLDIES

• Australian artist Smoky Dawson (b. March 19, 1913) is the ★ **oldest act to issue a new album.** Aged 92 years 156 days, he released *Homestead Of My Dreams* on August 22, 2005.

• In November 2006, Tony Bennett (U.S.A., b. August 3, 1926) became the ★ **oldest act to make the Top 20 of the UK albums chart** with *Duets: An American Classic.*

• The ★ **oldest act to have a No. 1 with a newly recorded album** is Bob Dylan (U.S.A.). He was 65 years 105 days old when *Modern Times* topped The Billboard 200 on September 6, 2006.

SONG & DANCE

Singing and dancing! The **largest song and dance routine (multi-venue)** involved 7,596 children from 40 schools across London, UK, performing the song "To the Show" for five minutes on March 22, 2002.

The ★ **largest song and dance routine (single-venue)** saw 4,431 people at Exhibition Place in Toronto, Ontario, Canada, performing the "hokey-pokey" with Elmo from *Sesame Street* on August 25, 2003.

SONG

★ **Most participants in a karaoke** To celebrate the Eurovision Song Contest victory of the Finnish hard-rock band Lordi, a crowd of 80,000 fans

★HIGHEST CONCERT The UK band Jamiroquai, fronted by lead singer Jay Kay (UK), performed a gig on an aircraft. It was the highest performance on a plane and the highest and fastest gig ever—at 35,000 ft. (10,668 m) on a 737 that had been refitted for the event. Lights and speakers were placed in the overhead bins, and a "stage" area was equipped with room for percussion, guitars, and a keyboard. The audience—who flew with the band from Munich, Germany, to Athens, Greece, on February 27, 2007—comprised winners of a competition organized by Sony Ericsson.

gathered on May 26, 2006, in Helsinki's Market Square Kauppatori, transformed for the occasion into a giant karaoke by Karaoke Service Finland, and sang "Hard Rock Hallelujah."

Although Lordi notched up 292 points—the ☆ **highest Eurovision score ever**—Finland remains the **worst Eurovision entrant,** having scored "nil points" three times and finished last eight times! (Ireland is the **most successful Eurovision entrant,** with seven wins.)

☆ **Longest singing marathon** Thomas Vijayan (India) sang for 73 hr. at the India Campus Crusade for Christ auditorium, Karnataka, India, on February 5–8, 2007. The **longest singing marathon by a group** lasted 31 hr. 45 min., by the Durg-Bhilai Lifecraft singers in Bhilai, Chhattisgarh, India, on February 5–6, 2005.

★HIGHEST CONCERT IN A HOT AIR BALLOON On May 31, 2006, the rock band The Girls (UK), made up of Steven Evansson (vocals, keys) and Joseph Short (vocals, guitars), and featuring Andrew "Mushroom" Vowles (decks), Clive Deamer (drums), and Jon Head (double bass), performed at 6,063 ft. (1,848 m). Their Virgin Balloon, piloted by Mark "Nobby" Simmons (UK), took off from Bath, Somerset, UK, and landed one hour later in Westbury, Wiltshire, UK, during which time the band performed their set, including a specially written song, "What I Did Today," to two paying audience members.

★ **DEEPEST CONCERT** On October 1, 2006, Katie Melua (UK) and her band—Henry Spinetti (drums), Jim Watson (piano), Tim Harries (bass), Denzil Daniels (back-line tech), and Stephen Croxford (tour manager)—performed a concert 994 ft. (303 m) below sea level, inside the leg of Statoil's Troll A gas rig, off the coast of Bergen, Norway. Melua performed two 30-minute concerts to an audience of 20 oil-rig workers, each of whom had won a ticket to see the performance. Pictured are Melua with Statoil's Geir Amland and GWR's Editor-in-Chief Craig Glenday; top right is Melua undergoing helicopter-crash training and (bottom) during the "gig in the rig."

☆ **Largest yodel** The world's largest simultaneous yodel involved 1,795 people all yodeling at the "Yahoo! Yodel Challenge" for more than one minute at the Yahoo! HQ in Sunnyvale, California, U.S.A., on November 19, 2004.

☆ **Largest group of carol singers** A group of 7,514 carolers sang at Bob Jones University, South Carolina, U.S.A., on December 3, 2004.

☆ **Largest collection of recordings made of the same song** Allan Chasanoff and Raymon Elozua (both U.S.A.) have amassed 3,049 recorded versions of the hymn "Amazing Grace" written by John Newton (GB) in 1772.

☆ **Largest sing-along** Young Voices (UK) staged a sing-along with 293,978 singers at 1,616 locations in the UK on December 9, 2005.

DANCE

☆**Largest dances** •On July 8, 2006, 475 participants took part in the ★**largest clog dance,** for an event organized by Introdans Education and Dance and Child International at the Spuiplein in the Hague, Netherlands.
•The **largest dance ever** involved 72,000 people flapping their elbows along to "The Birdie Song" at the 1996 Canfield Fair in Canfield, Ohio, U.S.A.
•The ☆**largest maypole dance** involved 128 participants who successfully performed three traditional English maypole dances in Bradworthy, Devon, UK, on July 12, 2006.
•The ☆**largest simultaneous quadrille (multi-venue)** consisted of 23,628 participants in 36 towns across Serbia and Montenegro, Slovenia, Croatia, Hungary, and Austria on May 19, 2006.

★**Most consecutive breakdance six-step routines** On November 4, 2006, Jonas Gothberg (Sweden) completed 501 six-step routines in 28 min. 17 sec. at the Galleria in Stockholm, Sweden.

☆**Longest dance party** Unique Events Limited (Ireland) organized a dance party at the Quay Front, Wexford, Ireland, that began on October 27, 2006, at midday with 40 dancers and finished 55 hours later with 31 dancers still on their feet!

★**Longest line of dancing drag queens** A chorus line of 58 men—all students at the Allen Hall Junior Common Room at the University of Manchester, UK—performed a charity "cha-cha slide" dance at the university's Owens Park Campus on March 25, 2006, while dressed as women!

☆**Largest dance class (single-venue)** The largest dance class in one place involved 250 participants and was organized by Dance FX Academy of the Arts in Northwood, Ohio, U.S.A., on May 26, 2006.

☆**Largest dance class (multi-venue)** On July 22, 2006, a total of 8,962 people took part in the BBC Local Radio Big Dance Class—a lesson choreographed by Luca Silvestrini (Italy) at multiple locations throughout the UK. Highlights were shown on the

★**MOST HEAD SPINS IN A MINUTE** Aichi Ono (Japan) achieved 89 consecutive head spins on the set of *Guinness World Records: Die größten Weltrekorde* (RTL, Germany) in Cologne, Germany, on September 9, 2006.

★ MOST STYLES DANCED TO ONE TRACK The most dance styles performed simultaneously to one music track is 44 and was achieved by 752 dancers as part of "The Big Dance for the Mayor of London" and broadcast as part of the BBC live show *Dancing in the Street* in Trafalgar Square, London, UK, on July 22, 2006. The styles included ballet, tap, belly, salsa, flamenco, bhangra, and even synchronized swimming in the fountains!

BBC's *Dancing in the Street* TV show on July 22, 2006, hosted by Bruce Forsyth and Zöe Ball.

On the same TV show: Russell Sargeant (UK) broke the record for the ☆ **most swing flips in one minute,** lifting his four dance partners head over heels 33 times; 116 pupils from the Barrett Semple-Morris School of Irish Dancing performed the ★ **longest Riverdance line;** Paul "Steady" Steadman (UK) set the record for the ★ **most break-dance windmills in 30 seconds** with 42; and Pierre "Punisher" Bleriot (France) set a record for the ★ **most vertical spins on one hand,** achieving 10 rotations of his body while standing on one hand.

TV SHOWS

Spoiled for choice According to the CIA World Facebook, the ★ **country with the most broadcasting TV stations** is Russia, which had a staggering 7,306 stations at its peak in 1998. In second place—yet with less than half of Russia's figure—is China, with 3,240 stations (1997 figure). Third is the U.S.A., with 2,218 (2006 figure). Several nations, particularly those in more remote island groups in the South Pacific, have no broadcasters.

★ **MOST DAYS IN THE FIELD FILMING A NATURE DOCUMENTARY** More than 2,000 days were spent in the field filming footage for the groundbreaking natural world documentary *Planet Earth* (BBC, UK). The entire 11-part series, first screened in the UK in 2006, was shot (entirely in high-definition) by 40 camera crews in 200 locations on every continent. The series was produced by Alastair Fothergill (UK).

★ **Most TV sets thrown out of a window** Two members of staff at Kerrang! Radio had three minutes to throw as many TV sets out of a window as possible during *The Ugly Phil Breakfast Show* in Birmingham, UK, on January 19, 2007. They set the record at 61 televisions!

☆ **Most-watched live sports event** An estimated 300 million viewers watched Italy beat France in the 2006 FIFA World Cup soccer final on July 9. FIFA claimed that the tournament was seen by 30 billion (non-unique) viewers, the result of an increased fan base among women and also its Euro time-zone: the games were shown when the majority of global fans could watch—unlike the 2002 tournament, which was broadcast from Japan and Korea.

★ **Best-selling TV comedy series DVD** The DVD of *Little Britain* (BBC, UK), a character-based sketch show starring its creators Matt Lucas and David Walliams (both UK), sold an unprecedented 645,457 units internationally between March 2006 and March 2007. The sales of the DVD generated a revenue of $5,436,151 (£2,769,985).

DID YOU KNOW?

Four new Latin American versions of *Desperate Housewives,* each with its own cast and cultural references, began production in 2006. Spanish versions will be broadcast in Argentina, Colombia, and Ecuador, with a Portuguese version shown in Brazil. Each version is filmed on one set, making it the show with the ★ **most simultaneous foreign-language remakes.**

☆ **LARGEST GLOBAL TV BEAUTY PAGEANT** On September 30, 2004, a record 107 women descended on the Crown of Beauty Theater in Sanya, China, to compete for the title of *Miss World,* the longest-running TV beauty pageant. The show was founded in 1951 by Eric Morley (UK) as a bikini contest to promote his dance hall, the Lyceum Ballroom, on the Strand in London, UK. The most recent winner (2006) was Miss Peru, Tatána Kuchařová (pictured).

☆ **BEST-SELLING TV DRAMA** When *Desperate Housewives* debuted in China on December 19, 2005, it established itself as the world's most licensed TV drama. The agreement to air the show on the state-run TV channel CCTV8 brought the number of territories in which the show is licensed to 203. The series ranked as No. 1 in 2005 in Australia, New Zealand, the UK, Italy, Singapore, South Africa, and Germany, and was the most watched new drama in Australia's history.

★ **MOST POPULAR TV SHOW** A 2006 Informa Telecoms & Media study of viewing figures from 20 countries found the most popular TV show was *CSI: Miami* (CBS, U.S.A.). The show follows Horatio Caine (David Caruso, pictured on the right with costar Adam Rodriguez, both U.S.A.) and his team as they unravel crimes in Miami, Florida, U.S.A.—a "city to die for." *See table on next page for the complete top 10.*

☆**Longest visual-effects shot (TV)** "Machine Dreams," the pilot episode of *Total Recall 2070* (Alliance Atlantis, Canada; aired January 1999), boasted a three-minute-long effects shot in the opening titles. It was created by a 10-strong design and technical team at GVFX in Toronto, Canada.

★ WORLD'S TOP TV SHOWS OF 2006 ★

SHOW	PRODUCTION DETAILS	FIRST RELEASED
1. *CSI: Miami*	CBS Productions/CBS Television (U.S.A.)	2002*
2. *Lost*	Touchstone Television/ABC (U.S.A.)	2004*
3. *Desperate Housewives*	Cherry Allen Productions/ABC (U.S.A.)	2004*
4. *Te Voy a Ensenar a Querer (I Will Teach You to Love)*	RTI Television (Colombia)	2004
5. *The Simpsons*	20th Century Fox Television (U.S.A.)	1989*
6. *CSI:Crime Scene Investigation*	Jerry Bruckheimer Television/CBS (U.S.A.)	2000*
7. *Without a Trace*	Jerry Bruckheimer Television/CBS (U.S.A.)	2002*
8. *Inocente de Ti (Innocent of You)*	Televisa S.A. de C.V. (Mexico)	2004–05
9. *Anita, No Te Rajes! (Anita, Don't Give Up!)*	Telemundo Network, Inc. (Colombia/U.S.A.)	2005
10. *The Adventures of Jimmy Neutron: Boy Genius*	DNA Productions/Nickelodeon Network (U.S.A.)	2002–06

Source: Informa Telecoms & Media, based on top 10 rankings from the 20 largest TV markets

*Original series still showing

TV FIRSTS...

• **Public TV service (September 30, 1929)** John Logie Baird (UK) transmits television from BBC's Long Acre Studio in London, UK.

• **Color transmission (July 3, 1928)** Red and blue scarves, a UK policeman's helmet, a man poking his tongue out, the glowing end of a cigarette, and a bunch of roses were the world's first color TV images.

★Most expletives The first episode of *Strutter* (Objective; aired November 2006), contained 201 swear-words. Host Mike Strutter (aka Paul Kaye, UK) describes his show as "like a public toilet—seriously filthy and always out of order!"

Longest running ... ☆**Sports show:** *Hockey Night in Canada,* or *HNIC* (CBC), debuted on TV on October 11, 1952, to cover the first televised National Hockey League match. Since then, *HNIC* has aired every Saturday night. Its current host is Ron MacLean (Canada).
☆**Sci-fi show:** *Doctor Who* has chalked up 749 episodes to date, encompassing 727 regular episodes, numerous specials, two spin-off series, and 10 Doctors. The Time Lord's latest generation is in the form of Scottish actor David Tennant, dubbed the "Perfect Ten" by fans.

★First live murder on TV The shooting of Lee Harvey Oswald (U.S.A.)—the man accused of killing U.S. President John F. Kennedy—by Jack Ruby (U.S.A.) on November 24, 1963, was broadcast live on national television and is the first known human killing seen live on TV.

★Most TV shows watched as a studio audience member From 1969 to the present, Alessandro Cocco (Italy) has watched 9,076 different shows. His personal record is seven shows in one day!

TV STARS

★Oldest TV "child" Although now in semi-retirement, Janette Tough (UK, b. May 16, 1947) regularly played the role of preteen schoolboy Jimmy Krankie alongside her husband Ian (UK), who plays Jimmy's father. Even though she celebrated her 60th birthday in 2007, Tough, at a diminutive 4 ft. 5 in. (1.3 m) tall, still occasionally dons her schoolboy cap and short trousers—most recently on the 2007 Comic Relief/Proclaimers (UK) single "(I'm Gonna Be) 500 Miles." In 2003, Jimmy Krankie was voted by readers of the *Glasgow Herald* as the Most Scottish Person in the World.

☆**HIGHEST PAID TV ACTRESS** According to *Variety* magazine, *Law & Order: Special Victims Unit* star Mariska Hargitay (U.S.A.) earns over $330,000 per episode of the NBC crime drama. The show is the first spin-off from the long-running *Law & Order* series and stars Emmy- and Golden Globe-winner Hargitay as Detective Olivia Benson.

Roma-Farnesina in diretta
Enzo Nucci

☆ **MOST TV LINKS HIJACKED** As of August 23, 2006, Gabriele Paolini (Italy) has hijacked an incredible 20,000 links. He regularly sabotages journalists and show hosts on national TV in Italy as part of his campaign to encourage the use of condoms in his civil battle against AIDS.

★ **Most hours of live TV in a week** Mino Monta (aka Norio Minorikawa, Japan) is the regular host of a total of 11 live-broadcast programs every week. He appears on TV for a combined total of 21 hr. 42 min. every week, and is considered the "host among hosts" in Japan today.

☆ **Most hours on camera** Host Regis Philbin (U.S.A.), whose career spans 48 years up to August 2006, has logged 15,188 hours on TV. This is an average of almost an hour a day throughout his career. He is best known for *Live with Regis and Kelly* (alongside Kelly Ripa), *Who Wants to Be a Millionaire,* and *America's Got Talent.*

Emmy awards ★ **Most shows to feature the same Emmy-nominated character:** Kelsey Grammer (U.S.A.) has appeared in three TV shows as Dr. Frasier Crane, and for each series received Emmy acknowledgment: twice for *Cheers,* once for his guest appearance on *Wings,* and nine times (winning four) for the title role in *Frasier.*

☆ **HIGHEST PAID ACTOR** Kiefer Sutherland's (Canada) contract with FOX (U.S.A.), signed in April 2006, will earn him $40 million for playing the lead character of Jack Bauer through series 7, 8, and 9 of *24* until May 2009—that is, approximately $555,555 per episode. Presented in real time, each episode of the crime thriller covers one hour in the day of federal agent Jack Bauer's life.

★HIGHEST PAID TV CAST According to *Forbes'* Celebrity 100, the cast of *The Sopranos* (HBO, U.S.A.) earned a combined salary of $52 million for the seventh series of the New Jersey-based Mob drama. James Gandolfini (U.S.A.), who plays Mob boss Tony Soprano, reportedly secured himself a $1 million fee for each of the last eight episodes.

★**Most wins by an individual:** James L. Brooks (U.S.A.)—a writer, producer, and director best known for his work on *The Simpsons*—and Dwight Hemion (U.S.A.)—a variety show producer/director—have both won a record 18 Emmys each.

★**Most nominations for an individual:** PBS (Public Broadcasting Service) producer Jac Venza (U.S.A.) has been nominated for an Emmy award 57 times (and won 11).

★**Most BAFTA nominations** The British Academy of Film and Television Arts (BAFTA) TV Awards are the UK equivalent of the Emmys, and the

★ HIGHEST EARNING TV CHARACTERS ★

CHARACTER	SHOW
★1. Jeff Tracy (far right, with Lady Penelope Creighton-Ward)	*Thunderbirds* (1965)
★2. C. Montgomery Burns (right)	*The Simpsons* (1989)
★3. Richie Rich	*Richie Rich* (1980)
★4. Lex Luthor	*Lois & Clark* (1993), *Smallville* (2001)
★5. Gomez Addams	*The Addams Family* (1964)
★6. Thurston J. Howell III	*Gilligan's Island* (1964)
★7. Jed Clampett	*The Beverly Hillbillies* (1962)
★8. Bruce Wayne (far bottom right, with Dick "Robin" Grayson)	*Batman* (1966), *The Adventures of Batman and Robin* (1992)
★9. J. R. Ewing	*Dallas* (1978)
★10. John Beresford Tipton	*The Millionaire* (1955)

most frequent nominee is comedienne Victoria Wood (UK), whose record 12th nomination came in 2007 for her role in *Housewife, 49*.

★**Most phone votes for a TV talent show contestant** Taylor Hicks (U.S.A.) won the final of *American Idol 5* on May 24, 2006, after receiving a large majority of the 63.4 million votes cast on the night (the exact percentages were not revealed). During season five's run, 580 million phone votes were cast.

The **most votes ever cast in a single TV phone vote** occurred during the 2004 series final of *American Idol,* when 65,491,313 votes were cast by telephone and SMS; the winner, Fantasia Barrino (U.S.A.), won by a margin of just 2%.

★**Most money raised by a telethon** Comedian Jerry Lewis (U.S.A.) hosts the world's most successful "telethon"—or televised fund-raising marathon. The 2006 edition of the annual *Jerry Lewis MDA Telethon* raised a record $61,013,855 during the Sunday of Labor Day weekend (September 3). To date, the show has raised over $1 billion for the Muscular Dystrophy Association.

★**Richest reality TV host** Richard Branson (UK), star of reality TV show *The Rebel Billionaire: Branson's Quest for the Best,* is worth an estimated $3.8 billion, making him the wealthiest person to feature regularly on a TV show. Donald Trump, star of *The Apprentice,* trails Branson with an estimated worth of $2.9 billion, as does Oprah Winfrey, worth "just" $1.5 billion.

WORTH (EST.)	ASSETS	
$50 billion	Private island, spaceships, space station, submarine, supersonic transporter, etc.	
$16.8 billion	Nuclear power station; once owned an oil well	
$10.7 billion	Large inheritance, conglomerates	
$8.4 billion	Island; real estate in Metropolis; technology, medicine, and food investments	
$8.2 billion	Crocodile farm, buzzard farm, tombstone factory, uranium mine	
$8 billion	Large industrial complex	
$7.7 billion	Oil and gas wells, a bank	
$6.8 billion	Inheritance, software company	
$2.9 billion	Oil and gas wells	
$2.5 billion	Unknown industries	

PERFORMANCE ARTS

Heavy handling In 1975, while performing with Gerry Cottle's Circus (UK), Khalil Oghaby (Iran) lifted an elephant using a harness and a platform above the elephant. At 4,400 lb. (2 metric tons), this was the **heaviest elephant ever lifted.**

★ **Most siblings in the same role in a musical** The lead role of Mrs. Johnstone in Willy Russell's (UK) musical *Blood Brothers* has been played by four sisters of the Nolan family (Ireland). In 1998, Bernie (b. October 17, 1960) took on the role for a UK touring production; in 2000, Linda (b. February 23, 1959) played the role at the Phoenix Theatre in London, UK; their sister Denise (b. April 9, 1952) was then chosen for the UK tour of the show; and, finally, Maureen (b. June 14, 1954) took over the role in the London performances from April 11, 2005, to date.

★ **MOST KNIVES THROWN IN A MINUTE** Patrick Brumbach (Germany) threw 96 knives around a human target in one minute on the set of *Guinness World Records: Die größten Weltrekorde* (RTL, Germany) in Cologne, Germany, on September 9, 2006.

★ **Most people performing Shakespeare on a single day** On July 3, 2005, a total of 7,104 schoolchildren performed in an estimated 368 productions as part of the UK Shakespeare Schools Festival.

☆ **Longest theater performance marathon** From September 19 to 22, 2006, a team of students performed 13 plays in 72 hours at the Bertram Hall, Loyola College Campus in Tamil Nadu, India.

★ **Longest theatrical run by the same cast** Michel Côté, Marcel Gauthier, and Marc Messier (all Canada) have performed all the characters in the play *Broue* ("Brew"), from its first performance on March 21, 1979, to the present, in cities all over Canada.

★ **Largest drag show** On September 23, 2005, 25 men performed together in a drag show at the Statler Terrace Ballroom in New York, U.S.A. It was organized by Lauren Fox (aka Ben Kuhns, U.S.A.) to celebrate his 25 years in the entertainment world.

★ **Olivier awards ·Most wins (show):** *Nicholas Nickleby* (1980) won six Oliviers in total, for best actor in a new play, best actor and actress in a supporting role, and best design, director, and play.

☆ **HIGHEST FLAME BLOWN BY A FIRE-BREATHER** Tim Black (Australia) was able to blow a flame to a height of 17 ft. 8 in. (5.4 m) on the set of *Guinness World Records,* Seven Network Studios at Sydney, New South Wales, Australia, on June 19, 2005. Black repeated this feat on the set of *Zheng Da Zong Yi—Guinness World Records Special* in Beijing, China, on December 17, 2006.

MOST HOOPS HULA-HOOPED SIMULTANEOUSLY Alesya Goulevich (Belarus) hula-hooped 101 hoops at the same time on the set of *Guinness World Records: El Show de Los Records* in Madrid, Spain, on June 11, 2006.

☆ **MOST TONY AWARDS BY A COMPOSER** Composer Stephen Sondheim (U.S.A.) has won a record seven Tony Awards: best music and best lyrics for *Company* (1971); and best score for *Follies* (1972), *A Little Night Music* (1973), *Sweeney Todd* (1979), *Into the Woods* (1988), and *Passion* (1994). Pictured are Michael Cerveris and Patti LuPone (both U.S.A.) in the 2006 Broadway revival of the composer's bloody magnum opus, *Sweeney Todd.*

•**Most wins (actor):** Sir Ian McKellen (UK) has won six Olivier Awards: actor of the year in a revival for *Pillars of the Community* (1977), best comedy performance for *The Alchemist* (1978), best actor in a new play for *Bent* (1979), best actor of the year in a revival for *Wild Honey* (1984), best actor for *Richard III* (1991), and The Society's Special Award (2006).

•**Most wins (actress):** Dame Judi Dench (UK) has won seven Oliviers: actress of the year in a revival for *Macbeth* (1977), actress of the year in a revival for *Juno and the Paycock* (1980), actress of the year in a new play for *Pack of Lies* (1983), best actress for *Antony and Cleopatra* (1987), best actress for *Absolute Hell* (1996), best actress in a musical for *A Little Night Music* (1996), and The Society's Special Award (2004).

☆ **Tony Awards** •**Most wins (individual):** Harold Prince (U.S.A.) has 21 Tony Awards, including eight for directing, eight for producing, two as producer of the year's best musical, and three special Tony Awards. He received his 21st award in June 2006 for lifetime achievement in the theater.

LARGEST ENSEMBLES

•The ☆ **largest accordion ensemble** consisted of 989 players who squeezed and pulled their way through the 29th Annual Newfoundland and Labrador Festival in Canada on August 6, 2005.

•The ☆ **largest drum ensemble** was organized by the Meghalaya Tourism Development Forum in Shillong, Meghalaya, India. It involved 7,951 participants who played together on October 28, 2006.

•On April 12, 2006, the ★ **largest harp ensemble** (with 201 harpists) played at the 25th Edinburgh International Harp Festival in Edinburgh, UK.

•The ★ **largest triangle ensemble** took place on *Guinness World Records: 50 Years, 50 Records* at The London Studios, UK, on September 11, 2004.

☆ MOST TONY AWARDS WON (PLAY) In 2006, Alan Bennett's (UK) *The History Boys* won six Tony Awards, more than any other play in Tony history. It won best play, best performance by a leading actor in a play (Richard Griffiths, UK), best performance by a featured actress in a play (Frances de la Tour, UK), best direction of a play (Nicholas Hytner, UK), best scenic design of a play (Bob Crowley, Ireland), and best lighting design of a play (Mark Henderson, UK). Pictured is the original UK National Theatre cast from the 2006 movie based on the original play.

•**Most wins (actor):** Hinton Battle (U.S.A.) has won three best actor Tony Awards (all in the category of featured role in a musical), for *Sophisticated Ladies* (1981), *The Tap Dance Kid* (1984), and *Miss Saigon* (1991).

•**Most wins (actress):** Julie Harris (U.S.A.) has won a record five best actress Tony Awards: *I Am a Camera* (1952), *The Lark* (1956), *Forty Carats* (1969), *The Last of Mrs. Lincoln* (1973), and *The Belle of Amherst* (1977). She also won a special lifetime achievement Tony in 2002.

•**Most wins (musical):** *The Producers* (2001) won 12 Tonys, including best musical, breaking the previous record of 10 held since 1964 by *Hello, Dolly!*

•**Longest title to win:** *The Persecution and Assassination of Jean-Paul Marat as Performed by the Inmates of the Asylum of Charenton Under the Direction of the Marquis de Sade* (1966) won four Tony Awards. The 26-word title was known as simply *Marat/Sade*.

•**Shortest title to win:** *Da* (1978) provided Barnard Hughes (U.S.A.) with a best actor award.

ADVERTISING

★**First 3-D ad created for movie theaters** Norwegian postproduction, design, and animation studio BUG created the first digital 3-D movie theater ad, which premiered on June 19, 2006. The advertisement, for Mitsubishi cars, was presented in digital 3-D, giving a three-dimensional effect without requiring special glasses.

★**First company to be successfully sued for spamming** In December 2005, Media Logistics UK became the first company to have the dubious honor of being sued successfully for sending unwanted e-mail advertising (spam). The company agreed to pay £270 ($465) in compensation plus costs to internet businessman Nigel Roberts (UK).

First trade ad The first printed trade ad appeared in the British newspaper *The Daily Courant* on March 17, 1703. It was for a patented chocolate maker.

★**Shortest radio advertisement** BBDO Oslo Reklamebyrå AS (Norway) created a 0.954-second-long radio ad. It was first broadcast on Norway's Channel 24 radio station on March 10, 2006.

★**Longest running advertising campaign** The character Smokey the Bear was first portrayed along with his famous phrase "Only you can prevent forest fires" on a fire-prevention poster displayed on August 9, 1944.

The wording was altered slightly by the U.S. Ad Council in April 2001 (to read "Only you can prevent wildfires").

★**Most advertisers on one search engine** Search engine Google has attracted 150,000 advertisers to its website in a business that continues to grow year after year. A Google banner ad is believed to be up to five times more effective than an ordinary banner ad.

★ MOST OFFENSIVE ADS [UK] ★

ADVERTISEMENT	COMPLAINTS	VERDICT
★KFC "Mouths Full" (see box page 360)	1,671	Not upheld
Living TV "The L Word"	650	Not upheld
Pot Noodle "Horn"	620	Not upheld
Mazda "Mannequins"	425	Not upheld
Ryanair "Churchill"	319	Not upheld
★Jamster "Crazy Frog" (pictured)	298	Upheld
Barclays Bank "Insect Sting"	293	Upheld
Damart "Debt Letter"	273	Upheld
Fanta Z "Spitting"	272	Upheld
Channel Five "Serial Killer"	197	Upheld

Source: www.news.bbc.co.uk

☆ **MOST TV COMMERCIALS FOR THE SAME PRODUCT IN EIGHT HOURS** On September 26, 2006, a total of 30 TV commercials were broadcast on Mexican television for one product—the cream Complett, produced by Genomma Laboratories Mexico.

Pictured left, GWR's Kelly Garrett presents Rodrigo Herrera of Genomma Laboratories with a certificate acknowledging this record-breaking achievement.

★ **Highest paid advertising executive** Sir Martin Sorrell (UK), head of the advertising company WPP, which also owns advertising industry giants J. Walter Thompson and Ogilvy & Mather, earned £17.1 million ($32.2 million) in the year ending July 2006.

☆ **LARGEST ADVERTISING BILLBOARD** An advertising billboard produced for AMTEL-Vredestein (Russia) measured 118 ft. 2 in. (36 m) high and 546 ft. 3 in. (166.5 m) long, with a surface area of 64,518 ft.² (5,994 m²). It was displayed on the side of a building in Moscow, Russia, from September 20, 2005, until December 20, 2005.

DID YOU KNOW?

The 2005 KFC Zinger Crunch Salad ad featured staff at a call center talking with their mouths full. Despite receiving record complaints, the UK's Advertising Standards Authority did not consider the ad to be offensive.

★ **LARGEST TELEVISION ADVERTISER** Procter & Gamble spent an unprecedented $3.3 billion on television advertising in 2006, a 3.3% increase on 2005. One of the company's major endorsement deals was with soccer player David Beckham (UK, left), who promoted Gillette razors.

★ **OLDEST BRANDING** Tate & Lyle's Golden Syrup (UK) has featured the same branding (packaging) since 1885, with only slight technical changes during World War I owing to a shortage of materials.

★ **LARGEST REMOTE-CONTROLLED BLIMP** A nonrigid airship made by Skywork Media in Turkey has a volume of 7,416 ft.³ (210 m³) and measures 60 ft. (18 m) long and 17 ft. 4 in. (5.3 m) wide. It has an advertising space of 860 ft.² (80 m²).

★**FIRST MOVIE BASED ON A COMMERCIAL** The character Ernest P. Worrell, played by actor Jim Varney (U.S.A.), was originally created by U.S. advertising agency Carden and Cherry in 1980. He proved extremely popular and a spin-off television series, *Hey Vern, It's Ernest!,* was subsequently produced. Ernest's first movie, *Dr. Otto and the Riddle of the Gloom Beam,* was released in 1986, and he went on to star in a further nine productions.

WRITTEN IN THE SKY

• The ★ **largest fleet of advertising blimps** numbers 17. All are operated by The Lightship Group, part of the American Blimp Corporation (U.S.A.).

• The "Suchard" airship, a human-powered craft financed by the Swiss chocolatiers Suchard in 1912–13, was the ★ **earliest advertising blimp.** It was built to fly the Atlantic but failed to do so owing to operational difficulties. However, it was the first time a commercial airship was sponsored for advertising purposes.

ENGINEERING

CONTENTS

COLOSSAL CONSTRUCTIONS

★**Heaviest building** The Palace of the Parliament in Bucharest, Romania, is made from 1.5 billion lb. (700,000 metric tons) of steel and bronze, plus 35.3 million ft.³ (1 million m³) of marble, 7.7 million lb. (3,500 metric tons) of crystal glass, and 31.7 million ft.³ (900,000 m³) of wood.

★**Tallest grain silo** The Henninger Turm in Frankfurt, Germany, which was originally used to store barley for the Henninger brewery, is 394 ft. (120 m) tall. The building once featured a revolving restaurant, but this was closed in 2002.

★**Largest masonry dome** The concrete dome of the Pantheon in Rome, Italy—which measures 142 ft. (43 m) across—has the greatest span of any dome constructed purely from masonry (that is, unreinforced stone or brick). Built by the emperor Hadrian in AD 118–128, it rises 71 ft. (22 m) above its base and has a greater span than the famous domes of the medieval cathedrals of Santa Maria del Fiore in Florence, St. Peter's in Rome, and St. Paul's in London.

★**Largest hemispherical building** The Stockholm Globe Arena in Sweden has a diameter of 361 ft. (110 m), stands 288 ft. (85 m) tall, and has a total volume of 21 million ft.³ (600,000 m³). The Globe Arena opened on February 19, 1989, and is the home arena of two of Stockholm's Elite League ice hockey teams: AIK and Djurgårdens IF.

★**Longest high-reach excavator** On September 19, 2005, Kobelco Construction Machinery Co., Ltd. (Japan) announced the completion of the SK3500D excavator, which has a reach of 213 ft. 8 in. (65.126 m).

★**Largest unoccupied building** By the time construction was halted on the Ryugyong Hotel in Pyongyang, North Korea, in 1992, it had a floor space of 3.9 million ft.² (360,000 m²). It had also reached its full height of 1,082 ft. (330 m), making it the world's ★**tallest unoccupied building.** At 105 stories, the hotel is the tallest structure in North Korea, the 18th tallest building in the world, and would be the world's tallest hotel if completed. Work ceased owing primarily to a lack of funding.

DID YOU KNOW?

The all-suite Burj Al Arab (Arabian Tower), situated 9 miles (15 km) south of Dubai, United Arab Emirates, is the world's **tallest hotel,** standing at 1,052 ft. (320.94 m) high from ground level to the top of its mast. The hotel, shaped like a sail, has 202 suites.

LARGEST OFFSHORE GAS PLATFORM The Troll A Offshore Gas Platform, located near the coast of Norway in the North Sea, is the tallest man-made object ever moved, standing 1,210 ft. 7 in. (369 m) tall—around 147 ft. (45 m) taller than the Eiffel Tower. The dry weight of the gravity base structure is 1.4 billion lb. (656,000 metric tons), and the platform is made from 8.6 million ft.³ (245,000 m³) of concrete and 220.4 million lb. (100,000 metric tons) of steel.

★ **LARGEST IRRIGATION PROJECT** The Great Man-Made River Project was initiated in 1984, with the aim of transporting water from vast underground natural aquifers to the coastal cities of Libya. To date, more than 3,100 miles (5,000 km) of pipelines have been completed, capable of carrying 229.5 million ft.³ (6.5 million m³) of water per day from wells in the Libyan desert.

★ **Largest hypostyle (pillared) hall** The hypostyle (pillared) hall at the temple of Amon-Re in Karnak, Egypt, originally had a roof supported by 134 giant columns. It is 335 ft. (102 m) long and 174 ft. (53 m) wide, and has a floor area of around 54,000 ft.² (5,000 m²)—almost large enough to accommodate 26 tennis courts!

The temple was commissioned by Pharaoh Ramses I in 1290 BC.

☆ **LARGEST HOTEL COMPLEX** The First World Hotel in Pahang Darul Makmur, Malaysia, has 6,118 rooms. The hotel, which is part of the Genting Highlands Resort, was completed during 2005. Facilities include a theme park, golf course, and sky-diving simulator.

★LARGEST HYDROELECTRIC PROJECT The Three Gorges Dam in China is a huge project that will generate power for China's expanding economy, as well as helping to control flooding of the Yangtze River. The huge dam wall was completed in May 2006 and measures 7,575 ft. (2,309 m) long by 607 ft. (185 m) high.

★Largest slaughterhouse The Smithfield Packing Company runs the world's largest slaughterhouse in Tar Heel, North Carolina, U.S.A. Established in 1992, the facility can process 32,000 pigs each day.

WOODEN WONDERS

• The **largest wooden structure** in the world is the Woolloomooloo Bay Wharf in Sydney, Australia. Built in 1912, the wharf is 1,312 ft. (400 m) long and 206 ft. (63 m) wide, and stands on 3,600 piles. The building on the wharf is five stories high, 1,150 ft. (350.5 m) long, and 141 ft. (43 m) wide, with a total floor area of 688,890 ft.² (64,000 m²). It has been converted into a hotel, apartments, and a marina complex.

• The **★ tallest ever wooden structure** was believed to have been the 623-ft. (190-m) Mühlacker transmission tower in Mühlacker, Germany. It was demolished in 1945.

• Although not the tallest wooden structure ever known, the 387-ft. (118-m) wooden truss tower at Gliwice, Poland, is currently the **★ tallest standing wooden structure**. It was constructed in 1935 and was originally used for radio transmissions, but today forms part of a cellular-telephone network.

• *Eureka* is the last of the traditional, wooden-hulled, side-paddle ferries that served as inland passenger vessels, connecting commuters and travelers with the railroad system in San Francisco, California, U.S.A. It is 227 ft. (69 m) long and 42 ft. 8 in. (13 m) wide, and is currently the **largest floating wooden structure.**

• The **longest single-span, self-supporting wooden structure** is the Odate Jukai Dome in Odate, Japan, which is a dome-shaped building that measures 584 ft. (178 m) on its longest axis and 515 ft. (157 m) on its shortest axis. It consists of an opaque membrane stretched over a cedar-and-steel frame constructed from 25,000 Akita cedar trees.

★ **LARGEST MAN-MADE ARCHIPELAGO** Surrounded by an oval-shaped breakwater, the World Islands, 2.5 miles (4 km) off the coast of Dubai in the United Arab Emirates, are 300 small artificial islands that collectively resemble the shape of the Earth's continents (artist's impression, above). When complete, the land for sale will cover an area of 5.5 × 3.7 miles (9 × 6 km), with each island measuring 247,500–925,600 ft.² (23,000–86,000 m²).

Tallest structure The top of the drilling rig on the Ursa tension-leg platform—a floating oil-production facility operated by Shell in the Gulf of Mexico—is 4,285 ft. (1,306 m) above the ocean floor. The platform is connected to the sea floor by oil pipelines and four huge steel tethers at each corner, with a total weight of approximately 35 million lb. (16,000 metric tons).

★ **Largest surviving Roman aqueduct** The Pont du Gard near Nîmes in France stands 155 ft. (47 m) tall and is 902 ft. (275 m) long. It was built in the late 1st century BC or the early 1st century AD and carried water across the Gard River.

Largest man-made floating island On August 10, 1999, the Mega-Float island was opened to the public at Yokosuka Port, Tokyo Bay, Tokyo, Japan. The steel-built structure measures 3,281 ft. (1,000 m) in length, 397 ft. (121 m) wide, and 10 ft. (3 m) deep.

ENORMOUS ENGINEERING

★ **Tallest indoor ice climbing wall** The tallest indoor ice climbing wall measures 65 ft. 7 in. (20 m) tall and 42 ft. 8 in. (13 m) wide. The wall is in the O2 World building in Seoul, South Korea, and was opened on November 19, 2005.

Largest mud building The Grand Mosque in Djenne, Mali, is the largest mud building in the world, measuring 328 ft. (100 m) long and 131 ft.

☆ **LONGEST BRIDGE TUNNEL** The Chesapeake Bay Bridge-Tunnel—a series of road bridges that dip into tunnels—extends 17.65 miles (28.40 km) from the Virginia Peninsula to Virginia Beach in the U.S.A. Its longest bridged section is Trestle C at 4.56 miles (7.34 km); its longest tunnel is the Thimble Shoal Channel Tunnel at 1.09 miles (1.75 km).

(40 m) wide. The present structure was built in 1905 and was based on the design of an 11th-century mosque. Rendered annually, it is surmounted by two giant towers and inside is a forest of vast columns taking up almost half the floor space.

★ **LARGEST INDOOR SKI RESORT** Ski Dubai in the desert state of the United Arab Emirates opened in December 2005 with a total area of 242,187 ft.^{2} (22,500 m^2). It is covered with up to 13 million lb. (6,000 metric tons) of "real" snow all year round and features a 1,312-ft.-long (400-m) slope and a 295-ft. (90-m) quarter pipe for trick practice.

☆ **LONGEST ROAD SYSTEM** The country with the greatest road network is the U.S.A., which had 3,981,527 miles (6,407,637 km) of graded roads in 2004. Pictured is a complex cloverleaf of roads in Los Angeles, California, U.S.A.

Highest mosque The King Abdullah Mosque on the 77th floor of the Kingdom Centre building in Riyadh, Saudi Arabia, is 600 ft. (183 m) above ground level and was completed on July 5, 2004. The Kingdom Centre, the tallest building in Saudi Arabia, dominates the skyline and is a former winner of the Emporis "Best New Skyscraper" Award.

★ **Largest sliding doors** A pair of sliding doors used at the vehicle assembly building of the Japan Aerospace Exploration Agency's (JAXA) Tanegashima Space Center in Kagoshima, Japan, are 221 ft. 4 in. (67.46 m) high, 88 ft. 5 in. (26.95 m) wide, and 8 ft. 2 in. (2.5 m) thick. Each door weighs 882,000 lb. (400 metric tons).

☆ **Largest railroad system** The U.S.A. has 141,198 miles (227,236 km) of railroad lines running the length and breadth of the country.

★ **Largest building site** Three palm-shaped artificial islands, built on the coast of Dubai, UAE, from 100 million m³ (3.5 billion ft.³) of sand and rock, will eventually make up the Palm Island project. When finished, say the architects, each "palm" will add 60 km (37 miles) of shoreline to Dubai and increase the beachfront by 166%. *See p. 369 for more.*

DID YOU KNOW?

The AquaDom takes 72,750 lb. (33 metric tons) of salt to reach the same salinity as the ocean.

LARGEST DIESEL ENGINE The 14-cylinder Wärtsila Sulzer RTA96C two-stroke diesel engine has a rated output of 108,920 hp (80,080 kW), weighs 5 million lb. (2,300 metric tons), and is 44 ft. 4 in. (13.5 m) tall and 89 ft. 6 in. (27.3 m) wide. It is designed for the world's largest container ships.

Largest palace The Imperial Palace in the center of Beijing, China, covers a rectangle measuring 3,150 × 2,460 ft. (960 × 750 m) over an area of 178 acres (72 ha). The outline survives from its construction by the third Ming emperor, Yongle (1402–24), but owing to constant reconstruction work most of the intramural buildings (five halls and 17 palaces) are from the 18th century.

★**LARGEST CYLINDRICAL AQUARIUM** The AquaDom, located in the Radisson SAS Berlin, Germany, opened in December 2003. Sitting on a 29-ft. 6-in.-tall (9-m) concrete foundation, it measures 46 ft. (14 m) high, 38 ft. (11.5 m) in diameter, holds 264,000 gallons (1 million liters) of salt water, and is home to 1,500 tropical fish of over 50 different species.

LARGEST UNIVERSITY BUILDING The largest university building in the world is the M. V. Lomonosov Moscow State University on the Lenin Hills, south of Moscow, Russia. It stands 787.5 ft. (240 m) tall and has 32 stories and 40,000 rooms. It was constructed between 1949 and 1953.

LONGEST...

• The Kiev Dam across the Dnieper River, Ukraine, was completed in 1964. It has a crest length of 25.6 miles (41.2 km), making it the **longest dam wall** in the world.

• The **longest bridge** is the Second Lake Pontchartrain Causeway, which joins Mandeville and Metairle, Louisiana, U.S.A., at 23.87 miles (38.422 km) long.

• The railroad bridge over the Thames River in Maidenhead, Surrey, UK, has a maximum span of 128 ft. (39 m)—the ★ **longest-span brick arch.**

• The world's **longest road and rail bridge system** is the Seto-Ohashi Bridge in Japan, which consists of six bridge sections stretching across a total distance of 5.8 miles (9.4 km).

• The **longest wooden bridge** is the Lake Pontchartrain Railroad Trestle in Louisiana, U.S.A. It is made of creosoted yellow pine timber and stretches for 5.82 miles (9.369 km).

• The Chiba Urban Monorail near Tokyo, Japan, is the **longest suspended monorail** train system in the world, at 9.45 miles (15.2 km). It opened on March 20, 1979, and the line has been expanded three times since then.

Largest levees The largest system of levees ever built is that around the Mississippi River and its tributaries in the U.S.A. Begun in 1717, it now extends for over 3,700 miles (6,000 km), largely thanks to the disastrous floods of 1927 that resulted in a huge federal building program. Over 1 billion yd³ (765 million m³) of soil was used in this project.

Tallest dam The Nurek dam, on the Vakhsh River, Tajikistan, is 984 ft. (300 m) high and was completed in 1980. The Rogunskaya dam, also across the Vakhsh River, was due to reach 1,098 ft. (335 m) in height, but the break-up of the former Soviet Union in 1991 prevented its completion.

Largest commercial building In terms of floor space, the world's largest commercial building under one roof is the flower auction building Bloemenveiling Aalsmeer (VBA) in Aalsmeer, the Netherlands. The floor surface of the building measures 10.7 million ft.² (1 million m²).

Longest car A 100-ft.-long (30.5-m), 26-wheeled limo was designed by Jay Ohrberg (U.S.A.). Its features include a swimming pool with diving board and a king-sized water bed.

UNDERGROUND

Largest railroad station The world's largest rail station by number of platforms is Grand Central Terminal, Park Avenue and 42nd Street, New York City, U.S.A., built from 1903 to 1913. Its 44 platforms are situated on

MOST ESCALATORS IN A SUBWAY SYSTEM The subway system in Washington D.C., U.S.A., has 557 escalators, which are run by the costliest in-house escalator service contract in North America, employing 90 technicians. One of the stations on the subway—Wheaton—has the longest escalator in America, at 248 ft. (75.5 m).

☆**LARGEST MODERN UNDERGROUND HOUSE** Microsoft billionaire Bill Gates (U.S.A.) lives in a vast earth-sheltered mansion overlooking Lake Washington in Medina, Washington, U.S.A. The building, much of which is concealed underground, occupies 50,000 ft.² (4,600 m²) of space and was completed in 1995. Included in the $60-million (£30-million) cost of the building were 40 miles (64 km) of fibre optic cables and a team of up to 300 electricians to hook up the state-of-the-art electronics features.

two underground levels with 41 tracks on the upper level and 26 on the lower. The station covers 48 acres (19 ha), and on average some 660 Metro North trains and 125,000 commuters use it daily.

Underground railroad with the most stations The New York City subway has 468 stations (277 of which are underground) in a network that covers 230 miles (370 km). It opened on October 27, 1904, with 28 stations.

★Fastest time to visit every station on the New York City subway Kevin Foster (U.S.A.) traveled the entire New York City subway system in 26 hr. 21 min. 8 sec. on October 25–26, 1989.

Most extensive underground railroad system The subway system of New York City, U.S.A., has a total track length of 842 miles (1,355 km)— sufficient to stretch to Chicago, Illinois—including 186 miles (299 km) of track in yards, workshops, and storage.

Shortest subway The shortest operating subway system is the Carmelit, in Haifa, Israel. Opened in 1959, the Carmelit is just 1.1 miles (1,800 m) long.

The only subway in Israel, the Carmelit is a funicular running at a gradient of 12 degrees. Starting at Paris Square and finishing at Carmel Central, it has only six stations.

Lowest railroad line The Seikan Tunnel, which crosses the Tsugaro Strait between Honshu and Hokkaido, Japan, reaches a depth of 786 ft. (240 m) below sea level. Opened on March 13, 1988, the tunnel is 33.46 miles (53.85

★ DEEPEST SWIMMING POOL
Designed to prepare divers for underwater expeditions, the world's deepest swimming pool is "Nemo 33" in Brussels, Belgium, which stretches to depths of over 108 ft. (33 m). The pool contains 661,000 gal. (2.5 million liters) of springwater heated to 86°F (30°C) by an array of solar panels.

km) long. Trains stop in the middle of the tunnel for two minutes so that passengers can take pictures through the windows of panels on its walls.

Busiest underground network The Greater Moscow Metro has been serving the Russian capital since 1935. It has 3,135 rail cars covering 159 stations and 132 miles (212 km) of track. At its peak, the system had 3.3 billion passenger journeys in a year, although by 1998 the figure had declined to 2.55 billion.

The network currently carries 8 to 9 million passengers per day, making it

★ LARGEST STORM DRAIN The G-Cans project beneath Tokyo, Japan, is designed to prevent the flooding of the city's waterways during typhoon season, which reaches its peak during September. It consists of five circular containment silos, each measuring 213 × 104 ft. (65 × 32 m), and connected together by 40 miles (64 km) of tunnels, as well as a huge water-containment tank measuring 580 × 255 ft. (177 × 78 m) wide and 83 ft. (25.4 m) high. The system connects to turbines that can pump 440,900 lb. (200 tons) of water per second into the Edogawa River.

the world's busiest metropolitan railroad system. By comparison, the New York City subway carries 4.5 million people per day, and the London Underground just under 3 million.

★Longest undersea road tunnel Norway's Bomlafjord Tunnel, completed in December 2000, measures 4.92 miles (7.93 km) long.

Deepest road tunnel The Hitra Tunnel in Norway, linking the mainland to the island of Hitra, reaches a depth of 866 ft. (264 m) below sea level. The three-lane tunnel was opened in December 1994.

☆Longest sewage tunnel When complete in 2019, the Chicago TARP (Tunnels and Reservoir Plan) in Illinois, U.S.A., will involve 131 miles (211 km) of machine-bored sewer tunnels measuring 9–33 ft. (2.7–10 m) in diameter. Phase one was due for completion on March 1, 2006, meaning 109.4 miles (176 km) have since been operational. The project was commissioned in the mid-1970s to better regulate flooding and sewage flow, and has cost $3 billion so far.

Largest underground shopping complex The PATH Walkway in Toronto, Canada, has 16.7 miles (27 km) of shopping arcades with 4 million ft.^{2} (371,600 m^2) of retail space accommodating around 1,200 stores and services. More than 50 buildings, five subway stations, and a rail terminal are accessible through the complex.

☆FASTEST TIME TO VISIT EVERY LONDON UNDERGROUND STATION
Håkan Wolgé (pictured) and Lars Andersson (both Sweden) traveled through all 275 stations on the London Underground network in a time of 18 hr. 25 min. 3 sec. on September 26, 2006.

SUPERSIZE ME

LARGEST . . .

★ **Silver spoon** A silver spoon measuring 51.75 in. (131.45 cm) long was commissioned by Michael D. Feldman of Argenteus Ltd., London, UK. Known as "The Great Basting Spoon of 2002," it was made for Queen Elizabeth II's Golden Jubilee in that year.

★ **Candy dispenser** Gary Doss (U.S.A.) created a PEZ candy dispenser 7 ft. 10 in. (2.4 m) high in Burlingame, California, U.S.A. It was measured on January 13, 2007.

Car seat A car seat 11 ft. 2 in. (3.4 m) high, 7 ft. 2 in. (2.17 m) wide, and 8 ft. 4 in. (2.54 m) deep was made for the Lust am Auto Exhibition in Mannheim, Germany, in September 2004. The seat was acquired at auction by Hemhofen Primary School, Bavaria, Germany, and measured on December 10, 2006.

★ **Floor lamp** Charbel Barouky and Abdo Barouky (both Lebanon) created a floor lamp measuring 25 ft. 2 in. (7.69 m) high in September 2003.

☆ **CHOPSTICKS** The world's longest chopsticks are 20 ft. 8 in. (6.295 m) long and weigh 118.4 lb. (53.7 kg). The enormous eating implements were made by the Museum of Chinese Diet Culture in Shenyang, China, and displayed on October 24, 2006.

★**ANGLEPOISE LAMP** To celebrate the 70th anniversary of the original 1227 Anglepoise lamp—designed in the 1930s by George Carwardine (UK)—Anglepoise (UK) released a model three times larger than the original. Known as the Type3, it has a reach of 8 ft. 9 in. (2.7 m) and a shade diameter of 1 ft. 5 in. (44.5 cm).

The lamp shade is made of iron and fabric and measures 8 ft. 2 in. (2.5 m) in diameter. The lamp's supporting pole is made from a single oak tree.

★**Fondue set** On March 1, 2007, Terrance Brennon (UK) unveiled the world's largest fondue set. It weighed 2,500 lb. (1,133 kg), and measured 7 ft. 7 in. (2.3 m) wide and 32 in. (81 cm) deep. Each fork was 36 in. (91 cm) long.

★**Garden gnome** With the help of Ken Brown and John Hutchison, Maria Reidelbach (all U.S.A.) created a garden gnome that measured 13 ft. 6 in. (4.11 m) tall on August 31, 2006.

The gargantuan gnome now resides at the Gnome on the Grange Mini Golf Range at Kedler's Farm, Kerhonkson, New York, U.S.A.

Handwoven carpet A team of 40 weavers from the Bakharden Art Carpet-Making Enterprise (Turkmenistan) created a carpet 45 ft. 11 in. (14 m) long and 70 ft. 6 in. (21.5 m) wide on October 10, 2001. The pure wool carpet has an area of 3,240 ft.^{2} (301 m^2).

Kettle A copper kettle built in Taunton, Somerset, UK, for hardware merchants Fisher & Son *ca.* 1800 stood 3 ft. (0.9 m) high with a 6-ft. (1.8-m) girth. It had a 24-gal. (90-liter) capacity.

☆**CHAIR** A chair measuring 85 ft. 4 in. (26 m) tall with a seat 32 ft. 10 in. (10 m) wide was made by Grupo Hermanos Huertas (Spain) to advertise its furniture factory. The chair was constructed in April 2005 and sits outside Grupo's factory in Lucena, Spain.

★**Onigawara** The largest onigawara (Japanese gargoyle) measures 29 ft. 6 in. (9 m) tall and 28 ft. 10 in. (8.8 m) wide. It was made by INO KAWARA Industry Co., Ltd. in Aichi Prefecture, Japan, and completed on December 15, 2005.

☆**Shopping bag (paper)** A shopping bag 9 ft. 10 in. (3 m) wide and 21 ft. 1 in. (6.45 m) tall, made by Jens Pauw (Germany), was shown at the CentrO shopping mall, in Oberhausen, Germany, on September 23, 2006.

Shower A shower built by Lever 2000 Pure Rain Body Wash at Jones Beach State

★**WHEELED LUGGAGE** A wheeled case measuring 5 ft. 9 in. × 3 ft. 9 in. × 1 ft. 6 in. (1.75 m × 1.15 m × 0.46 m) was made by Shanghai Newest Luggage Co., Ltd. in Shanghai, China, during September 2006. The colossal case—three times larger than the regular model—was made to commemorate the luggage company's 10th anniversary.

☆ BED Created by Hervormd Jeugdwerk of Westbroek, the Netherlands, the largest full-size bed measures 38 ft. 4 in. (11.7 m) long, 34 ft. 9 in. (10.6 m) wide, and 6 ft. 4 in. (1.94 m) tall, and was completed on February 7, 2004.

Park, Wantagh, New York, U.S.A., on May 27, 2000, measured 80 ft. 3.5 in. (24.47 m) long, 8 ft. (2.43 m) wide, and 12 ft. (3.65 m) tall. Hundreds of people could shower underneath it simultaneously.

★ **Stainless-steel cooking spoon** Made by Rösle GmbH & Co. KG, Germany, on January 27, 2006, the largest stainless-steel cooking spoon measures 32 ft. 8 in. (10.01 m).

★ **Tankard of beer** The largest beer tankard is made of bronze and is 17 ft. 8 in. (5.4 m) tall, has a circumference of 27 ft. 6 in. (8.40 m), and can hold

★ PUNCHING BAG Made by Mandarin Entertainment (Holdings) Ltd. during November 2005 as a prop for the movie *Dragon Tiger Gate* (Hong Kong, 2006), the largest punching bag measures 8 ft. 2 in. (2.5 m) tall and 5 ft. 10 in. (1.8 m) wide, and weighs 400 lb. (181 kg). It is filled with sand.

more than 1,849 gal. (7,000 liters). It was manufactured to celebrate the opening of a new section of the commercial and cultural center Stary Browar, in Poznań, Poland, on March 11, 2007.

★ **Vertical blinds** The world's largest vertical blinds measure 65 ft. 11 in. (20.1 m) wide and 27 ft. 3 in. (8.3 m) tall. They were created by Hillarys Blinds of Nottingham, UK, in January 2003.

★ **Wardrobe** A three-door wardrobe standing 15 ft. (4.57 m) high was created by Majestic Furniture and Interior Design, Kowloon, Hong Kong, China, in February 2004. It measures 6 ft. 9 in. (2.02 m) wide and 2 ft. (61 cm) deep—giving a total volume of 198 ft.^{3} (5.63 m^3)—and is equipped with a password-protected lock.

Window Three matching windows in the Palace of Industry and Technology at Rondpoint de la Défense in Paris, France, have an extreme width of 715 ft. (218 m) and a maximum height of 164 ft. (50 m). Each window is made from a large number of glass panes.

Working light switch The largest working light switch has a switch plate measuring 40 ft. (12.19 m) tall by 24 ft. (7.13 m) wide. Its mechanical toggle base is approximately 8 ft. (2.43 m) high and moves through 7 ft. 6 in. (2.28 m) in either the "on" or "off" position. It is located on the Broadway-facing facade of the Marriott Marquis Hotel in Times Square, New York City, U.S.A.

VEHICLES

LARGEST CRUISE SHIP Royal Caribbean International's *Freedom of the Seas* is 1,112 ft. (339 m) long (54 ft.—or 16 m—longer than the Eiffel Tower in Paris, France), with a beam (width) of 183 ft. (56 m), and space for 4,375 passengers and 1,365 crew. With a volume in excess of 150,000 gross tons, it is the biggest cruise ship (although it is smaller dimensionally than some of its competitors).

☆ **FASTEST FURNITURE** Marek Turowski (UK) achieved a speed of 92 mph (148 km/h) while driving a motorized sofa, designed and built by Edd China (UK) for sofa.com, at Bruntingthorpe Aerodrome, Leicestershire, UK, on May 11, 2007.

SEA STATS

• The **first known vessel** is a pine logboat or dugout found in Pesse, the Netherlands, dated to between 8040 and 7510 BC. It is almost 10 ft. (3 m) long but only 16 in. (40 cm) wide.

• The ★ **smallest submarine** was made by Pierre Poulin (Canada) and has a displacement of 1,366 lb. (620 kg). Its first official dive was made in Lake Memphremagog in Magog, Quebec, Canada, on June 26, 2005.

• On September 23, 1980, NATO announced the launch of the first Russian 941 Akula (a.k.a. "Typhoon")—the **largest submarine**—at the secret covered shipyard in Severodvinsk on the White Sea coast of Russia. The vessels are thought to have a dive displacement of 58 million lb. (26,500 tons), measure 562 ft. 7 in. (171.5 m) overall, and be armed with 20 multiple-warhead SS-N-20 missiles with a range of around 5,157 miles (8,300 km; 4,481 nautical miles).

• The **largest sailing ship (by weight)** was the *France II*, which was 418 ft. (127.4 m) long and weighed 5,800 tons. *France II* was launched at Bordeaux, France, in 1911 and was a steel-hulled, five-masted barque. It was wrecked off New Caledonia on July 12, 1922.

• Although there are other ships that can potentially carry more passengers, the **vessels with the largest "standard" passenger loads** are the Staten Island ferry (New York City, U.S.A.) sister ships *Andrew J. Barberi* and *Samuel I. Newhouse*. Each carries 6,000 passengers.

• The ★ **highest speed reached in a Formula One powerboat** is 159.22 mph (256.25 km/h) by Guido Capellini (Italy) on Lake D'Iseo in northern Italy on April 29, 2005.

CARS

Best-selling car Global sales of the Ford Focus totaled 941,938 in 2000 (the latest year for which statistics are available). This means that one in every 40 cars sold around the world is a Focus.

More than 650,000 Toyota Prius hybrid cars have been sold globally since 1997, making it the **best-selling hybrid car.**

Fastest car The official land-speed record (measured over one mile) is 763.035 mph (1,227.985 km/h; Mach 1.020), set by Andy Green (UK) in *Thrust SSC* in Nevada, U.S.A., on October 15, 1997. It is powered by two Rolls-Royce Spey 202 jet engines, which generate 50,000 lb. (222 kN) of thrust.

Smallest production car The Peel P50 was 53 in. (134 cm) long, 39 in. (99 cm) wide, and 53 in. (134 cm) high. It was constructed by Peel Engineering Co. at Peel, Isle of Man, UK, from 1962 to 1965.

LARGEST MONSTER TRUCK *Bigfoot 5,* built in the summer of 1986, is one of a fleet of 17 Bigfoot trucks created by Bob Chandler (U.S.A.). It weighs an incredible 38,000 lb. (17,236 kg) and stands 15 ft. 6 in. (4.7 m) high, with 10-ft.-tall (3-m) tires. The truck is permanently parked in St. Louis, Missouri, U.S.A., where it is regularly admired by fans such as Nick Ahart (U.S.A., above). It also makes occasional exhibitory appearances at local shows.

★ **MOST TRANSFORMATIONS OF A VEHICLE** An Ellert—a type of three-wheeled car—was successfully transformed into a hot rod, a rocket-powered hydrofoil, and finally, on September 8, 2006, an aircraft. Each of these transformations took two weeks to complete and was shown on the Danish TV show *NØRD*.

The Daimler-Benz Smart car is the ☆ **smallest four-wheeled car in mass production,** with an exterior length of just under 8 ft. 4 in. (2.5 m).

★ **Most prolific year for motor-vehicle production** Motor-vehicle production peaked in the year 2005, when a total of 64.496 million vehicles were made, according to the Organisation Internationale des Constructeurs d'Automobiles (OICA), Paris, France. This is a production rate of around 176,700 cars per day.

☆ **FASTEST POLICE CAR** With a top speed of 197 mph (317 km/h), the fastest police car in service is the Lamborghini Gallardo. In 2005, there were two on regular patrol with the Italian Polizia Stradale in Rome, Italy. As well as crime-fighting, the cars are used for medical activities, public relations duties and traffic control.

☆ **HIGHEST SPEED ON A QUADBIKE** Terry Wilmeth (U.S.A.) achieved an unprecedented speed of 149.4 mph (240.4 km/h) on the IbaAction/Fullbore/Powroll Rocket Raptor version RR 4.0 quadbike (ATV) at Madras Airport, Madras, Oregon, U.S.A., on June 3, 2006.

MOTORCYCLES

First motorcycle Gottlieb Daimler (Germany) built a wooden-framed motorized bicycle with an internal combustion engine at Bad Cannstatt, Germany, in 1885. Its top speed was 12 mph (19 km/h).

★**Fastest motorcycle** Chris Carr (U.S.A.) reached an average speed of 351.062 mph (564.979 km/h) riding the *BUB-Lucky 7* streamliner over one kilometer (flying start), and 350.884 mph (564.693 km/h) over one mile (flying start) at Bonneville Salt Flats, Utah, U.S.A., on September 5, 2006.

The Suzuki GSX1300R Hayabusa is the **fastest production motorcycle.** It is reported to reach speeds of 194 mph (312 km/h).

X-REF

• Some people travel the *world* in their vehicles—see page 175.

• Turn to page 388 for some of the craziest tricks ever seen on land or in the air!

• If you're mad about military hardware, shoot straight to page 392.

• For a "wheel" good time, check out our cycling records on page 390.

• Want to try a record-breaking roller-coaster ride? Then page 397 is for you!

☆ **LARGEST PEDAL-POWERED VEHICLE On September 3, 2005, in Örnsköldsvik, Sweden, the Hägglunds Marine Septoped Sällskap constructed a pedal-powered vehicle capable of carrying 82 riders. The vehicle was 244 ft. 3 in. (74.45 m) long and 6 ft. (1.85 m) wide.**

★**Largest parades** The ★**largest parade of scooters** comprised 449 Yamaha TMax scooters in Piazza del Campo, Siena, Italy, on May 7, 2006.

On September 11, 2005, the Shadow Motorclub Nederland formed the ★**largest parade of Honda motorcycles,** with 884 in Alkmaar, the Netherlands.

AIRCRAFT

★**Fastest human-powered aircraft** On October 2, 1985, Holger Rochelt (Germany) reached a top speed of 27.5 mph (44.2 km/h) in *Musculair II* at Oberscheißheim, Bavaria, Germany. The lightweight flying machine, constructed by the pilot's father, Gunther Rochelt (Germany), weighed only 55 lb. (25 kg) empty, despite its huge wingspan of 64 ft. (19.5 m).

Fastest speed for a manned aircraft Captain Eldon W. Joersz and Major George T. Morgan Jr. (both U.S.A.) reached 2,193.17 mph (3,529.56 km/h)—the same speed as a bullet from a rifle—in a Lockheed SR-71A "Blackbird" near Beale Air Force Base, California, U.S.A., on July 28, 1976. The aircraft has flown from New York to London in an incredible 1 hr. 55 min.

☆**Largest active airline fleet** As of February 2006, the American Airlines fleet comprised 996 planes, including 45 Boeing 777 models.

VEHICLE SKILLS

★ **Longest unicycle jump** David Weichenberger (Austria) jumped 9 ft. 8 in. (2.95 m) on a unicycle during the Vienna World Records Day in Vienna, Austria, on September 16, 2006.

☆ **Highest skateboard drop onto a quarter pipe** On April 7, 2006, Danny Way (U.S.A.) dropped 28 ft. (8.53 m) on a skateboard from the Fender Stratocaster guitar outside the Hard Rock Hotel & Casino in Las Vegas, Nevada, U.S.A., onto a quarter pipe.

TWO WHEELS

★ **Fastest speed in a human-powered vehicle (female)** Lisa Vetterlein (U.S.A.) reached a speed of 66.585 mph (107.15 km/h) on a flat road surface pedaling the streamlined recumbent bicycle *Varna II* at the World Human Powered Speed Challenge 2005 near Battle Mountain, Nevada, U.S.A., on October 7, 2005.

UCI BMX World Championships The Union Cycliste Internationale (UCI) sponsors an annual BMX world championship race.

★ **Most wins (male):** The most men's world championships won by an individual is two by five riders: Gary Ellis (U.S.A., 1985, 1987); Christophe Leveque (France, 1991, 1995); Dale Holmes (UK, 1996, 2001); Tomas Allier (France, 1998, 2000); and Kyle Bennett (U.S.A., 2002–03). Bennett holds the record for the ★ **most consecutive wins (male)** for his two victories.

★ **Most wins (female):** Gabriela Diaz (Argentina) has won three UCI BMX world championships, in 2001, 2002, and 2004. Equally, Diaz holds the record for the ★ **most consecutive wins (female)** for her first two back-to-back titles.

☆ **Fastest motorcycle wheelie (1 km)** Terry Calcott (UK) reached a speed of 156.50 mph (251.86 km/h) over 1 km at Elvington Airfield in Yorkshire, UK, on September 12, 2005.

★ **FASTEST BICYCLE WHEELIE (100 M)** Omar Cheeseman (Barbados) covered 100 m (328 ft.) on his back wheel in just 16.68 seconds as part of the 2006 Barbados World Record Festival at the National Stadium in St. Michael, Barbados, on March 25.

☆ MOST 360° MOTORCYCLE PIROUETTES IN 30 SECONDS Horst Hoffmann (Germany) beat his own record of 16 pirouettes (or 360° spins) on a motorcycle in 30 seconds by successfully achieving 21 complete spins during the CentrO Festival in Oberhausen, Germany, on September 9, 2006.

★ Longest backward motorcycle ride Mark Frymoyer (U.S.A.) covered 14.43 miles (23.2 km) while riding a Harley Davidson FLH *backward* at El Mirage Dry Lake in California, U.S.A., on September 7, 2005.

FOUR WHEELS

☆ Fastest time to do 10 donuts (spins) Terry Grant (UK) performed 10 donuts in 14.81 seconds in Birmingham, UK, on January 7, 2006. He also holds the record for the ★ most consecutive donuts, with 73 achieved in Madrid, Spain, on June 4, 2006.

★ Most tractors plowing simultaneously An impressive 2,141 tractors

★ MOST 180-DEGREE JUMPS ON A BICYCLE IN ONE MINUTE Kenny Belaey (Belgium) managed a total of 31 180-degree jumps in one minute on the set of *Zheng Da Zong Yi— Guinness World Records Special* in Beijing, China, on December 20, 2006.

☆ **FARTHEST DISTANCE SIDE-WHEEL DRIVING (TRUCK)** Johann Redl (Austria) drove a 16,358-lb. (7,420-kg) Steyr 891 delivery truck a distance of 10.19 miles (16.4 km) on two wheels at Wels Airport, Austria, on June 18, 2004.

BMX SKILLS

• The **most consecutive tail whips (half-pipe)** is seven, set by Romuald Noirot (France) on the set of *L'Été De Tous Les Records,* Port Medoc, France, on July 19, 2005.

• The record for the **highest air off a half-pipe ramp** is 9 ft. 6 in. (2.9 m), set by John Parker (U.S.A.) on the set of *L'Été De Tous Les Records,* La Tranche Sur Mer, France, on July 26, 2005.

• Benoit Mendiboure (France) jumped a record height of 15 ft. 9 in. (4.8 m) using a dirt ramp—the **highest dirt-ramp jump**—on the set of *L'Été De Tous Les Records* in Argelès-Gazost, France, on July 13, 2004.

• The record for the **most pinky squeaks performed in one minute** is 33, set by Michael Steingraeber (Germany) in the Sydney Olympic Village, Sydney, Australia, on November 18, 2005.

• The **longest power-assisted ramp jump by bicycle** was set by professional stunt rider Colin Winkelmann (U.S.A.), who jumped 116 ft. 11 in. (35.63 m) after being towed to approximately 60 mph (100 km/h) behind a motorcycle at Agoura Hills, California, U.S.A., on December 20, 2000, for the *Guinness World Records Primetime* TV show.

• At the Royal International Air Tattoo in Swindon, UK, on July 16, 2006, Sam Foakes (UK) broke his own record for the **most gyrator spins in one minute,** with 37.

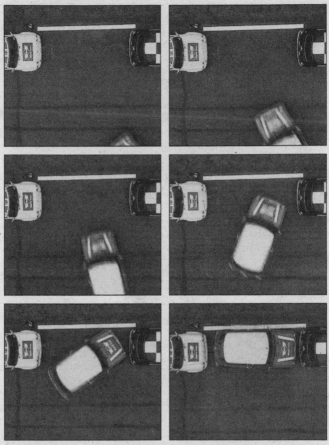

TIGHTEST PARALLEL PARKING At Bruntingthorpe Proving Ground in Leicestershire, UK, on April 17, 1999, stunt driver Russ Swift of Darlington, County Durham, UK, parked a Mini in a space that was only 13 in. (33 cm) longer than the car.

plowed together at the British Tractor Challenge 2006, organized by John and Lynda Collingborn (both UK) and held at Hullavington Air Base, Wiltshire, UK, on June 25, 2006.

★ **Side-wheel driving through smallest gap** Terry Grant (UK) drove a Vauxhall Astra VXR on two wheels through a gap just 26.77 in. (68 cm) wider than the car's height, in Wellingborough, UK, on October 17, 2006.

TAKING FLIGHT

★**Largest helicopter formation** On May 29, 2005, a formation of 16 NH-500-E helicopters from the Italian Air Force (72nd Wing) flew in a "72" formation over Frosinone, Italy.

★**Greatest weight difference during formation flight** On January 26, 2007, at the Al Ain Aerobatic Show in the UAE, an Etihad Airways Airbus A330–300 (takeoff weight: 507,063 lb.; 230,000 kg) flew in formation with a Sukhoi Su-26 (1,840 lb.; 835 kg) and an Extra-300S (1,862 lb.; 845 kg). The pilots were Granger Narara (UAE), Jurgis Kairis (Lithuania), and Zoltán Veres (Hungary).

★**Fastest airship speed** The Federation Aeronautique Internationale (FAI) top airship speed is 69.6 mph (112 km/h) by Steve Fossett (U.S.A.) in a Zeppelin Luftshifftechnik LZ N07–100 on October 27, 2004, at Friedrichshafen, Germany.

★**MOST CONSECUTIVE ROLLS IN AN AIRCRAFT** Zoltán Veres (Hungary) achieved 408 consecutive rolls during the Al Ain Aerobatic Show in Al Ain, United Arab Emirates (UAE), on January 29, 2007.

MILITARY HARDWARE

AIR WARFARE

★**First person to take off from a moving ship** Commander Charles Samson (UK) of the British Royal Navy flew a Short S27 biplane from the deck of HMS *Hibernia* during the Royal Fleet Review in Weymouth, UK, on May 2, 1912.

★ **LARGEST HELICOPTER MANUFACTURER** Eurocopter, a subsidiary company of the European Aeronautic Defense and Space Company (EADS) based in Germany and France, sold 381 new military and civilian helicopters in 2006, representing €3.8 billion ($5 billion) in sales.

★ **First air launch from a ship** The first time that a ship was used for airborne operations was in 1806, when the British Navy's Lord Thomas Cochrane, 10th Earl of Dundonald, launched kites from the 32-gun frigate HMS *Pallas* to distribute propaganda leaflets over French territory.

Most complex aircraft weapons system The weapons system on the U.S. Air Force AC-130U Spooky gunship is regarded as the most complex

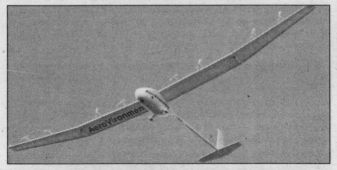

★ **FIRST LIQUID-HYDROGEN-POWERED UNMANNED AIRCRAFT** *Global Observer,* a 50-ft. (15-m) wingspan UAV (Unmanned Aerial Vehicle) that first flew in Arizona, U.S.A., on May 26, 2005, is the first to be powered by liquid hydrogen. It uses fuel-cell-powered electric motors to drive eight propellers and is able to store enough energy to remain in operation at altitudes of up to 65,000 ft. (19,810 m) for longer than a week at a time.

★LARGEST CONTRACT TO SUPPLY WEAPONS The Lockheed Martin F-35A Lightning II is being built in cooperation with Australia, Canada, Denmark, Norway, Italy, Netherlands, UK, and Turkey at an estimated cost of $250 billion.

in current use. Its computer software has over 609,000 lines of code, and it employs television, radar, and infrared sensors to pinpoint targets in all conditions. Equipped with a 105-mm tank-sized cannon, a 40-mm cannon, and a 25-mm Gatling gun, it can simultaneously lock onto targets up to 0.6 miles (1 km) apart. It is also equipped with nine countermeasure systems against attack.

☆Most produced military jet aircraft It is estimated that more than 11,000 Russian MIG-21 "Fishbed" jet fighters have been made since the first prototype in 1955, making it the most common jet-powered military aircraft, and the military aircraft produced in the greatest numbers since World War II.

★Most powerful jet engine on a fighter aircraft The F-135 engine—manufactured by Pratt & Whitney (U.S.A.) for the single-engine, single-seat F-35 Lightning II Joint Strike Fighter (JSF)—can achieve a thrust of over 40,000 lb. (178 kN). The F-35 enters operational service in 2012.

MOST POWERFUL JET ENGINE A General Electric GE90-115B turbofan engine (pictured above) achieved a steady-state thrust of 127,900 lb. (568 kN) during final certification testing at Peebles, Ohio, U.S.A., in December 2002.

☆ **LARGEST ARMED FORCES** According to 2005 estimates, the manpower available for military service in China was 342,956,265 people, of whom 281,240,272 were fit for active duty. The People's Liberation Army makes up the majority, but the figure also includes the internal People's Armed Police Force, which is considered in China to be an "armed force."

TANKS

★ **Oldest tank design** Italian artist and inventor Leonardo da Vinci (1452–1519) drafted early concepts for a tank. Provision was made for outward-facing guns, and the body was covered in wood for protection. It was designed for locomotion with wheels rather than tracks. Like his submarine and helicopter, Leonardo's tank was never built at the time, although a model was constructed for display in 2007 at Sofia City Art Gallery in Bulgaria.

Most tanks produced More than 50,000 Soviet T-54/55 series tanks were built between 1954 and 1980, the height of the Cold War, in the former USSR alone. There were further tanks produced in the countries of the one-time Warsaw Pact in central and eastern Europe, as well as in China.

SEA WARFARE

Largest battleships ever The largest battleships to enter service were the *Yamato*—commissioned in December 1941 and sunk by 11 torpedoes

> The *USS* Ronald Reagan *is nearly as long as the Empire State Building is tall, at 1,040 ft. (317 m).*

and 7 bombs southwest of Kyushu, Japan, by U.S. planes on April 7, 1945—and the *Musashi,* commissioned in August 1942 and sunk in the Philippine Sea by 20 torpedoes and 17 bombs on October 24, 1944. Each had a displacement of 156.7 million lb. (71,111 tons), a length of 863 ft. (263 m), a beam of 127 ft. (38.7 m), and a full-load draft of 35 ft. 6 in. (10.8 m).

Largest Navy The United States Navy is the world's largest in terms of manpower. In early 2006, there were 345,254 uniformed personnel on active duty, supported by 175,418 civilian employees.

Most warships The navy with the most ships is the United States Navy, which in early 2006 had 281 deployable battle-force ships (including submarines).

SUBMARINE WARFARE

• The U.S. Civil War Confederate ship *H.L. Hunley* became the **first submarine to sink another vessel during wartime** when it successfully torpedoed the Union navy's *Housatonic* off Charleston Harbor, South Carolina, U.S.A., on February 17, 1864.

• On February 9, 1945, toward the end of World War II, HMS *Venturer,* a British "V"-class submarine, made history by becoming the ★ **first submarine to be sunk by another submerged submarine,** in the North Sea west of Bergen, Norway.

• The ★ **first ship to have been sunk by a nuclear submarine** in conflict was the ARA *Belgrano,* a cruiser belonging to the Argentine Navy. It was sunk on May 2, 1982, by the nuclear hunter-killer submarine HMS *Conqueror,* using three Mk 8 torpedoes, during the Falklands War between the UK and Argentina. Two of these warheads struck the *Belgrano,* and it sank with a loss of 323 crew members.

• The **highest number of submarine kills by one ship** was 15, achieved by HMS *Starling,* captained by Frederic John Walker (DSO***, RN, CB) during World War II. Ships under Captain Walker's command sank a total of 20 U-boats between 1941 and the time of his death on July 9, 1944.

• The world's **first nuclear-powered submarine** was USS *Nautilus,* launched in Groton, Connecticut, U.S.A., on January 21, 1954. Built by General Dynamics Electric Boat, *Nautilus* was 324 ft. (98.7 m) long and was capable of reaching speeds of over 20 knots (23 mph or 37 km/h).

• The Russian Alpha class nuclear-powered submarines had a reported top speed of over 40 knots (46 mph; 74 km/h), making them the **fastest nuclear-powered submarines**. It is thought that only one now remains in service, as a trials boat.

LARGEST WARSHIP Five of the U.S. Navy Nimitz-class aircraft carriers, which includes USS *Abraham Lincoln* and *Ronald Reagan* (pictured), displace approximately 224.8 million lb. (102,000 tons). They are 1,040 ft. (317 m) long, have 4.49 acres (1.82 ha) of flight deck, and are driven by four nuclear-powered 260,000 shp (194,000 kW) steam turbines. They can reach speeds in excess of 30 knots (34.5 mph; 56 km/h).

FIND OUT MORE

For more about weapons and military hardware, see pages 245–49.

ROLLER COASTERS

Fastest roller coaster Opened on May 20, 2005, *Kingda Ka* at Six Flags Great Adventure near Jackson, New Jersey, U.S.A., has a top speed of 128 mph (206 km/h), which is reached in just 3.5 seconds.

★**Floorless** The 4,025-ft.-long (1,226-m) *Superman Krypton Coaster* at Six Flags Fiesta Texas, San Antonio, Texas, U.S.A., has a top speed of 70 mph (112.6 km/h).

★**Flying** *Tatsu* at Six Flags Magic Mountain, Valencia, California, U.S.A., places riders in a face-down position and reaches a speed of 62 mph (100 km/h).

★**Inverted** *Alpengeist* at Busch Gardens, Williamsburg, Virginia, U.S.A., can reach 67 mph (107.8 km/h).

★**Shuttle-design** *Superman: The Escape* at Six Flags Magic Mountain,

LARGEST NUMBER OF INVERSIONS IN A ROLLER COASTER The *Colossus* steel-track roller coaster at Thorpe Park, Chertsey, Surrey, UK, turns riders upside down 10 times during each 2,789-ft. (850-m) run.

Valencia, California, U.S.A., and *Tower of Terror* at Dreamworld, Gold Coast, Australia, both of which opened in 1997, have a top speed of 100 mph (161 km/h).

★**Stand-up** *Riddler's Revenge* at Six Flags Magic Mountain in California, U.S.A., has a top speed of 65 mph (104.6 km/h) and a maximum *g* force of 4.2.

Tallest roller coaster Designed by Werner Stengel (Germany) and built by Intamin AG of Switzerland, *Kingda Ka* at Six Flags Great Adventure near Jackson, New Jersey, U.S.A., is 456 ft. (139 m) tall.

★**Floorless** The *Superman Krypton Coaster* at Six Flags Fiesta Texas in San Antonio, Texas, U.S.A., is 168 ft. (51.2 m) tall.

★**Flying** Opened on May 13, 2006, *Tatsu* at Six Flags Magic Mountain in Valencia, California, U.S.A., measures 170 ft. (52 m) high. *Tatsu* is a Japanese word meaning "flying beast."

★**Inverted** *Alpengeist* at Busch Gardens, Williamsburg, Virginia, U.S.A., is 195 ft. (59.4 m) high. *Alpengeist* is German for "Ghost of the Alps."

★**Shuttle-design** *Superman: The Escape* at Six Flags Magic Mountain, Valencia, California, U.S.A., is 415 ft. (126.5 m) tall.

☆**LONGEST FLYING ROLLER COASTER** The longest flying roller coaster is *Tatsu* at Six Flags Magic Mountain, Valencia, California, U.S.A., at 3,602 ft. (1,098 m) long. Opened on May 13, 2006, it has a top speed of 62 mph (100 km/h) and reaches 170 ft. (52 m) at its highest point.

LONGEST ROLLER COASTER MADE OF WOOD *Beast,* at Paramount's Kings Island in Kings Mills, Ohio, U.S.A., is the longest wooden, laminated track roller coaster at 7,400 ft. (2,286 m). Rides reach a top speed of 65 mph (104 km/h).

★**Stand-up** Opened on April 4, 1998, *Riddler's Revenge* at Six Flags Magic Mountain in California, U.S.A., measures 156 ft. (47.5 m) tall.
Wood The first hill of *Son of Beast* at Paramount's Kings Island in Kings Mills, Ohio, U.S.A., is 218 ft. (66.4 m) tall. Designed by the Roller Coaster Corporation of America and opened on April 27, 2000, it is also the world's **fastest wooden roller coaster** at 78.3 mph (126 km/h).

Largest drop on a roller coaster ★**Floorless** The largest drop on a floorless roller coaster measures 150 ft. (45.7 m) and is found on *Medusa* at Six Flags Discovery Kingdom, Vallejo, California, U.S.A.
★**Inverted** Opened in 1997, *Alpengeist* at Busch Gardens in Williamsburg, Virginia, U.S.A., has a drop of 170 ft. (51.8 m).
★**Stand-up** *Riddler's Revenge*

OLDEST ROLLER COASTER (CONTINUOUS OPERATION) The *Scenic Railway* at Luna Park, Melbourne, Australia, opened to the public on December 13, 1912, and has remained in operation ever since.

LARGEST TEMPORARY AMUSEMENT PARK The world's largest temporary amusement park springs up around the Oktoberfest Beer Festival in Munich, Germany, each year, attracting up to 50 portable mechanical rides every October.

at Six Flags Magic Mountain in California, U.S.A., has a drop of 146 ft. (44.5 m).

★ **Wood** *Son of Beast* at Paramount's Kings Island in Kings Mills, Ohio, U.S.A., has a drop measuring 214 ft. (65.2 m).

•**Steel** *Kingda Ka* at Six Flags Great Adventure, which is located near Jackson, New Jersey, U.S.A., has a drop of 418 ft. (127.4 m)—the largest drop of any steel roller coaster.

Longest roller coaster Opened in 2000—the Year of the Dragon—in Nagashima Spaland, Japan, *Steel Dragon 2000* measures 8,133 ft. (2,479 m) long.

COASTER TYPES

Floorless roller coasters have no floors! Seats are suspended in the air around a central frame.

Flying roller coasters are rides in which passengers are suspended in harnesses, horizontally beneath the coaster, parallel to the track.

Inverted roller coasters are those where the train runs under the track, with upright seats hanging from the wheel carriage above.

Shuttle-design roller coasters are those that have a string of connected cars or shuttles for passengers to sit in.

Stand-up roller coasters are designed so that passengers stand during the ride, restrained by an upright bicycle-like seat with overhead harnesses.

•**Floorless** Opened on May 5, 2000, *The Dominator* at Geauga Lake, Ohio, U.S.A., is 4,210 ft. (1,283 m) long.

★**Inverted** *The Pyrenees* at Parque Espana-Shima Spain Village in Japan measures 4,048 ft. (1,233.8 m) long.

★**Shuttle-design** Manufactured by Premier Rides, *Mr. Freeze* at the Six Flags Over Texas in Arlington, Texas, U.S.A., is 1,480 ft. (451 m) long.

Stand-up *Riddler's Revenge* at Six Flags Magic Mountain in California, U.S.A., is 4,370 ft. (1,332 m) in length.

SPORTS

CONTENTS

ACTION SPORTS

★ **MOST SOMERSAULTS ON SKIS IN 10 MINUTES** Christian Rijavec (Austria) performed 29 somersaults in 10 minutes in Pitzal Tyrol, Austria, on April 8, 2006. In this record, the somersaults can be either forward (head first) or backward (feet first).

BASE JUMPING

Oldest jumper James Talbot Guyer (U.S.A., b. June 16, 1928) BASE jumped off the 486-ft. (148-m) Perrine Memorial Bridge near Twin Falls, Idaho, U.S.A., on August 2, 2002, aged 74 years 47 days.

★**Highest jump** The highest altitude point for a BASE jump is 21,666 ft. (6,604 m), by Glenn Singleman and Heather Swan (both Australia). The daredevil duo made a wingsuit jump from a ledge on Mt. Meru in the Garhwal Himalayas, India, on May 23, 2006.

★**Largest indoor base jump** Ten parachutists performed an indoor jump at the Tropical Islands Resort near Berlin, Germany, on January 31, 2005, at an event organized by the German BASE Association.

SKATEBOARDING

★**Most consecutive ollies** Ross West (UK) performed a total of 128 consecutive ollies at the Royal Bath and West Show Ground in Somerset, UK, on July 10, 2005.

★ **MOST BASE JUMPS IN 24 HOURS** Dan Schilling (U.S.A.) made 201 BASE (Building, Antenna, Span, Earth) jumps at the Perrine Memorial Bridge near Twin Falls, Idaho, U.S.A., on July 7–8, 2006.

★MOST SKATEBOARD 360 KICKFLIPS IN ONE MINUTE Marc Haziza (France) performed nine skateboard 360 kickflips in one minute on the set of *L'Été De Tous Les Records* in Cabourg, France, on August 1, 2005.

★**Highest wall ride** Brad Edwards and Aaron Murray (both U.S.A.) rode a 7-ft. 6-in.-long (2.29-m) wall for the opening of The Board Gallery at the Hollywood and Highland Center in Los Angeles, California, U.S.A., on August 25, 2006. The attempt was organized in conjunction with *Juice* magazine, the United States Skateboarding Association (USSA), and the World Skateboarding Association (WSA).

MORE TECHNICAL BOARD MOVES...

• The ★ **longest coping grind,** along a ramp measuring 22 ft. 5 in. (6.83 m), was achieved by Micky Iglesias (Switzerland) on the set of *L'Été De Tous Les Records,* Port Médoc, France, on July 20, 2005.

• Matthias Ringstrom (U.S.A.) set the record for the ★ **most consecutive front-side, front-foot impossibles,** with four on the set of *L'Été De Tous Les Records* in La Tranche-sur-Mer, France, on June 26, 2005.

• The ★ **most consecutive half-cab heelflips** is 10, a feat also achieved by Matthias Ringstrom (U.S.A.), on the set of *L'Été De Tous Les Records* in La Tranche-sur-Mer, France, on July 26, 2005.

• Stefan Akesson (Sweden) maintained the ★ **longest one-wheel manual (wheelie)** with a 128-ft. (39-m) wheelie at the Gallerian Shopping Center in Stockholm, Sweden, on November 4, 2006.

• Trevor Baxter (UK) cleared a bar set at 5 ft. 5 in. (1.65 m) to establish the record for the **highest jump from a skateboard.** He jumped off his moving skateboard and landed on it after it had passed under the bar in Grenoble, France, on September 14, 1982.

• Terence Bougdour (France) performed the **highest skateboard 540 McTwist off a half pipe.** It measured 4 ft. 11 in. (1.5 m) and was achieved on the set of *L'Été De Tous Les Records,* La Tranche-sur-Mer, France, on July 27, 2005.

☆ **MOST POINTS IN A RED BULL AIR RACE SEASON** Kirby Chambliss (U.S.A.) won a total of 38 points in the 2006 Red Bull Air Race World Series. This is the most points ever won by an individual pilot over the course of a Red Bull Air Race season.

Longest board slide Christian Pujola Hernandez (Spain) performed a 21-ft. 4-in. (6.5-m) rail grind on *El Show de Los Records* in Madrid, Spain, on November 22, 2001.

★ **Most heelflips in one minute** Claire Alleaume (France) pulled off eight heelflips in one minute in Benodet, France, on August 26, 2005.

IN-LINE SKATING

Highest ramp jump José Félix Henry (Spain) cleared a bar raised to 14 ft. 8 in. (4.5 m) on in-line skates on the set of *El Show de Los Records,* Madrid, Spain, on December 14, 2001.

★ **Greatest distance in 24 hours (men)** Mauro Guenci (Italy) covered 337.7 miles (543.5 km) on in-line skates on June 11–12, 2004, in Senigallia, Italy.

Guenci also holds the record for the **greatest distance skated in one hour,** at 24 miles (38.63 km).

Fastest speed On September 26, 1998, Graham Wilkie and Jeff Hamilton (both U.S.A.) reached a speed of 64.02 mph (103.03 km/h) skating downhill in Arizona, U.S.A.

DID YOU KNOW?

The Red Bull Air Race was established in 2003. It is an international series of air races in which competitors have to navigate an aerial obstacle course in the fastest time possible.

☆ **MOST BOULDERING WORLD CUP VICTORIES (FEMALE)** Sandrine Levet (France) has won five world cup titles in the women's bouldering competition, in 2000–01 and 2003–05.

PARACHUTING

★**Highest speed "canopy piloting"** Jason Moledzki (Canada) completed a piloting course in 2.72 seconds in Vienna, Austria, on August 25, 2006. Canopy piloting ("swooping") is a growing and extremely dangerous activity that involves the parachutist deploying their canopy at 5,000 ft. (1,524 m), before entering a course in a steep rotating dive, competing for distance, speed, or freestyle maneuvers. The **farthest swooping distance** is 678 ft. (206.85 m), also by Jason Moledzki, in Longmont, Colorado, U.S.A., on September 15, 2005.

★**Largest free-flying head-down formation** An international team of 53 sky divers flew head-down (a very dangerous upside-down position) in formation over Perris Valley, California, U.S.A., on April 29, 2005.

FOOTBALL

★**First NFL player to score two interception returns over 100 yards** The Philadelphia Eagles' Lito Sheppard (U.S.A.) became the first player in NFL history with two interception returns of over 100 yards. Both touchdown returns came against the Dallas Cowboys: a 101-yarder on November 15, 2004, and a 102-yard interception return for a touchdown on October 8, 2006.

★**Most ArenaBowl victories** The Tampa Bay Storm have won five times: in 1991, 1993, 1995–96, and 2003. The ArenaBowl has been contested annually since 1987 and is the championship game of the Arena Football League, a version of gridiron football played indoors.

★**Highest team score in an ArenaBowl game** The highest score recorded by one team in the annual ArenaBowl game is 69 points by the San Jose SaberCats (U.S.A.) at ArenaBowl XVIII, on June 27, 2004, when they defeated the Arizona Rattlers 69–62.

★**Most World Bowl victories** The most wins of the World Bowl is three by the Berlin Thunder in 2001–02 and 2004. The World Bowl has been contested since 1991, first as the final game of the World League of American Football in 1991–92 and then as the final game of the NFL Europe Championship in 1995–2005.

☆**Longest pass completion** A record pass completion of 99 yards has been achieved on 10 occasions and has always resulted in a touchdown. The most recent was a pass from quarterback Jeff Garcia to Andre Davis (both U.S.A.) of the Cleveland Browns in a game on October 17, 2004.

☆**Most combined net yards gained in a career** Jerry Rice (U.S.A.) gained 23,546 yards playing for the San Francisco 49ers from 1985 to 2000, Oakland Raiders from 2001 to 2004, and Seattle Seahawks in 2004.

☆**Most combined net yards gained in a season** The most combined net yards gained by a single player in an NFL season is 2,690 by Derrick Mason (U.S.A.) playing for the Tennessee Titans in 2000.

★**Most pass completions in a career by a quarterback** Brett Favre (U.S.A.) of the Green Bay Packers completed 5,021 passes between 1992 and

★**FASTEST TIME TO RECEIVE 1,000 PASSES** On December 10, 2006, Marvin Harrison (U.S.A.) of the Indianapolis Colts reached 1,000 career receptions in 167 games played.
•With Colts quarterback Peyton Manning (U.S.A.), Harrison set an NFL record for the ★**most passing yardage for a quarterback and wide receiver duo**, with 11,908 yards as of 2006.
•The same duo also set a record for the ☆**most pass completions by an NFL quarterback and wide receiver duo**, with 878 completions as of 2006.

★MOST SEASONS PASSING 4,000 YARDS IN AN NFL CAREER BY AN INDIVIDUAL Peyton Manning (U.S.A.) of the Indianapolis Colts set an NFL record in 2006 by reaching 4,000 passing yards in a season for the seventh time in his career (1999–2004, 2006).

2006. He also extended two of his quarterback records in 2006 by throwing for at least 3,000 yards in a season for the 15th consecutive year (see page 412), and by starting in his 237th consecutive regular-season game.

★First player with 20 interceptions and 20 quarterback sacks During the 2005 season, Ronde Barber (U.S.A.) of the Tampa Bay Buccaneers became the first player in NFL history to record 20 career interceptions (28) and 20 career quarterback sacks (20), proving Barber's rare dual ability to rush the quarterback as well as defend the receivers in pass coverage.

★MOST CARRIES IN AN NFL SEASON BY A RUNNING BACK Larry Johnson (U.S.A., above, wearing number 27) of the Kansas City Chiefs had the most carries in a season with 416 in 2006, surpassing the previous 410 set by Jamal Anderson (U.S.A.) of the Atlanta Falcons in 1998. Johnson rushed for 1,789 yards in the season.

★ **MOST 100-YARD RUSHING GAMES FOR A QUARTERBACK** Michael Vick (U.S.A.) of the Atlanta Falcons holds the NFL record for the most career 100-yard games by a quarterback, with seven, through 2006.

FIELD GOALS

• Morten Andersen (Denmark) has recorded the ★ **most NFL games played in a career by an individual,** with 681, as a place-kicker with the New Orleans Saints, Atlanta Falcons, New York Giants, Kansas City Chiefs, and Minnesota Vikings since 1982.

• Andersen also scored 540 field goals—the ☆ **most field goals by an individual in a career.**

• Adam Vinatieri (U.S.A.) set a record for the ☆ **most field goals by an individual in a postseason career,** with 40, while playing for the New England Patriots and Indianapolis Colts since 2002.

• During the 2006 postseason, Vinatieri scored five field goals for the Indianapolis Colts against the Baltimore Ravens on January 13, 2007, the ★ **most field goals scored in a postseason game by an individual.**

• The record for the ☆ **most field goals by an individual in an NFL game** is seven and has been accomplished by four placekickers. The most recent was Billy Cundiff of the Dallas Cowboys against the New York Giants on September 15, 2003.
  The other holders are Jim Bakken (U.S.A.) for the St. Louis Cardinals against the Pittsburgh Steelers on September 24, 1967; Rich Karlis (U.S.A.) for the Minnesota Vikings against the L.A. Rams on November 5, 1989; and Chris Boniol (U.S.A.) for the Dallas Cowboys against the Green Bay Packers on November 18, 1996.

★ MOST CONSECUTIVE SEASONS PASSING 3,000 YARDS Brett Favre (U.S.A.) of the Green Bay Packers set the NFL quarterbacking record in 2006 by throwing for at least 3,000 yards in a season for the 15th consecutive year.

★**Largest comeback in a championship game** The Indianapolis Colts overcame a 21–3 deficit and won the American Football Conference championship game in 2007 over the New England Patriots 38–34, pulling off the biggest comeback in conference championship game history.

☆**Most touchdowns in a career** Jerry Rice (U.S.A.) of the San Francisco 49ers, Oakland Raiders, and Seattle Seahawks scored a record 208 touchdowns between 1985 and 2004.

☆**Youngest NFL coach** Lane Kiffin (U.S.A., b. May 9, 1975) was 31 years 259 days old when he signed on to coach the Oakland Raiders on January 23, 2007.

★ LARGEST COMEBACK WITH UNDER 10 MINUTES LEFT TO PLAY Vince Young (U.S.A.), playing for the Tennessee Titans, engineered the largest and most spectacular comeback in NFL history, with less than 10 minutes left in the game. Having trailed 21–0 in the fourth quarter, the Titans came back and secured a 24–21 win over the New York Giants on November 26, 2006.

★**Most fumbles in a career** Warren Moon (U.S.A.) recorded 161 fumbles playing for the Houston Oilers from 1984 to 1993, Minnesota Vikings from 1994 to 1996, Seattle Seahawks in 1997/98, and Kansas City Chiefs in 1999/2000.

★**Youngest person to play in the Super Bowl** At 21 years 155 days, Jamal Lewis (U.S.A., b. August 26, 1979) of the Baltimore Ravens is the youngest player to appear in the Super Bowl (2001).

TRACK & FIELD

Five world records in 35 minutes! Jesse Owens (U.S.A.) set five records in 35 minutes in Ann Arbor, Michigan, U.S.A., on May 25, 1935: a 26-ft. 8.25-in. (8.13-m) long jump at 3:25 p.m., a 20.3-sec. 220 yd. (and 200 m) at 3:45 p.m., and a 22.6-sec. 220 yd. low hurdles (and 200 m) at 4 p.m.

Earlier that day, at 3:15 p.m., he equaled another world record, with a 9.4-second 110 yd. dash.

★**Earliest evidence of organized running** Historical research indicates that organized running took place in Memphis, Egypt, as long ago as 3800 BC.

HIGHEST POLE VAULT (FEMALE) Yelena Isinbayeva (Russia) recorded a 16-ft. 5.2-in. (5.01-m) pole vault in Helsinki, Finland, on August 12, 2005.
On February 10, 2007, in Donetsk, Ukraine, she produced the ☆ **highest indoor pole vault by a woman,** measuring 16 ft. 2 in. (4.93 m).

MOST GOLD MEDALS IN TRACK & FIELD WORLD CHAMPIONSHIPS The World Championships, as distinct from the Olympic Games, were inaugurated in 1983, when they were held in Helsinki, Finland. The most golds won to date is nine by Michael Johnson (U.S.A., left), in the 200 m (1991 and 1995), 400 m (1993, 1995, 1997, and 1999), and 4 × 400 m relay (1993, 1995, and 1999).

The most track & field gold medals won by a woman in the same competition is five by Gail Devers (U.S.A.) for the 100 m (1993), 100 m hurdles (1993, 1995, and 1999), and 4 × 100 m relay (1997).

☆**Fastest indoor 4 × 400 m relay (women)** A Russian team (Yulia Gushchina, Olga Kotlyarova, Olga Zaytseva, and Olesya Krasnomovets) ran the indoor 4 × 400 m relay in 3 min. 23.37 sec. in Glasgow, UK, on January 28, 2006.

★ MARATHON ENDEAVORS ★

ACHIEVEMENT	TOTAL	ATHLETE (COUNTRY)
★ Most London Marathon wins (male)	3	Antonio Pinto (Portugal) Dionicio Ceron (Mexico)
★ Most London Marathon wins (female)	4	Ingrid Kristiansen (Norway)
★ Most New York Marathon wins (male)	4	Bill Rogers (U.S.A.)
★ Most New York Marathon wins (female)	9	Grete Waitz (Norway)
★ Most consecutive Hawaiian Ironman wins (male)	4	Mark Allen (U.S.A.)
★ Most consecutive Hawaiian Ironman wins (female)	5	Paula Newby-Fraser (U.S.A.)
★ Most World Road Running Championship wins (male)	1	Zersemau Tadesse (Eritrea)*
★ Most World Road Running Championship wins (female)	1	Lornah Kiplagat (Netherlands)*

*The IAAF World Road Running Championships were first held in 2006, the year of these victories. This competition replaced the World Half-Marathon Championships.

☆ **FASTEST 110 M HURDLES**
Xiang Liu (China) ran the
110 m hurdles in 12.88
seconds in Lausanne,
Switzerland, on July 11, 2006.

☆ **Fastest 4 × 800 m relay
(men)** Kenya (Joseph Mutua,
William Yiampoy, Ismael Kombich, and Wilfred Bungei) ran
the 4 × 800 m relay in 7 min.
2.43 sec. in Brussels, Belgium,
on August 25, 2006.

☆ **Fastest indoor 4 × 800 m relay (women)** On February 11, 2007,
Russia (Anna Balakshina, Anna Emashova, Natalya Pantelyeva, and Olesya
Chumakova) ran the indoor 4 × 800 m relay in 8 min. 18.54 sec. in Volgograd,
Russia.

☆ **Fastest 20 km road run (female)** Lornah Kiplagat (Netherlands)
won the 20 km road run in 1 hr. 3 min. 21 sec. in Debrecen, Hungary, on October 8, 2006.

★ **Fastest road relay** The Kenyan team set a time of 1 hr. 57 min. 6 sec.
in Chiba, Japan, on November 23, 2005.

The record for the **fastest women's road relay** is held by the People's
Republic of China, with a time of 2 hr. 11 min. 41 sec. in Beijing, China, on
February 28, 1998.

★ **Fastest 1,000 km ultra-distance track (male)** Yiannis Kouros
(Greece) completed the 1,000 km ultra-distance track event in a time of
5 days 16 hr. 17 min. in Colac, Victoria, Australia, from November 26 to December 1, 1984.

Eleanor Robinson (UK) ran the **fastest women's 1,000 km ultra-
distance track event** in 8 days 27 min. 6 sec. in Nanango, Queensland,
Australia, from March 11 to 18, 1998. The term "ultra-distance" applies to
events staged over a greater than standard course and, sometimes, for events
carried out under more exacting conditions than usual.

X-REF

• There's more marathon magic on page 125.

• Teamwork is sometimes the key to success—as you'll see on
page 150.

• You'll find a wealth of sports stats 'n' facts from page 403 on . . .

• . . . including the GWR sports reference tables, starting on page 528.

☆ **FASTEST OUTDOOR 5,000 M (FEMALE)** Meseret Defar (Ethiopia) ran the 5,000 m in 14 min. 24.53 sec. in New York City, U.S.A., on June 3, 2006.

Most World Championships medals won
Merlene Ottey (Jamaica) won 14 World Championships medals: three gold, four silver, and seven bronze, 1983–97.

She also holds the record for the **most Olympic track & field medals won by a woman,** with eight: three silver and five bronze, 1980–2000.

The **most medals won in the World Championships by a man** is 10, by Carl Lewis (U.S.A.), comprising eight gold, one silver, and one bronze, 1983–93.

FASTEST 100 M (MALE) On June 14, 2005, Asafa Powell (Jamaica, above left) set a new world record of 9.77 seconds for the 100 m sprint in Athens, Greece—a time that he has since matched on two separate occasions. Justin Gatlin (U.S.A.) also ran the 100 m in exactly the same time on May 12, 2006, in Doha, Qatar.

★**Most World Cup wins (women)** East Germany has won the International Association of Athletics Federations (IAAF) World Cup four times, in 1979, 1983, 1985, and 1989.

The ★**most wins of the track & field World Cup by a men's team** is also four, by Africa in 1992, 1994, 1998, and 2002. (Both national and continental teams feature.)

★**Most European Cup wins (men)** East Germany won the European Cup six times, in 1970 and 1975–83. Germany has also won the title six times, in 1994–96, 1999, and 2004–05. (Held every two years from 1965 to 1993, the European Cup became an annual event in 1994.)

The ★**most wins by a women's team** is 12, by Russia, in 1993, 1995, and 1997–2006.

Oldest Olympic medalist Tebbs Lloyd Johnson (UK) was aged 48 years 115 days when he came in third in the 50,000 m walk in London, UK, in 1948.

The **oldest female Olympic medalist** was the Czech Dana Z. Topkov (b. September 19, 1922), who was 37 years 348 days old when she came in second in the 1960 Olympic javelin contest.

Oldest marathon The Boston Marathon was first held on April 19, 1897, when it was run over a distance of 24 miles 1,232 yd. (39 km).

John A. Kelley (U.S.A.) finished the Boston Marathon 61 times from 1928 to 1992, winning in 1935 and 1945.

Fastest half-marathon (male) Samuel Wanjiru (Kenya) ran a time of 58 min. 53 sec. in the Ras al-Khaimah international half-marathon in Ras al-Khaimah, United Arab Emirates, on February 9, 2007.

Elana Meyer (South Africa) recorded the **fastest half-marathon by a woman** with a time of 66 min. 44 sec. in Tokyo, Japan, on January 15, 1999.

Fastest marathon On September 28, 2003, Paul Tergat (Kenya) ran a marathon in a time of 2 hr. 4 min. 55 sec. in Berlin, Germany.

FARTHEST LONG JUMP Mike Powell (U.S.A., pictured) made a 29-ft. 4.3-in. (8.95-m) long jump in Tokyo, Japan, on August 30, 1991. Carl Lewis (U.S.A.) achieved the farthest indoor long jump—28 ft. 10 in. (8.79 m)—in New York City, U.S.A., on January 27, 1984.

Paula Radcliffe (UK) achieved the **fastest marathon by a woman** with a time of 2 hr. 15 min. 25 sec. in the London Marathon, UK, on April 13, 2003.

☆Fastest time to run three marathons in three days

Johan Oosthuizen (South Africa) ran three marathons in a combined time of 8 hr. 11 min. 8 sec. during the Lake Tahoe Triple marathon event in Lake Tahoe, Nevada, U.S.A., from September 28 to 30, 2006.

Shortest duration to complete a marathon on each continent

Tim Rogers (UK) completed a marathon on each of the seven continents in 99 days, from February 13 to May 23, 1999. He began his "marathon" feat with the Antarctica Marathon on King Jorge Island and went on to complete a marathon in the U.S.A. (North and Central America), South Africa (Africa), France (Europe), Brazil (South America), and Hong Kong (Asia)

FIRST IN THE FIELD

• On August 15, 2006, in Tallinn, Estonia, Tatyana Lysenko (Russia) achieved the ☆ **farthest hammer throw by a woman,** with a distance of 255 ft. 3 in. (77.8 m). In fact, the "hammer" is a metal ball on one end of a steel wire, at the other end of which is a grip. Not much good for pounding in nails, though . . .

• The **farthest javelin throw by a man,** one of 323 ft. 1.1 in. (98.48 m), was achieved by Jan Zĕlezný (Czech Republic), in Jena, Germany, on May 25, 1996. And the **farthest women's javelin throw?** See page 420.

• It's time to call the shots. Randy Barnes (U.S.A.) recorded the **farthest shot put** in Los Angeles, California, U.S.A., on May 20, 1990, with a put of 75 ft. 10.2 in. (23.12 m). The **farthest shot put by a woman** measured 74 ft. 3 in. (22.63 m) and was produced by Natalya Lisovskaya (USSR), in Moscow, Russia, on June 7, 1987.

• Leaping ahead, on June 11, 1988, in Leningrad, U.S.S.R. (now St. Petersburg, Russia), Galina Chistyakova (U.S.S.R.) produced the **farthest long jump by a woman,** measuring 24 ft. 8 in. (7.52 m). Heike Drechsler (GDR) holds the record for the **farthest indoor long jump by a woman,** with a distance of 24 ft. 2.1 in. (7.37 m), in Vienna, Austria, on February 13, 1988.

• One-two-three . . . Jonathan Edwards (UK) produced the **farthest triple jump by a man** in Gothenburg, Sweden, on August 7, 1995, with a leap of 60 ft. 0.7 in. (18.29 m). On August 10, 1995, Inessa Kravets (Ukraine) made the **farthest triple jump by a woman—**50 ft. 10.2 in. (15.5 m)—also in Gothenburg. Imagine that: one venue, two triple records in three days!

☆**FASTEST 50 KM ROAD WALK** Nathan Deakes (Australia, above) completed a 50 km road walk in an unprecedented 3 hr. 35 min. 47 sec. in Geelong, Australia, on December 2, 2006.

before finishing with a marathon in Huntly, New Zealand (Oceania) over three months later.

★**Shortest duration to complete a marathon on each continent (female)** Noelle Sheridan (U.S.A.) set a new record for the shortest overall time to complete a marathon on each of the seven continents by a woman. She took just 208 days from May 19 to December 13, 2006.

Fastest lunge mile To "lunge," an athlete starts from a standing position and extends one leg forward, bending the other leg until its knee touches the ground. The athlete then repeats the movement with the other leg. The ★**fastest time to lunge a mile by a woman** is 37 min. 58 sec. and was set by Dorothea Voegeli (Switzerland) in Dachau, Germany, on November 6, 2005.

The record for the **fastest lunge mile by a man** is 30 min. 50 sec., set by Ashrita Furman (U.S.A.) at the Sport Park in Neufahrn, Germany, on October 27, 2002.

Ashrita also recorded the ★**fastest mile hopping on a pogo stick while juggling three balls,** in 24 min. 49 sec., at the Brooklyn Promenade, Brooklyn Heights, New York City, U.S.A., on May 17, 2006. The ★**fastest time to hula hoop 10 km** is 1 hr. 25 min. 9 sec., and was set at Hechsler Park, Huntington, New York City, U.S.A., on June 12, 2006. The holder? You've guessed it—Ashrita Furman!

DID YOU KNOW?

The marathon was inspired by the story (probably a myth) of Greek runner Pheidippides. He ran 21.4 miles (34.5 km), from a battlefield near the town of Marathon to Athens, to announce a Greek victory over the Persians, then died.

MOST DECATHLON POINTS (FEMALE) Austa Skujyte (Lithuania) scored 8,358 points in the decathlon event in Columbia, Missouri, U.S.A., on April 14–15, 2005.

☆ **FARTHEST JAVELIN THROW (FEMALE)** Osleidys Menéndez (Cuba) achieved a record-breaking throw of 235 ft. (71.7 m) in the javelin event in Helsinki, Finland, on August 14, 2005.

★ **FASTEST HULA HOOPING OVER 10 KM (FEMALE)** Betty Hoops (U.S.A.) ran a distance of 10 km, while continuously hula hooping, in a time of 1 hr. 43 min. 11 sec. at the Bolder Boulder 10 km race in Colorado, U.S.A., on May 30, 2005.

★ FASTEST TIME TO HOP 100 M Andre Miller (Barbados, pictured left, far right) hopped 100 m in 17.4 seconds during the Barbados World Record Festival at Barbados National Stadium in St. Michael, Barbados, on March 25, 2006.

FEATS OF ENDURANCE

• Horst Preisler (Germany) completed 1,305 races of 26 miles 385 yd. (42.195 km) or longer from 1974 to 2004—the **most marathons completed by an individual.**

• The **longest annual running race** is the Sri Chinmoy 3,100 Mile Race, held in Jamaica, New York City, U.S.A. The fastest time to complete the race is 42 days 13 hr. 24 min. 3 sec. by Wolfgang Schwerk (Germany) in 2002. Suprabha Beckjord (U.S.A.) is the **only woman to have completed this race and is also the only person to have completed all of the 10 races held to date.**

• The **most wins of the Triathlon World Championship (male)** is four, by Simon Lessing (UK), in 1992, 1995, 1996, and 1998.
    He has also won the **most medals overall in the Triathlon World Championship (male)** to date, adding two silver medals (1993 and 1999) and one bronze (1997).
    The **fastest time achieved in winning the Triathlon World Championship (male)** is 1 hr. 39 min. 50 sec. by Simon Lessing (UK) in Cleveland, Ohio, U.S.A., in 1996.

• The **most wins of the ITU Triathlon World Championship (female),** in the Elite Women's event, is three, all by Emma Snowsill (Australia) in 2003, 2005, and most recently in Lausanne, Switzerland, on September 3, 2006.
    Michellie Jones has won the **most medals in the Triathlon World Championship (female)** overall. As well as her two gold medals, she has won two silver (1998 and 2001) and three bronze (1997, 2000, and 2003).
    The **fastest time to win the Triathlon World Championship (female)** is 1 hr. 50 min. 52 sec. by Jackie Gallagher (Australia) in Cleveland, Ohio, U.S.A., in 1996.

• The **highest score in a decathlon (male)** is 9,026 points, by Roman Šebrle (Czech Republic), in Götzis, Austria, on May 26–27, 2001.

LONGEST EVER RUNNING RACE The 1929 transcontinental race from New York City to Los Angeles, California, U.S.A., was 3,635 miles (5,850 km) long. The Finnish-born Johnny Salo (above right) was the winner, in 79 days, from March 31 to June 17. His time of 525 hr. 57 min. 20 sec. (averaging 6.91 mph or 11.12 km/h) left him only 2 min. 47 sec. ahead of Pietro "Peter" Gavuzzi (UK, above left).

☆**Fastest time to skip a marathon** The record for the fastest marathon run while skipping with a rope is 4 hr. 49 min. 39 sec. and was set by Chris Baron (Canada) at the ING Ottawa Marathon, Ottawa, Ontario, Canada, on May 29, 2005.

Oldest marathon finisher Greek runner Dimitrion Yordanidis ran a 26-mile marathon in Athens, Greece, on October 10, 1976, aged 98, in 7 hr. 33 min.

The **oldest female marathon finisher** is Jenny Wood-Allen (UK, b. 1911). She completed the 2002 London Marathon aged 90 years 145 days in 11 hr. 34 min. on April 14, 2002.

☆**FASTEST JOGGLING** The record for the fastest marathon while juggling three objects is held by Zach Warren (U.S.A., left), who ran the full Philadelphia Marathon—a distance of 26.22 miles (42.2 km)—while juggling three balls, in 3 hr. 7 min. 5 sec. in Philadelphia, U.S.A., on November 20, 2005.

FASTEST BACKWARDS MARATHON Xu Zhenjun (China, far left in the main group left) ran the Beijing International Marathon, China, backwards, in 3 hr. 43 min. 39 sec. on October 17, 2004.

AUTO SPORTS

The legend of Le Mans Instituted on May 26–27, 1923, Le Mans is the world's most famous endurance race. It is staged over the famous Circuit de la Sarthe course and organized by L'Automobile Club de l'Ouest (ACO).

The **most wins by an individual at the Le Mans 24-hour race** is seven by Tom Kristensen (Denmark) in 1997 and 2000–05.

Daytona 500 The ★**winner of the first Daytona 500,** in 1959, was Lee Petty (U.S.A.). He reached an average speed of 135.52 mph (218 km/h), driving an Oldsmobile.
•Kevin Harvick's (U.S.A.) 0.02-second margin of victory in the 2007 Daytona 500 was the ★**closest Daytona 500 victory** since the advent of electronic scoring in 1993.
•Driving a No. 48 Lowe's Chevrolet Monte Carlo in 2006, Jimmie Johnson (U.S.A.) became the ★**first driver to win the Daytona 500, Allstate 400, and NASCAR Nextel Cup Championship in the same year.**

Formula One Alberto Ascari (Italy) enjoyed a run of nine Formula One grand prix wins in 1952–53 driving for Ferrari, the **most consecutive Formula One grand prix victories.**
•Inaugurated in 1950, the World Drivers' Championship has been won seven times by Michael Schumacher (Germany) in 1994–95 and 2000–04, the **most Formula One World Championships won.**
•Schumacher also achieved the **most Formula One grand prix wins by a driver in a season,** with 13 victories in 2004.

The fastest lap in the Le Mans 24-hour race is 3 min. 21.27 sec. by Alain Ferté (France) on June 10, 1989

★MOST WOMEN RACING AT A MOTOR-SPORTS EVENT A total of 62
women took part in the Crash.net Formula Woman Novice Cup
Challenge staged at Pembrey Circuit, Pembrey, Wales, UK, on
November 19–20, 2005.

•The **most Formula One constructors' World Championships won** is 14
by Ferrari in 1961, 1964, 1975–77, 1979, 1982–83, and 1999–2004.

IndyCar Mario Andretti (U.S.A.) is the **★only racer to have won the
Indianapolis 500** (1969), the **Daytona 500** (1967), **and a Formula One
world title** (1978).
•Al Unser Jr. beat Scott Goodyear (both U.S.A.) in the **closest finish in the
history of the Indianapolis 500 race,** on May 24, 1992. The margin of victory was 0.043 seconds.
•Nigel Mansell (UK) made history in 1993 by becoming the **first rookie to
win the IndyCar Championship.**
   Mansell was also the 1992 Formula One World Driving Champion, making him the **★first driver to win the IndyCar and Formula One titles in
consecutive seasons.**
•In 1989, Emerson Fittipaldi (Brazil) and Patrick Racing shared winnings of
$1,001,604, becoming the **★first driver and team to earn $1 million in
one year for winning the Indianapolis 500.**
•Sam Hornish Jr. (U.S.A.) won the Indianapolis 500 with the **★first last-
lap pass** in the 90-year history of the race, on May 28, 2006. Hornish took
the lead on the final lap, passing rookie Marco Andretti (U.S.A.) just before
the checkered flag to capture his first Indy 500 win.

DID YOU KNOW?

The **youngest Formula One World Championship race winner** is
Fernando Alonso (Spain, b. July 29, 1981), who was aged 22 years 26
days when he won the Hungarian Grand Prix on August 24, 2003,
driving for Renault.

★ **YOUNGEST INDYCAR WINNER** Marco Andretti (U.S.A., b. March 13, 1987) is a third-generation driver from one of motor racing's most famous families. Aged 19 years 167 days, he became the youngest winner of a major open-wheel racing event when he scored his first career Indy Racing League victory at Infineon Raceway in Sonoma, California, U.S.A., on August 27, 2006. Andretti beat Dario Franchitti (UK) by 0.66 seconds to win the Indy Grand Prix in Sonoma.

NASCAR Jeff Gordon (U.S.A.) holds the record for the ☆ **highest National Association for Stock Car Auto Racing (NASCAR) career earnings,** with winnings of $82,373,526 to the end of the 2006 season.

★ **HIGHEST EARNINGS IN A SINGLE NASCAR SEASON (MALE)** Jimmie Johnson (U.S.A., above and in No. 48) earned $15,952,125 in 2006. He also achieved the ★ **most consecutive wins of the Coca-Cola 600 race,** with three in 2003–05. This 600-mile (965-km) race is the longest in NASCAR.

- In 2006, Denny Hamlin (U.S.A.) amassed prize money of $6,725,332, the ★ **highest single-season NASCAR earnings by a rookie.**
- The ★ **most money won by a rookie in his first season of NASCAR** is $4,759,020 by Kasey Kahne (U.S.A.) in 2004.
- The ★ **most consecutive race wins in NASCAR** is 10 by Richard Petty (U.S.A.) in 1967.
- Ricky Rudd (U.S.A.) started 788 consecutive races during his career from 1975 to 2005, the ★ **most consecutive starts in NASCAR.**
- The ★ **most pole positions achieved in a NASCAR season** is 20 by Bobby Isaac (U.S.A.) in 1969.
- The record for ★ **most cars in a 400-mile NASCAR race** is 35, set at the 2006 Allstate 400.
- The record for ★ **most cars in a 500-mile NASCAR race** is 31 on the lead lap at the 2006 Daytona 500.
- Juan Pablo Montoya (Colombia) became the ★ **first Formula One driver to switch to racing full-time in the NASCAR Nextel Cup series** in 2006.

NHRA For a gas-driven piston-engined car, the ★ **highest speed in Pro Stock National Hot Rod Association (NHRA) Drag Racing** is 209.75 mph (337.48 km/h) by Jason Line (U.S.A.) in a Pontiac GTO at Dinwiddie, Virginia, U.S.A., on October 15, 2006.
- The ★ **most NHRA Pro Stock championships won** is 10 by Bob Glidden (U.S.A.) in 1974, 1975, 1978, 1979, 1980, and 1985–89.
- Anthony Schumacher (U.S.A.) holds the record for ☆ **most consecutive Top Fuel NHRA round wins,** with 21 consecutive victories in 2005 and 2006 in the U.S. Army dragster.

★ **FASTEST SPEED IN TOP FUEL NHRA DRAG RACING (FEMALE)** The highest terminal velocity at the end of the 440-yd. (402-m) run by a female Top Fuel drag racer is 330.31 mph (531.58 km/h) by Melanie Troxel (U.S.A.) at the Texas Motorplex in Dallas, U.S.A., on October 7, 2005.

•The ★ **youngest NHRA Pro Stock winner** is Richie Stevens (U.S.A., b. September 27, 1978), who won the Winston Finals in Pomona, California, U.S.A., on November 18, 1998, aged 20 years 51 days.

•The ☆ **most NHRA Funny Car championships won** is 14 by John Force (U.S.A.) in 1990–91, 1993–2002, 2004, and 2006. Force is also the career leader in Funny Car victories, with 122 wins, and the season leader, with 13 wins in 1996.

•Warren Johnson (U.S.A., b. July 7, 1943) became the ★ **oldest driver to win an NHRA event,** at the age of 62 years 234 days. His record-breaking victory came at the Checker Schuck's Kragen NHRA Nationals at Firebird International Raceway, in Chandler, Arizona, U.S.A., on February 26, 2006.

MOTOCROSS

★ **Most arenacross championships** Arenacross is a U.S. indoor motocross competition. Two riders have won five championships: Dennis Hawthorne (U.S.A.), with wins in 1986–90, and Buddy Antunez (U.S.A.), in 1997–2001.

Motocross world championship The **most wins of the 125cc motocross world championship** is three, by three riders: Gaston Rahier (Belgium) in 1975–77, Harry Everts (Belgium) in 1979–81 and Alessio Chiodi (Italy) in 1997–99.

•The **most wins of the 500cc motorcross world championship** is five. It is shared by Roger de Coster (Belgium), with victories in 1971–73 and 1975–76, and Joel Smets (Belgium), with wins in 1995, 1997–98, 2000, and 2003.

☆ MOST MOTOCROSS DES NATIONS WINS Also known as the "Olympics of Motocross," the Motocross des Nations has been contested annually since 1947.

Two teams have won 16 times: Great Britain in 1947, 1949–50, 1952–54, 1956–57, 1959–60, 1963–67, and 1994; and the U.S.A. in 1981–93, 1996, 2000, and 2005.

Youngest motocross champion Dave Strijbos (Netherlands, b. November 9, 1968) won the 125cc motocross title aged 18 years 296 days on August 31, 1986.

MOTORCYCLE

Most world championship career race wins Between April 24, 1965 and September 25, 1977, Giacomo Agostini (Italy) won 122 races—68 at the 500cc class and 54 at the 350cc class.

Most world championship wins by a manufacturer Honda (Japan) won 48 World Championships in 1961–99.

★ MOST MOTO GRAND PRIX TITLES The Moto GP classification was instituted in 2002 and replaced the motorcycle World Championship 500cc Grand Prix.

The greatest number of Moto Grand Prix championships won by an individual is four, by Valentino Rossi (Italy) in 2002–05.

★ **MOST SUPERBIKE TITLES BY A MANUFACTURER** In 1977–2005, Kawasaki and Suzuki (both Japan) each won nine titles. Britain's Chris Walker is pictured on a Kawasaki ZX-7RR in the 2002 World Championship at Silverstone, UK.

Most world championship race wins in a season Two riders have won 19 motorcycle world championships in a season: Giacomo Agostini (Italy) in 1970, and Mike Hailwood (UK) in 1966.

Most superbike world championships Carl Fogarty (UK) won 59 races, 1992–99. He has also won the **most superbike world championship titles,** with four (1994–95, 1998–99).

☆ **Most Suzuka 8 Hours wins by a manufacturer** Honda (Japan) provided the winning motorcycle 20 times in the Suzuka 8 Hours endurance race, in 1979–2005.

☆ **MOST MOTORCYCLE SIDE-CAR WORLD CHAMPIONSHIPS** Steve Webster (UK) has won an unprecedented 10 motorcycle side-car World Championships, with victories in 1987–89, 1991, 1997–2000, and 2003–04.

First held on May 28, 1907, the Isle of Man TT Races are the world's oldest motorcycle races.

NHRA

★**Most NHRA titles in all categories (female)** Angelle Sampey (U.S.A.) won 40 National Hot Rod Association (NHRA) Pro Stock motorcycle titles between 1996 and 2006.

Sampey is the ★**first female to win an NHRA Pro Stock motorcycle championship,** winning three in a row between 2000 and 2002.

Drag racing The ★**most NHRA championships won in the Pro Stock motorbike category** is six by Dave Schultz (U.S.A.) in 1987–88, 1991, 1993–94, and 1996.
•The ☆**fastest speed achieved by a petrol-driven, piston-engined motorcycle (Pro Stock)** is 197.45 mph (317.69 km/hr.) by G.T. Tonglet (U.S.A.) on a Harley-Davidson on March 18, 2005, and Andrew Hines (U.S.A.)—also on a Harley-Davidson—on March 19, 2005. Both feats were achieved at Gainesville, Florida, U.S.A.
•The ☆**fastest time to cover 440 yd. on a Pro Stock motorbike** is 6.011 seconds and was achieved by Chip Ellis (U.S.A.) at Sonoma, California, U.S.A., on July 30, 2006.

RALLYING

Most rally world championship race wins in a season Didier Auriol (France) won six rally world championship races in 1992.

Most rally world championship race wins Carlos Sainz (Spain) recorded a total of 26 world championship race wins between 1990 and 2004.

TT RACES

Longest motorcycle race circuit The "Mountain" circuit on the Isle of Man, over which the principal TT Races have been run since 1911 (with minor amendments in 1920), has 264 curves and corners and is 37.73 miles (60.72 km) long.

TT RACES

The year 2007 marks a century of the TT (Tourist Trophy) Races, staged in the last week of May and the first week of June. Public roads on the Isle of Man are closed off to become the race circuit—now the oldest motorcycle course in regular use—and crowds of picnickers turn out to watch the racers hurtle round the roads at breakneck speeds.

☆**Fastest lap speed** The Isle of Man TT circuit record for the highest lap speed is 129.451 mph (208.33 km/hr.) by John McGuinness (UK, riding for England) on a Honda CBR1000 Fireblade on June 9, 2006.

Most wins in one year The greatest number of events won in one year in the TT Races is four—in the Formula One, Junior, Senior and Production categories—by Phillip McCallen (Ireland) in 1996.

Most wins in a career Joey Dunlop (Ireland) recorded 26 wins at the TT races between 1977 and 2000.

☆**Most wins by a manufacturer** The greatest number of wins by a manufacturer at the Isle of Man TT Races is 183, by Yamaha (Japan), from 1965 to 2005.

BALL SPORTS

AUSTRALIAN FOOTBALL

Most AFL games The career record for most Australian Football League (AFL) games played is 426 by Michael Tuck (Australia) for Hawthorn in 1972–91.

★**Most matches won** In the 2000 season, Essendon won 24 out of 25 matches.

LARGEST DISCIPLINARY FINES FOR A SINGLE AFL MATCH Following the match between the Western Bulldogs and St. Kilda on May 4, 2003, disciplinary fines totaling AUS$67,500 (U.S.$49,773) were imposed on players.

Highest team score Geelong scored 239 (37–17) against Brisbane on May 3, 1992. Geelong also recorded the **longest winning streak,** with 23 consecutive Premiership wins in 1952–53. The **most consecutive games lost** in the AFL Premiership is 51 by University in 1912–14.

Most goals John Coleman (Australia) scored 12 goals for Essendon v. Hawthorn in the 1949 season, the **most goals scored on an AFL debut.** •The **most goals in a season** is 150, by Bob Pratt (for South Melbourne) in 1934 and Peter Hudson (for Hawthorn; both Australia) in 1971.

CANADIAN FOOTBALL

★**Most pass attempts in a CFL career by a quarterback** Quarterback Damon Allen (U.S.A.) had achieved 9,071 pass attempts in his Canadian Football League (CFL) career through the 2006 season.

He also set a new record for the ★**most career pass completions in Canadian football** with 5,113 through the 2006 season.

Finally, Allen set a new record for the ★**most career touchdown passes in Canadian football,** with 391, through the 2006 season.

Allen's CFL career began in 1985.

CANADIAN FOOTBALL—MOST YARDS PASSING IN A CAREER Damon Allen (U.S.A.) threw for a record 71,590 yards during his CFL career for Edmonton, Ottawa, Hamilton, Memphis, British Columbia, and Toronto between 1985 and 2006.

☆GAELIC FOOTBALL: MOST ALL-IRELAND FINAL WINS Kerry has won 34 All-Ireland finals between 1903 and 2006. The greatest number of successive wins in an All-Ireland Final is four by Wexford (1915–18) and by Kerry twice (1929–32 and 1978–81). Pictured is Kerry's John Crowley (Ireland) in action against Mayo's Gary Ruane (Ireland).

GAELIC FOOTBALL

Highest combined score in an All-Ireland final The greatest aggregate score by both teams in an All-Ireland final was 45 points, when Cork (26, 3–17)* beat Galway (19, 2–13) in 1973.

Largest attendance The Down v. Offaly final at Croke Park in Dublin, Ireland, in 1961 attracted 90,556 spectators.

HANDBALL

Most men's world championships Sweden has won four titles, in 1954, 1958, 1990, and 1999, as has Romania in 1961, 1964, 1970, and 1974.

☆**Most women's European championships** Two teams have won these championships three times: Denmark in 1994, 1996, and 2002; and Norway in 1998, 2004, and 2006.

The **most women's handball world championships** won is three by East Germany in 1971, 1975, and 1978; and by the U.S.S.R. in 1982, 1986, and 1990.

★**Most wins of the beach world championships (men)** The men's beach handball world championships has been staged on two occasions, and the most wins is one, by Egypt in 2004 and Brazil in 2006.

*NB: in Gaelic football records, the aggregate score is listed first. The goals and points, respectively, are given separately afterward.

MOST OLYMPIC HANDBALL GOLD MEDALS—WOMEN The Danish women's team has won three consecutive Olympic gold medals—in 1996, 2000, and 2004. Pictured is Kristine Andersen (Denmark) of the 2004 winning team taking on Korea.

The ★most wins of the beach handball world championships (women) is one, by Russia in 2004 and Brazil in 2006.

Highest score at the handball Olympic games (women) Austria scored 45 points against Brazil in 2000.

MOST EUROPEAN HANDBALL CHAMPIONSHIPS WON—WOMEN The most European Handball Championships won by a women's team is three: by Denmark in 1994, 1996, and 2002; and by Norway in 1998, 2004, and 2006. The Norwegian team is pictured playing against Russia on their way to winning the 2006 European Handball Championships (by 27 points to 24) on December 17 in Stockholm, Sweden.

HOCKEY

☆ **MOST WOMEN'S FIELD HOCKEY WORLD CUP WINS** The Netherlands has won the women's field hockey world cup six times, in 1974, 1978, 1983, 1986, 1990, and 2006. Pictured far left is the Netherlands' Maartje Goderie with Mariana Gonzalez (Argentina) in the semifinal in Spain on October 6, 2006.

★**Most gold medals won by an individual (female)** Rechelle Hawkes (Australia), captain of the Australian women's field hockey team (also known as the Hockeyroos), has won three golds—in 1988, 1996, and 2000.

Highest score in international hockey (women) The England women's hockey team beat France 23–0 at Merton, London, UK, on February 3, 1923.

☆ **MOST FIELD HOCKEY CHAMPIONS TROPHY WINS** Three teams have won this trophy eight times: Germany in 1986–88 (as West Germany), 1991–92, 1995, 1997, and 2001; the Netherlands in 1981–82, 1996, 1998, 2000, 2002–03, and 2006; and Australia in 1983–85, 1989–90, 1993, 1999, and 2005. Pictured is Australia's Michael McCann in 2005.

★ MOST APPEARANCES IN INTERNATIONAL FIELD HOCKEY Jeroen Delmee (Netherlands, pictured at right with France's Nicolas Gaillard) made a record 338 appearances for the Netherlands men's team from 1994 to 2006.

Most World Cups (men) Pakistan has won four times, in 1971, 1978, 1982, and 1994.

☆ **Most international goals scored by an individual** The greatest number of goals scored in international field hockey is 288 by left full back Sohail Abbas (Pakistan, b. June 9, 1977) between 1998 and 2006. Sohail is a field hockey defender and penalty corner specialist.

NETBALL

☆ **Most Commonwealth Games titles** Netball has been played three times at the Commonwealth Games, first in Kuala Lumpur, Malaysia, in 1998, then Manchester, UK, in 2002, and Melbourne, Australia, in 2006, with Australia winning on the first two occasions and New Zealand the third.

★ **Most consecutive passes** Pupils of Brookfield Community School, Chesterfield, Derbyshire, UK, achieved 164 netball passes in a row on September 22, 2006.

Most international appearances (female) Irene van Dyk (New Zealand) made a record 129 appearances at international level playing for South Africa and New Zealand between 1994 and 2005.

Longest marathon The world's longest game of netball lasted 55 hours and was played by members of Capital NUNS netball club at the Shell Centre, Waterloo, London, UK, from July 22 to 24, 2005.

VOLLEYBALL

☆ **Highest career earnings in beach volleyball** Karch Kiraly (U.S.A.) has won a record $3,172,461 in official Association of Volleyball Professional (AVP) Tour earnings through to the end of the 2006 season. He also won a record 148 AVP Tour titles between 1979 and 2006.

★Most times to win AVP best offensive player award (male) The most AVP Pro Beach Tour offensive player of the year awards won by a male player is four by Jose Loiola (Brazil) from 1995 to 1998.

★Most times to win AVP best defensive player award (male) The most Pro Beach defensive player of the year awards won by a male is four by Mike Dodd (U.S.A.) in 1994–97.

OTHER BALL SPORTS

• The record for the **most consecutive foot-bag kicks with two foot-bags** is held by Juha-Matti Rytilahti (Finland) with 68 kicks by one foot on September 30, 2001.

• The **most foot-bag kicks in five minutes** is 1,019 by Andy Linder (U.S.A.) on June 7, 1996.

• In 2006, England hosted the inaugural Commonwealth Korfball Championships, and went on to win it. By default, therefore, England secured the record for the **★ most wins of the Commonwealth Korfball Championships.**

• The **longest game of korfball played** is 26 hr. 2 min., set by the Korfball Club De Vinken in Vinkeveen, the Netherlands, on May 23–24, 2001.

• The **largest korfball tournament** was held on June 14, 2003, when 2,571 men and women participated in the Kom Keukens/Ten Donck international youth korfball tournament in Ridderkerk, the Netherlands.

• The record for the **longest hurling hit** is a "lift and stroke" of 387 ft. (118 m; 129 yd.) credited to Tom Murphy of Three Castles, Kilkenny, Ireland, in a "long puck" contest in 1906.

• The **lowest combined score in an All-Ireland hurling final** is four, when Tipperary (one goal, one point) beat Galway (zero) in the first championship, held at Birr, Offaly, Ireland, in 1887.

• The **most team wins of the shinty Challenge Cup** is a record 28 by Newtonmore, Highland, UK, in 1907–86.

• The Camanachd Cup is shinty's most prestigious trophy. The **most consecutive Camanachd Cup wins by a team** is seven, by Kingussie (Scotland), from 1997 to 2003.

• The record for the **most goals scored in a Major League lacrosse career** is 206, held by Mark Millon (U.S.A.) of the Baltimore Bayhawks and the Boston Cannons between 2001 and 2005.

• The **longest recorded lacrosse throw** is 488 ft. 5 in. (148.91 m; 162.86 yds.), by Barnet Quinn of Ottawa, Canada, on September 10, 1892.

★ **MOST TIMES TO WIN THE AVP BEST OFFENSIVE PLAYER AWARD (FEMALE)** The greatest number of Association of Volleyball Professionals (AVP) Pro Beach Tour offensive player of the year awards won by a female player is three by Misty May-Treanor (U.S.A.) in 2004–06.

★ **MOST TIMES TO WIN THE AVP BEST DEFENSIVE PLAYER AWARD (FEMALE)** Holly McPeak (U.S.A.) has won the defensive player of the year award three times, in 2002–04.

★ **MOST WINS OF THE VOLLEYBALL GRAND PRIX (WOMEN)** Brazil has won the women's volleyball Grand Prix six times: 1994, 1996, 1998, and 2004–06. Pictured is Brazil's Fabiana Claudino in the Fédération Internationale de Volleyball (FIVB) World Grand Prix in Tokyo, Japan, on August 20, 2006.

★ **Most consecutive wins of the world championships (men)** Italy has won the indoor volleyball world championships three times, in Brazil in 1990, Greece in 1994, and Japan in 1998. The **most successive wins of the women's world championships** is three by the U.S.S.R.: in 1952 in the Soviet Union, 1956 in France, and 1960 in Brazil.

FASTEST BALL The fastest speed a projectile moves in any ball game is around 188 mph (302 km/hr.)—in jai alai, a sport that originates from the Basque areas of Spain and France. The jai alai ball is three-quarters the size of a baseball and harder than a golf ball. It is propelled through the air—and caught—using a 27-in. (70-cm) scoop-shaped cesta basket-glove (or *xistera* in the Basque language).

★**Most wins of the European championships** The U.S.S.R. men's team has won the indoor volleyball European championships a record 12 times between 1950 and 1992. The **most wins of the volleyball European championships by a women's team** is 13, also by the U.S.S.R., between 1949 and 1991.

Most national championships won by a team Changos de Naranjito won 20 championships in the Puerto Rico men's volleyball national league between 1958 and 2004.

DID YOU KNOW?

In electronically timed tests, a golf ball driven off a tee was found to have a top speed of 169.6 mph (273 km/h), compared with Jose Ramon Areitio's jai alai throw of 188 mph (302 km/h)!

BASEBALL

IN A CAREER . . .

☆**Most strikeouts** The Major League Baseball (MLB) record for the most strikeouts in a career is 5,714 by Nolan Ryan (U.S.A.) playing for the New York Mets, California Angels, Houston Astros, and Texas Rangers (all U.S.A.) from 1966 to 1993.

★**Most consecutive games played** From the beginning of his career with the New York Yankees (U.S.A.) on January 14, 2003, Hideki Matsui (Japan) played 518 consecutive games until May 11, 2006, when he injured his wrist.

Most games lost by a pitcher The pitcher who lost the most games in a career was Denton True "Cy" Young (U.S.A.), with 316 losses between 1890 and 1911, while playing for the Cleveland Spiders, St. Louis Cardinals, Boston Red Sox, Cleveland Indians, and Boston Braves (all U.S.A.).

★**Most consecutive 200-hit seasons** Ichiro Suzuki (Japan) had six consecutive 200-hit seasons for the Seattle Mariners (U.S.A.) from 2001 to 2006.

★**Most bases on balls** Playing for the Pittsburgh Pirates and San Francisco Giants (both U.S.A.) from 1986 to 2006, Barry Bonds (U.S.A.)

★ **MOST SAVES IN A CAREER** Trevor Hoffman (U.S.A., above) made an unprecedented 482 saves playing for the Florida Marlins and San Diego Padres (both U.S.A.) from 1993 to 2006. The record for the ★ **most saves in the American League in a career** is held by Mariano Rivera (Panama), with 413 for the New York Yankees (U.S.A.) from 1995 to 2006.

★LARGEST BASEBALL MITT On display at the San Francisco Giants' home stadium in San Francisco, California, U.S.A., this giant mitt measures 26 ft. (8 m) high, 32 ft. (9.7 m) wide, and 12 ft. (3.6 m) deep. It weighs 20,000 lb. (9,070 kg).

★LARGEST BASEBALL The largest baseball measured 12 ft. (3.6 m) in diameter and went on display at the David L. Lawrence Convention Center in Pittsburgh, Pennsylvania, U.S.A., from July 7 to 11, 2006. The ball is signed by famous players such as Ted Williams and Hank Aaron (both U.S.A.).

recorded 2,426 bases on balls. Bonds's achievement also represents the record for the ★ most intentional bases on balls in a career—confirming that he truly is a dangerous batter.

★Most strikeouts by a left-handed pitcher Randy Johnson (U.S.A.) threw 4,544 left-handed strikeouts playing for the Montreal Expos (Canada), and the Seattle Mariners, Houston Astros, Arizona Diamond-backs, and New York Yankees (all U.S.A.) from 1988 to 2006.

★Most times hit by pitches The MLB modern record (i.e., post-1900) for the most times to be hit by pitches in a career is 282, held by Craig Biggio (U.S.A.) playing for the Houston Astros (U.S.A.) from 1988 to 2006.

MOST HOME RUNS...

★Under one manager from start of career Chipper Jones (U.S.A.) hit 357 home runs while playing for manager Bobby Cox (U.S.A.) of the Atlanta Braves (U.S.A.) from 1993 to 2006.

DID YOU KNOW?

The baseball mitt shown above is a replica of a vintage 1927 four-fingered glove, scaled up to 36 times its actual size!

☆**By a switch-hitter** Switch-hitter Mickey Mantle (U.S.A.) hit 536 home runs playing for the New York Yankees (U.S.A.) from 1951 to 1968.

The record for **most career home runs by a switch-hitter in the National League** is 357 by Chipper Jones (U.S.A.), playing for the Atlanta Braves (U.S.A.) from 1993 to 2006.

★**By a second baseman** Jeff Kent (U.S.A.) hit 319 home runs while playing for the Toronto Blue Jays (Canada), and the New York Mets, Cleveland Indians, San Francisco Giants, Houston Astros, and Los Angeles Dodgers (all U.S.A.) from 1992 to 2006.

★**By a left fielder** Playing for the Pittsburgh Pirates and San Francisco Giants (both U.S.A.) from 1986 to 2006, Barry Bonds (U.S.A.) hit 698 home runs.

★**By a catcher** Mike Piazza (U.S.A.) hit 396 home runs while playing for the Los Angeles Dodgers, Florida Marlins, New York Mets, and San Diego Padres (all U.S.A.) from 1992 to 2006.

★**By a designated hitter in a season** David Ortiz (Dominican Republic) hit 47 home runs playing for the Boston Red Sox (U.S.A.) in 2006.

★**By a rookie second baseman in a season** Playing for the Florida Marlins (U.S.A.) in 2006, Dan Uggla (U.S.A.) hit 27 home runs in a single season.

☆**MOST RUNS BATTED IN BY A SWITCH-HITTER IN A SEASON** Mark Teixeira (U.S.A.) achieved 144 RBIs playing for the Texas Rangers (U.S.A.) in 2005. The National League (NL) record is 136 by Lance Berkman (U.S.A., pictured above right) playing for the Houston Astros (U.S.A.) in 2006.

★ ONLY MEMBERS OF THE "40–40" CLUB Just four MLB players have hit at least 40 home runs and stolen at least 40 bases in the same season (the "40–40" club). The most recent was Alfonso Soriano (Dominican Republic, left) playing for the Washington Nationals (U.S.A.) in 2006.

SOLD AT AUCTION

• The **most valuable baseball bat** in the world is the one used by George Herman Ruth (aka "Babe" Ruth, U.S.A.) to hit the first home run on opening day April 18, 1923, at Yankee Stadium in New York City, U.S.A. The bat was purchased by MastroNet, Inc. (an Illinois-based auction house in America) at an auction at Sotheby's, New York City, U.S.A., for a record $1,265,000 on December 2, 2004.

• The record for the **most valuable baseball** was set on January 12, 1999, when Todd McFarlane (U.S.A.) paid $3,054,000, including commission, for a ball at Guernsey's auction house in New York City, U.S.A. The baseball in question was the one hit by Mark McGwire (U.S.A.) of the St. Louis Cardinals for his 70th and final home run in his record-setting 1998 season.

• At an auction in Dallas, Texas, U.S.A., on May 5, 2006, Heritage Auction Galleries sold a baseball signed in 1961 by legendary baseball player Joe DiMaggio and movie star Marilyn Monroe (both U.S.A.). It secured $191,200, making it the ★ **most valuable autographed baseball.**

• The ☆ **most valuable baseball card** was a rare 1909 tobacco card, known as T206 Honus Wagner, sold by SCP Auctions in Los Angeles, California, U.S.A., to an anonymous collector for $2.35 million on February 27, 2007.

• The glove used by legendary U.S. baseball star Lou Gehrig during his final game on April 30, 1939, became the **most valuable baseball glove** in history when it sold for $389,500 at Sotheby's, New York City, U.S.A., on September 29, 1999.

★ **FIRST CATCHER TO LEAD THE MAJOR LEAGUES IN BATTING AVERAGE** Joe Mauer (U.S.A.) batted .347 while playing for the Minnesota Twins (U.S.A.) in 2006.

☆ **MOST TIMES HIT BY PITCHES IN A GAME** Several players have been hit three times by pitches. The most recent were Nomar Garciaparra (U.S.A.), playing for the Los Angeles Dodgers (U.S.A.) on July 3, 2006, and Reed Johnson (U.S.A., right), playing for the Toronto Blue Jays (Canada) on April 29, 2006.

BASKETBALL

☆ **Longest time to spin a basketball on one finger** Joseph Odhiambo (U.S.A.) spun a regulation basketball continuously for 4 hr. 15 min. on February 19, 2006, in Houston, Texas, U.S.A., during the NBA All-Star Jam Session.

☆ **Most successful free throws in one hour** Michael Campbell (U.S.A.) managed a total of 1,197 successful free throws in one hour at the Princeton Family YMCA in Princeton, New Jersey, U.S.A., on July 21, 2006.

☆ **FARTHEST BASKETBALL SLAM DUNK FROM A TRAMPOLINE** Daisuke Nakata (Japan, above) slam-dunked a basketball from a trampoline set 20 ft. 8 in. (6.3 m) from the backboard, on the set of the *Muscle Musical* show in Tokyo, Japan, on December 29, 2006. The record was matched on the same show by Shunsuke Nagasaki (Japan).

★ **BEST THREE-POINT FIELD-GOAL SHOOTING PERCENTAGE IN A CAREER** Steve Kerr (Lebanon) is the NBA's most accurate three-point shooter. He shot 45.4% from beyond the three-point line, making 726 of his 1,599 regular-season attempts while playing for six different teams from 1988 to 2003.

★ MOST POINTS SCORED IN A WNBA GAME On August 10, 2006, Diana Lurena Taurasi (U.S.A., left) scored a record 47 points to lead the Phoenix Mercury to a 111–110 triple-overtime win over the Houston Comets in the highest-scoring game in WNBA history.

★ MOST POINTS SCORED IN A PROFESSIONAL GAME (FEMALE) Anat Draigor (Israel) scored 136 points for Hapoel Mate Yehuda against Elitzur Givat Shmuel in Mesilat Zion, Israel, on April 5, 2006, the greatest number of points scored in a female professional basketball game.

DID YOU KNOW?

Diana Lurena Taurasi joined the University of Connecticut, U.S.A., in the 2000–01 season. While she was there, she won the 2003 and 2004 Naismith College Player of the Year awards, the 2003 Wade Trophy, and the 2003 AP Player of the Year Award.

NBA

★**Fastest coach to 900 victories** Phil Jackson (U.S.A.) recorded 900 victories out of 1,264 games while coaching the Chicago Bulls (1989–97) and Los Angeles Lakers (1999–2003, 2005–06). Jackson surpassed the feat that Pat Riley (U.S.A.) accomplished in 1,278 games with the Lakers (1981–89), New York Knicks (1991–94), and Miami Heat (1995–2002, 2005–06).

★**Best three-point field-goal shooting percentage in a single postseason** Derek Fisher (U.S.A.) shot 61.7% from beyond the three-point line, making 29 of his 47 attempts for the Los Angeles Lakers in the 2002–03 postseason.

★**Oldest player to record 20 rebounds in a game** At the age of 40 years 251 days, Dikembe Mutombo (Congo, b. June 25, 1966) recorded 22 rebounds playing for the Houston Rockets (U.S.A.) in their 108–97 victory over the Denver Nuggets on March 2, 2007.

★**First All-Star Game held outside an NBA city** The Western Conference All-Stars defeated the Eastern Conference All-Stars 153–132 in the NBA All-Star Game, played in Las Vegas, U.S.A., on February 18, 2007. It was the first All-Star Game not held in an NBA city.

Most... The ★**most consecutive three-point field goals scored** is 13, a feat achieved by two players: Brent Price (U.S.A.) for the Washington Wizards (1995–96); and Terry Mills (U.S.A.) for the Detroit Pistons (1996–97).

★**FASTEST COACH TO 100 NBA VICTORIES** Avery Johnson (U.S.A., pictured with Devin Harris) recorded 100 victories out of a record 131 games as coach of the Dallas Mavericks. The 100th win came in the Mavericks' win over the Denver Nuggets in Denver, Colorado, U.S.A., on December 31, 2006.

★ MOST THREE-POINT FIELD GOALS SCORED IN AN NBA SEASON Ray Allen (U.S.A.) scored 269 three-point goals playing for the Seattle SuperSonics during the 2005–06 season. He also holds the record for **most three-point field goals scored in one half** with eight against the Charlotte Hornets on April 14, 2002.

• The Dallas Mavericks' 110–87 win over the Atlanta Hawks on February 26, 2007, gave them the record for the **★ most winning streaks of 12 or more games in a single season,** with three. They are the first team in NBA history to achieve this feat.

• Reggie Miller (U.S.A.) scored the **☆ most career three-point field goals,** with 2,560 three-pointers for the Indiana Pacers from 1987 to 2005.

WNBA

The Women's National Basketball Association was formed in 1996, with league play beginning in 1997.

• The **★ most points scored by a team in a game** is 114 by the Minnesota Lynx (U.S.A.) in a 114–71 victory over the Los Angeles Sparks (U.S.A.) on May 31, 2006.

• Diana Taurasi (U.S.A.) became the **★ first player to score 800 points in a season,** finishing the 2006 campaign with 860 points while playing for the Phoenix Mercury.

• Lisa Leslie (U.S.A.) holds the record for the **☆ most field goals,** with 2,000 playing for the Los Angeles Sparks (U.S.A.) between 1997 and 2006. Leslie also holds the record for the **☆ most free throws in a career,** with 1,295 in 307 games playing for the Los Angeles Sparks from 1997 to 2006.

• Margo Dydek (U.S.A.) achieved the **☆ most blocks,** with 811 in 289 games playing for the Utah Starzz (1998–2002), the San Antonio Silver Stars (2003–04), and the Connecticut Sun (2005–06).

• The **☆ greatest number of steals in a career** by an individual player is 584 in 259 games by Sheryl Swoopes (U.S.A.), playing for the Houston Comets between 1998 and 2006.

•Phil Jackson (U.S.A.) has won 178 play-off games as coach of the Chicago Bulls (1989–97) and Los Angeles Lakers (1999–2003, 2005–06), ☆ **the most play-off games won by a coach.** Pat Riley (U.S.A.) is second, with 171 postseason wins as coach of the Lakers (1981–89), New York Knicks (1981–89), and Miami Heat (1995–2002, 2005–06).

•Three people share the record for the ★ **most consecutive NBA All-Star Game selections.** These players are: Shaquille O'Neal (U.S.A.), playing for the Orlando Magic, Los Angeles Lakers, and Miami Heat from 1994 to 2007; Jerry West (U.S.A.) of the Los Angeles Lakers, from 1961 to 1974; and Karl Malone (U.S.A.) of the Utah Jazz, from 1988 to 2001. All have been selected for the NBA All-Star Game 14 years in a row.

•Allen Iverson (U.S.A.) scored 40-plus points in five consecutive games for the Philadelphia 76ers in April 1997, the ★ **most consecutive games in which a rookie has scored 40-plus points.**

•As of March 15, 2007, Jerry Sloan (U.S.A.) had committed 413 technical fouls in his NBA career—as a player with the Baltimore Bullets (1965–66) and Chicago Bulls (1966–67 to 1975–76), and as a coach with the Bulls (1979–80 to 1981–82) and Utah Jazz (1988–89 to 2006–07). This represents the ★ **most technical fouls in an NBA career.** Sloan is the only person to record over 400 technical fouls since the league officially began recording this statistic in 1970.

COMBAT SPORTS

BOXING

Longest fight The longest world title fight (under Queensberry Rules) was that between lightweights Joe Gans (U.S.A.) and Oscar Matthew "Battling" Nelson (Denmark) in Goldfield, Nevada, U.S.A., on September 3, 1906. It was ended in the 42nd round when Gans was declared the winner on a technicality.

Youngest world champion Wilfred Benitez (U.S.A.) of Puerto Rico was 17 years 176 days when he won the WBA light welterweight title in Puerto Rico on March 6, 1976.

Oldest champion Archie Moore, aka "Ol' Mongoose" (U.S.A.)—who was recognized as a light heavyweight champion up to February 10, 1962, when his title was removed—was then believed to be between 45 and 48 years old.

Most knockdowns in a bout Vic Toweel, South Africa's first boxing world champion, knocked down Danny O'Sullivan (UK) 14 times in 10 rounds in their Commonwealth bantamweight fight in Wembley Stadium,

HIGHEST ANNUAL EARNINGS FOR A BOXER Oscar de la Hoya (U.S.A., pictured above left) is the world's highest paid boxer, with estimated earnings of $38 million in 2005, according to the *Forbes Rich List*.

Johannesburg, South Africa, on December 2, 1950. O'Sullivan eventually retired.

★ **Most consecutive world middleweight title defenses** The most consecutive successful defenses of the WBC middleweight world title is 14 by Carlos Monzon (Argentina) between 1970 and 1977. He achieved this despite being shot in the leg, in 1973, by his wife. In that year, he defended the title twice, then continued boxing for four more years!

☆ **MOST CONSECUTIVE WORLD SUPERMIDDLEWEIGHT TITLE DEFENSES** Joe Calzaghe (UK)—aka the "Italian Dragon"—made his 19th title defense on October 14, 2006, when he successfully beat Sakio Bika (Cameroon) in Manchester, UK, in a highly aggressive and frequently "dirty" fight.

Most knockouts in a career The greatest number of finishes classed as "knockouts" in a career is 145 (129 in professional bouts) by Archie Moore (U.S.A., b. Archibald Lee Wright). The "Ol' Mongoose" from Mississippi fought in a career lasting from 1936 to 1963, and for almost 10 years he reigned as light heavyweight world champion.

TAE KWON DO

Most Olympic gold medals won Ha Tae-kyung (South Korea) holds two Olympic titles in men's tae kwon do—winning gold in the flyweight in 1988 and welterweight in 1992. Chen Yi-an (Taiwan) matched this record for female competitors, winning the bantamweight title in 1988 and the lightweight in 1992.

Most men's world championship titles The most tae kwon do world titles won by a man is four, by Chung Kook-hyun (South Korea). He held light middleweight titles in 1982 and 1983, and welterweight titles in 1985 and 1987.

MARTIAL ARTS

• The record for the **most sumo wrestling bouts won** is held by *ozeki* Tameemon Torokichi (Japan), alias Raiden (1767–1825). In 21 years (1789–1810) he won 254 bouts and lost 10 to gain the highest ever winning percentage of 96.2.

• The ☆ **most competitive full-contact rounds** contested in boxing and martial arts is 6,264 by multiple record-holder Paddy Doyle (UK) from 1993 to November 2005.

• The ☆ **most full-contact kicks in one hour** is 5,545 by Ron Sarchian (U.S.A.) at Premier Fitness, Encino, California, U.S.A., on June 16, 2006.

• The **most kumite karate titles won by an individual** is four, by Guusje van Mourik (Netherlands) in the Female Over 60 kg category in 1982, 1984, 1986, and 1988.

• The record for the ☆ **most martial arts punches in one minute** is 548, and was achieved by Mick Fabar (Australia) at the Aussie Stadium in Sydney, Australia, on June 22, 2006.

• Csaba Mezei and Zoltán Farkas (both Hungary) of the Szany Judo Sport Team completed the **most judo throws in 10 hours,** achieving 57,603 at the Szany Sports Hall, Szany, Hungary, on May 1, 2003. The lucky "victims" were 27 members of the team.

• Don "The Dragon" Wilson (U.S.A.) won the **most world kickboxing titles,** taking 11 titles in three weight divisions (light heavyweight, super light heavyweight, and cruiserweight) in 1980–1999.

★ Most pine boards broken with feet in one minute (2 people)
Alejandro Marín and Angel Sáchez (both Spain) used moves associated with the Korean martial art tae kwon do to break a record 18 pine boards with their feet on the set of *Guinness World Records—El Show de los Records* in Madrid, Spain, on June 4, 2006.

★ Fastest time to break five glass bottles Tae kwon do expert Alberto Delgado (Spain) smashed five glass bottles with his right hand in a time of 1 min. 39 sec. on the set of *Guinness World Records—El Show de los Records* in Madrid, Spain, on June 11, 2006.

WRESTLING

Most consecutive sumo wrestling wins
The *yokozuna* Sadaji Akiyoshi (Japan), alias Futabayama, set an all-time record of 69 consecutive wins (1937 to 1939).

★ OLDEST AND YOUNGEST WRESTLERS TO WIN THE WWE
CHAMPIONSHIP The oldest wrestler to win the World Wrestling
Entertainment (WWE) Championship is Vince McMahon (U.S.A.,
above left), who took the title aged 54 years 21 days on September 14,
1999. The ★ youngest person to win the WWE Championship is
Brock Lesnar (U.S.A., above right). He was just 25 years 44 days when
he beat The Rock on August 25, 2002.

★ Most wins of the WWE Royal Rumble The most wins of the Royal
Rumble by an individual is three, by "Stone Cold" Steve Austin (U.S.A.) in
1997, 1998, and 2001. His consecutive wins (1997–98) is also a record,
shared with Hulk Hogan (U.S.A., 1990–91) and Shawn Michaels (U.S.A.,
1995–96).

★ Most wins of the WWE Royal Rumble from entry no. 30 The
Royal Rumble begins with 30 men—two in the ring and the rest outside; at
regular intervals, one wrestler after another enters the fight, and the last man
standing is the winner. Although the best position to enter the fight is last, at
number 30, only one wrestler, The Undertaker (U.S.A.), has won from this
position. It was achieved at the 2007 Royal Rumble on January 27.

CRICKET

WORLD CUP

★ Most wins With their victory in 2007, Australia won their third International Cricket Council (ICC) World Cup in a row. They also have the
★ longest unbeaten streak in World Cup matches, having gone 29 games
without losing.

★ **MOST WORLD CUP RUNS** Sachin Tendulkar (India) scored a record 1,796 runs from 1992 to 2007. He also holds records for the **most runs in a single World Cup**, with 673 runs in the 2003 tournament in South Africa, the ☆ **most centuries in ODI matches in a career**, with 41 from 1989 to 2007, and ☆ **most ODI runs in a career**, with 14,847 at an average of 44.05.

☆ **Most runs in a match** Australia (377–6) and South Africa (294 all out) scored a one-day international (ODI) record total 671 runs at Warner Park, Basseterre, St. Kitts, on March 24, 2007.

This included the ☆ **fastest World Cup century** by Matthew Hayden (Australia), who hit 101 runs from 66 balls.

★ **Most wickets** Glenn McGrath of Australia has taken 71 wickets in 39 World Cup matches, including 26 in the 2007 tournament—the ★ **most wickets in a single World Cup.**

★ **Most catches** Australian wicketkeeper Adam Gilchrist has held the most catches in World Cups, with 45 from 1999 to 2007. He also has the ★ **fastest World Cup final century** in 72 balls against Sri Lanka at Kensington Oval in Bridgetown, Barbados, on April 28, 2007.

☆ **MOST WINS OF THE CRICKET WORLD CUP (FEMALE)** The most women's cricket World Cup wins by a national side is six by Australia, in 1978, 1982, 1988, 1997, 2000, and 2005.

☆Highest margin of victory India scored 413–5 to beat Bermuda (156 all out) by 257 runs at Queen's Park Oval, Port of Spain, Trinidad, on March 19, 2007. India's total was also the ★ **highest innings by a team.**

★Most consecutive international wickets Lasith Malinga (Sri Lanka) became the first bowler to achieve four consecutive dismissals in any form of international cricket against South Africa in Guyana on March 28, 2007.

Fewest runs in a game This record stands at 73, when Sri Lanka (37–1) beat Canada (36 all out) at Boland Bank Park, Paarl, South Africa, on February 19, 2003.

INTERNATIONAL CRICKET

☆Highest partnership in a one-day international Sachin Tendulkar and Rahul Dravid (both India) amassed 331 runs against New Zealand in Hyderabad, India, on November 8, 1999.

☆Highest score in a one-day international by a team Sri Lanka reached 443–9 against the Netherlands in a match held on Amstelveen, the Netherlands, on July 4, 2006. They also have the **highest Test score,** with 952–6 against India at Colombo, Sri Lanka, on August 4–6, 1997.

☆Most wickets taken in Test matches Shane Warne (Australia) is the leading Test match wicket-taker, with 708 wickets (average 25.41 runs per wicket) in 145 matches, from August 1992 to his retirement after the final Test of the Ashes series in 2007.

☆Most Test matches umpired Steve Bucknor (Jamaica) has officiated at 117 Test matches between 1989 and 2007. He also holds the record for **most World Cup finals umpired,** with five between 1992 and 2007.

★Most Test matches as captain Allan Border (Australia) played as captain of his national side record 93 times

☆MOST INTERNATIONAL WICKETS TAKEN Muttiah Muralitharan (Sri Lanka) has taken 1,129 wickets playing for Sri Lanka, the ICC XI and the Asia XI between 1992 and 2007. The figure comprises 674 Test and 455 ODI wickets.

between 1978 and 1994. All his games as captain were played consecutively, which is also a record. He also has the ★ **most Test games played consecutively,** playing 153 consecutive games (out of 156) for Australia between 1978 and 1994.

★**Highest partnership in a limited overs match** Mohammed Shaibaaz Tumbi and B. Manoj Kumar (both India) put on a record stand of 721 runs for St. Peter's School against St. Phillip's High School in Secunderabad, India, on November 15, 2006.

★**Most dismissals in the 90s in Test match cricket** Steve Waugh (Australia) has been dismissed 10 times in the 90s. Such a score is unenviable as it means getting out before reaching the milestone of a century (100 runs).

☆**Most ODI matches played in a career** Sanath Jayasuriya (Sri Lanka) has played 390 ODIs for his country between 1989 and 2007.

BIG HITTERS

• The ★ **highest limited overs total in professional circket** is 496—4 from 50 overs by Surrey v. Gloucestershire at the Brit Oval, London, UK, on April 29, 2007.

• At the 2007 World Cup, Herschelle Gibbs (South Africa) became the ★ **first person to score six sixes in one over in an International match** against the Netherlands at Basseterre, St. Kitts, on March 16.

• The ★ **most Test match centuries in a calender year** is nine by Mohammad Yousuf (formerly known as Yousuf Youhana, Pakistan) in 2006.

• The **highest batting average in Test cricket** is held by Sir Don Bradman (Australia), with an average of 99.94 playing for Australia in 52 Tests (6,996 runs in 80 innings) between 1928 and 1948.

• Brian Lara (Trinidad and Tobago) scored 501 not out in 7 hr. 54 min. for Warwickshire v. Durham at Edgbaston on June 3–6, 1994—the **highest innings score.**

• Lara also holds th erecord for the **highest Test innings,** when he scored 400 not out for the West Indies v. England at the Antigua Recreation Ground, St. John, Antigua, on April 10–12, 2004.

• In a Junior House match between Clarkes House (now Poole's) and North Town at Clifton College, Bristol, UK, in June 1899, Arthur Edward Jeanne Collis (UK) scored a total of 628 not out in 6 hr. 50 min.—the **highest ever score.**

☆ **HIGHEST-SCORING TEST PARTNERSHIP** Between July 27 and 31, 2006, Kumar Sangakkara (287) and Mahela Jayawardene (374) scored 624 for the third wicket for Sri Lanka v. South Africa at the Sinhalese Sports Club in Colombo, Sri Lanka.

☆ **WICKET-KEEPING: MOST CATCHES IN TEST CRICKET** Mark Boucher (South Africa) made 376 catches in 102 Tests playing for South Africa between 1997 and 2007.

☆ **BATTING: MOST RUNS IN TEST CRICKET** Brian Lara (Trinidad and Tobago) scored 11,953 runs in 232 Test innings (at an average of 52.88) for the West Indies between 1990 and 2007.

CYCLING

FASTEST...

☆**Time to cycle across Australia—Perth to Sydney (male)**
Richard Vollebregt (Australia) cycled from Perth, Western Australia, to
Sydney, New South Wales, Australia, in 8 days 10 hr. 57 min. from October
13 to 21, 2006.

The **fastest time for a woman to cycle across Australia—Perth to
Sydney**—was achieved by Helen Shelley (Australia). She cycled between
the two cities in 13 days 2 hr. 55 min. from April 24 to May 7, 1999.

★**Major tour time trial over 20 km** Rubin Plaza Molina (Spain), rid-
ing for team Comunidad Valenciana-Puerta Castalla, averaged a record
speed of 34.93 mph (56.21 km/h) over a 24-mile (38.9-km) time trial from
Guadalajara to Alcalá de Henares in the 2005 Vuelta a España (Tour of
Spain), the fastest time trial achieved in any of the three major cycling tours
(Italy, France, Spain).

★**FASTEST TIME TO CYCLE 10 M ON GLASS BOTTLES** Wang
Jianguang (China) cycled 10 m (32 ft. 9 in.) on glass bottles in 29
seconds. He achieved the record using a standard bicycle on the set of
Zheng Da Zhong Yi—Guinness World Records Special in Beijing, China,
on December 20, 2006.

★Cycle journey across America (average speed) Pete Penseyres (U.S.A.) cycled coast-to-coast across the U.S.A. in 8 days 9 hr. 47 min. during the 1986 Race Across America event. He achieved an average speed of 15.4 mph (24.78 km/h) over a 3,100-mile (5,000-km) course between Huntington Beach, California, and Atlantic City, New Jersey.

The record for the **★fastest cycle journey across America by a woman (average speed)** was set by Seana Hogan (U.S.A.), who cycled coast-to-coast in just 9 days 4 hr. 2 min. during the 1995 Race Acros America ultracycling event. She set an average speed of 13.92 mph (22.4 km/h) over a 2,912-mile (4,686-km) course between Irvine, California, and Savannah, Georgia, U.S.A.

MOST WINS . . .

★Consecutive UCI cycling trials world championships (male) Benito Ros Charral (Spain) won the Union Cycliste Internationale (UCI) men's trial world championships three times consecutively from 2003 to 2005, the most by an individual rider.

★Cyclo-cross world championships (male) Eric De Vlaemink (Belgium) won the cyclo-cross world championships seven times, the most won by a man, in 1966 and from 1968 to 1973.

The ☆ **most wins of the cyclo-cross world championships by a woman** is three, by Hanka Kupfernagel (Germany) in 2000–01 and later in 2005.

☆ **Cross-country mountain biking world championships (female)** The most cross-country mountain biking world championships won by a woman is three, by Alison Sydor (Canada) from 1994 to 1996, and by Gunn-Rita Dahle Flesjaa (Norway) from 2004 to 2006.

☆ **Trials cycling world championships (male)** Two riders have won three elite men's trials cycling world championships: Marco Hösel (Germany) in 1999, 2002, and 2006, and Benito Ros Charral (Spain) from 2003 to 2005.

The **★most trials cycling world championship titles won by a woman** is six, consecutively, by Karin Moor (Switzerland) from 2001 to 2006.

Professional world championship cycling titles Koichi Nakano (Japan) won 10 world championship cycling titles in the professional sprint event between 1977 and 1986.

DID YOU KNOW?

The **largest attendance for a sports event** anywhere in the world is the annual Tour de France race. Over a period of three weeks, an estimated 10,000,000 spectators attend the event each year.

The **most world championship cycling titles won by a woman** is 12 by Jeannie Longo (France): for 3 km pursuit in 1986 and from 1988 to 1989; road from 1985 to 1987, 1989, and 1995; track 1989; and time trial from 1995 to 1997.

Olympic cycling medals Daniel Morelon (France) has won five Olympic cycling medals. He won two gold medals in 1968, a third in 1972, a silver in 1976, and a bronze in 1964.

Tour de France Lance Armstrong (U.S.A.) won the Tour de France seven times between 1999 and 2005. He finished his last race, on July 24, 2005, in 86 hr. 15 min. 2 sec.—clocking up another record: his average speed of 25.88 mph (41.65 km/h) beat his previous record of 25.02 mph (40.26 km/h) set in 1999.

★ MOST UCI MEN'S ROAD TIME TRIAL WORLD CHAMPIONSHIP WINS
Michael Rogers (Australia) won the Union Cycliste Internationale (UCI) road time trial world championships three times, from 2003 to 2005, the most times it has been won by an individual.

★ **MOST UCI ROAD RACE WORLD CHAMPIONSHIP WINS (MALE)** The most Union Cycliste Internationale (UCI) road race world championships won by an individual is three by four riders: Alfredo Binda (Italy) in 1927, 1930, and 1932; Rik Van Steenbergen (Belgium) in 1949, 1956, and 1957; Eddy Merckx (Belgium) in 1967, 1971, and 1974; and most recently Óscar Freire Gómez (Spain, above) in 1999, 2001, and 2004.

CYCLING SUCCESSES

• The **longest distance cycled backward** was set on August 11, 1985, by Alan Pierce (Australia). He cycled 62.5 miles (100 km) in reverse in Brisbane, Australia, in 4 hr. 5 min. 1 sec., sitting on the handlebars of a regular bicycle.

• The **highest downhill speed on a bicycle,** attained cycling downhill on snow or ice, is 132 mph (212.13 km/h). The record was set by downhill mountain bike racer Christian Taillefer (France) on a Peugeot bicycle at the speed ski slope in Vars, France, in March 1998.

• The world's **largest cycling event** was the Udine Pedala 2000, held at Udine, Italy, on June 11, 2000. Organized by Italian financial services provider Rolo Banca 1473, the event attracted 48,615 cyclists who completed a circuit of 18.2 miles (29.3 km) around the city.

• The **greatest vertical distance cycled in 24 hours** was 59,362 ft. (18,093 m) by Marcel Knaus (Switzerland) on July 16–17, 2005, in Wildhaus, Switzerland.

• The **youngest ever winner of the Tour de France** was Henri Cornet (France) in 1904, aged 19 years 350 days. He actually finished the race in fifth position, but was awarded the victory after the first four riders were all disqualified.

☆ **MOST CROSS-COUNTRY MOUNTAIN BIKING WORLD CHAMPIONSHIP WINS (MALE)** From 2004 to 2006, the Union Cycliste Internationale (UCI) cross-country mountain biking world championships was won three times by Julien Absalon (France). Henrik Djernis (Denmark) achieved the same feat between 1992 and 1994.

Tour of Italy The record for the most wins of the Giro d'Italia (Tour of Italy) is five and is shared by three people: Alfredo Binda (Italy) in 1925, 1927–29, 1933; Fausto Coppi (Italy) in 1940, 1947, 1949, 1952–53; and Eddy Merckx (Belgium) in 1968, 1970, 1972–74.

Tour of Spain Roberto Heras Hernández (Spain) won the Vuelta a España (Tour of Spain) four times—in 2000, and from 2003 to 2005—as well as 10 stage victories. However, following a two-year suspension by the Spanish Cycling Federation (RFEC) for testing positive for the synthetic hormone erythropoietin (EPO), the 2005 title went to runner-up Denis Menchov (Russia).

FISHING

★ **Farthest cast into a fishbowl** Maria Dolores Montesinos Fernández (Spain) managed to cast a weighted fly into a fishbowl with a neck diameter of 6.8 in. (17.5 cm)—without the fly touching the sides of the fishbowl—from a distance of 22 ft. 11 in. (7 m). The record was set at the studios of *El Show de los Récords,* Madrid, Spain, on December 11, 2001.

★ **HEAVIEST BLUEFIN TUNA** On October 26, 1979, at Aulds Cove, Nova Scotia, Canada, Ken Fraser (Canada) landed the heaviest bluefin tuna ever. The immense fish weighed 1,496 lb. (678.58 kg), heavier than many sharks!

★HEAVIEST HAMMERHEAD On May 23, 2006, Bucky Dennis (U.S.A.) used a live-lined stingray to land a great hammerhead shark weighing 1,280 lb. (580.59 kg) at Boca Grande, Florida, U.S.A. It took Dennis and his crew almost six hours to land the record-breaking fish.

Largest fishing rod The largest fly-fishing rod measures 71 ft. 4.5 in. (21.75 m) in length, while the reel measures 4 ft. (1.21 m) in diameter and 1.2 in. (3.1 cm) wide. The immense rod was assembled by Tiney Mitchell (U.S.A.) at the Pirates' Landing Restaurant, Port Isabel, Texas, U.S.A., on June 12, 1999.

★Largest ice-fishing competition The Veljekset Keskinen Miljoonap-Pilkki has been organized annually since 1997. The largest ever event took place on Lake Ponnenjärvi, Töysä, Finland, with 26,462 participants on March 15, 2003.

Most fly-fishing team titles World fly-fishing championships were inaugurated by CIPS (Confédération Internationale de la Pêche Sportive) in 1981. The most team titles held is five, by Italy in 1982–84, 1986, and 1992.

Most freshwater world championships The individual title at this competition has been won three times, by Robert Tesse (France), 1959–60, 1965; and Bob Nudd (England), 1990–91, 1994.

Most participants at a sea-angling competition The most people to have participated in a sea-angling competition is 679. The contestants were taking part in the 20th Torskfestivalen (Cod Festival) held at Öresund, Helsingborg, Sweden, which took place from January 15 to 17, 1999.

Smallest eyed fly-fishing hook The smallest eyed fly-fishing hook was produced by Tiemco Ltd., Tokyo, Japan, on June 12, 1999. The inner diameter of the eye was 0.01 in. (0.265 mm), while the outer diameter was 0.03 in. (0.8 mm). The hook shank was 0.14 in. (3.60 mm) long.

★ HEAVIEST FRESH- AND SALTWATER FISH ★

SPECIES	WEIGHT	NAME	YEAR
★ Albacore	88 lb. 2 oz. (40 kg)	Siegfried Dickemann (Germany)	1977
★ Barracuda, Guinean	101 lb. 3 oz. (45.9 kg)	Cyril Fabre (France)	2002
★ Barracuda, Hellers	4 lb. 8 oz. (2.04 kg)	Dan Stockdon Jr. (U.S.A.)	2005
★ Bass, European	20 lb. 14 oz. (9.48 kg)	Robert Mari (France)	1999
★ Bass, meanmouth	8 lb. 8 oz. (3.88 kg)	Dru Kinslow (U.S.A.)	2006
★ Batfish, tiera	4 lb. 3 oz. (1.92 kg)	Steven Wozniak (U.S.A.)	2006
★ Bonito, Atlantic	18 lb. 4 oz. (8.30 kg)	D. Gama Higgs (U.S.A.)	1953
★ Bonito, Pacific	21 lb. 5 oz. (9.67 kg)	Kim Larson (U.S.A.)	2003
★ Bream	13 lb. 3 oz. (6.01 kg)	Luis Rasmussen (Sweden)	1984
★ Bream, gilthead	16 lb. 3 oz. (7.36 kg)	Jean Serra (France)	2000
★ Carp, common	75 lb. 11 oz. (34.35 kg)	Leo van der Gugten (Netherlands)	1987
★ Carp, silver	35 lb. 4 oz. (16 kg)	Josef Windholz (Austria)	1983
★ Catfish, giant (Mekong)	138 lb. 14 oz. (63 kg)	Richard Ainsworth (UK)	2004
★ Catfish, redtail	101 lb. 6 oz. (46 kg)	Johnny Hoffman (U.S.A.)	2006
★ Char, whitespotted	17 lb. 8 oz. (7.96 kg)	Hajime Murata (Japan)	2006
★ Chub, European	5 lb. 12 oz. (2.62 kg)	Luis Rasmussen (Sweden)	1987
★ Cod, Atlantic	98 lb. 12 oz. (44.79 kg)	Alphonse Bielevich (U.S.A.)	1969
★ Cornetfish, red	2 lb. 5 oz. (1.05 kg)	Junzo Okada (Japan)	2006
★ Dainanumihebi	2 lb. 12 oz. (1.25 kg)	Takashi Nishino (Japan)	2006
★ Eel, conger	15 lb. (6.8 kg)	Ryan Dougherty (U,S,A.)	2002
★ Featherback, giant	13 lb. 6 oz. (9.08 kg)	Anongnat Sungwichien-Helias (Thailand)	2006
★ Flounder, olive	25 lb. 2 oz. (11.4 kg)	Masayuki Jinnou (Japan)	2006
★ Flounder, stone	5 lb. 11 oz. (2.6 kg)	Norikazu Fukinaga (Japan)	2006
★ Graysby, Panama	2 lb. (0.9 kg)	Karrie Ables (U.S.A.)	2006
★ Grouper, areolate	1 lb. 5 oz. (0.62 kg)	Jean-Francois Helias (France)	2006
★ Grouper, cloudy	1 lb. 6 oz. (0.63 kg)	Supachai Boongayson (Thailand)	2006
★ Grouper, duskytail	1 lb. 13 oz. (0.85 kg)	Wathini "Nid" Thisami (Thailand)	2006
★ Grouper, snowy	37 lb. 9 oz. (17.03 kg)	Jason Ferguson (U.S.A.)	2006
★ Grunt, burrito	10 lb. (4.53 kg)	Harold Lance Rigg (U.S.A.)	2006
★ Grunt, tomtate	1 lb. 4 oz. (0.56 kg)	John Overton (U.S.A.)	2006
★ Haddock	14 lb. 15 oz. (6.8 kg)	Heike Neblinger (Germany)	1997
★ Hake, European	15 lb. 9 oz. (7.08 kg)	Knut Steen (Norway)	2000
★ Halibut, Atlantic	418 lb. 13 oz. (190 kg)	Thomas Nielsen (Norway)	2004
★ Kitsune-mebaru	5 lb. 15 oz. (2.7 kg)	Kouichirou Morikawa (Japan)	2006
★ Korai-Nigoi	6 lb. 8 oz. (2.97 kg)	Junichi Inada (Japan)	2006
★ Ladyfish, Machnata	15 lb. 6 oz. (7 kg)	Frederik Hendrikss (Denmark)	2006
★ Lizardfish, wanieso	7 lb. 14 oz. (3.6 kg)	Harunori Kinjo (Japan)	2006
★ Mackerel, atka	2 lb. 10 oz. (1.2 kg)	David Witherell (U.S.A.)	2006
★ Mackerel, Atlantic	2 lb. 10 oz. (1.2 kg)	Jorg Marquard (Norway)	1992
★ Mullet, striped	7 lb. 10 oz. (3.45 kg)	Krag Ross (U.S.A.)	2004
★ Nigoi	5 lb. 6 oz. (2.45 kg)	Yoshiro Saito (Japan)	2006
★ Palometa	1 lb. 12 oz. (0.81 kg)	Henry Flores Jr. (U.S.A.)	2006
★ Perch, European	3 lb. 4 oz. (1.5 kg)	Johnny Hogll (Norway)	1998
★ Permit	60 lb. (27.21 kg)	Renato Fiedler (Brazil)	2002
★ Pike, Northern	55 lb. 1 oz. (25 kg)	Lothar Louis (Germany)	1986
★ Piranha, black	6 lb. 15 oz. (3.175 kg)	Alejandro Mata (Venezuela)	1995
★ Pompano, gafftopsail	3 lb. 12 oz. (1.7 kg)	Brett Philip (U.S.A.)	2006

★ Porcupine fish, black-blotched	2 lb. 5 oz. (1.05 kg)	Lootjirot Panthrapat (Thailand)	2006
★ Porgy, black	8 lb. 5 oz. (3.78 kg)	Ryushiro Omote (Japan)	2006
★ Queenfish, doublespotted	6 lb. 8 oz. (2.94 kg)	Jodie Johnson (U.S.A.)	2006
★ Ray, bluespotted ribbontail	3 lb. 2 oz. (1.43 kg)	Steven Wozniak (U.S.A.)	2006
★ Rock cod, bluelined	1 lb. 8 oz. (0.7 kg)	Jean-Francois Helias (France)	2006
★ Sailfin, vermiculated	3 lb. (1.36 kg)	Jay Wright Jr. (U.S.A.)	2006
★ Salmon, Atlantic	79 lb. 2 oz. (35.89 kg)	Henrik Henriksen (Norway)	1928
★ Sea bass, blackfin	21 lb. 4 oz. (9.66 kg)	Yuki Inoue (Japan)	2006
★ Shark, banded (hound)	33 lb. 9 oz. (15.25 kg)	Takashi Nishino (Japan)	2006
★ Shark, brownbanded bamboo	4 lb. 10 oz. (2.12 kg)	Steven Wozniak (U.S.A.)	2006
★ Shark, great hammerhead	1,280 lb. (580.59 kg)	Bucky Dennis (U.S.A.)	2006
★ Shark, lemon	405 lb. (183.7 kg)	Colleen Harlow (U.S.A.)	1988
★ Shimazoi	4 lb. 1 oz. (1.85 kg)	Masahiko Kikuchi (Japan)	2006
★ Snakehead, great	9 lb. 13 oz. (4.46 kg)	Jean-Francois Helias (France)	2006
★ Snapper, mangrove red	25 lb. 9 oz. (11.62 kg)	Takuya Kano (Japan)	2006
★ Sole, lemon	3 lb. 15 oz. (1.8 kg)	Robert Stalcrona (Sweden)	2004
★ Stingray, Atlantic	10 lb. 12 oz. (4.87 kg)	David Anderson (U.S.A.)	1994
★ Swordfish	1,182 lb. (536.15 kg)	Louis Marron (U.S.A.)	1953
★ Tilefish, blueline	17 lb. 6 oz. (7.9 kg)	Jenny Manus (U.S.A.)	2006
★ Trevally, giant	160 lb. 7 oz. (72.8 kg)	Keiki Hamasaki (Japan)	2006
★ Trout, lake	72 lb. (32.65 kg)	Lloyd Bull (Canada)	1995
★ Trout, rainbow	42 lb. 2 oz. (19.1 kg)	David White (U.S.A.)	1970
★ Tuna, bluefin	1,496 lb. (678.58 kg)	Ken Fraser (Canada)	1979

★ HEAVIEST BARRACUDA
Cyril Fabre (France) caught a Guinean barracuda weighing a massive 101 lb. 3 oz. (45.9 kg). Fabre caught the IGFA world-record fish while fishing near Olende, Gabon, on December 27, 2002. Barracuda can be found in the waters of the eastern Atlantic and can grow to a length of around 6 ft. 6 in. (2 m).

IGFA ALL-TACKLE RECORDS

The tabulated records on these pages are sourced from the IGFA (International Game Fish Association) Freshwater and Saltwater All-Tackle Records for the largest of each species caught in any line-class category. Since its inception in 1939, IGFA has taken an active, global role in fisheries management and fish conservation.

★ **HEAVIEST LEMON SHARK** On November 28, 1988, Colleen Harlow (U.S.A.) landed a lemon shark weighing 405 lb. (183.7 kg), off Buxton, North Carolina, U.S.A., the heaviest All-Tackle IGFA record for this species. On May 17, 2006, a 385-lb. (174.6-kg) lemon shark (pictured above) was caught by Dr. Martin Arostegui (U.S.A.)—and guided by Ralph Delph (U.S.A.)—near the Marquesas Keys, Florida, U.S.A. IGFA officially nominated the shark as the ★ **heaviest fish ever documented on fly.**

SOCCER

UEFA CHAMPIONS LEAGUE

★ **Biggest match win** On December 10, 2003, Italy's Juventus—the most successful team in the country's soccer history—beat the Greek side Olympiakos 7–0 on their home turf in Turin.

☆ **Fastest goal** Roy Makaay (Netherlands) scored the opening goal for Bayern Munich (Germany) against Real Madrid (Spain) in just 10 seconds in Munich, Germany, on March 7, 2007.

Paolo Maldini (Italy) took just 51 seconds to score for AC Milan against Liverpool on May 25, 2005, the **fastest goal scored in a Champions League final.**

Maldini (b. June 26, 1968) is also the **oldest player to score a goal in a Champions League final**—he was aged 36 years 333 days in AC Milan's game against Liverpool at the Atatürk Stadium in Turkey on May 25, 2005.

★ **YOUNGEST PLAYER IN THE ENGLISH PREMIERSHIP** Matthew Briggs (UK, left) was brought on as a 77th-minute substitute for Fulham against Middlesbrough, aged 16 years 65 days, on May 13, 2007.

He was 64 days younger than the previous record-holder, Tottenham Hotspur's Aaron Lennon (UK).

★ TOP-DIVISION LEAGUE WINNERS ★

COUNTRY	CHAMPIONSHIP*	TEAM	WINS	DATES
Scotland	Premier League	Glasgow Rangers	51	1891–2005
Greece	Super League	Olympiakos	35	1931–2007
Portugal	Liga	SL Benfica	31	1935–2005
Spain	La Liga	Real Madrid	29	1931–2003
Netherlands	Eredivisie	Ajax Amsterdam	29	1917–2004
Belgium	Jupiler League	RSC Anderlecht	29	1947–2007
Hungary	Borsodi Liga	Ferencváros	28	1903–2004
Italy	Serie A	Juventus	27	1904–2003
Finland	Veikkausliiga	HJK	21	1911–2003
Norway	Tippeligaen	Rosenborg	20	1967–2006
Germany	Bundesliga	Bayern Munich	20	1931–2006
England	Premiership	Liverpool	18	1901–1990
Sweden	Allsvenskan	IFK Göteborg	17	1908–1996
Denmark	Superliga	Kjøbenhavns Boldklub	15	1913–1980
Ireland	Premier Division	Shamrock Rovers	15	1923–1994
France	Ligue 1	AS Saint-Etienne	10	1956–1981
Japan	J-League	Kashima Antlers	4	1996–2001
U.S.A.	MLS	DC United	4	1996–2004

*This is the current name of the top division in each country.

★MOST EXPULSIONS IN A SINGLE WORLD CUP FINALS TOURNAMENT MATCH On June 25, 2006, a total of four red cards were awarded (two to each side) when Portugal met Holland in a World Cup match in Nuremberg, Germany.

As well as the four reds, 16 yellow cards were issued—nine to Portugal and seven to Holland.

EUROPEAN

★ **Most widely supported team** Portugal's Sport Lisboa e Benfica—or simply Benfica to fans—has a record 160,398 fully paid-up club members.

★ **Most wins of the English top division** Ryan Giggs (UK) claimed a record ninth Championship winner's medal in 2007 when Manchester United won the FA Premiership, having previously shared the record with Liverpool's Phil Neal and Alan Hansen (both UK) who have won eight domestic titles each.

★ **HIGHEST UK PREMIERSHIP ATTENDANCE** A crowd of 76,073 attended Old Trafford, Manchester, UK, for the match between Manchester United and Aston Villa on January 13, 2007. United's Michael Carrick (UK) is pictured scoring the second goal of the game.

★ **Most wins of the English top division** Liverpool won the top division of English league soccer 18 times between 1901 and 1990.

In 1992, the Premiership replaced the old First Division as English soccer's top flight.

☆ **Most consecutive seasons in the English top division** Arsenal has been in English soccer's top division for 81 consecutive seasons from 1920 to 2007 (excluding 1939–45, during World War II).

Most English Premiership goals The most goals scored in the English Premiership is 260 by Alan Shearer (UK). Shearer spent his Premiership career with Blackburn Rovers (1992–96) before moving to Newcastle United in 1996 for a record fee (at that time) of £15.6 million ($22.4 million). He retired in 2006.

★ **Most Premiership appearances** Between 1993 and 2007, midfielder and Welsh national team captain Gary Speed (UK) appeared 519 times—playing for Leeds United, Everton, Newcastle United, and Bolton Wanderers.

★ **Most Premiership manager of the month awards** Manchester United's Alex Ferguson (UK) won 19 manager of the month awards between 1993 and 2007. He also holds the record for the ☆ **most Champions League games managed,** with 118—a landmark passed when his team met Spain's Villareal in November 2005.

☆**Most Major League goals** Jason Kreis (U.S.A.) scored 108 goals in 301 games (1996–2004). Jaime Moreno (Bolivia) matched this feat, in only 203 games (1996–2007).

INTERNATIONAL

★**Confederations Cup: Most wins** Two countries have won the Confederations Cup (see box page 472) twice: France (2001 and 2003) and Brazil (1997 and 2005).

★**Oceania Cup: Most wins** Instituted in 1973 and contested by Oceania Football Confederation member nations, the Oceania Cup has been won a record four times by Australia, in 1980, 1996, 2000, and 2004.

★**CONCACAF Gold Cup: Most wins** Mexico has won the Confederation of North and Central American and Caribbean Association Football (CONCACAF) Gold Cup four times, in 1993, 1996, 1998, and 2003. The cup was instituted in 1991.

The U.S.A. has won the women's CONCACAF Gold Cup (instituted in 2000) three times—every time it has been held—in 2000, 2002, and 2006. Unsurprisingly, this gives the U.S.A. the record for the ★**most women's CONCACAF wins.**

THE CHAMPIONS LEAGUE

• The ☆**most Champions League matches won by a team** is 70 by Real Madrid between 1992 and 2007. An unprecedented 247 goals were scored in the process.

• The ☆**most goals in Champions League matches** is 56, by Raúl González Blanco (Spain)—for Real Madrid (1992–2007)—and Andriy Shevchenko (Ukraine)—for Dynamo Kyiv, AC Milan, and Chelsea (1994–2007). From 1992 to 2007, Raúl also made the ☆**most Champions League appearances:** 107.

• Two players share the record for the ☆**most appearances in a European Cup/Champions League final,** with eight finals each. They are Paulo Maldini between 1989 and 2007 and "Paco" Francisco Gento (Spain) between 1956 and 1966. Maldini became the ☆**oldest player to captain a Champions League team** (and the ☆**oldest captain of a European Cup/Champions League-winning team in a final**) when he led AC Milan out against Liverpool in Athens, Greece, on May 23, 2007. AC Milan's win that night also saw Maldini (at 38 years 331 days) become the ☆**oldest captain to win the Champions League** and Clarence Seedorf (Suriname) become the ★**first player to win four Champions League titles.**

MOST GOALS IN INTERNATIONAL SOCCER (MALE) The most international goals scored by a man is 109, by Ali Daei (Iran, in white), between 1993 and 2006.

☆ **South American Championship (Copa América): Most wins** Argentina and Uruguay have both won the South American championship (Copa América since 1975) 14 times. First held in 1916, this cup competition is the **oldest surviving international soccer competition.**

★ **Most African player of the year awards** The African player of the year title has been awarded since 1970. Three players have won three times: George Weah (Liberia), in 1989 and 1994–95; Abedi Pele (Ghana), in 1991–93; and Samuel Eto'o (Cameroon), in 2003–05.

CONFEDERATIONS CUP COMPETITION

Every four years, the FIFA World Cup host nation and winner (or runner-up if the host nation wins) join the Confederations Cup with the champions of the six FIFA confederations: African (CAF), South American (CONMEBOL), European (UEFA), Asian (AFC), Oceania (OFC), and North and Central America and the Caribbean (CONCACAF). The tournament began in 1992 (as the biannual King Fahd Cup) and was taken over by FIFA in 1997. As of 2005, the cup is played every four years, with the next to be staged in South Africa in 2009.

★ **MOST SOCCER TEAMS SPONSORED BY ONE INSTITUTION** Saudi Telecom sponsored the jerseys of all 12 soccer teams of the First Division in Saudi Arabia, in September 2006, setting a record for the most teams to be sponsored by just one institution simultaneously.

☆ **MOST GOALS SCORED BY A GOALKEEPER** Goalkeeper Rogério Ceni (Brazil, left) scored 66 goals for Brazil's São Paulo Football Club from 1997 to 2006.

☆ **LONGEST SOCCER MARATHON** A match played between FC EDO Simme (pictured) and FC Spiez in Erlenbach, Switzerland, on July 8–9, 2006, lasted 30 hr. 10 min. The final score was 243–210 to FC Spiez. The teams played from noon on July 8 to 6:10 p.m. on July 9.

★LARGEST SOCCER STICKER A 5-ft. × 6-ft. (153 × 188-cm) soccer sticker was unveiled at Charlton Athletic's stadium, The Valley, on February 8, 2007. It depicts Charlton striker Darren Bent (UK), and was created to launch FIFA's official FA Premier League 07 Sticker Collection.

★ Most FIFA world player of the year awards (female) Birgit Prinz (Germany) was awarded the Fédération Internationale de Football Association (FIFA) player of the year award in three consecutive years, 2003–05.

☆ Most international caps (female) The greatest number of international appearances by a woman for a national team is officially 319, by Kristine Lilly (U.S.A.) from 1987 to 2007.

BALL CONTROL

Martinho Eduardo Orige (Brazil) juggled a soccer ball for 19 hr. 30 min. nonstop with feet, legs, and head—without the ball touching the ground—at Padre Ezio Julli gym in Araranguá, Brazil, on August 2–3, 2003, the **longest time to control a soccer ball.**

☆SOCCER BALL TOUCHES: MOST IN 30 SECONDS BY A FEMALE The most touches of a soccer ball in 30 seconds by a female, while keeping the ball in the air, is 155 by Chloe Hegland (Canada) in Victoria, British Columbia, Canada, on December 12, 2006. Chloe is just 10 years old, but her amazing feat (or feet?) beats the record for both men and women in this category!

☆**LONGEST TIME CONTROLLING A SOCCER BALL WHILE LYING DOWN**
Tomas Lundman (Sweden) managed to keep a regulation-size soccer
ball up in the air using his feet while lying on his back for 9 min. 57 sec.
at the Gallerian Shopping Center in Stockholm, Sweden, on November
4, 2006.

•Cláudia Martini (Brazil) juggled a soccer ball for 7 hr. 5 min. 25 sec. in
Caxias do Sul, Brazil, on July 12, 1996, the **longest time to control a soc-
cer ball by a woman.**
•The **longest time to keep a soccer ball in the air using just the head
while seated** is 4 hr. 2 min. 1 sec. by Agim Agushi (Kosovo, Serbia and
Montenegro, now Republic of Serbia) in Flensburg, Germany, during the
Tummelum Festival, on August 14, 2005.
•Amadou Gueye (France) kept a soccer ball airborne using his chest for
30.29 seconds for *L'Emission Des Records* in Paris, France, on September 7,
2001, the **longest time to control a soccer ball using only the chest.**
•The ☆**longest time to keep a soccer ball spinning on the forehead** is
19.96 seconds, a feat achieved by Victor Rubilar (Argentina) at the Galler-
ian Shopping Center in Stockholm, Sweden, on November 4, 2006.
•Ferdie Adoboe (U.S.A.) managed 266 touches of a ball at the Schwan's
U.S.A. Cup in Blaine, Minnesota, U.S.A., on July 19, 2000, the **most soccer
ball touches in one minute.**

DID YOU KNOW?

Tomas Lundman (see photo above) also holds the record for the
longest time to head a soccer ball. He controlled a ball with his head,
without dropping it, for 8 hr. 32 min. 3 sec. in Lidingo, Sweden, on
February 27, 2004.

★MOST SOCCER BALLS JUGGLED On November 4, 2006, Victor Rubilar (Argentina) juggled five regulation-size balls for 10 seconds at the Gallerian Shopping Center in Stockholm, Sweden.

•Jan Skorkovsky (Czechoslovakia, now Czech Republic) kept a soccer ball up while he traveled 26.2 miles (42.2 km) for the Prague City Marathon on July 8, 1990. His time of 7 hr. 18 min. 55 sec. represents the **fastest time to run a marathon keeping a soccer ball airborne.**

BEACH SOCCER

An offshoot of association soccer, beach soccer had been played informally on beaches the world over for many years. It was not until 1992, however, that the sport's rules were formalized. Today, it is an international sport.

•The ★ **most goals scored by an individual player in a beach soccer world cup** is 21 by Madjer (aka João Victor Tavares), playing for Portugal at the tournament staged in Rio de Janeiro, Brazil, in 2006.

•The ★ **most goals scored by an individual player in a beach soccer world cup career** is 33 by Madjer, playing for Portugal at the tournaments staged in Rio de Janeiro, Brazil, in 2005 and 2006.

•The FIFA beach soccer world cup has been contested twice. The record for the ☆ **most beach soccer world cup wins** is tied, by France (the winners of the inaugural world cup, in 2005) and Brazil (winners in 2006).

•The precursor to the beach soccer world cup (organized by FIFA) was the beach soccer world championships (organized by Beach Soccer Worldwide), instituted in 1995. Brazil holds the record for the ★ **most beach soccer world championships,** with nine victories between 1995 and 2004.

GOLF

★ **Oldest golf course** The Old Links golf course in Musselburgh, Scotland, UK, is thought to be the oldest in the world. It is believed that Mary, Queen of Scots, played there in 1567, and in 1811 it became the first course to hold an all-women golf competition.

★ **Highest course** The Yak golf course is situated at an altitude of 13,025 ft. (3,970 m) above sea level and is located in Kupup, East Sikkim, India.

★ **Largest range** With 300 individual bays, the largest golf range in the world is the SKY72 Golf Club Dream Golf Range, which opened in Joong-Ku, Incheon, Korea, on September 9, 2005. The driving range is a circle with a diameter of 1,176 ft. (358.8 m) and has a total area of 2,900,529 ft.^{2} (269,468 m^2).

★ **Lowest stroke average in a PGA season** The lowest stroke average ever achieved during a single Professional Golfers Association (PGA) season is 68.33, by Byron Nelson (U.S.A.) during the 1945 season.

★ **Most PGA tour titles won consecutively** The most golf tour titles won in a row is 11, by Byron Nelson (U.S.A.) in 1945. The run, which has since become known as "The Streak," was among a total of 18 tour titles that Nelson won in the same year, adding to a career total of 52 PGA titles. He turned professional in 1932 and retired in the 1946 season to spend more time in Texas, where he was born.

☆ **Most golfers on one course in 24 hours (walking)** The greatest number of walking golfers—that is, no carts allowed—to complete a full round on the same course within 24 hours is 623, achieved by GP7 at the Shenzhen Green Bay Golf Club, China, from June 24 to 25, 2006.

☆ **MOST WOMEN'S BRITISH OPEN TOURNAMENT WINS** Karrie Webb (Australia, left) has won the women's British Open golf tournament three times—in 1995, 1997, and 2002. This record was equaled by Sherri Steinhauer (U.S.A.) with wins in 1998, 1999, and 2006.

☆ **LARGEST GOLF TEE** An 11-ft. 5-in.-tall (3.5-m) tee with a head diameter of 29 in. (75.2 cm) and a shaft width of 11.88 in. (30.2 cm) was made by Volvo Auto Polska and measured at the First Warsaw Golf & Country Club in Rajszew, Warsaw, Poland, on September 17, 2006.

★ **Most balls hit in two minutes** With the help of Scott "Speedy" McKinney, David Ogron (both U.S.A.) drove a record 113 balls in two minutes on the set of the *Zheng Da Zong Yi—Guinness World Records Special* TV show in Beijing, China, on December 21, 2006.

★ **Most balls hit in 12 hours** The most balls driven over a distance of 100 yards into a target area in 12 hours is 7,350, by Sylvain Ménard (Canada) at the Club de Golf des Erables in Gatineau, Quebec, Canada, on October 1, 2004.

Longest putt The longest recorded holed putt in a professional tournament is 110 ft. (33.5 m), a record shared by Jack Nicklaus (U.S.A.) in the 1964 Tournament of Champions and Nick Price (Zimbabwe) in the 1992 U.S. PGA.

Bob Cook (U.S.A.) sank a putt measured at an incredible 140 ft. 3 in. (42.74 m) on the 18th hole at St. Andrews, UK, in the International Fourball Pro Am Tournament—which is not classed as a professional tournament—on October 1, 1976.

☆ **LARGEST GOLF FACILITY** The Mission Hills Golf Club, stretching across Shenzhen and Dongguan in China, boasts 12 fully operational 18-hole courses as of February 2007. Additional amenities include a large pro shop, a clubhouse of 300,000 ft.² (27,871 m²), a ballroom, swimming pools, no fewer than 51 tennis courts, and extensive changing rooms that can accommodate up to 3,000 guests.

★ MOST HOLES-IN-ONE BY A RYDER CUP TEAM The European team has achieved the most holes-in-one during the history of the Ryder Cup, with six from 1927 to 2006. Over the same period, the U.S.A. team has made just one hole-in-one! Pictured is European team member Darren Clarke (UK) during the 2006 Cup, in which he scored three points in three matches, helping Europe beat the U.S.A. 18½–9½.

LOWEST U.S. PGA ROUND SCORE Gary Player (South Africa, pictured) is one of eight players to have finished a U.S. PGA Championship round of 18 holes in just 63 shots. He achieved this record low score at Shoal Creek in Birmingham, Alabama, in 1984. His fellow record holders are:

- **Bruce Crampton** (Australia), Firestone, Akron, Ohio, U.S.A., 1975
- **Ray Floyd** (U.S.A.), Southern Hills, Tulsa, Oklahoma, U.S.A., 1982
- **Vijay Singh** (Fiji) at Inverness Club, Toledo, Ohio, U.S.A., 1993
- **Michael Bradley** (U.S.A.) and **Brad Faxon** (U.S.A.), both at Riviera Pacific Palisades, California, U.S.A., 1995
- **Jose Maria Olazabal** (Spain) at Valhalla, Louisville, Kentucky, U.S.A., 2000
- **Mark O'Meara** (U.S.A.) at Atlanta Athletic Club, Georgia, U.S.A., 2001

★FARThEST GOLF SHOT Flight Engineer Mikhail Tyurin (Russia, pictured left practicing his swing on Earth), assisted by caddy Commander Michael Lopez-Alegria (U.S.A.), teed off during a six-hour space walk outside the International Space Station (ISS) on February 23, 2006. Element 21 Golf (Canada) paid an undisclosed sum for the stunt, which was permitted by the Russian space agency as a means of raising cash. NASA estimated that the ball would orbit for three days before burning up in the atmosphere—a distance of 2.2 billion yards (1.26 million miles; 2.02 million km). The Russians put their estimate at 810 billion yards (460 million miles; 740 million km)!

GOLF TOURNAMENTS

• The ★ **most Ladies Professional Golf Association Women's Championships won** is four by Mickey Wright (U.S.A.) in 1958, 1960–61, and 1963.

• The **oldest player to compete in the Ryder Cup** is Raymond Floyd, U.S.A., in 1993, aged 51 years 20 days.

• The ★ **most Kraft Nabisco Championships won by an individual** is three, by three golfers: Amy Alcott (U.S.A.) in 1983, 1988, and 1991; Betsy King (U.S.A.) in 1987, 1990, and 1997; and Annika Sorenstam (Sweden) in 2001–02 and 2005.

• The **lowest single-round score at the Masters** is 63 by Nick Price (Zimbabwe) in 1986 and Greg Norman (Australia) in 1996.

• The ★ **most Senior PGA Championships won by an individual** is six by Sam Snead (U.S.A.) in 1964–65, 1967, 1970–71, and 1973.

• The record for the ★ **most wins of the Tradition Championship** is held by Jack Nicklaus (U.S.A.), who has won four times, in 1990–91 and 1995–96.

• The ★ **most U.S. Senior Open Championships won by an individual** is three by Miller Barber (U.S.A.) in 1982 and 1984–85.

• The ★ **most Vare trophies won by a female** is seven by Kathy Whitworth (U.S.A.) in 1965–67 and 1969–72.

Most nations represented in a single competition A record 72 nations were represented at the 2000 Junior Open Championships, held at Crail Golf Club in Fife, Scotland, UK, in July 2000.

☆**Greatest distance between two rounds of golf played on the same day** John Knobel (Australia) played two full 18-hole rounds on May 21, 2006: the first at The Coast Golf Club in Sydney, Australia, and the second at Forest Park Golf Club in Woodhaven, New York, U.S.A. The distance between the two rounds was 9,931 miles (15,982 km).

★**Most miniature golf played in 24 hours (fourball)** Two teams from MGC Olympia Kiel e.V. (Germany) played 80 rounds of 18 holes—a total of 1,140 holes—of miniature golf in 24 hours at Miniaturegolfhalle in Rendsburg, Germany, on March 19–20, 2005.

ICE HOCKEY

European competition The ★**most ice hockey world championships (men)** won by a nation is four by Sweden in 1921, 1923–24, and 1932. After 1932 and until 1991, European teams could be awarded only European championship medals.

NHL

★**Longest scoring streak by a rookie** Paul Stastny (Canada), of the Colorado Avalanche (U.S.A.), achieved a 20-consecutive-game scoring streak, the most by a rookie. He had 11 goals and 18 assists during the streak, which began on February 3 and ended March 17, 2007.

★**Longest serving captain** The longest period as captain of any team in National Hockey League (NHL) history is a mammoth 20 seasons by

★FASTEST TIME TO SCORE A HAT TRICK (FEMALE) Melissa Horvat (Canada) scored three times in just 35 seconds for the Burlington 1 Bantams (Canada) against Stoney Creek (Canada) in Burlington, Ontario, Canada, on March 4, 2006.

☆ **FIRST PLAYER TO SCORE IN FIRST SIX GAMES** Playing for the Pittsburgh Penguins (U.S.A.) in 2006, Evgeni Malkin (Russia) became the first player in 89 years to score in his first six games.

Steve Yzerman (Canada), who served as captain of the Detroit Red Wings (U.S.A.) from 1986 to 2006. Yzerman led the Red Wings to three Stanley Cup championships (1997–98, 2002) and had his jersey, No. 19, retired in a ceremony at Joe Louis Arena in Detroit, Michigan, U.S.A., on January 2, 2007.

★ **Longest contract** The longest contract in NHL history is the 15-year deal given to goalkeeper Rick

★ **SHORTEST NHL PLAYER** At 5 ft. 7 in. (1.7 m), forward Brian Gionta (U.S.A.) of the New Jersey Devils (U.S.A.) is the shortest active player in the league. The ★ **tallest NHL player** is defenseman Zdeno Chara (Czech Republic) of the Boston Bruins (U.S.A.), who is 6 ft. 9 in. (2.05 m).

★ **MOST OVERTIME GAME-WINNING GOALS** The NHL play-off record for the most overtime game-winning goals is seven by Joe Sakic (Canada) playing for the Quebec Nordiques (Canada) and Colorado Avalanche (U.S.A.) from 1992 to 2006.

DiPietro (U.S.A.) by the New York Islanders (U.S.A.) on September 12, 2006. DiPietro's contract managed to top the previous longest NHL contract, a 10-year deal the New York Islanders had given to Alexei Yashin (Russia) in 2001.

Longest winning streak to end a season The New Jersey Devils (U.S.A.) won their last 11 regular-season games of the 2005–06 season to set the NHL record for the longest winning streak at the end of a season, which ran from March 28 to April 18, 2006.

★ **Most victories in a season by a goalie** The NHL record for the most victories by a goalkeeper in a single season is 48, set by Martin Brodeur (Canada) while playing for the New Jersey Devils (U.S.A.) during the 2006–07 season.

★ **Most severe suspension** The NHL record for the longest suspension is 25 games, which was given to Chris Simon (Canada) of the New York Islanders (U.S.A.). It was his punishment for a two-handed stick attack to the face of Ryan Hollweg (U.S.A.) of the New York Rangers (U.S.A.) in a 2–1 loss on March 8, 2007, at the Nassau Coliseum, New York.

MOST GOALS SCORED BY A TEAM IN AN NHL SEASON The Edmonton Oilers scored 446 goals in the 1983–84 NHL season, the most by any team. The Oilers also achieved a record 1,182 scoring points in the same season. Pictured is the Oilers' Chris Pronger (front) during the 2006 Stanley Cup, against the Carolina Hurricanes in Raleigh, North Carolina, U.S.A.

Most minutes played in a season The NHL record for the most minutes played in a season is 4,434 minutes by Martin Brodeur (Canada) as goalkeeper for the New Jersey Devils (U.S.A.) during the 1995–96 season.

Most shutouts in a regular season The most NHL shutouts by a goalie in a season is 15 by Tony Esposito (Canada) for the Chicago Blackhawks (U.S.A.) in the 1969–70 season.

★ MOST CONSECUTIVE... ★

EVENT	TEAM/PLAYER	NUMBER	DATE
☆ Wins to start a season	Buffalo Sabres (U.S.A.)	10	Oct. 4–26, 2006
★ Road wins to start a season	Buffalo Sabres (U.S.A.)	10	Oct. 4–Nov. 11, 2006
★ Games scoring a goal, NHL Team	Calgary Flames (Canada)	264	Nov. 1981–Jan. 1985
★ Games scoring the winning goal	Newsy Lalonde (Canada)	5	Feb. 1921
★ Games played by an NHL defenseman	Karlis Skrastins (Russia)	495	Feb. 21–25, 2007
★ Team wins to start a season, NHL goalie	Martin Brodeur (Canada)	38	2006–07 season
☆ Seasons winning 30 games, NHL goalie	Martin Brodeur (Canada)	11	1995–96 to 2006–07 season
☆ Seasons winning 35 games, NHL goalie	Martin Brodeur (Canada)	10	1996–97 to 2006–07 season
☆ Seasons winning 40 games, NHL goalie	Martin Brodeur (Canada)	6	1997–98, 1999–2001, 2002–03, 2005–07 seasons

Most shutouts in a career The NHL record for the most career shutouts by a goalie is 103 by Terry Sawchuk (Canada). During his career, which ran for 21 years from 1949 to 1970, he played with a number of teams: the Detroit Red Wings (U.S.A.), Boston Bruins (U.S.A.), Toronto Maple Leafs (Canada), Los Angeles Kings (U.S.A.), and New York Rangers (U.S.A.).

★**First consecutive 40-goal seasons by an over 35-year-old** By scoring two power-play goals against the Vancouver Canucks on March 11, 2007, Teemu Selanne (b. July 3, 1970, Finland) of the Anaheim Ducks (U.S.A.) became the first NHL player over 35 to record consecutive 40-goal seasons.

★**First player in 400 games with three teams** Chris Chelios (U.S.A.) became the first player in NHL history to appear in 400 or more games for three different teams: the Montreal Canadiens (1984–90), Chicago Blackhawks (1990–99), and the Detroit Red Wings (1999–2007).

YOUNG GUNS

• The ★ **youngest player to start in the NHL All-Star Game** is Sidney Crosby (Canada b. August 7, 1987) of the Pittsburgh Penguins (U.S.A.). At 19 years 5 months, he was in the starting lineup for the Eastern Conference in the NHL All-Star Game on January 24, 2007, becoming the youngest ever player elected by the fans since All-Star fan balloting began in 1986. Crosby also became the ★ **youngest NHL player to reach 200 career points** with a goal in the first period of a game against the Carolina Hurricanes (U.S.A.) on March 2, 2007. He was also the ★ **youngest player in NHL history with two 100-point seasons** after reaching the century mark for the 2006–07 season with a goal in a 3–2 overtime win over the New York Rangers (U.S.A.) at Mellon Arena in Pittsburgh, Pennsylvania, U.S.A., on March 10, 2007.

• At 29 years 243 days, Martin Brodeur (b. May 6, 1972, Canada) playing for the New Jersey Devils (U.S.A.), became the **youngest goalkeeper to win 300 career NHL regular-season games.** His 300th victory was against the Ottawa Senators (Canada), at the Corel Center in Ottawa, Canada, on December 15, 2001.

At 31 years 322 days, Brodeur became the **youngest goalkeeper to win 400 career NHL regular-season games.** His 400th victory was an overtime win over the Florida Panthers (U.S.A.) at the Office Depot Center in Miami, Florida, U.S.A., on March 23, 2004.

• The NHL single-season record for **most goals scored by an NHL rookie** is 76 by Teemu Selanne (Finland) playing for the Winnipeg Jets (Canada) in 1992–93. The **most points scored by a rookie** is 132 points, also by Selanne while playing for the Winnipeg Jets (Canada) in 1992–93.

RUGBY

League The ★ **most points scored in a national rugby league career** by an individual player is 1,754, by Hazem El Masri (Lebanon), between 1996 and 2006, playing for the Canterbury Bulldogs (Australia).

•The ★ **most points scored in a national rugby league season** by an individual player is 342, also by Hazem El Masri (Lebanon), playing for the Bulldogs in 2004.

•The rugby league Tri-Nations international competition was inaugurated in 1999 as a contest between Australia, Great Britain, and New Zealand. Between 1999 and 2006, Darren Lockyer (Australia) and Joe Vagana (New Zealand) both scored nine tries in rugby league Tri-Nations matches, the ★ **most tries scored by a player in the history of the Tri-Nations tournament.**

•The ☆ **most wins in Australia's rugby league State of Origin series** is 12 by New South Wales between 1980 and 2005.

•The ★ **most wins of the rugby league City against Country match** (played every year in Australia) is 63 by the City team from 1930 to 2006.

•The Super League is the UK's premier rugby league competition, instituted in 1996. The ☆ **most Super League titles** won by a team is five, by St. Helens in 1996, 1999, 2000, 2002, and 2006.

Union •The ★ **most appearances in Guinness Premiership matches by an individual** is 174, by Tony Diprose (UK), between 1997 and 2006, playing for Saracens and Harlequins.

•The ★ **most tries scored in a Guinness Premiership match by an individual player** is six, by Ryan Constable (Australia) for Saracens against Bedford on April 16, 2000.

•The ★ **most tries scored in Guinness Premiership matches by an individual player** is 75, by Steve Hanley (UK) between 1998 and 2006 playing for Sale Sharks.

•The ★ **most points scored in an English Premiership rugby union match by an individual player** is 32, by Niall Woods (Ireland) playing for London Irish against Harlequins on April 23, 1998.

•The ★ **most Test tries scored in rugby union test matches in one year** is 17

★ **FASTEST TRY IN THE ENGLISH PREMIERSHIP** Tom Voyce (UK) scored a try in 9.63 seconds playing for Wasps against Harlequins on November 5, 2004, the fastest by an individual player in a Guinness Premiership match.

★ **MOST WINS OF THE LANCE TODD TROPHY** The Lance Todd trophy is awarded to the outstanding player in each rugby league season's Challenge Cup Final and has been won three times by St. Helens' Sean Long (UK, above), in 2001, 2004, and 2006.

and was achieved by Joe Rokocoko for New Zealand in 2003—equaling the record held by Daisuke Ohata (Japan).

• The ★ **highest attendance for a Heineken Cup pool match** is 44,100 at Parc des Princes in Paris, France, for a game played between Stade Français and Sale Sharks on December 10, 2006.

• The ☆ **most Six Nations Championship wins** is four, by France, in 2002, 2004, 2006, and 2007.

• Jonny Wilkinson (UK), playing for England, scored a record 89 points in the five games of the Six Nations Championship series in 2001, the ☆ **most points scored in a Six Nations season by an individual player.**

• The ★ **most penalty goals kicked in a Five/Six Nations Championship match** is seven: by Simon Hodgkinson for England v. Wales at Cardiff on January 19, 1991; Rob Andrew for England v. Scotland at Twickenham, Greater London, UK, on March 18, 1995; Jonny Wilkinson for England v. France at Twickenham on March 20, 1999; Neil Jenkins for Wales v. Italy at Cardiff, UK, on February 19, 2000; Gerald Merceron for France v. Italy on February 2, 2002; and Chris Paterson for Scotland v. Wales on February 10, 2007.

★ **MOST APPEARANCES IN RUGBY UNION SUPER RUGBY FINAL MATCHES** The most Super 12 and 14 Final appearances by an individual player is eight, by Reuben Thorne (New Zealand) playing for the Canterbury Crusaders from 1998 to 2000 and 2002 to 2006.

★ MOST RUGBY LEAGUE TRI-NATIONS TITLES Australia has won the rugby league Tri-Nations tournament on three occasions to date, in 1999, 2004, and 2006.

•Jason Leonard (UK) has played a total of 114 times for England, the **most international appearances by a rugby union forward.** The prop was awarded his first cap in July 1990 against Argentina in Buenos Aires and won his 100th playing against France in the Six Nations Championship at Twickenham, England, in February 2003.

•The ☆ **most tries scored in an international rugby union career** is 65 by Daisuke Ohata (Japan, b. November 11, 1975). He scored three tries in his debut international on November 9, 1996, and again on May 14, 2006 in his most recent test against Georgia, breaking David Campese's (Australia) record of 64 international tries.

•The ☆ **most international rugby union appearances by an individual** is by George Gregan (Australia), who competed in 127 internationals between 1990 and 2006.

Sevens •The ☆ most IRB Sevens Series titles won is six by New Zealand: in 1999–2000, 2000–01, 2001–02, 2002–03, 2003–04, and 2004–05. Fiji broke New Zealand's dominance to claim their first title in 2005–06.

★ MOST POINTS SCORED IN A GUINNESS PREMIERSHIP CAREER As of February 25, 2007, Jonny Wilkinson (UK) had scored 1,411 points for Newcastle Falcons.

He also holds the record for the **most points scored by an individual in an International Championship match,** with 35 for England (80) against Italy (23) at Twickenham, London, UK, on February 17, 2001.

★ **MOST TAG RUGBY PLAYERS** On July 6, 2006, 242 players took part in the Northwich and District Primary Schools Tag Rugby Tournament 2006, at Moss Farm sports complex, Northwich, UK.

OFF THE FIELD

• The record for the ★ **longest beach rugby try** is 18.3 ft. (5.60 m) and was set by Cedric Di Dio (France) on the set of *L'Été De Tous Les Records* in St. Cyprien, France, on June 29, 2005.

• The record for the ★ **most consecutive passes** of a rugby ball is 262 and was organized by Wooden Spoon and the Scottish Rugby Union as part of BT Finals day at Murrayfield, Edinburgh, UK, on April 30, 2005.

• The ☆ **most rugby tackles made in one hour** is 2,670 by Aberdeen Wanderers' under-18 squad (UK) at Aberdeen Wanderers Rugby Club, Aberdeen, UK, on June 10, 2006.

• The ☆ **most World Cup titles in women's rugby union** is three, by New Zealand in 1998, 2002, and 2006. The U.S.A. and England both have one win apiece. The women's World Cup has been contested five times between 1991 and 2006.

• First held in 1997, the **most wins of the women's Hong Kong Sevens** is five by New Zealand in 1997 and from 1999 to 2002.

• The **highest rugby union goal posts** measure 110 ft. (33.54 m). That is equivalent to the height of 7.5 double-decker buses stacked on top of each other! The record-breaking posts stand at the Roan Antelope Rugby Union Club, Luanshya, Zambia.

• The **largest rugby tour** was made by Ealing Rugby Club (UK) from April 11 to 14, 2003, with 264 players on a coach tour playing matches around Ireland.

• The **oldest rugby union competition,** The United Hospitals Cup, is played between teams representing hospitals in England. It was first contested in 1875.

• The ☆ **most points scored in IRB Sevens tournaments by an individual player** is 1,613, by Ben Gollings (UK) playing for England.

• The ☆ **most tries scored in IRB Sevens tournaments by an individual player** is 165, by Santiago Gomez Cora (Argentina) between 1999 and 2007.

• The ☆ **most goals scored in IRB Sevens tournaments by an individual player** is 449, by Ben Gollings (UK) playing for England.

TARGET SPORTS

Leaders of the lanes The Weber Cup is bowling's equivalent of the Ryder Cup—that is, bowlers from the U.S.A. and Europe compete against each other over three days of matches. The ★ **most wins of the Weber Cup** is four, by the U.S.A., in 2000, 2001, 2002, and 2006.

Archery The ☆ **most points scored in 24 hours of shooting Fédération Internationale de Tir à l'Arc (FITA) 18 rounds** (i.e., indoor archery rounds over 18 m, or 26 ft.) is 35,121 by Brian Williams and Mark Duggan (both UK) at Perriswood Archery Centre, Gower, Swansea, UK, on June 18, 2005.

• South Korea (Jang Yong-Ho, Choi Young-Kwang, and Im Bong Hyun) scored the ☆ **most points in a FITA round outdoor recurve (team),** with 4,074 out of a possible 4,320 in New York City, U.S.A., in July 2003.

★ **FASTEST TIME TO SHOOT 10 ARROWS** Luis Caídas Martín (Spain) shot 10 arrows in 1 min. 7 sec. on the set of *Guinness World Records—El Show de los Records* in Madrid, Spain, on June 4, 2006. Don't be fooled by the picture (above)—he shot the arrows one by one!

★ **MOST TIMES TO SCORE 180 IN A PRO DARTS CORPORATION FINAL** The greatest number of maximum scores recorded in a Pro Darts Corporation final by an individual is 21, by Raymond van Barneveld (Netherlands, pictured) in his match against Phil Taylor (UK) in Purfleet, UK, on January 1, 2007.

•The ☆ **most points scored in the men's individual 70 m outdoor recurve** (out of a possible 360 in a single round) is 351 by Kim Jae Hyung (South Korea) in Wonju, South Korea, on October 24, 2006.

Lawn Bowling Alex Marshall (UK) registered the ☆ **most wins of the indoor lawn bowling world championships,** with four titles (1999, 2003–04, and 2007).
•The ☆ **longest outdoor lawn bowling marathon** lasted 105 hours and was set by 12 members of Lloyd Hotel Bowling Club, Chorlton, UK, from October 14–18, 2006.

Croquet The President's Cup is the UK's premier invitation croquet event. Robert Fulford (UK) has achieved the ★ **most wins of the President's Cup,** with six victories (1989, 1998–99, 2001–02, and 2006).
•The MacRobertson Shield (instituted 1925) is the world's top croquet team event. The ★ **most wins of the MacRobertson Shield** is 13 by Great Britain (1925, 1937, 1956, 1963, 1969, 1974, 1982, 1990, 1993, 1996, 2000, 2003, and 2006).

Darts Phil Taylor (UK) has won the ☆ **most world championship titles,** with 13 victories, in 1990, 1992, 1995–2002 (consecutively), and 2004–06.
•Taylor also holds the record for the ★ **most World Matchplay titles,** with eight wins, in 1995, 1997, 2000–04, and 2006.
•Finally, Taylor holds the record for the ☆ **most World Grand Prix titles won by an individual player,** with seven, in 1998–2000, 2002–03, and 2005–06.

Pool The Mosconi Cup is a nine-ball pool tournament contested every year by two teams of the best players from the U.S.A. and Europe. The ☆ **most wins of the Mosconi Cup** is 11 by the U.S.A. in 1994, 1996–2001, and 2003–06.

On July 15, 2004, archer Jeremie Masson (France) scored a record three bull's-eyes in 90 seconds.

★ LONGEST SINGLES DARTS MARATHON Stephen Lye and Mick Kinney (both UK) played a darts match that lasted 24 hours at the Summerfield Tavern, Wilmslow, Cheshire, UK, on May 6–7, 2006.

•The ★ **most pool World Masters titles won** is five by Ralf Souquet (Germany)— 1994, 1996, 2000, 2002, and 2006.

•The ★ **most women's pool world championships won** is four by Allison Fisher (UK) in 1996–98 and 2001.

SHOOTING STARS

The first steps toward formalizing rules and regulations for shooting competitions were taken during the late 19th century. Shooting was one of the nine sports featured in the first modern Olympic Games, in 1896, and the inaugural shooting world championship took place in France the following year. The sport's governing body is the International Shooting Sport Federation (ISSF).

You'll find a wealth of shooting records in our comprehensive sports reference section (see page 528), but here are a few recent highlights:

•Alexei Klimov (Russia) holds the record for the ☆ **men's ISSF 25 m rapid-fire pistol shot event,** with a score of 591 in Granada, Spain, on October 6, 2006.

•On August 3, 2006, Espen Berg-Knutsen (Norway) set a new record for the ☆ **men's ISSF 300 m rifle three-positions event,** with a score of 1,181 in Zagreb, Croatia.

•Thomas Farnik (Austria) holds the record for the ☆ **men's 10 m air-rifle event,** with a score of 703.1 (599 + 104.1) in Granada, Spain, on October 4, 2006.

•Li Du (China) set a world record for the ☆ **women's 10 m air-rifle (40 shots) event** in Zagreb, Croatia, on June 4, 2003. Her overall score was 504.9 (400 + 104.9).

•Maria Grozdeva (Bulgaria) set a world record in the ☆ **women's 25 m pistol (60 shots) event** in Changwon, South Korea, on April 11, 2005. Her overall score was 796.7 (591 + 205.7).

•Sonja Pfeilschifter (Germany) scored 698.0 (594 + 104.0) in the ☆ **women's rifle 50 m three-positions (20 shots) event** in Munich, Germany, on May 28, 2006.

★**MOST CONSECUTIVE CENTURY SNOOKER BREAKS** John Higgins (UK) achieved four consecutive breaks of 100 or more in Preston, UK, on October 16, 2005. The "Wizard of Wishaw" recorded breaks of 103, 104, 138, and 128 in his match against Ronnie O'Sullivan (UK).

•Ralph Greenleaf (U.S.A.) won the **most World Pocket Billiards Championship titles,** with 19 from 1919 to 1937.

Snooker The ★**most Masters titles won by an individual** is six by Stephen Hendry (UK), in 1989–93 (consecutively) and 1996.
•Hendry also achieved the ★**most breaks of 100 or more in a professional career,** with 700 from 1985 to 2007.
•The final frame between Peter Ebdon (UK) and Graeme Dott (UK) at the Crucible in Sheffield, UK, on May 1, 2006 lasted for 74 minutes—the ★**longest frame in a world championship match.**

Bowling The ★**highest bowling score in 24 hours by an individual** is 59,702 points, by Cory Bithell (U.S.A.) at Eastways Lanes in Erie, Pennsylvania, U.S.A., on July 25–26, 1997.
•The bowling world cup (instituted in 1965) is contested annually by the national champions of the Fédération Internationale des Quilleurs (FIQ). The **most wins of the bowling world cup** is four by Paeng Nepomuceno (Philippines) in 1976, 1980, 1992, and 1996.

☆ **HIGHEST BACKWARD BOWLING SCORE IN A SINGLE GAME** Joe Scrandis (U.S.A.) scored 175 in a single game of backward bowling at The Lanes in Fort Meade, Maryland, U.S.A., on April 29, 2006.

•Three bowlers share the record for ★ **most world cup bowling titles won by a woman,** with two wins each. They are: Jeanette Baker (Australia) in 1982 and 1983; Pauline Smith (UK) in 1981 and 1993; and Shannon Pluhowsky (U.S.A.) in 2002 and 2004.

TENNIS & RACKET SPORTS

TENNIS

Speedy service The ☆ **fastest tennis serve** measured 155 mph (246.9 km/hr.) and was struck by Andy Roddick (U.S.A.) in a Davis Cup semifinal on September 24, 2006.

Brenda Schultz-McCarthy (Netherlands) produced a 130-mph (209-km/hr.) serve in the first round of the Western & Southern Financial Group Women's Open on July 15, 2006, the ☆ **fastest serve by a woman.**

★ **Most consecutive weeks as world tennis number one** Roger Federer (Switzerland) was ranked number-one male tennis player for 161 weeks, from February 2, 2004, to February 26, 2007.

Federer also holds the record for the ★ **most consecutive grass-court men's singles tennis match wins.** He won his 42nd match, beating Richard Gasquet (France) 6–3, 6–2, 6–2 at Wimbledon, London, UK, on June 26, 2006.

★ **Longest Wimbledon ladies singles final** In terms of minutes played, the longest ladies singles final in Wimbledon's history—indeed, one of the

★ **MOST CONSECUTIVE CLAY WINS (MALE)** On June 11, 2006, Rafael Nadal (Spain) won his 60th consecutive clay-court singles match, beating Roger Federer (Switzerland) 1–6, 6–1, 6–4, 7–6 (7–4) in the French Open final.

Chris Evert (U.S.A.) holds the ★ **women's—and overall—record for most consecutive wins** with 125.

longest of all women's tennis Grand Slam finals—occurred on July 2, 2005, when Venus Williams beat Lindsay Davenport (both U.S.A.) 4–6, 7–6 (7–4), 9–7 in a match lasting 2 hr. 45 min., at the Championships.in London, UK.

★ **Most prize money in a season** In 2006, Roger Federer (Switzerland) won $8.4 million from 17 tournaments.

Highest attendance An unprecedented 30,472 people filed into the Astrodome in Houston, Texas, U.S.A., on September 20, 1973, for the "Battle of the Sexes," when Billie-Jean King beat Robert Larimore Riggs (both U.S.A.).

The record for **highest attendance at a regular tennis match** was set at the 2004 Davis Cup final (December 3–5) between the U.S.A. and Spain in Seville's La Cartuja Olympic Stadium, Spain. It was seen by about 26,600 spectators.

WHAT'S IN A NAME?

Most historians believe tennis began in France around 800 years ago, as a game of handball played against walls or over a rope strung across a courtyard. As players served the ball, they called *"Tenez!"* ("Take this!"), which then evolved into the word "tennis."

★ **OLDEST PERSON TO BE RANKED WORLD TENNIS NUMBER ONE** The oldest male tennis player to be ranked number one by the Association of Tennis Professionals (ATP) is Andre Agassi (U.S.A., b. April 29, 1970), who became the highest-seeded men's player on May 11, 2003, aged 33 years 13 days. He held the ranking for 14 weeks.

☆ **MOST TENNIS CLUB SINGLES CHAMPIONSHIPS (MALE)** Mike Keat (UK) won 40 consecutive championships in the men's singles at Budehaven Tennis Club Championships in Bude, Cornwall, UK, 1959–98.

DID YOU KNOW?

Boris Becker (Germany) won the Wimbledon men's singles title in 1985 aged 17 years 227 days, making him the **youngest male Wimbledon champion.**

★ **MOST HOPMAN CUPS WON (FEMALE)** The greatest number of Hopman Cup titles won by a female player is two, by Arantxa Sánchez Vicario (Spain), playing for Spain in 1990 and 2002.

The ★ **highest attendance at Wimbledon for one day** was 42,457, for "First Wednesday" in 2002.

The ★ **highest attendance at a Wimbledon tournament** was 490,081 in 2001, when play was extended because of bad weather.

CUP GLORIES

•The Davis Cup, organized by the International Tennis Federation (ITF), is the ★ **largest annual team sport competition**. The 2006 competition saw 133 countries enter—one less than the previous year. The **most wins in the Davis Cup** has been 31 by the U.S.A. from 1900 to 1995.

•The women's equivalent of the Davis Cup is the ITF's Fed Cup (originally the Federation Cup), itself the **largest annual female team sports event,** with 89 countries represented in 2006. The U.S.A. has recorded the ★ **most consecutive wins of the Fed Cup by an international team,** with seven victories, 1976–82.

•The Hopman Cup is an invitational mixed-team contest that has been held in Perth, Australia, every year since 1989.

The ★ **greatest number of Hopman Cup titles** won by an international pairing is four, by the U.S.A., in 1997, 2003, 2004, and 2006.

The **most consecutive Hopman Cup wins by a country** is two, again by the U.S.A., in 2003–04.

James Blake holds the record for the ★ **most Hopman Cup titles won by a male player,** with two wins, playing for the U.S.A. in 2003 and 2004.

TABLE TENNIS

Longest rally The longest table-tennis rally was played between Brian and Steve Seibel (both U.S.A.) at the Christown YMCA, Phoenix, Arizona, U.S.A., on August 14, 2004. It lasted for 8 hr. 15 min. 1 sec.

Most team World Championships The ★most women's team World Championship titles (for the Corbillon Cup) is 17, by China, in 1965, 1971, 1975–89 (every two years), 1993, 1995, 1997, 2000–01, 2004, and 2006.

The ★most men's team World Championship titles (for the Swaythling Cup) is 15, by China, in 1961, 1963, 1965, 1971, 1975, 1977, 1981, 1983, 1985, 1987, 1995, 1997, 2001, 2004, and 2006.

☆ MOST OLYMPIC TABLE TENNIS TEAM GOLD MEDALS (MEN) The greatest number of gold medals won in Olympic competitions by a men's team is six by China from 1988 to 2004. Pictured above, left to right, are China's Qi Chen and Lin Ma on their way to Olympic gold in August 2004.

BADMINTON

☆**Most singles World Championships** Five Chinese players have won singles world titles twice. Yang Yang took the men's singles in 1987 and 1989. The women's singles has been won twice by: Li Lingwei (1983, 1989); Han Aiping (1985, 1987); Ye Zhaoying (1995, 1997); and Xie Xingfang (2005, 2006).

Longest match rally In the men's singles final of the 1987 All-England Championships between Morten Frost (Denmark) and Icuk Sugiarto (Indonesia), there were two successive rallies of more than 90 strokes.

☆**Fastest shuttlecock** During a Sudirman Cup match on June 3, 2005, Fu Haifeng (China) hit a shuttlecock at a speed of 206 mph (332 km/hr.), beating the previous record by 44 mph (72 km/hr.).

Most team badminton World Championships (men) Indonesia has won 13 men's team badminton World Championships, for the Thomas Cup: 1958, 1961, 1964, 1970, 1973, 1976, 1979, 1984, 1994, 1996, 1998, 2000, and 2002.

☆ **MOST TEAM BADMINTON UBER CUP WORLD CHAMPIONSHIPS (WOMEN)** The Chinese team has won the Uber Cup (instituted 1956) nine times, in 1984, 1986, 1988, 1990, 1992, 1998, 2000, 2002, and 2004. Pictured left is team member Zhang Ning in 2006.

UNUSUAL SPORTS

Farthest peanut throw On February 21, 1999, at Westfield Devils Junior Soccer Club in Launceston, Tasmania, Australia, Adrian Finch (Australia) threw a 0.1-oz. (4-mg) peanut a distance of 111 ft. 10 in. (34.11 m).

Farthest nira (Japanese chive) throw Junsuke Miyamoto (Japan) threw a nira (a type of oriental chive or leek) a distance of 36 ft. 5 in. (11.11 m) on June 20, 1997. Junsuke's record was ratified under the rules of "nira-tobashi" competitions held at the Sako Festival in Kochi-ken, Japan.

☆ **FARTHEST DISTANCE TO THROW A PERSON** Juha Rasanen (Finland) threw a person weighing 132 lb. (60 kg) a distance of 17 ft. 8 in. (5.4 m) onto a premarked mattress on the set of *Guinness World Records—El Show De Los Records* in Madrid, Spain, on June 11, 2006. In doing so, he broke his own record by over 4 ft. 11 in. (1.5 m).

Farthest distance to throw a rolling pin Lori La Deane Adams (U.S.A.) threw a 2-lb. (907-g) rolling pin a distance of 175 ft. 5 in. (53.47 m) at the Iowa State Fair, Iowa, U.S.A., on August 21, 1979.

Farthest distance to hurl a haggis Alan Pettigrew (UK) threw—or "hurled"—a haggis (of minimum weight 1 lb. 8 oz., or 680 g) a distance of 180 ft. 10 in. (55.11 m) at Inchmurrin, Argyll, UK, on May 24, 1984. The sport of haggis hurling dates back to 1977.

Fastest speed for "walking on water" Remy Bricka (France) covered 0.6 miles (1 km) in 7 min. 7.41 sec. on the Olympic pool in Montreal,

---

X-REF

• If you have a penchant for strange hobbies, check out our peculiar pastimes on page 142.

• Question: Where can you find some truly testing Scrabble, sudoku, and crossword conundrums? Answer: page 197.

• Enter the Olympic Hall of Fame on page 258.

• And for the latest records in every discipline from action sports to X Games, run along to page 528.

★ LONGEST RUNNING PUMPKIN RACE The Windsor Pumpkin Regatta and Parade in Nova Scotia, Canada, has been held annually since 1999. Competitors first parade their PVC (Personal Vegetable Craft)—giant hollowed-out pumpkins—then race them 0.5 miles (0.8 km) across Lake Pesaquid in either the motorized or paddler class.

Canada, on August 2, 1989. Monsieur Bricka "walks on water" by attaching ski floats to his feet and by moving in the same way as in cross-country skiing, using a double-headed paddle instead of ski poles.

★ **Fastest sandbag carrying** Peyo Mendiboure (France) carried a 176-lb. (80-kg) sandbag over a 393-ft. (120-m) course in 29.84 seconds on the set of *L'Été De Tous Les Records* in Argèles-Gazost, France, on July 6, 2005.

Largest crowd at a Camel-Wrestling Festival A crowd of 20,000 gathered to watch 120 dromedaries wrestle at the 1994 Camel-Wrestling Festival in Selçuk, Turkey.

★ LONGEST RUNNING FINGER-WRESTLING CONTESTS Finger-wrestling competitions, known as Fingerhakeln, have been staged in Bavaria, Germany, since the 14th century, when rivals competed in them for women's favor. Today, wrestlers contest various weight titles in the Bavarian Finger-Wrestling Championships held annually in Pflugdorf, near Munich. The aim is for each competitor to pull his rival across a table placed between them, using a finger lash wrapped around each contestant's digit.

☆**FASTEST 31-LEGGED RACE OVER 50 M** Students from the Ishii Higashi Elementary School ran a 31-legged race covering a total of 50 m (164 ft.) in 8.8 seconds at their school gym, in Matsuyama, Ehime Prefecture, Japan, on October 16, 2005. Thirty pupils from the sixth grade took part.

Most World Peashooting Championships Mike Fordham (UK) won seven peashooting World Championships, in 1977–78, 1981, 1983–85, and 1992.

Most Elephant Polo Championships The Tiger Top Tuskers won a record eight World Elephant Polo Association Championships, in 1983–85, 1987, 1992, 1998, 2000, and 2003.

Tiddlywinks Championships Larry Khan (U.S.A.) has won the ☆ **most world singles titles of the Tiddlywinks World Championships,** with 19.

Geoff Myers (UK) has won the ★ **most world pairs titles of the Tiddlywinks World Championships,** with 12.

Largest water pistol fight On April 28, 2005, 1,173 participants staged a colossal water fight at Loyola Marymount University, Los Angeles, California, U.S.A.

Longest running pillow fight The World Pillow-Fighting Championships in Kenwood, California, U.S.A., is the longest running annual competition of its kind: its 40th tournament was held on July 4, 2006. Around 100 contestants battled it out with wet, muddy pillows, sitting astride a steel pole over a mud-filled creek!

For more unusual record fights, look on the next page.

Nick and Alastair Benbow (both UK) ran the London Marathon three-legged in a record 3 hr. 40 min. 16 sec. on April 26, 1998.

★**LARGEST HIGH-HEELS RACE** The Glamour Stiletto Run, created by BSUR Concepting (Netherlands), takes place in cities worldwide. On March 9, 2006, 150 women ran 262 ft. (80 m) through a shopping mall in Amsterdam, Netherlands, wearing shoes with a minimum heel height of 2.75 in. (7 cm). Each hoped to win €10,000 ($12,600) of shopping money to be spent that day!

MORE FIGHTING TALK

•A total of 3,745 people created their own winter wonderland at Michigan Technological University, Houghton, Michigan, U.S.A., on February 10, 2006, with the **largest snowball fight.**

•Have you ever been asked to stop playing with your food? Clearly, no one's told the residents of Buñol in Spain. Every year, they amass around 275,500 lb. (125 tons) of tomatoes to throw at each other on the last Wednesday of August in the Tomatina, the **largest annual food fight.**

•The **largest water balloon fight** involved 2,849 people, who threw 51,400 balloons in the XBox 360 Water Balloon Challenge at Coogee Beach in Sydney, Australia, on April 22, 2006.

•Why eat a custard pie when it's so much more fun to throw it? On October 7, 1998, 50 people—including the band Electrasy and members of the Official Laurel and Hardy Fan Club—threw 4,400 custard pies in three minutes for the band's video of their single "Best Friend's Girl," in the **largest custard pie fight.** And why Laurel and Hardy? Well, a total of 3,000 pies were thrown in their silent two-reeler *The Battle of the Century* (U.S.A., 1927), the **largest custard pie fight in a movie.** As Ollie might have said, "That's another fine mess you've got me into!"

WATERSPORTS

SWIMMING

Fastest swimmer On March 23, 1990, Tom Jager (U.S.A.) achieved an average speed of 5.37 mph (8.64 km/hr.) over 50 yards (45.72 m) in Nashville, Tennessee, U.S.A.

•The **fastest female swimmer** is Le Jingyi (China), who achieved a speed of 4.56 mph (7.34 km/hr.) over 50 m on September 11, 1994.

☆ FASTEST 4 × 200 M FREESTYLE (WOMEN) Germany (Petra Dallmann, Daniela Samulski, Britta Steffen, Annika Liebs) completed the women's 4 × 200 m freestyle in 7 min. 50.82 sec. at the European Swimming Championships held in Budapest, Hungary, on August 3, 2006.

☆ **FASTEST 200 M BUTTERFLY (FEMALE)** Jessica Schipper (Australia) swam the women's 200 m butterfly in a time of 2 min. 5.4 sec. in Victoria, Canada, on August 17, 2006.

Most world records Ragnhild Hveger (Denmark) set 42 swimming world records from 1936 to 1942. For currently recognized events (only metric distances in 50-m pools), the **most swimming world records set by a woman** is 23, by Kornelia Ender (GDR) from 1973 to 1976.

•Arne Borg (Sweden) set 32 world records from 1921 to 1929, the **most swimming world records set by a man.** For currently recognized events, the record is 26 by Mark Spitz (U.S.A.), from 1967 to 1972.

Most Olympic golds at one games (female) At the 1988 Olympic Games, Kristin Otto (GDR) won six Olympic gold medals: the 50 m freestyle, the 100 m freestyle, the 100 m backstroke, the 100 m butterfly, the 4 × 100 m freestyle, and the 4 × 100 m medley.

50 m Jade Edmistone (Australia) swam the ☆**fastest women's 50 m breaststroke,** finishing in 30.31 seconds in Melbourne, Australia, on January 30, 2006.

☆ **FASTEST 100 M FREESTYLE (FEMALE)** Britta Steffen (Germany) swam the women's 100 m freestyle in 53.30 seconds in Budapest, Hungary, on August 2, 2006.

FASTEST 100 M BREASTSTROKE (MALE) Brendan Hansen (U.S.A.) swam the 100 m breaststroke in 59.13 seconds in Irvine, California, U.S.A., on August 1, 2006.

In Victoria, British Columbia, Canada, on August 20, 2006, he completed the ☆ **fastest men's 200 m breaststroke** in a time of 2 min. 8.50 sec.

Earlier—along with teammates Aaron Peirsol, Ian Crocker, and Jason Lezak—he had set the record for the **fastest men's short-course medley 4 × 100 m relay**, with a time of 3 min. 25.09 sec. in Indianapolis, U.S.A., on October 11, 2004.

100 m Leisel Jones (Australia) achieved the ☆ **fastest women's 100 m breaststroke** with a time of 1 min. 5.09 sec. in Melbourne, Australia, on March 20, 2006.

200 m Aaron Peirsol (U.S.A.) swam the ☆ **fastest men's 200 m backstroke** on August 19, 2006, in Victoria, Canada, with a time of 1 min. 54.44 sec.

•The ☆ **fastest women's 200 m breaststroke** record was set by Leisel Jones (Australia) on February 1, 2006, in Melbourne, Australia, with a time of 2 min. 20.54 sec.

4 × 100 m relay The U.S.A. (Michael Phelps, Neil Walker, Cullen Jones, Jason Lezak) recorded the ☆ **fastest 4 × 100 m freestyle relay** in 3 min. 12.46 sec. in Victoria, Canada, on August 19, 2006.

DID YOU KNOW?

The ★ **oldest woman to swim the Channel** was Carol Sing (U.S.A., b. August 24, 1941), who was 57 years 361 days old when she completed the journey on August 21, 1999.

☆ **FASTEST 400 M FREESTYLE (FEMALE)** Laure Manaudou (France) swam the women's 400 m freestyle in 4 min. 2.13 sec. in Budapest, Hungary, on August 6, 2006.

•On July 31, 2006, Germany (Petra Dallmann, Daniela Götz, Britta Steffen, Annika Liebs) recorded the ☆ **fastest women's 4 × 100 m freestyle relay**, finishing in 3 min. 35.22 sec. in Budapest, Hungary.

•Australia (Sophie Edington, Leisel Jones, Jessica Schipper, Lisbeth Lenton) swam the ☆ **fastest women's 4 × 100 m medley relay** in 3 min. 57.32 sec. in Melbourne, Australia, on March 21, 2006.

★ **Fastest 100 × 1,000 m relay (mixed team)** On September 2–3, 2006, a relay team of 100 swimmers (comprising 50 men and 50 women) took 22 hr. 48 min. 43.10 sec. to each successfully swim 1,000 m at Volkspark, Dortmund, Germany.

☆ **FASTEST 200 M BUTTERFLY (MALE)** Michael Phelps (U.S.A.) won the men's 200 m butterfly in a time of 1 min. 53.8 sec. in Victoria, Canada, on August 17, 2006.

He also holds the record for the **most swimming medals won by an individual at a single Olympic Games** with six golds (100 m and 200 m butterfly, 200 m and 400 m medley, 4 × 200 m freestyle, and 4 × 100 m medley) and two bronze (200 m freestyle and 4 × 100 m freestyle) at the 2004 Games.

DIVING

★**Oldest scuba diver** Herbert Kilbride (U.S.A., b. March 8, 1914), a qualified PADI instructor, celebrated his 90th birthday on March 8, 2004, and remains an active scuba enthusiast.

☆**Longest scuba dive in open freshwater** Jerry Hall (U.S.A.)—a Tennessee diver, not the Texan actress!—remained under water at a depth of 12 ft. (3.6 m) on a submerged platform in Watauga Lake, Tennessee, U.S.A., for 120 hr. 1 min. 9 sec. from August 29 to September 3, 2004. In accordance with the rules, he did not surface at any time.

Highest high dive Olivier Favre (Switzerland) recorded a dive of 176 ft. 10 in. (53.9 m) from a diving board at Villers-le-Lac, France, on August 30, 1987.

Greatest high-dive score In 2000, during the Cliff Diving World Championships in Kaunolu, Hawaii, U.S.A., Orlando Duque (Colombia) performed a double back somersault with four twists from 80 ft. (24.4 m). He earned a perfect 10 from all seven judges and scored 159.00 points.

Youngest cliff diver In December 2005, 12-year-old Iris Alvarez (Mexico) became the youngest person—and first female—to dive 59 ft. (18 m) off La Quebrada rock in Acapulco, Mexico. A person diving from the top of the cliff (at 100 ft.; 30 m) would hit the water at 56 mph (90 km/hr.)!

Canoeing The ★**longest journey by canoe or kayak** was made by Daniel Bloor (UK), who traveled 326.98 miles (526.22 km) from Tewitfield, Cumbria, to Little Venice, London, UK, from June 9 to 19, 2006.
•Three men share the record for the **greatest number of world and Olympic titles,** with 13: Gert Fredriksson (Sweden), 1948–60, Rüdiger Helm (GDR), 1976–83, and Ivan Patzaichin (Romania), 1968–84.

ENTER THE DRAGON...

Dragon boats are long, thin craft equipped with dragon heads and tails and propelled by paddlers. Dragon boat racing is a Chinese tradition dating back some 2,500 years, but it has become a modern sport, governed by the International Dragon Boat Federation (IDBF).

The International Dragon Boat Race was instituted in 1975 in Hong Kong and is held annually. The **fastest time** to complete this 2,100-ft. (640-m) course is 2 min. 27.45 sec. and was achieved by the Chinese Shun De team on June 30, 1985.

The **largest dragon boat regatta** consisted of 154 dragon boats in an event organized by Wanheimer Kanu-Gilde eV in Duisburg, Germany, from June 17 to 19, 2005.

YOUNGEST DIVING WORLD CHAMPION Fu Mingxia (China, b. August 16, 1978) won the women's world title for platform diving in Perth, Australia, on January 4, 1991, at the age of 12 years 141 days.

•The **longest canoeing race** was the Canadian Government Centennial Voyageur Canoe Pageant and Race from Rocky Mountain House, Alberta, to the Expo 67 site at Montreal, Quebec, from May 24 to September 4, 1967. The total length of the course was 3,283 miles (5,283 km).

Rowing The ★**most gold medals won in the World Championships and Olympic Games** is 13 by Sir Steven Redgrave (UK) who, in addition to his five Olympic successes, won world titles at coxed pairs (1986), coxless pairs (1987, 1991, 1993–95), and coxless fours (1997–99).

The rowing World Championships are distinct from the Olympic Games and were first held in 1962.

•The ★**greatest distance rowed in 24 hours (up- and downstream) by a man** is 163.42 miles (263 km), by Matthias Auer, Christian Klandt, and Olaf Behrend (all Germany) at DRUM Rowing Club, Berlin, Germany, on August 2–3, 2003.

•Maha Drysdale (New Zealand) set the ★**fastest men's single-sculls row** with a time of 6 min. 35.4 sec., in Eton, UK, on August 26, 2006.

•The ★**fastest men's double-sculls row** was achieved by Jean-Baptiste Macquet and Adrien Hardy (both France), with a time of 6 min. 4.25 sec. in Poznań, Poland, on June 17, 2006.

•Dongxiang Xu and Shimin Ya (both China) set a new record for the ★**fastest women's double-sculls lightweight-class row** in a time of 6 min. 49.77 sec. in Poznań, Poland, on June 17, 2006.

•China (Hua Yu, Haixia Chen, Xuefei Fan, and Jing Liu) set a new record for the ★**fastest women's quadruple-sculls lightweight-class row** with a time of 6 min. 23.96 sec. in Eton, UK, on August 27, 2006.

•The ☆**fastest women's coxed-eights row** was achieved by the U.S.A.

★ **FASTEST ROW BY COXLESS FOURS (WOMEN)** Australia (Selby Smith, Lutz, Bradley, Hornsey) completed a coxless fours race in 6 min. 25.35 sec. in Eton, UK, on August 26, 2006.

(Sickler, Cooke, Goodale, Shoop, Mickelson, Francia, Lind, Davies, and Whipple) with a time of 5 min. 55.5 sec. in Eton, UK, on August 27, 2006.

Surfing The ☆ **most ASP Tour World Championship titles won by a woman** is seven by Layne Beachley (Australia) from 1998 to 2004.
•Beachley also holds the record for the ★ **highest surfing career earnings by a woman,** with $567,935 to the end of the 2005 season.
•Last, in 1998, Beachley won $75,300 in surfing competitions, the **highest earnings from surfing in one season by a woman.**

★ **FASTEST SINGLE-SCULLS LIGHTWEIGHT-CLASS ROW (MALE)** Zac Purchase (UK) completed a single-sculls lightweight-class rowing race in a time of 6 min. 47.82 sec. in Eton, UK, on August 6, 2006. (This is a non-Olympic boat-class event.)

Water polo •The ☆ **most wins of the men's water polo World Championships** is two: Hungary in 1973 and 2003; the Soviet Union in 1975 and 1982; Italy in 1978 and 1994; Yugoslavia in 1986 and 1991; and Spain in 1998 and 2001. It was first held at the World Swimming Championships in 1973.

•Since it was introduced in 1986, the ☆ **women's water polo World Championships** has been won a record two times, by Italy (in 1998 and 2001) and by Hungary (in 1994 and 2005).

Waterskiing The ☆ **highest score for men's barefoot waterskiing tricks** is 10,880 points by Keith St. Onge (U.S.A.) at the 15th Barefoot Water Ski World Championships, Adna, Washington, U.S.A., on September 17, 2006.

•The ★ **fastest women's barefoot waterskiing speed** is 96.08 mph (154.63 km/hr.) by Teresa Wallace (U.S.A.) at Firebird International Raceway, Chandler, Arizona, U.S.A., on November 16, 2006.

CHANNEL CHAMPS

The Brits call it the English Channel; to the French, it's La Manche ("The Sleeve"). At its narrowest—between Dover (UK) and Cap Gris-Nez (France)—this slim stretch of water separating England and France measures just 21 miles (34 km), and to some people that represents a challenge...

•The **first person to swim the Channel** (without a life jacket) was Matthew Webb (UK), who made the crossing in 21 hr. 45 min. on August 24–25, 1875.

•The official Channel Swimming Association record for the **fastest time to swim the Channel** from Shakespeare Beach, Dover, UK, to Cap Gris-Nez, France, is 7 hr. 17 min. by Chad Hundeby (U.S.A.), on September 27, 1994.

•For some people, once is never enough. The ★ **greatest number of Channel crossings swum** is 39 by Alison Streeter (UK) from 1982 to 2000 (including a record seven in one year, 1992). The ★ **greatest number of Channel crossings swum by a man** is 33 by Michael Read (UK) from 1969 to 2004.

•Different strokes for different folks: the ★ **fastest crossing of the Channel using solely breaststroke** is 13 hr. 31 min. by Frederik Jacques (Belgium) on August 6, 2005.

The ★ **fastest crossing using solely backstroke** is 13 hr. 22 min. by Tina Neil (U.S.A.) on August 9, 2005.

Finally, ★ **the fastest crossing using solely the butterfly** is 14 hr. 18 min. by Julie Bradshaw (UK) on August 5, 2002.

★ **HIGHEST CAREER EARNINGS BY A SURFER** Kelly Slater (U.S.A.) earned an unprecedented $1,462,005 by the end of the 2006 season. Slater also holds the record for the ☆ **most wins of the Association of Surfing Professionals (ASP) World Championship Tour** with eight victories (1992, 1994–98, and 2005–06), and in 2005 became the ★ **first person to score two perfect-10 rides** under the ASP's two-wave scoring system.

★ **FASTEST TIME TO FINISH THE IJSBA PRO-AM WOMEN RUNABOUT SLALOM COURSE** The fastest electronically timed run for an international Jet Sports Boating Association (IJSBA) Pro-Am Women Runabout slalom course is 20.06 seconds by Karine Paturel (France, pictured) on Lake Havasu, Arizona, U.S.A., on October 13, 1995.

The ★ **fastest electronically timed run for an IJSBA Pro Runabout 785 slalom course** is 18.26 seconds by Minoru Kanamori (Japan) on Lake Havasu, Arizona, U.S.A., on October 14, 1995.

Wild-water racing West Germany is the ★ **most successful men's team at the International Canoe Federation (ICF) wild-water racing World Championships,** K1 class. The team has won eight titles, in 1963, 1965, 1969, 1971, 1973, 1979, 1983, and 1985.

•The ★ **most individual titles won at the ICF wild-water racing World Championships** is four by Vladimir Vala and Jaroslav Slucik (both Slovakia), who won the C2 events in 1996, 2000, and two titles in 2004.

The ★ **most successful women's team at the ICF wild-water racing World Championships** is France, having won three titles in the K1 team event, in 1996, 1998, and 2000.

Yachting The ☆ **highest speed reached on water by a yachtsman** is 48.70 knots (56.04 mph; 90.19 km/hr.) by Finian Maynard (Ireland) on a

---

AT THE OLYMPICS

•Two sportsmen share the record for the **most canoeing gold medals won at a single Olympic Games,** with three each: Vladimir Parfenovich (USSR) in 1980 and Ian Ferguson (New Zealand) in 1984.

Gert Fredriksson (Sweden) won six Olympic gold medals, from 1948 to 1960, the **most canoeing gold medals won at the Olympic Games.**

Fredriksson also picked up a silver medal in the 1952 Games and a bronze in the 1960 Games, giving him the record for ★ **most canoeing medals won at the Olympic Games,** with eight in total.

In short, Gert Fredriksson was the most successful men's canoeist in Olympic history.

•Five players share the record for **most water polo Olympic gold medals,** with three wins each: Britons George Wilkinson (in 1990, 1908, and 1912), Paulo "Paul" Radmilovic and Charles Sidney Smith (both in 1908, 1912, and 1920); and Hungarians Desz Gyarmati and Gyorgy Karpati (both in 1952, 1956, and 1964).

•The **first sportsman ever to win individual yachting gold medals in four successive Olympic Games** was Paul B. Elvstrøm (Denmark). He triumphed in the Firefly class in 1948 and the Finn class in 1952, 1956, and 1960. Elvstrøm also won eight other world titles in a total of six classes.

•The record for **longest span by an Olympic competitor** stands at 40 years. Of the four sportsmen who share this record, three are yachtsmen. Magnus Andreas Thulstrup Clasen Konow (Norway) in 1908–20, 1928, and 1936–48; Paul B. Elvstøm (Denmark) in 1948–60, 1968–72, and 1984–88; and Durward Randolph Knowles (UK 1948, then Bahamas) in 1948–72 and 1988).

The fourth, Dr. Ivan Joseph Martin Osiler (Denmark), competed in Olympic fencing in 1908–32 and 1948.

windsurfer at Saintes Maries de la Mer, France, on April 10, 2005. This achievement also gives Maynard the records for ☆ **highest speed reached under sail on water** and the ☆ **highest speed reached on a windsurfer.**

•The ☆ **women's record for the highest speed reached under sail on water by any craft over a 500 m timed run** is by windsurfer Karin Yaggi (Switzerland), who achieved 41.25 knots (47.4 mph; 76.4 km/hr.) on F2/arrows at Saintes Maries de la Mer, France, on April 10, 2005.

WILD WEST ARTS

★ **Largest gathering of Wild West artists** The Will Rogers Wild West International Expo, staged annually in Claremore, Oklahoma, U.S.A., by the Wild West Arts Club (WWAC), is the largest gathering of Wild West performers and competitors in the world. Each year, around 200 entrants compete across various "cowboy" disciplines (see page 518) for thousands of dollars in prize money. The event was previously held in Las Vegas until moving in 2005 to Claremore, Oklahoma—home of famous movie cowboy Will Rogers, (U.S.A., 1879–1935).

Most consecutive Texas skips Andrew Rotz (U.S.A.) achieved an incredible 11,123 consecutive Texas skips at the national convention of the Wild West Arts Club in Las Vegas, Nevada, U.S.A., on March 11, 2003,

★ **LARGEST TRICK-ROPING LOOP (FEMALE)** Kimberly Mink (U.S.A.) spun a loop around herself to a length of 76 ft. 2 in. (23.21 m)—measured from the end of the extended hondo (the eye of the rope) to her marked hand position—at Jerome High School in Jerome, Idaho, U.S.A., on January 25, 2003.

★**LARGEST TRICK-ROPING LOOP (MALE)**
Charles Keyes (U.S.A.) spun a rope to 114
ft. 5 in. (34.8 m) on April 21, 2007 at the
Will Rogers Wild West International Expo
in Claremore, Oklahoma, U.S.A. (see page
518 for more on this event), beating his
previous record of 107 ft. 2 in. (32.66 m)
set at the 2006 Expo. The secret of his
success is "bodybuilding, weight lifting,
running, and aerobics."

smashing the previous record set at 4,011.
The attempt took a bone-shattering 3 hr. 10
min. to complete.

★**Most Texas skips in one minute**
Daniel Ledda (Spain) achieved a record 80
Texas skips in 60 seconds on the set of *Guinness World Records—El Show de los Records*
in Madrid, Spain, on June 11, 2006.

★**Fastest Texas skip over 100 m** Ray
Kozak (U.S.A.) completed a 100-m sprint in
17.61 seconds while performing 23 consecutive Texas skips at the Warren County Middle
School, McMinnville, Tennessee, U.S.A., on
February 26, 2005.

A Texas skip is a vertical loop that is repeatedly pulled from one side of the body to
the other; with each pass, the roper jumps
through the center of the loop.

★**YOUNGEST WINNER OF THE TEXAS SKIP RACE** Cody Lamb (U.S.A.),
two-time winner of the "Rising Star" award at the Will Rogers Expo
(2005–06), is, at 11 years old, the youngest competitor to win the Texas
skip race. Cody was inducted along with mother Kim and father Dan
into the National Knife Throwers Hall of Fame in Austin, Texas, U.S.A.,
in 2007 as the "Western Performing Family of the Year."

★ **YOUNGEST WILD WEST ARTS COMPETITOR** At just seven years old, Maxwell William Mobley (U.S.A.) became the youngest registered entrant in a Wild West Arts event, when he participated in the youth "Wedding Ring" race, which involves running a race while maintaining a rope loop around the body.

★ **LONGEST WHIP CRACK** Wild West performance artist and whip maker Adam Winrich (U.S.A.) cracked a whip measuring 216 ft. (65.8 m) excluding the handle—almost as long as a jumbo jet!—in Fall Creek, Wisconsin, U.S.A., on May 24, 2006. (To "crack," the end must be made to travel above the speed of sound, breaking the sound barrier.)

Winrich also holds records for the ☆ **most stock-whip cracks in one minute**, with 272 on October 18, 2006, at the Stone's Throw bar in Eau Claire, Wisconsin, U.S.A.; the ☆ **most bullwhip cracks in one minute**, with 253, also at the Stone's Throw bar; and ★ **most whip cracks in one minute with two whips**, with a total of 420 at the 2007 Will Rogers Wild West Expo in Claremore, Oklahoma, U.S.A.

★ **FASTEST WHIP** The whip-cracking speed and accuracy world record is held by John Bailey (U.S.A.) of Ypsilanti, Michigan, U.S.A., who hit 10 targets consecutively with a cracking whip in 8.04 seconds at the 2007 Wild West Arts Expo in Claremore, Oklahoma, U.S.A., on April 21, 2007.

★ **Fastest draw (open style)** The record for the world's fastest draw has stood since 1982 when, on a given signal, Ernie Hill (U.S.A.) drew his gun from a standing position and fired a shot in a record 0.208 seconds!

★ **LARGEST MOUNTAIN-MAN EVENT** Chuck Weems (U.S.A., above) organizes the Texas State Knife and Tomahawk Championships, a mountain-man–style throwing contest that, in February 2007, attracted a record 54 entrants (winners pictured, inset).

★ **MOST KNIFE-THROWING WORLD TITLES WON** Dr. Michael Bainton (U.S.A.) has won four knife-throwing world championships, in 2003–05 and 2007. He is also the only thrower to throw a perfect score in the impalement category at the world championships.

WILD WEST ARTS CLUB

Guinness World Records is indebted to the Wild West Arts Club (WWAC) for the majority of the records on these pages. The WWAC is "dedicated to preserving the Western arts of trick roping, riding, shooting, whip cracking, and the throwing arts," and stages the annual Will Rogers Wild West International Expo in Claremore, Oklahoma, U.S.A.

The group—a nonprofit heritage foundation—currently boasts around 600 active members from 10 countries, and celebrated its 16th year at the Expo held in February 2007.

If you wish to take part in next year's Expo, contact the WWAC on **www.wwac.com.**

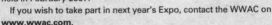

WINTER SPORTS

Bobsled The ☆**most wins of the women's bobsled world championships** is four, by Germany in 2000, 2003, 2004, and 2005.
•The **most individual Olympic bobsled medals won** is seven (one gold, five silver, and one bronze) by Bogdan Musiol (GDR) in 1980–92.

Skiing The ☆**highest recorded speed for a male skier** is 156.83 mph (252.40 km/hr.), achieved by Simone Origone (Italy) at Les Arcs, France, on April 20, 2006.

★ **MOST BIATHLON WORLD CUP PURSUIT MEDALS (WOMEN)** First held in 1997, the biathlon world cup 10-km pursuit has seen Germany win a record six medals: two gold (most recently in 2005 by Uschi Disl, pictured), two silver, and two bronze.

Germany has won a total of 14 medals in both men's and women's events, the ★ **most world cup pursuit medals won by a country.**

•The ☆ **highest recorded speed by a female skier** is 150.73 mph (242.59 km/hr.), by Sanna Tidstrand (Sweden), also at Les Arcs, France, on April 20, 2006.

•The ★ **oldest known ski** was found in a peat bog in Hoting, Sweden. It dates from *ca.* 2500 BC.

•The ☆ **greatest distance skied uphill** (using fur-covered skis) in 24 hours is 47,929 ft. (14,609 m), by Erwin Reinthaler (Austria) in Bad Gastein, Austria, on March 11–12, 2006.

•During the 1970s, Annemarie Moser-Pröll (Austria) achieved 62 world cup race wins—36 in the downhill, 16 in the giant slalom, three in the slalom, and seven in the combined, giving her the record for the ★ **most ski race world cup victories.**

•The ★ **youngest winner of a freestyle skiing world cup event** is Anais Caradeux (France), aged 15 years 199 days, at Les Contamines, France, on January 15, 2006.

•The ★ **oldest winner of a freestyle skiing world cup event** is Mike Nemesvary (UK), aged 83 years 77 days, at Angel Fire, New Mexico, U.S.A., on March 19, 1983.

•When Annelise Coberger (New Zealand) won a silver medal in the women's ski slalom at the XVI Olympiad in Albertville, France, in 1992, she became the ★ **first Winter Olympic medalist from the southern hemisphere.**

Ski jumping The ☆ **longest competitive ski jump by a man** is 784 ft. (239 m) by Bjørn Einar Romøren (Norway) in Planica, Slovenia, on March 20, 2005.

•Three ski fliers share the record for the ★ **most ski fly world championships,** with two wins each: Walter Steiner (Switzerland) in 1972 and 1977; Sven Hannawald (Germany) in 2000 and 2002; and Roar Ljøkelsøy (Norway) in 2004 and 2006.

Snowboarding The ★ **first competition for snow bodyboarders** was held in Switzerland in 2002.

MOST SKELETON TITLES Alex Coomber (UK) has won four world skeleton titles: the world cup in 2000, 2001, and 2002, and the world championships in 2000.

•The ★ **youngest winner of a snowboarding world cup event** is Sophie Rodriguez (France), aged 15 years 200 days, in Kreischberg, Austria, on January 23, 2004.

•Ursula Bruhin's (Switzerland) victory at Le Relais, Canada, on December 17, 2005, made her the ★ **oldest individual winner of a snowboarding world cup event,** at the age of 35 years 273 days.

•Snowboard cross was included in the Winter Olympics program for the first time in 2006. The women's gold medal was won by Tanja Freiden (Switzerland) in Bardonecchia, Italy, on February 17, 2006, giving her the record for the ★ **most snowboard cross Olympic medals won by a woman.**

SKATE GREATS

•Natalia Kanounnikova (Russia) recorded the ★ **fastest spin on ice skates,** with a maximum rotational velocity of 308 rpm (revolutions per minute) at Rockefeller Center Ice Rink, New York City, U.S.A., on March 27, 2006.

•The **most figure skating Olympic gold medals won by a man** is three, by Gillis Grafstrom (Sweden) in 1920, 1924, and 1928. Sonja Henie (Norway) achieved the **most figure skating Olympic gold medals won by a woman,** with three wins at the Winter Olympic Games of 1928, 1932, and 1936.

•The ☆ **fastest time in the men's 10,000 m speed skating event** is 12 min. 41.69 sec.* by Sven Kramer (Netherlands) in Salt Lake City, Utah, U.S.A., on March 10, 2007.

•The ☆ **fastest time in the women's 3,000 m speed skating event** is 3 min. 53.34 sec. by Cindy Klassen (Canada) in Calgary, Canada, on March 18, 2006.

•The ★ **oldest international speed skating competition** is the Alberto Nicolodi Trophy, organized by Sportivi Ghiaccio Trento, Trento, Italy, which had its 46th anniversary on February 11–12, 2006.

*awaiting ratification

★MOST WINS OF THE IDITAROD TRAIL SLED DOG RACE The Iditarod Trail Sled Dog Race is held annually in Alaska, U.S.A., and covers more than 1,150 miles (1,850 km). The most wins to date is five by Rick Swenson (U.S.A., pictured) in 1977, 1979, 1981–82, and 1991.

MOST OLYMPIC SNOWBOARD MEDALS Two snowboarders have won two Olympic medals each: Ross Powers (U.S.A., left), with gold (2002) and bronze (1998) in the half-pipe; and Karine Ruby (France), with gold (1998) and silver (2002) in the parallel giant slalom.

★LONGEST RUNNING SKIKJÖRING EVENT The longest running winter horse-racing event that requires the "jockeys" to be pulled on skis is Skikjöring, which has been held annually in February since 1907. Skikjöring takes place during White Turf St. Mortiz, an international horse race held on the frozen surface of Lake St. Mortiz, Switzerland.

★ **MOST WORLD ICE GOLF CHAMPIONSHIPS** Since the first World Ice Golf Championship was held in March 1999, in Uummannaq, Greenland, two players have won the championship title twice. Annika Östberg (Denmark, pictured) won in 2000 and 2001, followed by two consecutive wins by Roger Beames (UK) in 2002 and 2003.

•Likewise, Seth Wescott's (U.S.A.) victory in the men's event on February 16, 2006, gave him the record for the ★ **most snowboard cross Olympic medals won by a man.**

X GAMES

Highest attendance at an extreme sports event The 1999 ESPN Summer X Games, held in San Francisco, California, U.S.A., were attended by a record 268,390 visitors over its 10-day duration.

★ **Highest attendance at the Winter X Games** An unprecedented 85,100 spectators attended Winter X Games 5 in 2001 in Mount Snow, Vermont, U.S.A. This represents **the greatest attendance for any winter action sports event.**

By the late 20th century, the public profile of extreme action sports was on the rise and growing increasingly popular with a younger generation. In recognition of this, the Entertainment and Sports Programming Network (ESPN) organized the Extreme Games in Rhode Island, U.S.A., in 1995. Nine events featured, including BMX, bungee jumping, and skateboarding, and the competition attracted 198,000 spectators. In 1996, the contest was renamed X Games, and the next year saw the debut of the Winter X Games.

HIGHEST BMX VERTICAL AIR The highest unassisted air on a half-pipe is 19 ft. (5.8 m), by Dave Mirra (U.S.A., pictured) off an 18-ft.-tall (5.4-m) ramp in San Diego, California, U.S.A., in January 2001. Mat Hoffman (U.S.A.) achieved 26 ft. 6 in. (8.07 m) on a BMX from a quarter-pipe ramp on March 20, 2001, in Oklahoma City, Oklahoma, U.S.A., but was towed by a motorcycle in the run-up to the jump.

First skateboard 900 Skateboard legend Tony Hawk (U.S.A.) became the first person to achieve a "900" (two-and-a-half airborne rotations) in a competition, at X Games 5 in San Francisco, California, U.S.A., on June 27, 1999. The 900 (named after the fact that the skater spins through 900°) is regarded as one of the most difficult tricks in vert skateboarding.

★Longest handstand on a snowskate board Trenton R. Schindler (U.S.A.) performed a snowskate-board handstand lasting a record 4.38 seconds at Winter X Games 11 in Aspen, Colorado, U.S.A., on January 28, 2007.

★Longest ollie on a snowskate board Phil Smage (U.S.A.) performed an 11-ft. 4-in. (3.45-m) ollie on a snowskate board at Winter X Games 11 in Aspen, Colorado, U.S.A., on January 27, 2007. An ollie involves lifting the board off the snow with just the momentum of your body.

YOUNGEST X GAMES ATHLETE The youngest ever X Games athlete is Nyjah Huston (U.S.A., b. November 30, 1994), who was 11 years 246 days old when he made his competition debut in the men's Skateboard Street at X Games 12, staged from August 3 to 6, 2006.

★**Most consecutive ollies on a snowskate board** Phil Smage (U.S.A.) set another world snowskate record at Winter X Games 11 by achieving 14 consecutive ollies (or kickflips) on January 25, 2007.

SUMMER MEDAL WINNERS

Most medals The most individual medals of any kind won during the history of the Summer X Games is 20 by Dave Mirra (U.S.A.), who competes in BMX Freestyle. Mirra also holds the record for the ☆**most Summer X Games gold medals won by an individual,** with 18 wins as of March 2, 2007.

Skateboarding Tony Hawk and Andy Macdonald (both U.S.A.) have each won 16 X Games skateboard medals.

Moto X Travis Pastrana (U.S.A.) has won a total of 11 X Games medals during his career in Moto X Best Trick, Freestyle and Step Up, seven of them gold.

Moto X (Best Trick) was once also a discipline of the Winter X Games. The **most Moto X Winter X Games medals won** is two, by five U.S. riders: Mike Metzger, Mike Jones, Tommy Clowers, Caleb Wyatt and Brian Deegan, whose two medals (2002, 2005) were gold—another record!

★**FIRST MOTO X DOUBLE BACKFLIP** Travis Pastrana (U.S.A.) made history at X Games 12 in Los Angeles, California, U.S.A., on August 4, 2006, by performing the first double backflip on a motorcycle—an incredible stunt for which he was awarded gold for Best Trick. The following day, Pastrana went on to pick up his third gold of the games, in the rally event.

WINTER MEDAL WINNERS

Skier X Enak Gavaggio (France) holds six Skier X medals—gold in 1999 and bronze from 2001 to 2004 and 2007.

Skiing Tanner Hall (U.S.A.) has won a record nine Winter X Games skiing medals: a gold for Big Air, three golds and one silver for Slopestyle, and two golds and two silvers for SuperPipe Men's.

Ski SuperPipe Jon Olsson (Sweden) has won four Ski SuperPipe medals: gold in 2002, silver in 2004, and bronze in 2003 and 2005. Superpipes have 16-ft. 4-in.-high (5-m) walls that are almost 90° vertical.

SnoCross Canadian X Games competitor Blair Morgan has earned a total of eight medals for SnoCross: gold from 2001 to 2003 and 2005 to 2006, silver from 1999 to 2000, and bronze in 2004.

★ HIGHEST OLLIE ON A SNOWSKATE BOARD The highest ollie on a snowskate board is 27.75 in. (70.5 cm) by Phil Smage (U.S.A.) at ESPN's Winter X Games 11 in Aspen, Colorado, U.S.A., on January 26, 2007.

MOST SNOWBOARD SUPERPIPE MEDALS AT THE WINTER X GAMES (MALE) Danny Kass (U.S.A.) has won a total of four medals for Snowboard SuperPipe: gold in 2001, silver in 2003 and 2004, and bronze in 2005.

MOST INDIVIDUAL MEDALS AT THE WINTER X GAMES Barrett Christy (U.S.A.) won 10 Winter X Games medals in a variety of snowboard disciplines between 1997 and 2001. For Slopestyle, she won gold in 1997, silver in 1998 and 1999, and bronze in 2000 and 2002; in Big Air, she won gold in 1997 and 1999 and silver in 1998 and 2001; finally, she earned a silver for SuperPipe in 2000.

MOST GOLD MEDALS AT THE WINTER X GAMES Two X Games competitors have won six gold medals each—Shaun Palmer (U.S.A., above) and Shaun White (U.S.A.). Palmer won gold in Skier X (2000), Snowboarder X (1997–99), Snow Mountain Biking (1997), and Ultracross (2001). White won his golds in Snowboard SuperPipe (2003 and 2006) and Slopestyle (2003–06).

MOST SNOWBOARD SLOPESTYLE MEDALS AT THE WINTER X GAMES Shaun White (U.S.A.) has earned five Snowboard Slopestyle medals: gold in 2003, 2004, 2005, and 2006, and silver in 2002.

MOST SKI SLOPESTYLE MEDALS AT THE WINTER X GAMES Jon Olsson (Sweden, pictured) and Tanner Hall (U.S.A.) have each won four medals for Ski Slopestyle. Hall took gold in 2002–04 and silver in 2005. Olsson took bronze in 2002–05.

XTREMES OF XCELLENCE

•Ryan Sheckler (U.S.A., b. December 30, 1989) was 13 years 230 days old when he won the Skateboard Park gold medal at X Games 9 in Los Angeles, California, U.S.A., on August 17, 2003. This feat made him the **youngest X Games gold medalist.**

•Lindsey Adams Hawkins (U.S.A., b. September 21, 1989) became the **youngest female X Games gold medalist** when she won the Skateboard Vert competition, aged 14 years 321 days at X Games 10 in Los Angeles, California, U.S.A., on August 7, 2004.

•Ayumi Kawasaki (Japan) was 12 years old in 1997 when she won an X Games bronze medal in the women's Aggressive Inline Skate Vert competition. The achievement made her the **youngest X Games medalist.**

•The record for the **oldest X Games athlete** is held by Angelika Casteneda (U.S.A.), who was 53 years old when she competed in the X Venture Race in 1996.

Casteneda secured a gold medal in the race, a feat that also gives her the record for the **oldest X Games medalist.**

SPORTS REFERENCE

★ ARCHERY—OUTDOOR RECURVE ★

MEN	RECORD HOLDER	RECORD
30 m	Kye Dong-Hyun (South Korea)	360/17
50 m	Kim Kyung-Ho (South Korea)	351
70 m	Kim Jae-Hyung (South Korea)	349
70 m Round (72 Arr.)	Im Dong-Hyun (South Korea)	687
90 m	Jang Yong-Ho (South Korea)	337
12 Arr. Final Match	Choi Won-Jong (South Korea)	120/0
144 Arr. FITA Round	Oh Kyo-Moon (South Korea)	1,379
3 × 144 Arr. FITA Round	South Korea (Jang Yong-Ho, Choi Young-Kwang, Im Dong-Hyun)	4,074
24 Arr. Final Match	China (Xue Haifeng, Jiang Lin, Wu FengBo)	229
70 m Round (3 × 72 Arr.)	South Korea (Jang Yong-Ho, Kim Bo-Ram, Oh Kyo-Moon)	2,031

WOMEN	RECORD HOLDER	RECORD
30 m	Yun Mi-Jin (South Korea)	360/15
50 m	Park Sung-Hyun (South Korea)	350
60 m	Kim Yu-Mi (South Korea)	351
70 m	Park Sung-Hyun (South Korea)	351
70 m Round (72 Arr.)	Park Sung-Hyun (South Korea)	682
12 Arr. Final Match	Song Mi-Jin (South Korea)	118
144 Arr. FITA Round	Park Sung-Hyun (South Korea)	1,405
☆ 3 × 144 Arr. FITA Round	South Korea (Park Sung-Hyun, Yun Mi-Jin, Yun Ok-Hee)	4,129
☆ 24 Arr. Final Match	South Korea (Kim Yu-Mi, Lee Sung-Jin, Lee Tuk-Young)	226
70 m Round (3 × 72 Arr.)	South Korea (Park Sung-Hyun, Lee Sung-Jin, Yun Mi-Jin)	2,030

★ TRACK AND FIELD—INDOOR FIELD EVENTS ★

MEN	RECORD	NAME & NATIONALITY
High jump	2.43 m (7 ft. 11.66 in.)	Javier Sotomayor (Cuba)
Pole vault	6.15 m (20 ft. 2.12 in.)	Sergei Bubka (Ukraine)
Long jump	8.79 m (28 ft. 10.06 in.)	Carl Lewis (U.S.A.)
Triple jump	17.83 m (58 ft. 5.96 in.)	Aliecer Urrutia (Cuba)
	17.83 m (58 ft. 5.96 in.)	Christian Olsson (Sweden)
Shot put	22.66 m (74 ft. 4.12 in.)	Randy Barnes (U.S.A.)
Heptathlon*	6,476 points	Dan O'Brien (U.S.A.)

*60 m 6.67 seconds; long jump 7.84 m; shot put 16.02 m; high jump 2.13 m; 60 m hurdles 7.85 seconds; pole vault 5.20 m; 1,000 m 2 min. 57.96 sec.

PLACE	DATE
Cheongju, South Korea	Sep. 1, 2002
Wonju, South Korea	Sep. 1, 1997
Yecheon, South Korea	Oct. 24, 2006
Athens, Greece	Aug. 12, 2004
New York City, U.S.A.	Jul. 16, 2003
Ulsan, South Korea	Oct. 18, 2005
Wonju, South Korea	Nov. 1, 2000
New York City, U.S.A.	Jul. 16, 2003
Porec, Croatia	May 12, 2006
Atlanta, U.S.A.	Jul. 1, 1996

PLACE	DATE
Yecheon, South Korea	Oct. 27, 2004
Yecheon, South Korea	Mar. 12, 2003
Cheongju, South Korea	Aug. 26, 2004
Cheongju, South Korea	Oct. 9, 2004
Athens, Greece	Aug. 12, 2004
Cheongju, South Korea	Aug. 13, 2001
Cheongju, South Korea	Oct. 10, 2004
New Delhi, India	Nov. 10, 2005
Antalya, Turkey	Jun. 9, 2006
Athens, Greece	Aug. 12, 2004

24 ARROW FINAL MATCH Xue Haifeng (China, member of the record-holding team) is shown in action at the men's archery individual event in Athens, Greece, on August 16, 2004.

PLACE	DATE
Budapest, Hungary	Mar. 4, 1989
Donetsk, Ukraine	Feb. 21, 1993
New York City, U.S.A.	Jan. 27, 1984
Sindelfingen, Germany	Mar. 1, 1997
Budapest, Hungary	Mar. 7, 2004
Los Angeles, U.S.A.	Jan. 20, 1989
Toronto, Canada	Mar. 14, 1993

★ TRACK AND FIELD—INDOOR FIELD EVENTS ★

WOMEN	RECORD	NAME & NATIONALITY
High jump	2.08 m (6 ft. 9.8 in.)	Kajsa Bergqvist (Sweden)
☆ Pole vault	•4.93 m (16 ft. 2 in.)	Yelena Isinbayeva (Russia)
Long jump	7.37 m (24 ft. 2.15 in.)	Heike Drechsler (GDR)
Triple jump	15.36 m (50 ft. 4.72 in.)	Tatyana Lebedeva (Russia)
Shot put	22.50 m (73 ft. 9.82 in.)	Helena Fibingerová (Czechoslovakia)
Pentathlon†	4,991 points	Irina Belova (Russia)

•Still awaiting ratification/confirmation by the IAAF at the time of going to press

†60 m hurdles 8.22 seconds; high jump 1.93 m; shot put 13.25 m; long jump 6.67 m; 800 m 2 min. 10.26 sec.

★ TRACK AND FIELD—OUTDOOR FIELD EVENTS ★

MEN	RECORD	NAME & NATIONALITY
High jump	2.45 m (8 ft. 0.45 in.)	Javier Sotomayor (Cuba)
Pole vault	6.14 m (20 ft. 1.73 in.)	Sergei Bubka (Ukraine)
Long jump	8.95 m (29 ft. 4.36 in.)	Mike Powel (U.S.A.)
Triple jump	18.29 m (60 ft. 0.78 in.)	Jonathan Edwards (GB)
Shot put	23.12 m (75 ft. 10.23 in.)	Randy Barnes (U.S.A.)
Discus	74.08 m (243 ft. 0.53 in.)	Jürgen Schult (GDR)
Hammer	86.74 m (284 ft. 7 in.	Yuriy Sedykh (USSR)
Javelin	98.48 m (323 ft. 1.16 in.)	Jan Železný (Czech Republic)
Decathlon*	9,026 points	Roman Šebrle (Czech Republic)

*100 m 10.64 seconds; long jump 8.11 m; shot put 15.33 m; high jump 2.12 m; 400 m 47.79 seconds; 110 m hurdles 13.92 seconds; discus 47.92 m; pole vault 4.80 m; javelin 70.16 m; 1,500 m 4 min. 21.98 sec.

WOMEN	RECORD	NAME & NATIONALITY
High jump	2.09 m (6 ft. 10.28 in.)	Stefka Kostadinova (Bulgaria)
Pole vault	5.01 m (16 ft. 5.24 in.)	Yelena Isinbayeva (Russia)
Long jump	7.52 m (24 ft. 8.06 in.)	Galina Chistyakova (USSR)
Triple jump	15.50 m (50 ft. 10.23 in.)	Inessa Kravets (Ukraine)
Shot put	22.63 m (74 ft. 2.94 in.)	Natalya Lisovskaya (USSR)
Discus	76.80 m (252 ft.)	Gabriele Reinsch (GDR)
☆ Hammer	77.80 m (255 ft. 3 in.)	Tatyana Lysenko (Russia)
Javelin	71.70 m (235 ft. 2.83 in.)	Osleidys Menéndez (Cuba)
Heptathlon†	7,291 points	Jacqueline Joyner-Kersee (U.S.A.)
Decathlon**	8,358 points	Austra Skujyte (Lighuania)

†100 m hurdles 12.69 seconds; high jump 1.86 m; shot put 15.80 m; 200 m 22.56 seconds; long jump 7.27 m; javelin 45.66 m; 800 m 2 min. 8.51 sec.

**100 m 12.49 seconds; long jump 6.12 m; shot put 16.42 m; high jump 1.78 m; 400 m 57.19 seconds; 100 m hurdles 14.22 seconds; discus 46.19 m; pole vault 3.10 m; javelin 48.78 m; 1,500 m 5 min. 15.86 sec.

PLACE	DATE
Arnstadt, Germany	Feb. 4, 2006
Donetsk, Ukraine	Feb. 10, 2007
Vienna, Austria	Feb. 13, 1988
Budapest, Hungary	Mar. 6, 2004
Jablonec, Czechoslovakia	Feb. 19, 1977
Berlin, Germany	Feb. 15, 1992

WOMEN'S POLE VAULT
Yelena Isinbayeva (Russia) competes at the Norwich Union Grand Prix meeting on July 22, 2005 at Crystal Palace Athletics Stadium, London, UK. She holds both the indoor and outdoor pole vault world records.

PLACE	DATE
Salamanca, Spain	Jul. 27, 1993
Sestriere, Italy	Jul. 31, 1994
Tokyo, Japan	Aug. 30, 1991
Gothenburg, Sweden	Aug. 7, 1995
Los Angeles, U.S.A.	May 20, 1990
Neubrandenburg, Germany	Jun. 6, 1986
Stuttgart, Germany	Aug. 30, 1986
Jena, Germany	May 25, 1996
Götzis, Austria	May 27, 2001

PLACE	DATE
Rome, Italy	Aug. 30, 1987
Helsinki, Finland	Aug. 12, 2005
St. Petersburg, Russia	Jun. 11, 1988
Gothenburg, Sweden	Aug. 10, 1995
Moscow, Russia	Jun. 7, 1987
Neubrandenburg, Germany	Jul. 9, 1988
Tallinn, Estonia	Aug. 15, 2006
Helsinki, Finland	Aug. 14, 2005
Seoul, South Korea	Sep. 24, 1988
Columbia, U.S.A.	Apr. 15, 2005.

★ TRACK AND FIELD—INDOOR TRACK EVENTS ★

MEN	TIME	NAME & NATIONALITY
50 m	5:56	Donovan Bailey (Canada)
60 m	6:39	Maurice Greene (U.S.A.)
	6:39	Maurice Greene (U.S.A.)
200 m	19:92	Frank Fredericks (Namibia)
400 m	44:57	Kerron Clement (U.S.A.)
800 m	1:42:67	Wilson Kipketer (Denmark)
1,000 m	2:14:96	Wilson Kipketer (Denmark)
1,500 m	3:31:18	Hicham El Guerrouj (Morocco)
1 mile	3:48:45	Hicham El Guerrouj (Morocco)
3,000 m	7:24:90	Daniel Komen (Kenya)
5,000 m	12:49:60	Kenenisa Bekele (Ethiopia)
50 m hurdles	6:25	Mark McKoy (Canada)
60 m hurdles	7:30	Colin Jackson (GB)
4 × 200 m relay	1:22:11	Great Britain & N. Ireland (Linford Christie, Darren Braithwaite, Ade Mafe, John Regis)
☆ 4 × 400 m relay	3:02:83	U.S.A. (Andre Morris, Dameon Johnson, Deon Minor, Milton Campbell)
4 × 800 m relay	7:13:94	Global Athletics & Marketing, U.S.A. (Joey Woody, Karl Paranya, Rich Kenah, David Krummenacker)
5,000 m walk	18:07:08	Mikhail Shchennikov (Russia)

WOMEN	TIME	NAME & NATIONALITY
50 m	5:96	Irina Privalova (Russia)
60 m	6:92	Irina Privalova (Russia)
	6:92	Irina Privalova (Russia)
200 m	21:87	Merlene Ottey (Jamaica)
400 m	49.59	Jarmila Kratochvílová (Czechoslovakia)
800 m	1:55.82	Jolanda Ceplak (Slovenia)
1,000 m	2:30.94	Maria de Lurdes Mutola (Mozambique)
1,500 m	3:58.28	Yelena Soboleva (Russia)
1 mile	4:17.14	Doina Melinte (Romania)
☆ 3,000 m	*8:23.72	Meseret Defar (Ethiopia)
☆ 5,000 m	14:27.42	Tirunesh Dibaba (Ethiopia)
50 m hurdles	6.58	Cornelia Oschkenat (GDR)
60 m hurdles	7.69	Ludmila Engquist (Russia)
4 × 200 m relay	1:32.41	Russia (Yekaterina Kondratyeva, Irina Khabarova, Yuliva Pechonkina, Yulia Gushchina)
4 × 400 m relay	3:23.37	Russia (Yulia Gushchina, Olga Kotlyarova, Olga Zaytseva, Olesya Krasnomovets)
☆ 4 × 800 m relay	*8:18.54	Russia (Anna Balakshina, Natalya Pantelyeva, Anna Emashova, Olesya Chumakova)
3,000 m walk	11:40.33	Claudia Stef (Romania)

*Still awaiting ratification/confirmation by the IAAF at the time of going to press

PLACE	DATE
Reno, U.S.A.	Feb. 9, 1996
Madrid, Spain	Feb. 3, 1998
Atlanta, U.S.A.	Mar. 3, 2001
Liévin, France,	Feb. 18, 1996
Fayetteville, U.S.A.	Mar. 12, 2005
Paris, France	Mar. 9, 1997
Birmingham, UK	Feb. 20, 2000
Stuttgart, Germany	Feb. 2, 1997
Ghent, Belgium	Feb. 12, 1997
Budapest, Hungary	Feb. 6, 1998
Birmingham, UK	Feb. 20, 2004
Kobe, Japan	Mar. 5, 1986
Sindelfingen, Germany	Mar. 6, 1994
Glasgow, UK	Mar. 3, 1991
Maebashi, Japan	Mar. 7, 1999
Boston, U.S.A.	Feb. 6, 2000
Moscow, Russia	Feb. 14, 1995

PLACE	DATE
Madrid, Spain	Feb. 9, 1995
Madrid, Spain	Feb. 11, 1993
Madrid, Spain	Feb. 9, 1995
Liévin, France	Feb. 13, 1993
Milan, Italy	Mar. 7, 1982
Vienna, Austria	Mar. 3, 2002
Stockholm, Sweden	Feb. 25, 1999
Moscow, Russia	Feb. 18, 2006
East Rutherford, U.S.A.	Feb. 9, 1990
Stuttgart, Germany	Feb. 3, 2007
Boston, U.S.A.	Jan. 27, 2007
Berlin, Germany	Feb. 20, 1988
Chelyabinsk, Russia	Feb. 4, 1990
Glasgow, UK	Jan. 29, 2005
Glasgow, UK	Jan. 28, 2006
Volgograd, Russia	Feb. 11, 2007
Bucharest, Romania	Jan. 30, 1999

☆ WOMEN'S 5,000 M
Tirunesh Dibaba (Ethiopia)
waves to the crowd at the
Reebok Boston Indoor
Games in Boston,
Massachusetts, U.S.A.,
after winning the 5,000 m
in a time of 14 min. 27.42
sec. on January 27, 2007.

★ TRACK AND FIELD—OUTDOOR TRACK EVENTS ★

MEN	TIME/DISTANCE	NAME & NATIONALITY
100 m	9.77	Asafa Powell (Jamaica)
	•9.77	Justin Gatlin (U.S.A.)
☆	9.77	Asafa Powell (Jamaica)
☆	9.77	Asafa Powell (Jamaica)
200 m	19.32	Michael Johnson (U.S.A.)
400 m	43.18	Michael Johnson (U.S.A.)
800 m	1:41.11	Wilson Kipketer (Denmark)
1,000 m	2:11.96	Noah Ngeny (Kenya)
1,500 m	3:26.00	Hicham El Guerrouj (Morocco)
1 mile	3:43.13	Hicham El Guerrouj (Morocco)
2,000 m	4:44.79	Hicham El Guerrouj (Morocco)
3,000 m	7:20.67	Daniel Komen (Kenya)
5,000 m	12:37.35	Kenenisa Bekele (Ethiopia)
10,000 m	26:17.53	Kenenisa Bekele (Ethiopia)
20,000 m	56:55.60	Arturo Barrios (Mexico)
1 hour	21,101 m	Arturo Barrios (Mexico)
25,000 m	1:13:55.80	Toshihiko Seko (Japan)
30,000 m	1:29:18.80	Toshihiko Seko (Japan)
3,000 m steeplechase	7:53.63	Saif Saaeed Shaheen (Qatar)
☆110 m hurdles	12.88	Xiang Liu (China)
400 m hurdles	46.78	Kevin Young (U.S.A.)
4 × 100 m relay	37.40	U.S.A. (Michael Marsh, Leroy Burrell, Dennis Mitchell, Carl Lewis)
	37.40	U.S.A. (John Drummond Jr., Andre Cason, Dennis Mitchell, Leroy Burrell)
4 × 200 m relay	1:18.68	Santa Monica Track Club, U.S.A. (Michael Marsh, Leroy Burrell, Floyd Heard, Carl Lewis)
4 × 400 m relay	2:54.20	U.S.A. (Jerome Young, Antonio Pettigrew, Tyree Washington, Michael Johnson)
☆4 × 800 m relay	7:02.43	Kenya (Joseph Mutua, William Yiampoy, Ismael Kombich, Wilfred Bungei)
4 × 1,500 m relay	14:38.80	West Germany (Thomas Wessinghage, Harald Hudak, Michael Lederer, Karl Fleschen)

*Still awaiting ratification/confirmation by the IAAF at the time of going to press

WOMEN	TIME/DISTANCE	NAME & NATIONALITY
100 m	10.49	Florence Griffith-Joyner (U.S.A.)
200 m	21.34	Florence Griffith-Joyner (U.S.A.)
400 m	47.60	Marita Koch (GDR)
800 m	1:53.28	Jarmila Kratochvílová (Czechoslovakia)
1,000 m	2:28.98	Svetlana Masterkova (Russia)
1,500 m	3:50.46	Qu Yunxia (China)
1 mile	4:12.56	Svetlana Masterkova (Russia)
2,000 m	5:25.36	Sonia O'Sullivan (Ireland)
3,000 m	8:06.11	Wang Junxia (China)
☆5,000 m	14:24.53	Meseret Defar (Ethiopia)
10,000 m	29:31.78	Wang Junxia (China)

PLACE	DATE
Athens, Greece	Jun. 14, 2005
Doha, Qatar	May 12, 2006
Gateshead, UK	Jun. 11, 2006
Zürich, Switzerland	Aug. 18, 2006
Atlanta, U.S.A.	Aug. 1, 1996
Seville, Spain	Aug. 26, 1999
Cologne, Germany	Aug. 24, 1997
Rieti, Italy	Sep. 5, 1999
Rome, Italy	Jul. 14, 1998
Rome, Italy	Jul. 7, 1999
Berlin, Germany	Sep. 7, 1999
Rieti, Italy	Sep. 1, 1996
Hengelo, Netherlands	May 31, 2004
Brussels, Belgium	Aug. 26, 2005
La Fléche, France	Mar. 30, 1991
La Fléche, France	Mar. 30, 1991
Christchurch, New Zealand	Mar. 22, 1981
Christchurch, New Zealand	Mar. 22, 1981
Brussels, Belgium	Sep. 3, 2004
Lausanne, Switzerland	Jul. 11, 2006
Barcelona, Spain	Aug. 6, 1992
Barcelona, Spain	Aug. 8, 1992
Stuttgart, Germany	Aug. 21, 1993
Walnut, U.S.A.	Apr. 17, 1994
Uniondale, U.S.A.	Jul. 22, 1998
Brussels, Belgium	Aug. 25, 2006
Cologne, Germany	Aug. 17, 1977

☆ **4 × 800 M RELAY** The Kenyan relay team (Wilfred Bungei, Joseph Mutua, Ismael Kombich, and William Yiampoy, left to right) celebrate their world record in the 4 × 800 m men's relay race in Brussels, Belgium, on August 25, 2006.

WOMEN'S 200 M Florence Griffith-Joyner (U.S.A.) crosses the finish line at the Seoul Games, South Korea, on September 29, 1988, having run the 200 m in 21.34 seconds. Her record remains unbroken after nearly 20 years.

PLACE	DATE
Indianapolis, U.S.A.	Jul. 16, 1988
Seoul, South Korea	Sep. 29, 1988
Canberra, Australia	Oct. 6, 1985
Munich, Germany	Jul. 26, 1983
Brussels, Belgium	Aug. 23, 1996
Beijing, China	Sep. 11, 1993
Zürich, Switzerland	Aug. 14, 1996
Edinburgh, UK	Jul. 8, 1994
Beijing, China	Sep. 13, 1993
New York City, U.S.A.	Jun. 3, 2006
Beijing, China	Sep. 8, 1993

★ TRACK AND FIELD—OUTDOOR TRACK EVENTS ★

WOMEN	TIME/DISTANCE	NAME & NATIONALITY
20,000 m	1:05:26.60	Tegla Loroupe (Kenya)
1 hour	18,340 m	Tegla Loroupe (Kenya)
25,000 m	1:27:05.90	Tegla Loroupe (Kenya)
30,000 m	1:45:50.00	Tegla Loroupe (Kenya)
3000 m steeplechase	9:01.59	Gulnara Samitova-Galkina (Russia)
100 m hurdles	12.21	Yordanka Donkova (Bulgaria)
400 m hurdles	52.34	Yuliya Pechonkina (Russia)
4 × 100 m relay	41.37	GDR (Silke Gladisch, Sabine Rieger, Ingrid Auerswald, Marlies Göhr)
4 × 200 m relay	1:27.46	United States "Blue" (LaTasha Jenkins, LaTasha Colander-Richardson, Nanceen Perry, Marion Jones)
4 × 400 m relay	3:15.17	USSR (Tatyana Ledovskaya, Olga Nazarova, Maria Pinigina, Olga Bryzgina)
4 × 800 m relay	7:50.17	USSR (Nadezhda Olizarenko, Lyubov Gurina, Lyudmila Borisova, Irina Podyalovskaya)

★ TRACK AND FIELD—ROAD RACE ★

MEN	TIME	NAME & NATIONALITY
10 km	27:02	Haile Gebrselassie (Ethiopia)
15 km	41:29	Felix Limo (Kenya)
☆	•41:29	Samuel Wanjiru (Kenya)
☆ 20 km	•55:31	Samuel Wanjiru (Kenya)
☆ Half marathon	•58:35	Samuel Wanjiru (Kenya)
25 km	1:12:45	Paul Malakwen Kosgei (Kenya)
30 km	1:28:00	Takayuki Matsumiya (Japan)
Marathon	2:04:55	Paul Tergat (Kenya)
100 km	6:13:33	Takahiro Sunada (Japan)
☆ Road relay	1:57:06	Kenya (Josephat Ndambiri, Martin Mathathi, Daniel Mwangi, Mekubo Mogusu, Onesmus Nyerere, John Kariuki)

WOMEN	TIME	NAME & NATIONALITY
10 km	30:21	Paula Radcliffe (UK)
15 km	46:55	Kayoko Fukushi (Japan)
☆ 20 km	1:03:21	Lornah Kiplagat (Netherlands)
Half marathon	1:06:44	Elana Meyer (South Africa)
25 km	1:22:13	Mizuki Noguchi (Japan)
30 km	1:38:49	Mizuki Noguchi (Japan)
Marathon	2:15:25	Paula Radcliffe (UK)
100 km	6:33:11	Tomoe Abe (Japan)
Road relay	2:11:41	China (Jiang Bo, Dong Yanmei, Zhao Fengdi, Ma Zaijie, Lan Lixin, Li Na)

•Still awaiting ratification/confirmation by the IAAF at the time of going to press

PLACE	DATE
Borgholzhausen, Germany	Sep. 3, 2000
Borgholzhausen, Germany	Aug. 7, 1998
Mengerskirchen, Germany	Sep. 21, 2002
Warstein, Germany	Jun. 6, 2003
Iráklio, Greece	Jul. 4, 2004
Stara Zagora, Bulgaria	Aug. 20, 1988
Tula, Russia	Aug. 8, 2003
Canberra, Australia	Oct. 6, 1985
Philadelphia, U.S.A.	Apr. 29, 2000
Seoul, South Korea	Oct. 1, 1988
Moscow, Russia	Aug. 5, 1984

PLACE	DATE
Doha, Qatar	Dec. 11, 2002
Nijmegen, Netherlands	Nov. 11, 2001
Ras Al Khaimah, UAE	Feb. 9, 2007
The Hague, Netherlands	Mar. 17, 2007
The Hague, Netherlands	Mar. 17, 2007
Berlin, Germany	May 9, 2004
Kumamoto, Japan	Feb. 27, 2005
Berlin, Germany	Sep. 28, 2003
Tokoro, Japan	Jun. 21, 1998
Chiba, Japan	Nov. 23, 2005

PLACE	DATE
San Juan, Puerto Rico	Feb. 23, 2003
Marugame, Japan	Feb. 5, 2006
Debrecen, Hungary	Oct. 8, 2006
Tokyo, Japan	Jan. 15, 1999
Berlin, Germany	Sep. 25, 2005
Berlin, Germany	Sep. 25, 2005
London, UK	Apr. 13, 2003
Tokoro, Japan	Jun. 25, 2000
Beijing, China	Feb. 28, 1998

★ TRACK AND FIELD—ULTRA-LONG DISTANCE [TRACK] ★

MEN	TIME/DISTANCE	NAME & NATIONALITY
100 km	6:10:20	Don Ritchie (UK)
100 miles	11:28:03	Oleg Kharitonov (Russia)
1,000 miles	11 days 13:54:58	Piotr Silikin (Lithuania)
24 hours	303.306 km (188.46 miles)	Yiannis Kouros (Greece)
6 days	1,023.200 km (635.78 miles)	Yiannis Kouros (Greece)

WOMEN	TIME/DISTANCE	NAME & NATIONALITY
100 km	7:14:06	Norimi Sakurai (Japan)
100 miles	14:25:45	Edit Berces (Hungary)
1,000 miles	13 days 1:54:02	Eleanor Robinson (UK)
24 hours	250.106 km (155.40 miles)	Edit Berces (Hungary)
6 days	883.631 km (549.06 miles)	Sandra Barwick (New Zealand)

★ TRACK AND FIELD—RACE WALKING ★

MEN	TIME	NAME & NATIONALITY
20,000 m	1:17:25.6	Bernardo Segura (Mexico)
20 km (road)	1:17:21	Jefferson Pérez (Ecuador)
30,000 m	2:01:44.1	Maurizio Damilano (Italy)
50,000 m	3:40:57.9	Thierry Toutain (France)
☆ 50 km (road)	3:35:47	Nathan Deakes (Australia)

WOMEN	TIME	NAME & NATIONALITY
10,000 m	41:56.23	Nadezhda Ryashkina (U.S.S.R.)
20,000 m	1:26:52.3	Olimpiada Ivanova (Russia)
20 km (road)	1:25:41	Olimpiada Ivanova (Russia)

OFFICIAL BODIES

•**IAAF** International Association of Athletics Federations *www.iaaf.org*

•**IAU** International Association of Ultrarunners *www.iau.org.tw*

•**RWA** Race Walking Association
www.racewalkingassociation.btinternet.co.uk

PLACE	DATE
London, UK	Oct. 28, 1978
London, UK	Oct. 2, 2002
Nanango, Australia	Mar. 11–23, 1998
Adelaide, Australia	Oct. 4–5, 1997
Colac, Australia	Nov. 26–Dec. 2, 1984

PLACE	DATE
Verona, Italy	Sep. 27, 2003
Verona, Italy	Sep. 21–22, 2002
Nanango, Australia	Mar. 11–23, 1998
Verona, Italy	Sep. 21–22, 2002
Campbelltown, Australia	Nov. 18–24, 1990

PLACE	DATE
Bergen, Norway	May 7, 1994
Paris Saint-Denis, France	Aug. 23, 2003
Cuneo, Italy	Oct. 3, 1992
Héricourt, France	Sep. 29, 1996
Geelong, Australia	Dec. 2, 2006

PLACE	DATE
Seattle, U.S.A.	Jul. 24, 1990
Brisbane, Australia	Sep. 6, 2001
Helsinki, Finland	Aug. 7, 2005

MEN'S 20 KM RACE (WALKING)
Jefferson Pérez (Ecuador) crosses the finish line of the 20 km men's road walk at the IAAF World Athletics Championships in Paris, France, on August 23, 2003. He achieved a record time of 1 hr. 17 min. 21 sec.

★ FREE DIVING ★

MEN'S DEPTH DISCIPLINES	DEPTH/TIME	NAME & NATIONALITY
☆Constant weight with fins	364 ft. 2 in. (111 m)	Herbert Nitsch (Austria)
☆Constant weight without fins	269 ft. (82 m)	William Trubridge (New Zealand)
Variable weight	459 ft. 4 in. (140 m)	Carlos Coste (Venezuela)
☆No limit	600 ft. 4 in. (183 m)	Herbert Nitsch (Austria)
Free immersion	347 ft. 9 in. (106 m)	Martin Stepanek Czech Republic)

MEN'S DYNAMIC APNEA		
☆With fins	731 ft. 7 in. (223 m)	Tom Sietas (Germany)
☆Without fins	600 ft. 4 in. (183 m)	Tom Sietas (Germany)

MEN'S STATIC APNEA		
☆Without fins, duration	9 min. 8 sec.	Tom Sietas (Germany)

WOMEN'S DEPTH DISCIPLINES		
☆Constant weight with fins	288 ft. 8.5 in. (88 m)	Mandy-Rea Cruickshank (Canada)
Constant weight without fins	108 ft. 5 in. (55 m)	Natalia Molchanova (Russia)
Variable weight	400 ft. 3 in. (122 m)	Tanya Streeter (U.S.A.)
No limit	524 ft. 11 in. (160 m)	Tanya Streeter (U.S.A.)
☆Free immersion	262 ft. 5 in. (80 m)	Natalia Molchanova (Russia)

WOMEN'S DYNAMIC APNEA		
With fins	656 ft. 2 in. (200 m)	Natalia Molchanova (Russia)
Without fins	429 ft. 9 in. (131 m)	Natalia Molchanova (Russia)

WOMEN'S STATIC APNEA		
Without fins, duration	7 min. 30 sec.	Natalia Molchanova (Russia)

PLACE	DATE
Hurghada, Egypt	Dec. 9, 2006
Long Island, The Bahamas	Apr. 11, 2007
Sharm, Egypt	May 9, 2006
Zirje, Croatia	Aug. 28, 2006
Grand Cayman, Cayman Islands	Apr. 3, 2006
Tokyo, Japan	Aug. 28, 2006
Tokyo, Japan	Aug. 27, 2006
Hamburg, Germany	May 1, 2007
Grand Cayman, Cayman Islands	Apr. 29, 2007
Dahab, Egypt	Nov. 7, 2005
Turks and Caicos Islands	Jul. 19, 2003
Turks and Caicos Islands	Aug. 17, 2002
Dahab, Egypt	Jun. 3, 2006
Moscow, Russia	Apr. 23, 2006
Tokyo, Japan	Dec. 20, 2005
Moscow, Russia	Apr. 22, 2006

☆ MEN'S FREE DIVING
Herbert Nitsch (Austria) currently holds two free diving records: constant weight with fins (he dived to 364 ft. 2 in. or 111 m using his muscle power alone but using fins for propulsion), and the "deepest man" record (that is, a "no-limit" dive) of 600 ft. 4 in. (183 m), which he achieved using a weighted sled to pull him down and air-filled balloons to return to the surface.

★ ROWING ★

MEN	TIME	NAME & NATIONALITY
☆ Single sculls	6:35.40	Mahe Drysdale (New Zealand)
☆ Double sculls	6:03.25	Jean-Baptiste Macquet, Adrien Hardy (France)
☆ Quadruple sculls	5:37.31	Konrad Wasielewski, Marek Kolbowicz, Michal Jelinski, Adam Korol (Poland)
Coxless pairs	6:14.27	Matthew Pinsent, James Cracknell (UK)
Coxless fours	5:41.35	Sebastian Thormann, Paul Dienstbach, Philipp Stüer, Bernd Heidicker (Germany)
Coxed pairs*	6:42.16	Igor Boraska, Tihomir Frankovic, Milan Razov (Croatia)
Coxed fours*	5:58.96	Matthias Ungemach, Armin Eichholz, Armin Weyrauch, Bahne Rabe, Jörg Dederding (Germany)
Coxed eights	5:19.85	Deakin, Beery, Hoopman, Volpenheim, Cipollone, Read, Allen, Ahrens, Hansen (U.S.A.)

LIGHTWEIGHT

	TIME	NAME & NATIONALITY
☆ Single sculls*	6:47.82	Zac Purchase (UK)
Double sculls	6:10.80	Elia Luini, Leonardo Pettinari (Italy)
Quadruple sculls*	5:45.18	Francesco Esposito, Massimo Lana, Michelangelo Crispi, Massimo Guglielmi (Italy)
Coxless pairs*	6:26.61	Tony O'Connor, Neville Maxwell (Ireland)
Coxless fours	5:45.60	Thomas Poulsen, Thomas Ebert, Eskild Ebbesen, Victor Feddersen (Denmark)
Coxed eights*	5:30.24	Altena, Dahlke, Kobor, Stomporowski, Melges, März, Buchheit, Von Warburg, Kaska (Germany)

WOMEN	TIME	NAME & NATIONALITY
Single sculls	7:07.71	Rumyana Neykova (Bulgaria)
Double sculls	6:38.78	Georgina and Caroline Evers-Swindell (New Zealand)
Quadruple sculls	6:10.80	Kathrin Boron, Katrin Rutschow-Stomporowski, Jana Sorgers, Kerstin Köppen (Germany)
Coxless pairs	6:53.80	Georgeta Andrunache, Viorica Susanu (Romania)
☆ Coxless fours*	6:25.35	Robyn Selby Smith, Jo Lutz, Amber Bradley, Kate Hornsey (Australia)
☆ Coxed eights	5:55.50	Mickelson, Whipple, Lind, Goodale, Sickler, Cooke, Shoop, Francia, Davies (U.S.A.)

REGATTA	DATE
Eton, UK	Aug. 26, 2006
Poznań, Poland	Jun. 17, 2006
Poznań, Poland	Jun. 17, 2006
Seville, Spain	Sep. 21, 2002
Seville, Spain	Sep. 21, 2002
Indianapolis, U.S.A.	Sep. 18, 1994
Vienna, Austria	Aug. 24, 1991
Athens, Greece	Aug. 15, 2004

Eton, UK	Aug. 26, 2006
Seville, Spain	Sep. 22, 2002
Montreal, Canada	1992
Paris, France	1994
Lucerne, Switzerland	Jul. 9, 1999
Montreal, Canada	1992

REGATTA	DATE
Seville, Spain	Sep. 21, 2002
Seville, Spain	Sep. 21, 2002
Duisburg, Germany	May 19, 1996
Seville, Spain	Sep. 21, 2002
Eton, UK	Aug. 26, 2006
Eton, UK	Aug. 27, 2006

★ ROWING ★

LIGHTWEIGHT	TIME	NAME & NATIONALITY
☆ Single sculls*	7:28.15	Constanta Pipota (Romania)
☆ Double sculls	6:49.77	Dongxiang Xu, Shimin Yan (China)
☆ Quadruple sculls*	6:23.96	Hua Yu, Haixia Chen, Xuefei Fan, Jing Liu (China)
Coxless pairs*	7:18.32	Eliza Blair, Justine Joyce (Australia)

*Denotes non-Olympic boat classes

★ SHOOTING ★

MEN	SCORE	NAME & NATIONALITY
☆ 300 m rifle three positions	1,181	Epsen Berg-Knutsen (Norway)
300 m rifle prone	600	Harald Stenvaag (Norway)
	600	Bernd Ruecker (Germany)
300 m standard rifle 3 × 20	589	Trond Kjoell (Norway)
	589	Marcel Buerge (Switzerland)
50 m rifle three positions	1,186	Rajmond Debevec (Slovenia)
50 m rifle prone	600	This record has been achieved a total of 16 times. Most times: Sergei Martynov (Belarus) with 5.
10 m air rifle	600	Tevarit Majchacheeap (Thailand)
50 m pistol	581	Alexsander Melentiev (USSR)
☆ 25 m rapid fire pistol	591	Alexei Klimov (Russia)
25 m center fire pistol	590	Afanasijs Kuzmins (USSR)
	590	Sergei Pyzhianov (USSR)
	590	Mikhail Nestruev (Russia)
	590	Park Byung-Taek (South Korea)
	590	Mikhail Nestruev (Russia)
☆	590	Jaspal Rana (India)
25 m standard pistol	584	Erich Buljung (U.S.A.)
10 m air pistol	593	Sergei Pyzhianov (USSR)
50 m running target	596	Nicolai Lapin (USSR)
50 m running target mixed	398	Lubos Racansky (Czech Republic)
10 m running target	590	Manfred Kurzer (Germany)
10 m running target mixed	391	Manfred Kurzer (Germany)
☆	391	Lukasz Czapla (Poland)
Trap	125	Giovanni Pellielo (Italy)
	125	Ray Ycong (U.S.A.)
	125	Marcello Tittarelli (Italy)
	125	Lance Bade (U.S.A.)
	125	Pavel Gurkin (Russia)
☆	125	David Kostelecky (Czech Republic)
Double trap	147	Michael Diamond (Australia)

REGATTA	DATE
Paris, France	Jun. 19, 1994
Poznań, Poland	Jun. 17, 2006
Eton, UK	Aug. 27, 2006
Aiguebelette-le-Lac, France	Sep. 7, 1997

PLACE	DATE
Zagreb, Croatia	Aug. 3, 2006
Moscow, USSR	Aug. 15, 1990
Tolmezzo, Italy	Jul. 31, 1994
Boden, Sweden	Jul. 7, 1995
Lahti, Finland	Jul. 16, 2002
Munich, Germany	Aug. 29, 1992
Langkawi, Thailand	Jan. 27, 2000
Moscow, USSR	Jul. 20, 1980
Granada, Spain	Oct. 6, 2006
Zagreb, Yugoslavia	Jul. 15, 1989
Moscow, USSR	Aug. 5, 1990
Kouvola, Finland	Jul. 1, 1997
Lahti, Finland	Jul. 14, 2002
Belgrade, Serbia &	Jul. 10, 2005
Montenegro	
Doha, Qatar	Dec. 8, 2006
Caracas, Venezuela	Aug. 20, 1983
Munich, West Germany	Oct. 13, 1989
Lahti, Finland	Jul. 25, 1987
Milan, Italy	Aug. 4, 1994
Athens, Greece	Aug. 18, 2004
Pontevedra, Spain	Mar. 14, 2001
Zagreb, Croatia	Jul. 31, 2006
Nicosia, Cyprus	Apr. 1, 1994
Lahti, Finland	Jun. 9, 1995
Suhl, Germany	Jun. 11, 1996
Barcelona, Spain	Jul. 23, 1998
Americana, Brazil	Aug. 10, 2005
Granada, Spain	Oct. 5, 2006
Barcelona, Spain	Jul. 19, 1998

☆ MEN'S 25 M CENTER FIRE PISTOL Jaspal Rana (India) shows his gold medal won at the 15th Asian Games in Doha, Qatar, on December 8, 2006. Rana shot a combined tally of 590 in the precision and rapid rounds to equal the world mark set by Latvian shooter Afanasijs Kuzmins (USSR) in Zagreb in 1989. Three others have also achieved this record: Sergei Pyzhianov (USSR) in 1990, Mikhail Nestruev (Russia) in 1997 and 2005, and Park Byung-Taek (South Korea) in 2002.

★ SHOOTING ★

MEN	SCORE	NAME & NATIONALITY
Skeet	124	Vincent Hancock (U.S.A.)
	124	Vincent Hancock (U.S.A.)
	124	Ennio Falco (Italy)
	124	Mario Nunez (Spain)
	124	Tino Wenzel (Germany)
	124	Vincent Hancock (U.S.A.)
	124	Erik Watndal (Norway)
	124	Antonis Nicolaides (Cyprus)
	124	George Achilleos (Cyprus)
☆	124	Jin Di (China)
☆	124	Qu Ridon (China)
☆	124	Anthony Terras (France)

WOMEN	SCORE	NAME & NATIONALITY
300 m rifle three positions	588	Charlotte Jakobsen (Denmark)
☆	588	Charlotte Jakobsen (Denmark)
300 m rifle prone	597	Marie Enqvist (Sweden)
☆ 50 m rifle three positions	594	Sonja Pfeilschifter (Germany)
50 m rifle prone	597	Marina Bobkova (Russia)
	597	Olga Dovgun (Kazakhstan)
	597	Olga Dovgun (Kazakhstan)
☆	597	Olga Dovgun (Kazakhstan)
10 m air rifle	400	This record has been achieved a total of 12 times. Most times: Lioubov Galkina (Russia) with 3.
25 m pistol	594	Diana Iorgova (Bulgaria)
	594	Tao Luna (China)
10 m air pistol	393	Svetlana Smirnova (Russia)
10 m running target	391	Xu Xuan (China)
10 m running target mixed	390	Audrey Soquet (France)
Trap	74	Victoria Chuyko (Ukraine)
☆	74	Chen Li (China)
☆	74	Zuzana Stefecekova (Slovakia)
Double trap	115	Yafei Zhang (China)
Skeet	74	Elena Little (UK)
☆	74	Christine Brinker (Germany)
☆	74	Shi Hong Yan (China)
☆	74	Zemfira Meftakhetdinova (Azerbaijan)

PLACE	DATE
Changwon, South Korea	Apr. 16, 2005
Rome, Italy	May 22, 2005
Rome, Italy	May 22, 2005
Belgrade, Serbia & Montenegro	Jul. 18, 2005
Belgrade, Serbia & Montenegro	Jul. 18, 2005
Americana, Brazil	Aug. 13, 2005
Americana, Brazil	Aug. 13, 2005
Dubai, UAE	Nov. 22, 2005
Dubai, UAE	Nov. 22, 2005
Qingyuan, China	Apr. 10, 2006
Qingyuan, China	Apr. 10, 2006
Santo Domingo, Dominican Republic	Mar. 28, 2007

PLACE	DATE
Lahti, Finland	Jul. 12, 2002
Zagreb, Croatia	Aug. 3, 2006
Plzen, Czech Republic	Jul. 22, 2003
Munich, Germany	May 28, 2006
Barcelona, Spain	Jul. 19, 1998
Lahti, Finland	Jul. 4, 2002
Busan, Philippines	Oct. 4, 2002
Zagreb, Croatia	Jul. 29, 2006
Milan, Italy	May 31, 1994
Munich, Germany	Aug. 23, 2002
Munich, Germany	May 23, 1998
Lahti, Finland	Jul. 6, 2002
Lahti, Finland	Jul. 9, 2002
Nicosia, Cyprus	Jun. 13, 1998
Qingyuan, China	Apr. 4, 2006
Qingyuan, China	Apr. 4, 2006
Nicosia, Cyprus	Oct. 20, 2000
Belgrade, Serbia & Montenegro	Jul. 17, 2005
Qingyuan, China	Apr. 9, 2006
Qingyuan, China	Apr. 9, 2006
Cairo, Egypt	May 18, 2006

☆ MEN'S SKEET Skeet shooting is one of the major types of competitive shotgun shooting at clay targets. Left, Jin Di (China) competes in the men's final during the 15th Asian Games in Doha on December 8, 2006; he, and teammate Qu Ridon, scored a record 124.

MEN	TIME/POINTS	NAME & NATIONALITY
☆ 500 m	•34.25	Lee Kang-Seok (South Korea)
☆ 2 × 500 m	•68.69	Lee Kang-Seok (South Korea)
1,000 m	1:07.03	Shani Davis (U.S.A.)
☆ 1,500 m	•1:42.32	Shani Davis (U.S.A.)
3,000 m	3:37.28	Eskil Ervik (Norway)
☆ 5,000 m	•6:08.48	Sven Kramer (Netherlands)
☆ 10,000 m	•12:41.69	Sven Kramer (Netherlands)
500/1,000/500/1,000 m	137,230 points	Jeremy Wotherspoon (Canada)
500/3,000/1,500/5,000 m	146,365 points	Erben Wennemars (Netherlands)
500/5,000/1,500/10,000 m	145,742 points	Shani Davis (U.S.A.)
☆ Team pursuit (8 laps)	•3:37.80	Netherlands (Sven Kramer, Carl Verheijen, Erben Wennemars)

WOMEN	TIME/POINTS	NAME & NATIONALITY
☆ 500 m	•37.04	Jenny Wolf (Germany)
☆ 2 × 500 m	•74.42	Jenny Wolf (Germany)
1,000 m	1:13.11	Cindy Klassen (Canada)
1,500 m	1:51.79	Cindy Klassen (Canada)
☆ 3,000 m	3:53.34	Cindy Klassen (Canada)
☆ 5,000 m	•6:45.61	Martina Sáblíková (Czech Republic)
500/1,000/500/1,000 m	149,305 points	Monique Garbrecht-Enfeldt (Germany) Cindy Klassen (Canada)
500/1,500/1,000/3,000 m	155,576 points	Cindy Klassen (Canada)
500/3,000/1,500/5,000 m	154,580 points	Cindy Klassen (Canada)
Team pursuit (6 laps)	2:56.04	Germany (Daniela Anschütz, Anni Friesinger, Claudia Pechstein)

•Please note that these records were still awaiting ratification by the International Skating Union at the time of going to press.

☆ **MEN'S TEAM PURSUIT** Sven Kramer leads Carl Verheijen and Erben Wennemars as the Dutch team sets a world record at the 2007 ISU World Single Distances Speed Skating Championships in Salt Lake City, Utah, U.S.A. They won gold for the eight-lap team pursuit on March 11, 2007, in 3 min. 37.80 sec.

PLACE	DATE
Salt Lake City, U.S.A.	Mar. 9, 2007
Salt Lake City, U.S.A.	Mar. 9, 2007
Calgary, Canada	Nov. 20, 2005
Calgary, Canada	Mar. 4, 2007
Calgary, Canada	Nov. 5, 2005
Calgary, Canada	Mar. 3, 2007
Salt Lake City, U.S.A.	Mar. 10, 2007
Calgary, Canada	Jan. 18–19, 2003
Calgary, Canada	Aug. 12–13, 2005
Calgary, Canada	Mar. 18–19, 2006
Salt Lake City, U.S.A.	Mar. 11, 2007

PLACE	DATE
Salt Lake City, U.S.A.	Mar. 10, 2007
Salt Lake City, U.S.A.	Mar. 10, 2007
Calgary, Canada	Mar. 25, 2006
Salt Lake City, U.S.A.	Nov. 20, 2005
Calgary, Canada	Mar. 18, 2006
Salt Lake City, U.S.A.	Mar. 11, 2007
Salt Lake City, U.S.A.	Jan. 11–12, 2003
Calgary, Canada	Mar. 24–25, 2006
Calgary, Canada	Mar. 15–17, 2001
Calgary, Canada	Mar. 18–19, 2006
Calgary, Canada	Nov. 13, 2005

☆ **MEN'S 500 M LONG TRACK** Lee Kang-Seok (South Korea) skates in the second race of the men's 500 m at the 2007 ISU World Single Distances Speed Skating Championships at the Utah Olympic Oval in Salt Lake City, Utah, U.S.A. He won the gold medal for this race on March 9, 2007.

ISU

The International Skating Union is the sport's official regulating body. For more info, visit **www.isu.org**.

★ SPEED SKATING—SHORT TRACK ★

MEN	TIME	NAME & NATIONALITY
500 m	41.184	Jean-François Monette (Canada)
1,000 m	1:24.674	Jiajun Li (China)
1,500 m	2:10.639	Ahn Hyun-Soo (South Korea)
3,000 m	4:32.646	Ahn Hyun-Soo (South Korea)
5,000 m relay	6:39.990	Canada (Charles Hamelin, Steve Robillard, François-Louis Tremblay, Mathieu Turcotte)

WOMEN	TIME	NAME & NATIONALITY
500 m	43.671	Evgenia Radanova (Bulgaria)
1,000 m	1:30.037	Jin Sun-Yu (South Korea)
1,500 m	2:18.861	Jung Eun-Ju (South Korea)
3,000 m	5:01.976	Choi Eun-Kyung (South Korea)
3,000 m relay	4:11.742	South Korea (Choi Eun-Kyung, Kim Min-Jee, Byun Chun-Sa, Ko Gi-Hyun)

★ SWIMMING—LONG COURSE ★

MEN	TIME	NAME & NATIONALITY
50 m freestyle	21.64	Alexander Popov (Russia)
100 m freestyle	47.84	Pieter van den Hoogenband (Netherlands)
☆200 m freestyle	1:43.86	Michael Phelps (U.S.A.)
400 m freestyle	3:40.08	Ian Thorpe (Australia)
800 m freestyle	7:38.65	Grant Hackett (Australia)
1,500 m freestyle	14:34.56	Grant Hackett (Australia)
☆4 × 100 m freestyle relay	3:12.46	U.S.A. (Michael Phelps, Neil Walker, Cullen Jones, Jason Lezak)
☆4 × 200 m freestyle relay	7:03.24	U.S.A. (Michael Phelps, Ryan Lochte, Klete Keller, Peter Vanderkaay)
50 m butterfly	22.96	Roland Schoeman (South Africa)
100 m butterfly	50.40	Ian Crocker (U.S.A.)
☆200 m butterfly	1:52.09	Michael Phelps (U.S.A.)
50 m backstroke	24.80	Thomas Rupprath (Germany)
☆100 m backstroke	52.98	Aaron Peirsol (U.S.A.)
☆200 m backstroke	1:54.32	Ryan Lochte (U.S.A.)
50 m breaststroke	27.18	Oleg Lisogor (Ukraine)
☆100 m breaststroke	59.13	Brendan Hansen (U.S.A.)
☆200 m breaststroke	2:08.50	Brendan Hansen (U.S.A.)
☆200 m medley	1:54.98	Michael Phelps (U.S.A.)
☆400 m medley	4:06.22	Michael Phelps (U.S.A.)
4 × 100 m medley relay	3:30.68	U.S.A. (Aaron Peirsol, Brendan Hansen, Ian Crocker, Jason Lezak)

PLACE	DATE
Calgary, Canada	Oct. 18, 2003
Bormio, Italy	Feb. 14, 2004
Marquette, U.S.A.	Oct. 24, 2003
Beijing, China	Dec. 7, 2003
Beijing, China	Mar. 13, 2005

PLACE	DATE
Calgary, Canada	Oct. 19, 2001
Bormio, Italy	Nov. 13, 2005
Beijing, China	Jan. 11, 2004
Calgary, Canada	Oct. 22, 2000
Calgary, Canada	Oct. 19, 2003

WOMEN'S 500 M SHORT TRACK Evgenia Radanova (Bulgaria) skates in the women's 500 m heat at the Torino 2006 Winter Olympics in Turin, Italy, on February 12, 2006. She holds the world record for this event at 43.671 seconds.

PLACE	DATE
Moscow, Russia	Jun. 16, 2000
Sydney, Australia	Sep. 19, 2000
Melbourne, Australia	Mar. 27, 2007
Manchester, UK	Jul. 30, 2002
Montreal, Canada	Jul. 27, 2005
Fukuoka, Japan	Jul. 29, 2001
Victoria, Canada	Aug. 19, 2006
Melbourne, Australia	Mar. 30, 2007
Montreal, Canada	Jul. 25, 2005
Montreal, Canada	Jul. 30, 2005
Melbourne, Australia	Mar. 28, 2007
Barcelona, Spain	Jul. 27, 2003
Melbourne, Australia	Mar. 27, 2007
Melbourne, Australia	Mar. 30, 2007
Berlin, Germany	Aug. 2, 2002
Irvine, U.S.A.	Aug. 1, 2006
Victoria, Canada	Aug. 20, 2006
Melbourne, Australia	Mar. 29, 2007
Melbourne, Australia	Apr. 1, 2007
Athens, Greece	Aug. 21, 2004

☆ **MEN'S 100 M BACKSTROKE** Aaron Peirsol (U.S.A.) competes in the men's 100 m backstroke at the 12th FINA world championships on March 27, 2007, in Melbourne, Australia. He won in a record time of 52.98 seconds.

★ SWIMMING—LONG COURSE ★

WOMEN	TIME	NAME & NATIONALITY
50 m freestyle	24.13	Inge de Bruijn (Netherlands)
☆ 100 m freestyle	53.30	Britta Steffen (Germany)
☆ 200 m freestyle	1:55.52	Laure Manaudou (France)
☆ 400 m freestyle	4:02.13	Laure Manaudou (France)
800 m freestyle	8:16.22	Janet Evans (U.S.A.)
1,500 m freestyle	15:52.10	Janet Evans (U.S.A.)
☆ 4 × 100 m freestyle relay	3:35.22	Germany (Petra Dallmann, Daniella Goetz, Britta Steffen, Annika Liebs)
☆ 4 × 200 m freestyle relay	7:50.09	U.S.A. (Natalie Coughlin, Dana Vollmer, Lacey Nymeyer, Katie Hoff)
50 m butterfly	25.57	Anna-Karin Kammerling (Sweden)
100 m butterfly	56.61	Inge de Bruijn (Netherlands)
☆ 200 m butterfly	2:05.40	Jessicah Schipper (Australia)
☆ 50 m backstroke	28.16	Leila Vaziri (U.S.A.)
☆ 100 m backstroke	59.44	Natalie Coughlin (U.S.A.)
200 m backstroke	2:06.62	Krisztina Egerszegi (Hungary)
☆ 50 m breaststroke	30.31	Jade Edmistone (Australia)
☆ 100 m breaststroke	1:05.09	Leisel Jones (Australia)
☆ 200 m breaststroke	2:20.54	Leisel Jones (Australia)
200 m medley	2:09.72	Wu Yanyan (China)
☆ 400 m medley	4:32.89	Katie Hoff (U.S.A.)
☆ 4 × 100 m medley relay	3:55.74	Australia (Emily Seebohm, Leisel Jones, Jessicah Schipper, Lisbeth Lenton)

Long course swimming events are held in a pool measuring 50 m in length. This is the international standard and Olympic pool size. **Short course** swimming is done in a pool measuring 25 m. This means that a 100 m swim long course would consist of two lengths, whereas it would involve four lengths in a short-course pool. The swimmer "gains" some time because of the additional number of turns in short course, so short-course records (see pp. 554–557) are "faster" than long-course records.

FINA

The International Swimming Federation (FINA), based in Lausanne, Switzerland, is responsible for administering international competitions in aquatic sports. For more information, visit *www.fina.org*.

PLACE	DATE
Sydney, Australia	Sep. 22, 2000
Budapest, Hungary	Aug. 2, 2006
Melbourne, Australia	Mar. 28, 2007
Budapest, Hungary	Aug. 6, 2006
Tokyo, Japan	Aug. 20, 1989
Orlando, U.S.A.	Mar. 26, 1988
Budapest, Hungary	Jul. 31, 2006
Melbourne, Australia	Mar. 29, 2007
Berlin, Germany	Jul. 30, 2000
Sydney, Australia	Sep. 17, 2000
Victoria, Canada	Aug. 17, 2006
Melbourne, Australia	Mar. 28, 2007
Melbourne, Australia	Mar. 27, 2007
Athens, Greece	Aug. 25, 1991
Melbourne, Australia	Jan. 30, 2006
Melbourne, Australia	Mar. 20, 2006
Melbourne, Australia	Feb. 21, 2006
Shanghai, China	Oct. 17, 1997
Melbourne, Australia	Apr. 1, 2007
Melbourne, Australia	Mar. 31, 2007

☆ WOMEN'S 4 × 100 M
MEDLEY RELAY Australians
Lisbeth Lenton (front), Emily
Seebohm, Jessicah Schipper,
and Leisel Jones (back, left to
right) celebrate their victory
in the 4 × 100 m medley relay
final at the 12th FINA world
championships in Melbourne,
Australia. On March 31, 2007,
the Australian women's team
won the 4 × 100 m medley
relay gold medal and set a
new world record of 3 min.
55.74 sec. The U.S.A. took the
silver in a time of 3 min. 58.31
sec. and China won the
bronze in 4 min. 1.97 sec.

★ SWIMMING—SHORT COURSE ★

MEN	TIME	NAME & NATIONALITY
☆ 50 m freestyle	20.98	Roland Schoeman (South Africa)
100 m freestyle	46.25	Ian Crocker (U.S.A.)
	46.25	Roland Schoeman (South Africa)
200 m freestyle	1:41.10	Ian Thorpe (Australia)
400 m freestyle	3:34.58	Grant Hackett (Australia)
800 m freestyle	7:25.28	Grant Hackett (Australia)
1,500 m freestyle	14:10.10	Grant Hackett (Australia)
4 × 100 m freestyle relay	3:09.57	Sweden (Johan Nyström, Lars Frölander, Mattias Ohlin, Stefan Nystrand)
4 × 200 m freestyle relay	6:56.41	Australia (William Kirby, Ian Thorpe, Michael Klim, Grant Hackett)
50 m butterfly	22.60	Kaio Almeida (Brazil)
100 m butterfly	49.07	Ian Crocker (U.S.A.)
200 m butterfly	1:50.73	Franck Esposito (France)
50 m backstroke	23.27	Thomas Rupprath (Germany)
☆ 100 m backstroke	49.99	Ryan Lochte (U.S.A.)
☆ 200 m backstroke	1:49.05	Ryan Lochte (U.S.A.)
50 m breaststroke	26.17	Oleg Lisogor (Ukraine)
100 m breaststroke	57.47	Ed Moses (U.S.A.)
200 m breaststroke	2:02.92	Ed Moses (U.S.A.)
100 m medley	51.52	Ryk Neethling (South Africa)
☆ 200 m medley	1:53.31	Ryan Lochte (U.S.A.)
400 m medley	4:00.37	Laszlo Cseh (Hungary)
4 × 100 m medley relay	3:25.09	U.S.A. (Aaron Peirsol, Brendan Hansen, Ian Crocker, Jason Lezak)

PLACE	DATE
Hamburg, Germany	Aug. 12, 2006
New York City, U.S.A.	Mar. 27, 2004
Berlin, Germany	Jan. 22, 2005
Berlin, Germany	Feb. 6, 2000
Sydney, Australia	Jul. 18, 2002
Perth, Australia	Aug. 3, 2001
Perth, Australia	Aug. 7, 2001
Athens, Greece	Mar. 16, 2000
Perth, Australia	Aug. 7, 2001
Santos, Brazil	Dec. 17, 2005
New York City, U.S.A.	Mar. 26, 2004
Antibes, France	Dec. 8, 2002
Vienna, Austria	Dec. 10, 2004
Shanghai, China	Apr. 9, 2006
Shanghai, China	Apr. 9, 2006
Berlin, Germany	Jan. 21, 2006
Stockholm, Sweden	Jan. 21, 2002
Berlin, Germany	Jan. 17, 2004
New York City, U.S.A.	Feb. 11, 2005
Shanghai, China	Apr. 8, 2006
Trieste, Italy	Dec. 9, 2005
Indianapolis, U.S.A.	Sep. 11, 2004

☆ MEN'S 200 M MEDLEY Ryan Lochte (U.S.A.) celebrates his new world record of 1 min. 53.31 sec. in the men's 200 m individual medley at the FINA World Swimming Championships (short course) held at the Qi Zhong Stadium in Shanghai, China, on April 8, 2006. The next day, Lochte also broke the world records in the 100 m and 200 m backstroke.

★ SWIMMING—SHORT COURSE ★

WOMEN	TIME	NAME & NATIONALITY
50 m freestyle	23.59	Therese Alshammar (Sweden)
100 m freestyle	51.70	Lisbeth Lenton (Australia)
200 m freestyle	1:53.29	Lisbeth Lenton (Australia)
400 m freestyle	3:56.79	Laure Manaudou (France)
800 m freestyle	8:11.25	Laure Manaudou (France)
1,500 m freestyle	15:42.39	Laure Manaudou (France)
☆ 4 × 100 m freestyle relay	3:33.32	Netherlands (Inge Dekker, Hinkelien Schreuder, Chantal Groot, Marleen Veldhuis)
4 × 200 m freestyle relay	7:46.30	China (Xu Yanvei, Zhu Yingven, Tang Jingzhi, Yang Yu)
50 m butterfly	25.33	Anne-Karin Kammerling (Sweden)
☆ 100 m butterfly	55.95	Lisbeth Lenton (Australia)
200 m butterfly	2:04.04	Yang Yu (China)
50 m backstroke	26.83	Li Hui (China)
100 m backstroke	56.71	Natalie Coughlin (U.S.A.)
200 m backstroke	2:03.62	Natalie Coughlin (U.S.A.)
50 m breaststroke	29.90	Jade Edmistone (Australia)
☆ 100 m breaststroke	1:03.86	Leisel Jones (Australia)
200 m breaststroke	2:17.75	Leisel Jones (Australia)
100 m medley	58.80	Natalie Coughlin (U.S.A.)
200 m medley	2:07.79	Allison Wagner (U.S.A.)
400 m medley	4:27.83	Yana Klochkova (Ukraine)
☆ 4 × 100 m medley relay	3:51.84	Australia (Jessicah Schipper, Lisbeth Lenton, Tayliah Zimmer, Jade Edmistone)

★ TRACK CYCLING—ABSOLUTE ★

MEN	TIME/DISTANCE	NAME & NATIONALITY
☆ 200 m (flying start)	9.772	Theo Bos (Netherlands)
500 m (flying start)	25.850	Arnaud Duble (France)
1 km (standing start)	58.875	Arnaud Tournant (France)
4 km (standing start)	4:11.114	Christopher Boardman (UK)
Team 4 km (standing start)	3:56.610	Australia (Graeme Brown, Luke Roberts, Brett Lancaster, Bradley McGee)
1 hour	49.7 km*	Ondrej Sosenka (Czech Republic)

WOMEN	TIME/DISTANCE	NAME & NATIONALITY
200 m (flying start)	10.831	Olga Slioussareva (Russia)
500 m (flying start)	29.655	Erika Saloumiaee (U.S.S.R.)
3 km (standing start)	3:24.537	Sarah Ulmer (New Zealand)
1 hour	46.65 km*	Leontien Zijlaard-van Moorsel (Netherlands)

*Some athletes achieved better distances within an hour with bicycles that are no longer allowed by the Union Cycliste Internationale (UCI). The 1-hour records given here are in accordance with the new UCI rules.

PLACE	DATE
Athens, Greece	Mar. 18, 2000
Melbourne, Australia	Aug. 9, 2005
Sydney, Australia	Nov. 19, 2005
Trieste, Italy	Dec. 10, 2005
Trieste, Italy	Dec. 9, 2005
La Roche-sur-Yon, France	Nov. 20, 2004
Shanghai, China	Apr. 8, 2006
Moscow, Russia	Apr. 3, 2002
Gothenburg, Sweden	Mar. 12, 2005
Hobart, Australia	Aug. 28, 2006
Berlin, Germany	Jan. 18, 2004
Shanghai, China	Dec. 2, 2001
New York City, U.S.A.	Nov. 21, 2002
New York City, U.S.A.	Nov. 27, 2001
Brisbane, Australia	Sep. 26, 2004
Hobart, Australia	Aug. 28, 2006
Melbourne, Australia	Nov. 29, 2003
New York City, U.S.A.	Nov. 23, 2002
Palma de Mallorca, Spain	Dec. 5, 1993
Paris, France	Jan. 19, 2002
Shanghai, China	Apr. 7, 2006

☆ **WOMEN'S 4 × 100 M FREESTYLE RELAY** Inge Dekker (Netherlands) swims in the 100 m butterfly semifinal at the World Swimming Championships (short course) in Shanghai, China.

At the same event on April 8, 2006, the Dutch team (also including Chantal Groot, Hinkelien Schreuder, and Marleen Veldhuis) won the freestyle relay race in 3 min. 33.32 sec.

PLACE	DATE
Moscow, Russia	Dec. 16, 2006
La Paz, Bolivia	Oct. 10, 2001
La Paz, Bolivia	Oct. 10, 2001
Manchester, UK	Aug. 29, 1996
Athens, Greece	Aug. 22, 2004
Moscow, Russia	Jul. 19, 2005

PLACE	DATE
Moscow, Russia	Apr. 25, 1993
Moscow, U.S.S.R.	Aug. 6, 1987
Athens, Greece	Aug. 22, 2004
Mexico City, Mexico	Oct. 1, 2003

☆ **MEN'S 200 M TRACK CYCLING** Theo Bos (Netherlands) is shown in the men's sprint during the UCI Track Cycling World Championship on April 1, 2007, in Palma de Mallorca, Spain. Just a few months earlier, on December 16, 2006, Bos had set a new world record of 9.772 seconds for the 200 m (flying start) in Moscow, Russia.

★ WATERSHIING ★

MEN	RECORD	NAME & NATIONALITY
Slalom	1.5 buoy/9.75-m line	Chris Parrish (U.S.A.)
Barefoot slalom	20.6 crossings of wake in 30 seconds	Keith St. Onge (U.S.A.)
Tricks	12,400 points	Nicolas Le Forestier (France)
☆ Barefoot tricks	10,880 points	Keith St. Onge (U.S.A.)
Jump	239 ft. 6 in. (73 m)	Freddy Krueger (U.S.A.)
Barefoot jump	89 ft. 11 in. (27.4 m)	David Small (UK)
Ski fly	298 ft. 10 in. (91.1 m)	Jaret Llewellyn (Canada)
Overall	2,818.01 points*	Jaret Llewellyn (Canada)

WOMEN	RECORD	NAME & NATIONALITY
Slalom	1 buoy/10.25-m line	Kristi Overton Johnson (U.S.A.)
Barefoot slalom	17.0 crossings of wake in 30 seconds	Nadine de Villiers (South Africa)
☆ Tricks	8,740 points	Mandy Nightingale (U.S.A.)
Barefoot tricks	4,400 points	Nadine de Villiers (South Africa)
Jump	186 ft. (56.6 m)	Elena Milakova (Russia)
Barefoot jump	67 ft. 7 in. (20.6 m)	Nadine de Villiers (South Africa)
Ski fly	227 ft. 8.2 in. (69.4 m)	Elena Milakova (Russia)
☆ Overall	2,850.11 points**	Clementine Lucine (France)

*5@11.25 m, 10,730 tricks, 71.7 m jump

**4@11.25 m, 8,680 tricks, 52.1 m jump; calculated with the new 2006 scoring method (slalom base reduced by 24)

IWSF

Founded in Geneva, Switzerland, in July 1946, the International Water Ski Federation is the world governing body for towed water sports. These include all sports performed on the water in which the athlete is towed by a rope attached to any mechanical propulsion device. Barefoot waterskiing also operates under the IWSF umbrella. For more information, visit *www.iwsf.com.*

PLACE	DATE
Trophy Lakes, U.S.A.	Aug. 28, 2005
Bronkhorstspruit, South Africa	Jan. 6, 2006
Lac de Joux, Switzerland	Sep. 4, 2005
Adna, U.S.A.	Sep. 17, 2006
Polk City, U.S.A.	May 29, 2005
Mulwala, Australia	Feb. 8, 2004
Orlando, U.S.A.	May 14, 2000
Seffner, U.S.A.	Sep. 29, 2002

PLACE	DATE
West Palm Beach, U.S.A.	Sep. 14, 1996
Witbank, South Africa	Jan. 5, 2001
Santa Rosa, U.S.A.	Jun. 10, 2006
Witbank, South Africa	Jan. 5, 2001
Rio Linda, U.S.A.	Jul. 21, 2002
Pretoria, South Africa	Mar. 4, 2000
Pine Mountain, U.S.A.	May 26, 2002
Lacanau, France	Jul. 9, 2006

☆ **MEN'S BAREFOOT TRICKS** At the 15th Barefoot Water Ski World Championships held on September 17, 2006, in Adna, Washington, U.S.A., Keith St. Onge (U.S.A.) achieved 10,880 points for barefoot waterskiing tricks—the highest score ever in this discipline. He also holds the world record in barefoot slalom, with 20.6 crossings of the wake in 30 seconds.

★ WEIGHT LIFTING ★

MEN	CATEGORY	WEIGHT LIFTED	NAME & NATIONALITY
56 kg	Snatch	138 kg	Halil Mutlu (Turkey)
	Clean & jerk	168 kg	Halil Mutlu (Turkey)
	Total	305 kg	Halil Mutlu (Turkey)
62 kg	Snatch	153 kg	Shi Zhiyong (China)
	Clean & jerk	182 kg	Le Maosheng (China)
	Total	325 kg	World Standard*
69 kg	Snatch	165 kg	Georgi Markov (Bulgaria)
	Clean & jerk	197 kg	Zhang Guozheng (China)
	Total	357 kg	Galabin Boevski (Bulgaria)
77 kg	Snatch	173 kg	Sergey Filimonov (Kazakhstan)
	Clean & jerk	210 kg	Oleg Perepetchenov (Russia)
	Total	377 kg	Plamen Zhelyazkov (Bulgaria)
85 kg	Snatch	186 kg	Andrei Rybakov (Bulgaria)
	Clean & jerk	218 kg	Zhang Yong (China)
	Total	395 kg	World Standard*
94 kg	Snatch	188 kg	Akakios Kakhiasvillis (Greece)
	Clean & jerk	232 kg	Szymon Kolecki (Poland)
	Total	417 kg	World Standard*
105 kg	Snatch	199 kg	Marcin Dolega (Poland)
	Clean & jerk	242 kg	World Standard*
	Total	440 kg	World Standard*
+105 kg	Snatch	213 kg	Hossein Reza Zadeh (Iran)
	Clean & jerk	263 kg	Hossein Reza Zadeh (Iran)
	Total	472 kg	Hossein Reza Zadeh (Iran)

*From January 1, 1998, the International Weightlifting Federation (IWF) introduced modified body-weight categories, thereby making the then world records outdated. This is the new listing with the world standards for the new body-weight categories. Results achieved at IWF-approved competitions exceeding the world standards by 0.5 kg for snatch or clean & jerk, or by 2.5 kg for the total, will be recognized as world records.

PLACE	DATE
Antalya, Turkey	Nov. 4, 2001
Trencín, Slovakia	Apr. 24, 2001
Sydney, Australia	Sep. 16, 2000
Izmir, Turkey	Jun. 28, 2002
Busan, South Korea	Oct. 2, 2002
Sydney, Australia	Sep. 20, 2000
Qinhuangdao, China	Sep. 11, 2003
Athens, Greece	Nov. 24, 1999
Almaty, Kazakhstan	Apr. 9, 2004
Trencín, Slovakia	Apr. 27, 2001
Doha, Qatar	Mar. 27, 2002
Wladyslawowo, Poland	May 6, 2006
Ramat Gan, Israel	Apr. 25, 1998
Athens, Greece	Nov. 27, 1999
Sofia, Bulgaria	Apr. 29, 2000
Wladyslawowo, Poland	May 7, 2006
Qinhuangdao, China	Sep. 14, 2003
Athens, Greece	Aug. 25, 2004
Sydney, Australia	Sep. 26, 2000

IWF

The International Weightlifting Federation is the global governing body for the sport of weight lifting. The IWF was founded in 1905 and currently has 167 member nations. For more information about the sport, visit *www.iwf.net*.

★ WEIGHT LIFTING ★

WOMEN	CATEGORY	WEIGHT LIFTED	NAME & NATIONALITY
48 kg	☆ Snatch	98 kg	Yiang Lian (China)
	☆ Clean & jerk	119 kg	Yiang Lian (China)
	☆ Total	217 kg	Yiang Lian (China)
53 kg	Snatch	102 kg	Ri Song-Hui (North Korea)
	☆ Clean & jerk	128 kg	Qiu Hongxia (China)
	☆ Total	226 kg	Qiu Hongxia (China)
58 kg	☆ Snatch	111 kg	Chen Yanqing (China)
	☆ Clean & jerk	140 kg	Chen Yanqing (China)
	☆ Total	251 kg	Chen Yanqing (China)
63 kg	Snatch	116 kg	Pawina Thongsuk (Thailand)
	☆ Clean & jerk	142 kg	Pawina Thongsuk (Thailand)
	Total	256 kg	Pawina Thongsuk (Thailand)
69 kg	☆ Snatch	123 kg	Oxana Slivenko (Russia)
	Clean & jerk	157 kg	Zarema Kasaeva (Russia)
	Total	275 kg	Liu Chunhong (China)
75 kg	Snatch	130 kg	Natalia Zabolotnaia (Russia)
	Clean & jerk	159 kg	Liu Chunhong (China)
	☆ Total	286 kg	Svetlana Podobedova (Russia)
+75 kg	☆ Snatch	139 kg	Mu Shuangshuang (China)
	Clean & jerk	182 kg	Gonghong Tang (China)
	☆ Total	318 kg	Jang Mi-Ran (South Korea)

WOMEN'S 69 KG CLEAN & JERK Zarema
Kasaeva (Russia) is shown during the
women's 69 kg weight-lifting program at the
Athens 2004 Olympic Games. The following
year, on November 13, 2005, she broke the
world record in clean & jerk by achieving a
weight of 157 kg in Doha, Qatar.

PLACE	DATE
Santo Domingo, Dominican Republic	Oct. 1, 2006
Santo Domingo, Dominican Republic	Oct. 1, 2006
Santo Domingo, Dominican Republic	Oct. 1, 2006
Busan, South Korea	Oct. 1, 2002
Santo Domingo, Dominican Republic	Oct. 2, 2006
Santo Domingo, Dominican Republic	Oct. 2, 2006
Doha, Qatar	Dec. 3, 2006
Doha, Qatar	Dec. 3, 2006
Doha, Qatar	Dec. 3, 2006
Doha, Qatar	Nov. 12, 2005
Doha, Qatar	Dec. 4, 2006
Doha, Qatar	Nov. 12, 2005
Santo Domingo, Dominican Republic	Oct. 4, 2006
Doha, Qatar	Nov. 13, 2005
Athens, Greece	Aug. 19, 2004
Doha, Qatar	Nov. 13, 2005
Doha, Qatar	Nov. 13, 2005
Hangzhou, China	Jun. 2, 2006
Doha, Qatar	Dec. 6, 2006
Athens, Greece	Aug. 21, 2004
Wonju, South Korea	May 22, 2006

WOMEN'S +75 KG SNATCH Heavyweight gold medal winner Mu Shuangshuang (China) breaks the world snatch record in the +75 kg category of women's weight lifting. The 22-year-old lifted 139 kg at the 15th Asian Games in Doha, Qatar, on December 6, 2006, to beat the previous record by Jang Mi-Ran (South Korea) by 1 kg.

DISCIPLINE	MEDALS	NAME & NATIONALITY
☆ Overall	10	Barrett Christy, Shaun White (both U.S.A.)
☆ Skiing	9	Tanner Hall (U.S.A.)
☆ Snowboard	10	Barrett Christy, Shaun White (both (U.S.A.)
MEN		
Moto X	2	Tommy Clowers, Mike Jones, Mike Metzger, Caleb Wyatt, Brian Deegan (all U.S.A.)
☆ Skier X	6	Enak Gavaggio (France)
Skiing Slopestyle	4	Jon Olsson (Sweden), Tanner Hall (U.S.A.)
☆ Skiing SuperPipe	4	Jon Olsson (Sweden), Tanner Hall, Simon Dupont (both U.S.A.)
SnoCross	8	Blair Morgan (Canada)
☆ Snowboarder X	6	Seth Wescott (U.S.A.)
☆ Snowboard Slopestyle	6	Shaun White (U.S.A.)
☆ Snowboard SuperPipe	4	Danny Kass, Shaun White (both U.S.A.)
WOMEN		
Skier X	5	Aleisha Cline (Canada)
☆ Snowboarder X	4	Lindsey Jocobellis (U.S.A.)
Snowboard Slopestyle	5	Barrett Christy, Janna Meyen (both U.S.A.)
Snowboard SuperPipe	4	Kelly Clark (U.S.A.)

☆ **MEN'S SKIING SUPERPIPE** Tanner Hall (U.S.A.) competes in the men's skiing SuperPipe elimination at Winter X Games 11 on January 25, 2007. During his career, Hall has won a record nine medals for skiing: four in SuperPipe, four in Slopestyle, and one in Big Air.

DISCIPLINE	MEDALS	NAME & NATIONALITY
Overall	20	Dave Mirra (U.S.A.)
BMX Freestyle	20	Dave Mirra (U.S.A.)
☆ Moto X	11	Travis Pastrana (U.S.A.)
Skateboard	16	Tony Hawk, Andy Macdonald (both U.S.A.)
Aggressive inline skate	8	Fabiola da Silva (Brazil)
Wakeboard	6	Darin Shapiro, Tara Hamilton, Dallas Friday (all U.S.A.)

WOMEN'S WAKEBOARDING Gold medalist Dallas Friday (U.S.A.) competes in the women's wakeboarding finals at X Games 11 in Aspen, Colorado, U.S.A., in January 2007. Friday has won six medals in this discipline.

★ LONGEST SPORTS MARATHONS ★

SPORT	TIME	NAME & NATIONALITY
☆ Basketball	60 hr. 3 sec.	"Miyazaki 60" (Japan)
☆ Bowling	120 hours	Andy Milne (Canada)
Bowling (lawn, indoor)	36 hours	Arnos Bowling Club (UK)
☆ Bowling (lawn, outdoor)	105 hours	Lloyd Hotel Bowling Club (UK)
☆ Cricket	33 hr. 30 min.	Citipointe Church/Global Care (Australia)
Curling	33 hr. 10 min.	Rotary Club of Ayr/Ayr Curling Club (UK)
Futsal	30 hours	Max Cosi/Quinny and Christos Michael Keo teams (Cyprus)
Handball	70 hours	HV Mighty/Stevo (Netherlands)
Hockey (ice)	240 hours	Brent Saik and friends (Canada)
Hockey (indoor)	24 hours	Mandel Bloomfield AZA (Canada)
Hockey (in-line)	24 hours	8K Roller Hockey League (U.S.A.)
Hockey (street)	30 hours	Conroy Ross Partners (Canada)
Korfball	26 hr. 2 min.	Korfball Club de Vinken (Netherlands)
Netball	55 hours	Capital NUNS Netball Club (UK)
Parasailing	24 hr. 10 min.	Berne Persson (Sweden)
☆ Pétanque (boules)	40 hr. 9 min.	Bevenser Boule-Freunde (Germany)
Pool (singles match)	45 hr. 10 min.	Arie Hermans and Jeff Fijneman (Netherlands)
Punching bag	36 hr. 3 min.	Ron Sarchian (U.S.A.)
Rifle shooting	26 hours	St. Sebastianus Schützenbruderchaft (Germany)
Skiing	202 hr. 1 min.	Nick Willey (Australia)
Snowboarding	180 hr. 34 min.	Bernhard Mair (Austria)
☆ Soccer	30 hr. 10 min.	FC Edo and FC Spiez (Germany)
Softball	95 hr. 23 min.	Delmar and Renmark/Drive for 95 (Canada)
☆ Tennis (doubles match)	48 hr. 15 min.	Jahrsdoerfer, Lavoie, Okpokpo, Tse (U.S.A.)
Tennis (singles match)	25 hr. 25 min.	Christian Barschel and Hauke Daene (Germany)
Volleyball (indoor)	51 hours	Bunbury Indoor Beach Volleyball (Australia)
Water polo	24 hours	Rapido 82 Haarlem (Netherlands)
Waterskiing	56 hr. 35 min. 3 sec.	Ralph Hildebrand and Dave Phillips (Canada)
Windsurfing	71 hr. 30 min.	Sergiy Naidych (Ukraine)

GWR marathon guidelines are constantly updated—please contact us for information before you attempt a record.

PLACE	DATE
Miyazaki, Japan	Jun. 16–18, 2006
Ontario, Canada	Oct. 24–29, 2005
Southgate, UK	Apr. 20–21, 2002
Manchester, UK	Oct. 14–18, 2006
Brisbane, Australia	Jun. 10–11, 2006
Ayr, UK	Mar. 24–25, 2005
Limassol, Cyprus	Nov. 19–20, 2005
Tubbergen, Netherlands	Aug. 30–Sep. 2, 2001
Strathcona, Canada	Feb. 11–21, 2005
Edmonton, Canada	Feb. 28–29, 2004
Eastpointe, U.S.A.	Sep. 13–14, 2002
Edmonton, Canada	Sep. 17–18, 2004
Vinkeveen, Netherlands	May 23–24, 2001
London, UK	Jul. 22–24, 2005
Lake Graningesjön, Sweden	Jul. 19–20, 2002
Bad Bevensen, Germany	Jul. 22–23, 2006
Oosterhout, Netherlands	Feb. 12–14, 2004
Encino, U.S.A.	Jun. 15–17, 2004
Ettringen, Germany	Sep. 20–21, 2003
Thredbo, Australia	Sep. 2–10, 2005
Bad Kleinkirchheim, Austria	Jan. 9–16, 2004
Erlenbach, Switzerland	Jul. 8–9, 2006
Dollard-des-Ormeaux, Canada	Jun. 29–Jul. 3, 2005
Houston, U.S.A.	Apr. 13–15, 2006
Mölln, Germany	Sep. 12–13, 2003
Bunbury, Australia	Nov. 18–20, 2005
Haarlem, Netherlands	Apr. 30–May 1, 1999
Rocky Point, Canada	Jun. 10–12, 1994
Simerferopol, Ukraine	Jun. 6–9, 2003

INDEX

This year's index is organized into two parts: by subject and by superlative. **Bold** entries in the subject index indicate a main entry on a topic, and entries in BOLD CAPITALS indicate an entire chapter. Neither index lists personal names.

SUBJECT

A

abortions, 115
Abraham Lincoln, USS, 397
Abyss Live, 182
accordions, 82, 357
action sports, 405–408
Active Denial System, 246
actors, 216, 357, 358
 movies, 307–311, 314, 316
 TV, 350–354
adrenaline junkies, 93–97
advertising, 359–362
 blimps, 361, 362
 billboards, 369
aerobatics, 392
aestivation, 51, 53
Africa (wildlife), 66–70
AIDS, 118
airbeds, 157
aircraft, 387
 aerobatics, 392
 circumnavigation, 175–176
 crashes, 133, 134
 human-powered, 387
 liquid-hydrogen, 393
 military, 392–394
 paper, 142, 210
 passengers, 149
 races, 407
 weapons systems, 393
airlines, 387
airs (extreme sports), 390, 523
airships, 361, 362, 392
albinos, 108
alcohol, 117
ale, 195
Alison May, 163
alligators, 62

Al-Qaeda, 245
Amazon rainforest, 29
Amazon River, 29, 43
ambulances, 112
American Academy Awards
 see Oscars
American Airlines, 387
amphibians, 65
AMRAAM weapons systems, 248
amusement parks, 400
anatomical anomalies, 101–104
Andromeda Galaxy, 4
Anechoic Test Chamber, Minneapolis,
 USA, 275
Angel Falls (Salto Angel), 28
animals
 attacks on humans, 254
 in captivity, 250
 endangered, 52, 55
 furries, 223
 loudest, 275
 luminescent, 89–92
 mating, 72
 pets, 185–189
 phylum, 60
 rare, 52, 62
 wildlife, 49–79
 see also specific animals & groups of
  animals
animals & man, 249–254
animation, 313, 315, 318, 323, 326
ankylosaurids, 75
Antarctic hair grass, 75
Antarctica, 28, 36, 38, 75
 expeditions, 166–169
anthropology, forensic, 278
anti-aircraft missiles, 248
ants, 54, 58, 59
appendix, 101
applause, 275
apples, 138, 212, 213
AquaDorn, Berlin, 371, 372
aquariums, 371, 372
aqueducts, Roman, 369
arcade games, 300
archery, 490, 491, 528–529
arches, 28, 373
archipelago, man-made, 369
architecture, 366–374
Arctic Ocean, 40, 41

Solutions

From pages 200–201

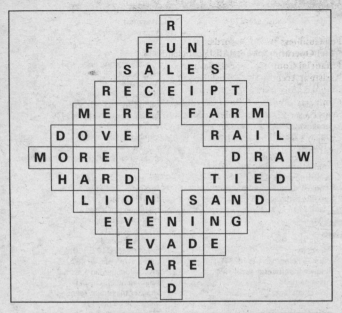

The crossword solution reads:

```
                R
              F U N
            S A L E S
            R E C E I P T
          M E R E   F A R M
        D O V E     R A I L
      M O R E         D R A W
      H A R D       T I E D
        L I O N   S A N D
          E V E N I N G
            E V A D E
            A R E
              D
```

1	3	7	4	2	9	6	5	8
5	8	9	6	1	3	4	2	7
2	6	4	7	5	8	3	1	9
7	2	5	8	4	6	1	9	3
8	9	6	1	3	7	5	4	2
3	4	1	5	9	2	7	8	6
9	5	2	3	7	1	8	6	4
4	7	8	9	6	5	2	3	1
6	1	3	2	8	4	9	7	5

2	8	6	9	4	5	1	7	3
7	1	4	6	3	2	9	5	8
9	3	5	7	8	1	4	2	6
4	2	7	3	5	6	8	1	9
6	5	8	1	9	7	3	4	2
1	9	3	4	2	8	7	6	5
3	6	1	5	7	9	2	8	4
5	4	2	8	1	3	6	9	7
8	7	9	2	6	4	5	3	1

ACHNOWLEDGMENTS

For Guinness World Records:
Chief Operating Officer Alistair Richards
Financial Controller Nicola Savage
Assistant Accountant Neelish Dawett
Finance Assistant Jack Brockbank
Contracts Administration Lisa Gibbs
Senior Vice President, Sales & Marketing Sam Fay
Senior Marketing Manager Laura Plunkett
English Language Sales Director Nadine Causey
International Sales Director Frank Chambers
Senior Brand Manager Kate White
Communications Officer Amarilis Espinoza
International Brand Manager Beatriz Fernandez
English Language Sales Executive John Pilley
Records Management (remote) Amanda Sprague
Director of Television Rob Molloy
Development Producer Simon Gold
Archiving & Production Assistant Denise Anlander
Software Manager Katie Forde
Software Engineer Kevin Wilson
IT Support Paul Bentley, Ryan Tunstall, James Herbert, Gordon Sherratt
Legal Jan Rowland, Juliette Bearman, Barry Kyle, Amanda Richards
Human Resources Kelly Garrett, Michel Ellis
Facilities Manager Fiona Ross
GWR overseas Chris Sheedy (Australia), Angela Wu (China), Jun Otsuki (Japan), Olaf Kuchenbecker (Germany)

Special thanks to
Jennifer Banks, Ellie Gibson, Nick Minter, Christopher Reinke, Nicola Shanks, Nick Watson, Jimmy Weight

The 2008 book team would also like to acknowledge the following people and organizations for their help during the production of this year's edition:

82ASK (Tom, Sarah, Rhod, Paul); 4Kids Entertainment (Bob Mitchell, Brian Simmons); Pedro Adrega, FINA; Animal Planet (Mike Kane, Krishna San Nicolas); Toby Anstis; Anthrocon; Ascent Media (Suzane, Carla, Simon, Esther, Keith); Florrie Baldwin; Zoe Ball; Sam and Kerri Baxter; BBC TV (Julia Cottrell, Leah Henry); Prof. Michael Besser; Luke and Joseph Boatfield; boxofficemojo.com; Nicky Boxall; Sir Richard Branson; Nikki Brin; Anna Browne; Bruntingthorpe Aerodrome; Claire Bygrave; Daniel Byles; Peter Cassidy, RWA; CCTV; Sasha Cestnik; Charlton Athletic Football Club;

Edd China, Cummfy Banana; Paulo Coelho; Scott Cory; David Crouch, Toyota; Davy's Wine Bar; Johnny Depp; Emmerdale; ESPN; Louis Epstein; Sian Evans, BVI, UK; Explorer's Club; exploresweb.com; Dick Fiddy; Neil Fingleton; Flix Marketing (Nic, Tam, Scott, Sharan, Jamie); Food Network (Art Edwards, Susie Fogelson, Keegan Gerhard, Tom Giesen, Allison Page); Ashrita Furman; Marion Gallimore, FISA; Jorge Garcia; Lois Gibson; Ryan Gibson-Judge; Terry Gilliam; Greenpeace; Jordan, Ryan and Brandon Greenwood; Victoria Grimsell; Debby de Groot; Ray Harper; Jan Hauge; Hayden Planetarium, New York; Gavin Hennessy; Lisa Holden, Bloomsbury Publishing, UK; Hotel Arts, Barcelona; Paul Hunn; Sue Hyman Associates; imdb.com; INP Media (Bryn, Martin); International Game Fishing Association; IWSF (Andy Harris, Gill Hill); Michael Jackson; Sarah Jackson, Consolidated, UK; Jamiroquai; Jason Joiner; Terry Jones; Joost (Aki, Dagmara, Tim); Maureen Kane; Damien Kindler; Adam Kirley; Hans Jakob Kvalheim; Murray and Ellie Lamont; Paul Landry; Orla and Thea Langton; Christopher Lee; Steve Lee; Anthony Liu; Ken Livingstone; Carey Low; Mad Macs II (Carol Kane, David Moncur); Sam Malone; Manda; Martyn, Acorn; MAX Entertainment, Kuala Lumpur (Alex, Faisal, Ann, Christy, Belle, Marcus); Mayor's office, Boise, Idaho; Iain McAvoy; Scotti McGowan, Liaison PR; Jan Meek; Katie Melua (Henry Spinetti, Jim Watson, Tim Harries, Denzil Daniels, Stephen Croxford); *Metro* (Bob Bohn, Daniel Magnus); Millbrook Proving Ground; Mino Monta; Dr. Alan Morgan (Zoobiotic Ltd., Bridgend, Wales); Clare Merryfield; *Muscle Musical,* Japan; Kevin Myers, BBC Wales; National Forensic Academy; *National Geographic Kids* (Rachel Buchholz, Eleanor Shannah); Aniko Nemeth-Mora, IWF; newlaunches.com; cast of Nøord; Ocean Rowing Society (Kenneth and Tatiana Crutchlow); Liam O'Connor; Ziggy Opoczynska, *National Geographic Kids UK;* Kenny Ortega and the cast of *High School Musical;* Palace Theatre, London, Crispin Ollington and the cast of *Spamalot;* Michael Perham and family; Phoenix Theatre, London, Iain McAvoy and the cast of *Blood Brothers;* Phoenix Theatre Bar; Fabrice Prahin, ISU; Ray Quinn; R et G Productions, France (Stephane Gateau, Jerome Revon, David Bensousan, Olivia Vandenhende, Jeff Peralta); Daniel Radcliffe; Red Lorry Yellow Lorry (Kim, Rob, Guy); Lee Redmond; Annabel Sally Reid; Beth Reynolds; Martyn Richards; Hugh Robertson, MP; J.K. Rowling; RTL (Tom, Sacha); San Manuel Indian Bingo; Shamrock Farms; Gene Simmons; Fredrik Skavlan; Alan Smithee; Stage3 Media; Paul Stanley; Statoil; Julien Stauffer, UCI; Chantal Steiner, FITA; Aaron Studman; Sunstate Equipment Co.; Russ Swift; Amanda Tapping; Taylor Herring; David Tennant; Mark Thomas; Julian Townsend; Sarah Trabucci, Scholastic Publishing, U.S.; Twin Galaxies (Walter Day, Ben Gold); Dr. Neil de Grasse Tyson; Kendra Voth and Smallville Productions; Jessica & Isabel Way; Steven Webb; Ellis Webster; Fran Weelen, Royal Bath and West Show; Wild West Arts Club (Chuck Weems "Walking Eagle", Joe Darrah, Matt and Max Mobley, John Bailey, "Doc"); Elijah Wood; Daniel Woods; World Puzzle Federation; X Games (Danny Chi, Lisa Fruggiero, Debbie McKinnis, Katie Moses, Marc Murphy, Kelly Robshaw); Xi Shun; YouTube; Zheng Da Zong Yi of CCTV.

In memoriam...

Julie Winnefred Bertrand (Canada, September 16, 1891–January 18, 2007, world's oldest woman at time of death); Elizabeth "Lizzie" Bolden (U.S.A., August 15, 1890–December 11, 2006, world's oldest person at time of death); Maria Esther de Capovilla (Ecuador, September 14, 1889–August 27, 2006, world's oldest person at time of death); Cedric (oldest pig); Florence Finch (New Zealand, b. UK, December 22, 1893–April 10, 2007, New Zealand's oldest person at time of death); Moses Hardy (U.S.A., January 6, 1893–December 7, 2006, U.S.A.'s oldest man at time of death); Florence Homan (U.S.A., November 18, 1893–August 13, 2006, Ohio, U.S.A.'s oldest person at time of death); Camille Loiseau (France, February 13, 1892–August 12, 2006, France's oldest person at time of death); Emiliano Mercado del Toro (Puerto Rico, August 21, 1891–January 24, 2007, world's oldest man at time of death); Giulia Sani-Casagli (Italy, September 15, 1893–September 4, 2006, Italy's oldest person at time of death); Mary Margaret Smith (U.S.A., October 7, 1893–May 23, 2006, Ohio, U.S.A.'s oldest person at time of death); Emma Tillman (U.S.A., November 22, 1892–January 28, 2007, world's oldest person at time of death).

BBC radio stations involved in GWR Day:

2CR FM•BBC 3CR•BBC Asian Network•BBC Coventry & Warwickshire•BBC GMR•BBC London Live•BBC Radio 2 (Chris Evans)•BBC Radio Berkshire•BBC Radio Bristol•BBC Radio Cambridgeshire•BBC Radio Cleveland•BBC Radio Cornwall•BBC Radio Cumbria•BBC Radio Derby•BBC Radio Devon•BBC Radio Essex•BBC Radio Five Live (Anita Anand)•BBC Radio Five Live Morning Reports•BBC Radio Gloucestershire•BBC Radio Guernsey•BBC Radio Humberside•BBC Radio Jersey• BBC Radio Kent•BBC Radio Lancashire•BBC Radio Leeds•BBC Radio Leicester•BBC Radio Lincolnshire•BBC Radio Merseyside•BBC Radio Newcastle•BBC Radio Norfolk•BBC Radio Northampton•BBC Radio Oxford•BBC Radio Shropshire•BBC Radio Solent•BBC Radio Somerset• BBC Radio Suffolk•BBC Radio Swindon•BBC Radio Ulster•BBC Radio Wales•BBC Radio York•BBC Southern Counties•BBC Wales•BBC West Midlands•BCB Radio (Bradford)•BFBS•BRMB (Birmingham)•IRN•Isle of Wight Radio•LBC (London)•Leicester Sound•Radio Clyde 1•Sky News Radio•Time FM (South East)•The Wave (Swansea)

PICTURE CREDITS

Rex Features; Gualter Fatia; Erik G. Svensson; Zuma Press; Eddie Cheng/ Corbis; **89–92:** Darwin Dale/SPL; Frank Borges LLosa/frankly.com; Advanced Cell Technology; Y. Kito/imagequest marine.com; Per Flood/ Bathbiologica; David M. Dennis/Photolibrary; AP/PA Photos; Paulo De Oliveira/Photolibrary; **93–97:** Christophe Vollmer/Reuters; Stephanie Thomet/Reuters; WENN; Richard Bradbury/GWR; Getty Images; John Wright/GWR; Gleb Garanich/Reuters; **101–104:** Juan Villasenor/AP/PA Photos; Monica Rueda/AP/PA Photos; Victor Ruiz/Reuters; **106–109:** Eleoi Correa/AP/PA Photos; News of the World; Getty Images; Oscar Izquierdo/ Getty Images; **110–113:** Colin Fisher/Zuma Press; Ron Hunt/Zuma Press; Jason Reed/Reuters; Paul Michael Hughes/GWR; **114–118:** Peter Andrews/Reuters; Chad Ehlers/Photolibrary; Paula Bronstein/Getty Images; Paul Michael Hughes/GWR; Michael Friedel/Rex Features; **121–124:** Jagadeesh Nv/Reuters; Paul Grover/PA Photos; Yui Mok/PA Photos; Warren Johnson/TopFoto; Camera Press; **126–129:** Jim Jurica/iStockphoto; Bonita Hein/iStockphoto; Paul Kane/Getty Images; Bradley Kanaris/Getty Images; **130–133:** China Photos/Getty Images; Tyne News/WENN; John Wright/ GWR; Ranald Mackechnie/GWR; Michael Kemter/iStockphoto; Pierre Landry/iStockphoto; **133–137:** Reuters; Mike Powell/Getty Images; John Lindsay/AP/PA Photos; Popperfoto; Barratts/PA Photos; Topham; Werner Herzog Film; John Wright/GWR; **138–140:** John Wright/GWR; Richard Bradbury/GWR; **142–145:** John Wright/GWR; Patrick Seeger/Corbis; Ranald Mackechnie/GWR; **146–150:** Rex Features; John Wright/GWR; EMAP Advertising; Drew Gardner/GWR; **151–157:** Dan Wooller; Romeo Ranoco/Reuters; Henny Boogert; **163–171:** oceanfours.com; Jon Nash/ Getty Images; Gilles Martin Raget/Getty Images; Gibsons of Scilly; David Brenchley/AP/PA Photos; Frank Perry/Getty Images; David De Lossy/ Photolibrary; thepoles.com; Sarah McNair-Landry; WellChild; **172–175:** Devendra Man Singh/Getty Images; Kenji Kondo/AP/PA Photos; Peter Macdiarmid/Getty Images; **176–179:** Frederick M. Brown/Getty Images; Sean Dempsey/PA Photos; Mike Hewitt/Getty Images; Marcel Mochet/ Getty Images; Charles Platiau/Reuters; Oceanfilmboat.com; **180–181:** Rex Features; Sandra Teddy/Getty Images; Richard Bradbury/GWR; **185–189:** Alexandra Beier/Reuters; Lee Jae-Won/Reuters; Debra Sally/Reuters; Keith Bedford/Reuters; **190–194:** John Wright/GWR; WENN; Cavendish Press; Paul Michael Hughes/GWR; Max Blain/iStockphoto; **198–200:** Paul Michael Hughes/GWR; iStockphoto; Deyan Razsadov; **203–205:** Drew Gardner/GWR; WENN; **207–214:** Norm Betts/Rex Features; Emap; Nigel Andrews; **215–219:** Tim Anderson/GWR; Deshakalyan Chowdhury/Getty Images; Robert Sullivan/Getty Images; Richard Bradbury/GWR; Richard Bradbury/GWR; **219–223:** Ron Heflin/AP/PA Photos; Rex Features; Anders Ryman/Corbis; Monoceros Media; **224–227:** www.santa-dash.com; Macedos Pirotecnia; Monika Adamczyk/iStockphoto; Drew Gardner/ GWR; Manan Vatsyayana/Getty Images; **229–232:** numismondo.com; iStockphoto; Mark Lennihan/AP/PA Photos; Tom Chao; Frazer Harrison/ Getty Images; **233–237:** Susan Blond, Inc; Anthony Harvey/PA Photos; Jacques Demarthon/Getty Images; Sergei Supinsky/Getty Images; Ross Land/Getty Images; **238–240:** Dirck Halstead/Getty Images; Peter

Macdiarmid/Getty Images; Mario Ruiz/Getty Images; Dimitar Dilkoff/ Getty Images; Alban Donohoe/Rex Features; Philippe Hays/Rex Features; **242–245:** Hulton Archive/Getty Images; Artothek; U.S. Army; Zohra Bensemra/Getty Images; Getty Images; Daniel Munoz/Reuters; **247–249:** Greg Hume; Elliott Minor/AP/PA Photos, Corbis; Eric T. Sheler/USAF; WENN; **249–254:** Adrees Latif/Reuters; Sukree Sukplang/Reuters; Chris Jackson/Getty Images; Ami Vitale; WENN; Incredible Feats/Barcroft Media; **255–265:** Science Photo Library; Ranald Mackechnie/GWR; Drew Gardner/GWR; Ranald Mackechnie/GWR; Pam Fraser/Alamy; Bettmann/ Corbis; Ron Kuntz/Getty Images; Hulton Archive/Getty Images; Lutz Bongarts/Getty Images; Don Emmert/Getty Images; Rich Clarkson/Getty Images; Hulton Archive/Getty Images; Getty Images; Mike Blake/Reuters; Darren England/Getty Images; Getty Images; Christophe Simon/Getty Images; Maximilien Brice/CERN; University of Alberta; **269–272:** Kamioka Observatory; **274–277:** Peter Dazeley/SPL; Fred Bayer; Erich Schrempp/ SPL; Charles D. Winters/SPL; Andrew Lambert/SPL; Joachim Angeltun/ iStockphoto; Lui Lennox/Photolibrary; **279–282:** Volker Steger/SPL; Pasieka/SPL; Arthur Turner/Alamy; Paul Michael Hughes/GWR; Michael Donne/SPL; Digital Art/Corbis; Gregory Spencer/iStockphoto; NASA; Getty Images; **284–290:** NASA/Getty Images; Maxim Marmur/Getty Images; Matt Stroshane/Getty Images; Victor Habbick/SPL; Nigel Cook/AP/ PA Photos; Toru Yamanaka/Getty Images; Rex Features; **291–294:** AP/PA Photos; Junko Kimura/Getty Images; Koichi Kamoshida/Getty Images; Paul Yeung/Reuters; Yoshikazu Tsuno/Getty Images; Shizuo Kambayashi/ AP/Empics; **295–299:** Yui Mok/PA Photos; Tony Cordell/Rex Features; Jen Lowery/Rex Features; YouTube; Google Earth; David Boily/AP/PA Photos; Regina Leader/AP/PA Photos; Wikipedia; Chrys Rynearson; **300–304:** Washington University in St. Louis; Fred Hayes/Disney Channel; Mark Mainz/Getty Images; **307–311:** New Line Cinema; Matt Baron/Rex Features; WENN; Dave Hogan/Getty Images; Evan Agostini/Getty Images; Disney Enterprises, Inc; **312–315:** 20th Century Fox; Columbia Pictures; DreamWorks Animation; Sony Pictures; Nathan Blaney/iStockphoto; **315–318:** Miramax; Ronald Grant; Rex Features; Picturehouse; Sony Pictures; Moviestore; **319–323:** Rex Features; www.marble head .net; hollywoodlostandfound.net; Walt Disney Pictures; Walt Disney/Ronald Grant; Danjaq/United Artists; Warner Bros; Platinum Studios; **324–328:** Scott Wishart; D. Dovarganes/AP/PA Photos; Gus Ruelas/Reuters; Bandai Visual Co. Ltd; Warner Bros Pictures; **328–341:** Ray Tang/Rex Features; Greg Wood/Getty Images; Reuters; Robert G. Bednarik; Daniel Aberg/ AP/PA Photos; M. Lorenzo/Corbis; John Wright/GWR; Dave Hogan/Getty Images; Warner Music; Pascal Guyot/Getty Images; Tommy Holl/Rex Features; Getty Images; Chung Sung-Jun/Getty Images; Bertrand Guay/Getty Images; Kristian Dowling/Getty Images; Mercury Music; Jonathan Ernst/ Reuters; John Wright/GWR; **342–345:** Chris Jackson/Getty Images; Rebecca Reid/PA Photos; Toby Melville/Reuters; Joe Short; Fredrik Arff/Dinamo; Ole Morten/AP/PA Photos; Fredrik Arff/Statoil; Dave Hogan/Getty Images; **346–349:** BBC; BBC; Chris Jackson/Getty Images; Cliff Lipson/ CBS; Andrew Eccles/ABC; CBS; Touchstone Television; Ron Tom/ABC;

20th Century Fox; Andy Ryan/Getty Images; **350–353:** Kevin Winter/Getty Images; HBO/Rex Features; Fox TV; Ronald Grant; Kobal; Big Pictures; Matt Baron/Rex Features; **355–358:** John Wright/GWR; José Carlos Pires Pereira/iStockphoto; Gilles Landry/iStockphoto; Rex Features; **359–362:** The Advertising Archives; Rex Features; Touchstone/Allstar; Richard Bradbury/GWR; Leif Berge/Statoil; **366–369:** Statoil; Behrouz Mehri/Getty Images; AP/PA Photos; Reuters; **370–372:** Chad Ehlers/Photolibrary; Ahmed Jadallah/Reuters; WENN; Alamy; Edogwa River Office; **374–377:** Reuters; Alex Wong; WENN; Olga Labrador/Corbis; **379–381:** Alvin Chan/ Reuters; AnglepoiseR; **382–387:** Roland Magunia/Getty Images; Joe McGorty/GWR; **388–392:** David Drais/Lockheed Martin; **393–397:** Robyn Beck/Getty Images; Sarah Foster/U.S. Navy; Patrick Penna/Eurocopter; Pratt & Whitney; Craig T. Mathew/Mathew Imaging; **398–400:** Joerg Koch/ Getty Images; Harjono Djoyobisono/Alamy; Pierre Tostee/Getty Images; **405–408:** M Thompson/AP/PA Photos; Alexis Huret; Paul Kane/Getty Images; Yves Boucau/Getty Images; Scott Boehm/Getty Images; **409–412:** Jonathan Daniel/Getty Images; Jed Jacobsohn/Getty Images; Andy Lyons/ Getty Images; Scott Boehm/Getty Images; John Amis/ AP/PA Photos; **413–417:** Adrian Dennis/Getty Images; Laurent Gillieron/ AP/PA Photos; Mike Powell/Getty Images; Fabrice Coffrini/Getty Images; Gary Hershorn/ Reuters; Brendan McDermid/Reuters; **419–423:** Mark Dadswell/Getty Images; Martin Meissner/AP/PA Photos; Andreas Schaad/AP/PA Photos; Bettmann/CORBIS; **424–429:** Mike Burley/AP/PA Photos; Gavin Lawrence/Getty Images; Joe Amato Racing; Robert Laberge/ Getty Images; Darrell Ingham/Getty Images; Gerry Penny/Getty Images; Joe Klamar/ Getty Images; Virginie Lefour/Getty Images; superside.com; supercross .com; Christian Fischer/Getty Images; **431–439:** Manan Vatsyayana/Getty Images; K. Kasahara/AP/PA Photos; Javier Soriano/ Getty Images; Al Bello/Getty Images; Christian Petersen/Getty Images; George Sal/Newspix; J. P. Moczulski/Reuters; Jonathan Ferrey/Getty Images; Sven Nackstrand/ Getty Images; Omar Martinez/Mexsport/AFP; Brian Lawless/Sportsfile; **440–444:** Jonathan Daniel/Getty Images; Jed Jacobsohn/Getty Images; Jason Cohn/Reuters; Ronald Martinez/Getty Images; Jeff Gross/Getty Images; Rich Pilling/Getty Images; Nick Laham/ Getty Images; **445–448:** T. Vaccaro/NBAE/Getty Images; Jeff Haynes/ Getty Images; B. Gossage/ NBAE/Getty Images; Mike Stone/Reuters; P. P. Marcou/Getty Images; **450–453:** Ethan Miller/Getty Images; Simon Galloway/PA Photos; John Gichigi/Getty Images; Szenes Jason/Corbis; E. Jayawardena/AP/PA Photos; **454–457:** Touchline/Getty Images; Saeed Khan/Getty Images; David Gray/ Reuters; Arif Ali/Getty Images; Alessandro Abbonizio/Getty Images; **458–460:** Dean Treml/Getty Images; Franck Fife/Getty Images; IGFA; **467–476:** Lee Smith/Reuters; Shaun Botterill/ Getty Images; Getty Images; Hassan Ammar/Getty Images; Rabih Mogrhabi/Getty Images; John Peters/ Getty Images; Henry Romero/ Reuters; Erik G. Svensson; **478–480:** Mark Lyons/Getty Images; Sven Nackstrand/Getty Images; Sergei Remezov/ Reuters; Tim Graham/Getty Images; **481–484:** Getty Images; PA Photos; Capozzola & Ringuette/ SIPictures.com; Jim McIsaac/Getty Images; Jack Dempsey/AP/PA Photos; **486–489:** Scott Miller/GWR; **490–494:** Tony